FELIX SMITH

CHINA PILOT

FLYING FOR CHENNAULT
DURING THE COLD WAR

SMITHSONIAN INSTITUTION PRESS
WASHINGTON AND LONDON

Grateful acknowledgment is made to the Society of Authors as literary representative on the Estate of A. E. Housman and Henry Holt & Co., Inc., for permission to reprint "Epitaph on an Army of Mercenaries" by A. E. Housman from *The Collected Poems of A. E. Housman*. Copyright 1939, 1940 by Holt, Rinehart & Winston, Inc. Copyright © 1967 by Robert E. Symons. Copyright 1965 by Henry Holt & Co., Inc.

Library of Congress Cataloging-in-Publication Data
Smith, Felix, 1918–
    China pilot : flying for Chennault during the Cold War / Felix Smith.
       p.   cm.
    Originally published: Washington : Brassey's, c1995.
    ISBN 1-56098-398-1 (alk. paper)
    1. Smith, Felix, 1918– . 2. China—History—Civil War, 1945–1949—Personal narratives, American. 3. Civil Air Transport—History. 4. Airlift, Military—Asia—History. 5. Humanitarian assistance, American—Asia—History. 6. Air pilots—United States—Biography.
D790.S5682 2000
951.04′2—dc21   00-022601

British Library Cataloguing-in-Publication Data is available

Manufactured in the United States of America
06 05 04 03 02 01 00   5 4 3 2 1

For whom there were no bugler's taps or names inscribed in stone. Their bones rest in alien ground unwet by tears.

Contents

Foreword

I have known Felix Smith for many years, ever since he went to Shanghai to join Civil Air Transport (CAT), the airline formed by my late husband, General Claire Lee Chennault. Mr. Smith is now able to share his many experiences not only as a pilot flying for CAT, but also as a friend of the Chinese people. He is to be congratulated as an astute observer of the changes in a great nation that was both proud and sad but not without glory.

Much has happened and been achieved during the five decades since 1945, and CAT played an important part in Sino-U.S. history. Smith's story is the account of many men and women who worked with General Chennault during a very difficult time and faced unique challenges. Yet they proved that by working together, they could accomplish the impossible. Many of them left their homes to work in an unknown land with an ancient civilization alien to their own. They worked closely with the Chinese people, and they saw the suffering and the hunger and how the Chinese tried to rebuild a country torn by many years of war. Courage is grace under pressure. Smith had it, and many pilots with Chennault did, too.

I am glad that my friend, Felix Smith, is sharing his exciting experiences. His account is most moving. General Chennault would be very proud of him.

Anna C. Chennault
Washington, D.C.

Preface

These, in the day when heaven was falling,
The hour when earth's foundations fled,
Followed their mercenary calling
And took their wages and are dead.

Their shoulders held the sky suspended;
They stood, and earth's foundations stay;
What God abandoned these defended,
And saved the sum of things for pay.
　　　　　—A. E. HOUSMAN,
　　　　　　　"EPITAPH ON AN ARMY OF MERCENARIES"

Housman's poem influenced President Roosevelt's decision to let the Flying Tigers—General Chennault's American Volunteer Group—support China before Pearl Harbor.

These fighter pilots were the only bright spot in the early days of World War II. They became a legend.

After the war, Chennault organized a collection of pilots to fly relief supplies into war-torn China. He called the outfit CAT (Civil Air Transport), and it expanded to become a bright spot in the long Cold War that was often hot. I was one of these pilots.

Chennault said, "CAT reminds me a lot of the Tigers. They were both one of those things you could sit in a corner and think about—but you couldn't actually do it."

We were a fragment of the Cold War. Like an iceberg, only our tip showed, and it became an elegant Chinese crest, an international airline, a favorite of business commuters and tourists who traversed Asia. They recognized the flag of Free China on the tail, the dragon on the nose. Inside, they relaxed in an ambience of luxury—a golden carpet, seats covered with shantung silk, a moon gate, menus on replicas of ancient scrolls, fine porcelain, patrician stewardesses in split-skirt cheongsams.

The pampered passengers had no way of knowing the mechanics in white coveralls who tended the planes with pit-stop speed also rigged unmarked birds with cargo rollers and parachutes, and the pilots changed hats and dropped supplies to people who were besieged by Soviet-backed forces. Warriors counted on us for ammunition, and their families knew that rice would rain from the sky.

Growing beyond two hundred planes and eight thousand employees, we became one of the largest aerial complexes in history, albeit secret. We participated in the tumultuous events that changed the face of Asia and played a strong hand in settling Free China on the island of Taiwan.

Civilians from fifteen nations, military veterans from five, knowing we were contributing to the collapse of the Evil Empire, we bonded. We laughed at petty chauvinism. A visiting Air Force general remarked with surprise, "CAT has the spirit of a fighter squadron."

Such a phenomenon is unlikely to recur. I wanted to see its spirit glimmer in sunlight for one brief moment, like a butterfly, before it died as a footnote of history.

Friends warned, "You're not a historian, not a scholar—just do a memoir," but I didn't have the brass. Not until I recalled histories by scholars and thought the masterpieces deserved companion pieces, however unpolished, by the spear carriers: a seaman on the *Santa María*, an Indian scout with Lewis and Clark, a mechanic who laid a hand on Lindbergh's monoplane.

I wanted to put readers in the cockpit, show what I saw and heard; what I wanted to remember and what I'd tried to forget.

If you feel you've jumped into a swirl of warlords, peasants, missionaries, and mercenaries, then you feel like a pilot in that twenty-three-year odyssey.

Sit comfortably beside me—we'll be airborne after I thank those who helped log the journey.

Ernest K. Gann treated me like a professional writer even though I'm not. In between stern admonitions he scrutinized my words with the same care he gave his own. Near the end of his earthly life, exhausted though he was, he edited my work and said, "You may have to get in touch with me in outer space." The tutelage of the disciplined artist, the warmth of his comradeship—these were Gann's gifts to me.

Renee (Lym) Robertson of Canton, Hong Kong, and San Francisco, follower of Kwan Yin, Goddess of Mercy. Friend, adviser on things Chinese, Renee introduced me to Gann, knowing we'd become brothers.

Journalist Dorothy Witte Austin. For decades never too busy to read my stuff, she still teaches me much about writing. With generosity and artistry, line by line, she edited the final manuscript.

Our writing group—University of Hawaii professors LaRene Despain and Robert Hughes, and poet Sue Cowan. The help of these scholars was priceless.

Barbara McLeod of Cheyenne, Wyoming, provided enthusiastic support and smoothed out the rough spots.

Sue (Buol) Hacker, Chennault's secretary and wife of a CAT pilot, contributed a chapter.

Dr. William Leary, historian, University of Georgia, shared significant documents he discovered in archives.

Samuel Vaughan, U.S. Marine Corps, editor emeritus at Random House, a combat veteran and great editor, shared his China experiences with me and endorsed my manuscript.

Leigh Lu Prasse, a spirited colleague in South Pacific Island Airways, sparked ideas as intelligently as she dispatched Boeing jets.

Cheryl Jordan, another vivacious and brainy executive in the South Pacific airline, championed the manuscript and set its final course.

Rosemary Montrose launched the book by reading the draft and then recommended it to a friend who is a fine agent.

Maria Downs, with the skill of a polished literary agent, piloted me around rocks and shoals in the sea of publishing.

George Thibault and Don McKeon, Brassey's editor, gave me unfailing support. Copy editor Ted Johnson, with artistry, refined the manuscript.

China Pilot

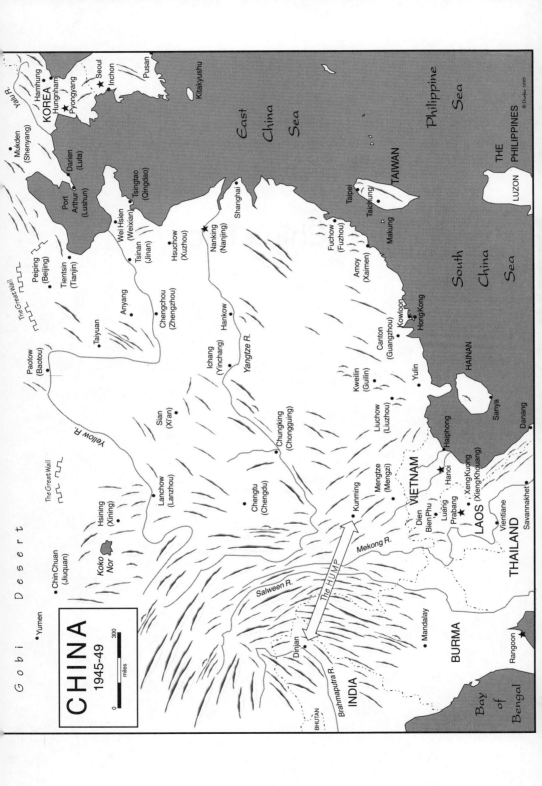

CHINA
1945-49

Gobi Desert

The Great Wall

Yellow R.

Yangtze R.

Mekong R.

Salween R.

Brahmaputra R.

The HUMP

miles
0   300

KOREA
Hamhung
Hungnham
Pyongyang ★
Seoul ★
Inchon
Pusan
Kitakyushu

Mukden (Shenyang)
Darien (Luta)
Port Arthur (Lushun)
Wei Hsien (Weixian)
Tsingtao (Qingdao)

Peiping (Beijing)
Tientsin (Tianjin)
Tsinan (Jinan)
Hsuchow (Xuzhou)
Nanking (Nanjing) ★
Shanghai

Anyang
Chengchou (Zhengzhou)
Taiyuan
Paotow (Baotou)

Ichang (Yinchang)
Hankow

Sian (Xi'an)
Lanchow (Lanzhou)
Hsining (Xining)
Koko Nor
ChinChuan (Jiuquan)
Yumen

Chungking (Chongqing)
Chengtu (Chengdu)

Kweilin (Guilin)
Liuchow (Liuzhou)
Yulin

Kunming
Mengtze (Mengzi)

Canton (Guangzhou)
Kowloon
Hong Kong

Fuchow (Fuzhou)
Amoy (Xiamen)

East China Sea

Taipei
Taichung
Makung
TAIWAN

Philippine Sea

THE PHILIPPINES
LUZON

South China Sea

HAINAN
Sanya
Danang

Haiphong
Hanoi
Dien Bien Phu
Luang Prabang
VIETNAM
XengKuang (XiengKhouang) ★
LAOS
Vientiane
Savannakhet
THAILAND

Mandalay
BURMA
Rangoon ★

Dinjan
INDIA
BHUTAN

Bay of Bengal

© Durfee 1995

1

The Yangtze River

Autumn 1945. I descended through ten thousand feet with the aplomb of a junior birdman. I should have been terrified. We saw buildings and streets, but the airport—a gravel island in a river a thousand feet below the level of the city—was obscured by smoke.

Beside me sat Wang, my copilot, hired for his linguistic—not flying—skill, and behind me, Mah, my Manchurian radio operator. He had learned his craft in his country's merchant marine and could talk his way past any curfew guard in China.

Twenty-one passengers—civilians in blue ankle-length gowns, a Western-dressed tobacco merchant from Shanghai, a few Kuomintang politicians, and two Chinese Army officers—sat in back with unwarranted confidence. They didn't know the depth of my ignorance, nor did I. I thought it was routine to land a DC-3 there. After all, it was a scheduled stop for my employer—the elite China National Aviation Corporation.

Some optimist had put eighteen hundred feet of cobblestones on the island and called it a runway. It ended in the water in the shadow of a Hsi Mountain peak where the Yangtze bent sharply around and joined the Kialing River flowing from the north. In their fork the rivers squeezed and eroded the V-shaped prow of another peak. A walled city sprawled on top, a medieval city, wispy in lazy smoke, a picture in a child's book of fairy tales. It was Chungking, the wartime capital of China. It had become the headquarters after Japan's imperial bombers—in the winter of 1937—made rubble of Nanking, then the capital.

Now there was peace, and thousands of people were cooking dinner on soft-coal fires. Smoke joined muggy air and settled into the gorge.

As if a mountain at the far end of the runway weren't hazard enough, the approach was obstructed by high-tension wires across the gorge. I had flown into Chungking often enough to believe I was a hot pilot—a myth common to beginning professionals. China National veterans, superb pilots, had taught me the secrets of hurdling the wires and swooping down without gaining speed. "Touch down at the beginning of the strip," they had warned, "and control your speed. Too fast, you'll skid off the end and go for a swim."

After flying precisely over Chungking's radio beacon, we headed south for ninety seconds, executed a standard rate turn to the right, and rolled out on the heading of the Yangtze.

"Gear down," I said. Mah moved the lever, and we felt the wheels thump into place. "Half flaps." They extended beneath the wings. I pushed the nose down and we submerged, like a submarine, into a sea of smog.

We couldn't see ahead, but if I plastered my face against the side window I could see straight down and follow the bank of the river. It felt like that parlor game of walking a line while peering at your feet through the wrong end of binoculars. I leveled off to hold at fifteen hundred feet until we crossed cables we wouldn't see. I'd been taught to ignore the wires and watch for the tower that supported them. I flirted with the stalling speed.

The tower suddenly appeared off our left wing. A silvery ghost. I pushed our nose down, pulled off all power, and called, "Full flaps." We dropped like a streamlined brick. Seconds later I saw the school. Its basketball court was our cue to turn to the compass heading of the runway. I slowed our descent by adding power and pulling our nose up. We watched warily, knowing the island would suddenly pop out of the fog. We skimmed the masts of junks before we saw the runway; it seemed as if we were landing in the river itself. We touched hard. The instrument panel rattled while we rolled over the cobblestones. We stopped in front of a lopsided bamboo terminal. This was the China of my boyhood daydreams. Modern Shanghai lay a thousand miles behind us. I mumbled, "Jeezus Keerist, this is what I call flying."

I waited with Mah and Wang until the airline's sampans ferried our passengers from the island to the riverbank. The Yangtze, flowing from Tibet's melting glaciers, ran swiftly and silently except for gurgling vortexes that whirled past. A flat cargo boat was propelled by a ballet of standing oarsmen in scrubbed denims and bamboo hats the size of umbrellas.

Along the riverbank a team of about fifty men on a grooved path, harnessed with diagonal sashes to a hawser of braided bamboo, towed a huge junk upstream. Its poop deck, high as a Spanish galleon, said it brought cargo from Shanghai. The oceangoing junks sailed up the Yangtze River to the city of Ichang at the foot of the Wu Ling Mountains to be towed the remaining 375 miles, step by step through the Yangtze's white-water gorges to Chungking. They trudged to a leader's chant and answered in chorus. A few who could swim were prepared to jump into the river to free the hawser when it snagged on a rock. Drowning was their occupational hazard. When they saw me with my camera they waved, shouted, laughed. They were Yangtze Trackers, the sturdy breed who'd kept western China open to the sea for centuries.

The rapids in the narrow gorges downstream sank one junk in ten. Merchants' shipments were pooled and spread around the fleet so that the loss would be shared whenever a junk shattered on the rocks. It was the beginning of insurance.

Our sampan dropped us at the base of a cliff. Steps chipped from stone zigzagged up to Main Street high above us. Bare-chested bearers in khaki shorts and rope sandals waited in the traces of sedan chairs. Their trips up the cliff were logged in calf muscles larger than baseballs. The veins bulged. My forward bearer leaped onto the first step, higher than his trailing partner, while I pitched awkwardly on my back, between poles, in the jouncing bamboo chair. When the steps switched from zigs to zags I looked over the arm of the chair and saw a frightening drop.

The bearers had started the climb with cheerful banter, but halfway up the mountain, sweat flowed, jolts and trembles of the chair telegraphed the agony of their muscles, and they lapsed into songs to get them to the top—working chants that had become familiar and haunting. Like sea chanteys with an Oriental lilt.

There'd be other sounds in years to come—toots of laughter from Earthquake Magoon, whose bones lie in a Buddhist shrine; scornful retorts from the Russian princess; yowls of professional mourners with the discordant brass band of Cheong's funeral that I was leading to Happy Valley; the gentle Louisiana drawl of a general named Chennault who trusted his pilots.

But all that lay in a future unexpected, unthought-of, when the sedan chair dumped me on the mountaintop outside Chungking's wall. I thought it was my final trip up the steps, the last I'd see of peasants hurrying through the city gates before they closed for the night.

I heard "Hi-hi, hi-hi" behind me and stepped aside to let a restaurant jog by. The pole on the chef's shoulder was swinging a pot of glowing charcoal from one end and a wicker cage from the other. Its shelves separated clattering plates and sauce bottles and bowls of green vegetables, pork, ginger. The springing of the pole, in rhythm to his pace, seemed to lighten the burden.

After a rickshaw pulled me through a portal in the wall, I twisted around to look back at my favorite calligraphy. Chinese characters chiseled into the mildewed stone arch announced "The Gate Connecting with Distant Places." Beyond it, past smoke-laden gorges and crazy-quilt patterns of terraced farms, the blue-tinted mountains waited. Told the calligraphy was new because it was only six hundred years old, I wondered how many city dwellers had been made restless by the stone carver's deed, for the Chinese are a curious and adventurous people.

Inside the wall, Chungking was grime and noise. Homes of black mud and straw backed against roads of stone and muck. Poverty and cheerfulness were easy companions.

Scrawny beggars brush stroked words of woe on thin papers and anchored them to the road with pebbles. A few Chinese Army jeeps, honking incessantly, rattled past and forced my rickshaw man to splash a wheel through a gutter's rivulet of sewage. My skinny guy (shaved head, remnants of jeep tires for sandals) strained forward and sang working songs to get uphill. Downhill, he became a speed maniac, leaning back in the traces, balancing on his craft's two wheels, roller-coastering down, slapping the ground with his feet infrequently. Some thrill, some hazard; but astonishing balance, coordination, timing. Had he been born in the USA, he'd be a motor-cycle daredevil rider at carnivals. A couple of years at MIT and he'd be a test pilot at Grumman.

We sped past a temple garden and caught a glimpse of women lighting joss. Other women squatted beside glowing charcoal and tended pots fashioned from bashed airplanes. Stringy-bearded old men sat patiently on their heels and puffed tall pipes made of American beer cans that had been soldered end to end.

A cyclist rounded a corner without banking, frantically wobbled his front wheel, and crashed. Other teetering cyclists collided. Chungking was the only place I saw head-on collisions of two bikes bound in the same direction. Humid air kept smells alive: opium, urine, sesame oil, garlic, nose-tickling mysteries.

For all its ugly face, Chungking was a monument to the human spirit. It became a Mecca after Japan plundered eastern China. Refugees trudged two thousand miles westward to Chungking because it perched above a fertile plateau behind forbidding mountains, beyond the Yangtze's turbulent gorges. They lugged, piece by piece, 300 million pounds of dismantled factory machinery, while students toted entire university libraries, and their professors held classes en route.

Dr. Wang's number two son recalled, "My father warned me about the hazards of crossing China, which was controlled by warlords. We needed to know the correct handshake and methods of accepting offers of cigarettes. It was such turmoil."

Remote in Szechwan Province, Chungking had become a citadel of Free China. And now the cave-pocked, polluted, slime-covered, uphill-and-downhill medieval city was a reminder of a magnificent exodus in human history.

Monument or not, this was the last time it would find Felix overnighting there. Which was why I smiled when my rickshaw expert jogged past stalls fringed with drying duck carcasses and drapes of stuffed pig intestines yet to be twisted into sausages.

My room in our hostel, oppressive with heat and a mildew stink, had a table, a shower stall, and a bunk with two-by-four posts that had been gnawed by rats. A khaki mosquito net hung from a nail in the ceiling.

A room boy stopped by with a pot of fresh tea and a tray full of miniature teacups that my seamstress aunt could have used for thimbles. I knew how to quench a raging thirst without acquiring dysentery. I aligned the cups on my table and filled them to the brim. The tea would cool while I was in the shower, and then I'd have a satisfying drink.

Covered in lather when the water trickled to a stop, I doused myself with a jug of cold drinking water—its best use. The kitchen staff had been taught to fill the jugs with water that had been boiled and cooled, but the procedure was seldom followed. Tap water looked clean enough to those who knew nothing of bacteria or amoebas. A demand that water be boiled and then cooled back to its original temperature seemed like another obtuse whim of foreign devils. Newcomers learned, after a series of panic dashes to toilets, to stick to tea.

By the time I emerged from the shower, the room boy had dumped my precious cool brew and was refilling the line of cups from the scalding pot. I shouted, "I cool it off and you dump it out. How the hell does a guy get a drink in this half-ass barn?"

"You no like China? Why no go home? Everybody say America very fine place."

Smart-ass but logical, that room boy. It was indeed time for me to go. The Second World War was over; it was late summer 1945. America, the British Commonwealth of Nations, Russia, and most of Europe had defeated the totalitarian Axis—Germany, Italy, Japan. It had been a long war: four years for America, six for the other Western Allies, fourteen for China. Around-the-clock supply flights from India—over the Himalayas to China's back door—were no longer needed. Terminations had been announced. When I got back to Shanghai, I'd be out of work. No longer under the aegis of the U.S. Army's Service of Supply, China National would revert to its former role—as the premier passenger carrier of China—with a nucleus of old-timers. It'd continue to be managed by William Bond, whose white hair and suave manner induced others to call him Mr.

Bond. He was one of the many vice presidents of Pan American
World Airways, the American corporation that owned a piece of
China's pioneer airline. George Robertson—Robbie, one of the original jewels selected to remain with China National—wrote this epitaph for the wartime Hump pilots:

> *After the war had finished I was flying between Nanking and Chungking*
> *with Mr. Bond as one of the passengers. We had to stop at Hankow for*
> *fuel, so we all went into the operations tent for a cup of coffee. As we*
> *were sitting there talking, Mr. Bond said, "Now, Robbie, the war is over,*
> *we're a scheduled airline, every one of you boys must be in uniform,*
> *shaven, and put on a respectful appearance for the passengers. No more*
> *chewing tobacco or coonskin caps, and put your .45 in your flight bag.*
> *Remember, we're a scheduled airline." Just then about six hogs ran*
> *through the tent, splattering mud over both of us. I said, "Yes sir, Mr.*
> *Bond, this is a scheduled airline."*

The next morning I'd fly out of the capital's tiny island airport and
land in Shanghai, and the genteel China National of Mr. Bond's
dream would become my alma mater.

I had been carrying items torn from the *Shanghai Evening Post
and Mercury*. "Flying Tiger General Organizing Airlift". . .
"Chennault to Distribute Relief Supplies Throughout War-Ravaged
China . . . Looking for Pilots Who Are Familiar with China's
Weather." My peers read them and laughed. "You've been flying
without your oxygen mask. We're going home."

Common sense made me agree. After I became somewhat accustomed to China I occasionally got flashes of my old perspective and
asked myself, What am I doing in this weird place? Other pilots got
these backward glimpses also. I called them sanity attacks. Now was
the time to begin a sensible life in my own country. Wisconsin
Central Airlines was hiring pilots. I'd ignore Chennault's airlift.

I dropped into my dank bunk in Chungking's miserable hostel and
kept my arms away from the netting so mosquitoes wouldn't get a
toehold and introduce me to malaria. I'd had dengue fever, and that
was enough.

My eyelids got heavy. The melody of a noodle seller's flute floated
in the stillness of the night. Its strange pentatonic scale drifted from
a great distance. It said I was a long way from home. Exotic caden-
zas conjured visions of junks and sedan chairs and a wall that was
new because it was only six hundred years old.

The roving noodle man could have been a sorcerer, because I found
myself wondering what distant places lay beyond the stone arch.

2

Footsteps

A master at rationalization, I told myself that any outfit run by the famous Flying Tiger general was bound to be all-American, almost as good as being home.

In Shanghai, General Chennault's aide, Colonel Wise, said, "Flew for China National? Hmm. . . . The Hump? Hmmm. . . . Hmmm. . . . You're hired, but there's been a delay. I'll call when we start up."

It sounded promising until the adage "Foreigners can't hold secrets in China" bore out. I soon heard that American investors had grown skittish over rumblings of civil war and backed out of "the harebrained China scheme." I took a room at Shanghai's YMCA and waited while Chennault searched for an angel with cash.

I slept fitfully that night and thought of my China National buddies who were settled comfortably in America. Did my lollygagging in Shanghai, waiting for a flying scheme that might never begin, make my father an oracle? I wondered.

A respected scholar, my father. Ran the music department of a fine high school in Milwaukee, played the organ brilliantly, taught his charges to compose music, nurtured the chorus and orchestra with an artist's sensitivity.

Teachers marched us from somber classrooms to the auditorium, where his musicians waited with brass, woodwinds, and strings. My father mounted the podium. A baton held high by one hand, his hernia pressed by the other, he silenced snickers with a downbeat.

Reverberations of Tchaikovsky pushed out the walls while I soared away on violin strings. Reedy flights of oboes put me in a Chinese shirt laundry where I first smelled incense, but bravura trumpets heralded more. Piccolos whistled to me from some ethereal place where horns tooted laughter, cellos promised noble deeds, while kettledrums spelled storms. And a bass-drum boom startled me back to school.

Books I carried home remained closed while I climbed from an attic window to lie on our roof and watch the sun at the time of day when it sinks and the universe says peace. And deep inside I knew I'd fly and see things I didn't yet know existed.

Sometimes my father called me to his study. In his brooding, Beethoven-like presence I heard a refrain he had dedicated to me. It went, "You'll only make a mess of it." My father didn't like airplanes, and when he intoned, "Be a fireman or a policeman, a job with a pension," I thought he didn't like me.

Nor did the Air Corps flight surgeon with the wooden tongue depressor who said, "Open your mouth." Like some damn horse trader, he tapped my buck teeth and muttered, "Malocclusion." Then he stuck the tip of his ruler on my nose, held a small card at the eighteen-inch mark, and said, "Read." I guessed, squirmed, dipped into my shirt pocket for my glasses, and found myself creeping out of his office like a beaten dog. The Air Corps could afford to be fussy; America was at peace.

Retracing these steps in my mind made my presence in China seem more reasonable, and my reverie was better than a movie. I recalled my flying lessons from a canny Scot named McPherson who tossed tidbits that I hoarded like gems. "Plan, think ahead, don't get behind the power curve, shun thunderstorms, don't be afraid of instrument flying—if you try to stay visual you'll wander into a cloud with rocks in it."

Eventually I myself became an instructor and taught green Air Corps cadets the rudiments of flying. After the Japanese bombed Pearl Harbor and the war matured, the Air Corps got less stuffy.

"Glasses? They won't blow off—the open-cockpit days are over. With your glasses you can see like a hawk—that's why they were invented. We'll give you transitional training and a commission, but you'll have to enter via your draft board."

"Yes, I'm the draft board chairman, but I can't touch you. War Manpower Act. Flight instructor. Essential to the war effort."

I asked for a hearing before the appeal board.

"Appeal? That's for guys who're trying to stay out. Goddam, I thought I'd heard everything. You can't appeal to get in!" He wanted me to just fade away, but I told him I'd pay the long-distance fee if he'd telephone his headquarters in Madison.

The phone call worked. That's how stupid I was. Bare-assed, in line with glum draftees, I knew that a stroke of a sergeant's pen could keep me a private in the walking army, a quick end to my short flying career. I'd have done it to myself; it would vindicate my father's gloomy prophecy.

I sighed with relief when the sergeant told me to go home and wait for transitional flight training.

After months of waiting, I was offered work by the China National Aviation Corporation. "I'm sorry, I can't. I'm in the Air Corps Reserve, waiting for active duty."

"We'll fix that," the telephone said. "China National has been chartered by the U.S. Army Service of Supply. You'll be based in the Assam Valley in India, flying war supplies to China. Over the Hump."

Great Britain's Dum-Dum Aerodrome near Calcutta was aptly named for a fledgling like me with a thousand hours in single-engine airplanes. China National ushered me to the seat of a camouflaged C-47, the Army Air Corps' name for a Douglas DC-3 that had been modified with large cargo doors and reinforced flooring.

If I try to land this huge airplane like I landed primary trainers, I thought, I'll only make a mess of it. So I leveled off at what I trusted was a few feet above Dum-Dum and hung on while the C-47 made a succession of short bounces, like a hungry crow hopping along the ground. Instructor Mahrt, a laconic veteran, droned, "I know you think you can't land this beast, but why don't you try—just for the hell of it?"

Graduated to line flying, I learned much from Check Airman Pottschmidt. Loose-jointed, casual, he resembled a contemplative bookkeeper. Much of the time he tilted his sandy-topped head down and thrust out his lower lip. If someone spoke to him he rolled his blue eyes up and peered past the fringes of his eyebrows. Outsiders never guessed he drove airplanes. He didn't have hair on his chest; he had feathers. He'd been flying in China since 1936, and his analytical brain never rested. He invented instrument approach procedures for China's airports and explored air routes across the Himalayas to India, skimming peaks to determine their exact height. Pilots called the wartime air link between India and China "the Hump," and it became notorious for granite peaks that stuck beyond the vertical reach of propeller workhorses; for its lack of navigation aides; for its terminus in India's Assam Valley that beckoned fog; for storms aloft that stuck ice to cargo-laden planes, changed the aerodynamic shape of wings, and sabotaged lift while crews sweated behind oxygen masks and watched altimeters unwind.

Pottschmidt insisted I memorize the position and height of every mountain that waited to destroy me and my crew if we strayed off course, and I had to recite the course and distance to every reachable airport outside the Assam Valley so I'd know without scrambling for charts how to escape India's humid basin if fog hid it before I arrived from China, low on fuel.

Even with Pottschmidt's easy mien, I was all thumbs when he flew with me. Critics hexed me; I focused on how instead of what I was doing. All my life I couldn't perform when watched. Had the weather been good during my final test, I would have flunked. But that night on the Hump I was too busy to care what any check airman thought. The last friendly object we saw was Old Baldy, the moon-lit chalk-blue cliff rising above Kunming's twenty-mile lake.

Thunderstorms where the horizon's supposed to be. Not dramatic zigzag flashes, just a boiling glow that spells trouble. Translucent orange churns for several seconds and then goes black. Left, right, dead ahead. I steer a compass course in between. The fringe of a thunder-bumper slams us down and then up, abruptly enough to jerk my neck. A blinding flash. Flip the white cockpit lights on, focus on the artificial horizon, keep the toy wings level, ignore the gyrating airspeed needle gone mad. Ice growing on windshield, wing lights on, it's white with rime. Don't activate deicer boots; wait for a two-inch layer. A thin coat can be stretched; the boot will pulsate ineffectively behind a growing wall. Too late and it won't budge. I guess—two inches—flip the switch and watch the wing's edge inflate, deflate, breathe in, breathe out. The ice crackles and vanishes into blackness.

One more shudder and the thunderhead spits us out while the Air Corps' traffic cop asks for our position report. Yunnani beacon should give good line of position, but our radio compass prefers lightning and hunts crazily for the thunderhead with the highest electrical charge. Give estimated position; been flying an hour and twenty minutes, should be near Mount Tali. Adjust heading to left, fudge south of course, just in case. Unpredicted south winds, sometimes a hundred miles an hour, have carried guys north into Mount Everest's cousins . . . five planes one night.

Pottschmidt in copilot seat, head down, contemplating, or snoozing, or maybe he wants to find out how I'd cope with a deaf, dumb copilot.

We must be over the spine of the Hump where the Mekong and Salween rivers parallel each other as they cascade from Tibet. On clear days the twin rivers are magnificent, one as imposing as the other, each with its own sheer canyon two miles deep, its own tumbling green water. But tonight everything is black. We're past the thunderstorms.

Our clock says we should be over Burma, but I want a positive fix. On my lap, a chart of green valleys, tan hills, brown mountains is pocked with ugly white blotches announcing, "Relief data incomplete. Maximum terrain elevation believed not to exceed 23,500 feet." That's higher than we are. The scary blanks aren't far north of our course. In clear weather last week I saluted Fox's Pass, where he died. Old-timers told me they wept when they flew over Mickey's Peak. Schroeder was shot down by Japs to the south. . . .

Blackness is bejeweled with millions of electric sparks as snowflakes collide with our windshield and spew their energy. Got a beacon, but snow static hides its tone, which means I can't fine-tune it accurately enough; the needle won't point. Volume higher, static louder; not much use. For the very first time, Pottschmidt speaks. Two words, mild voice: "Less volume." I rotate the knob and discover it's possible, in snow static, to distinguish a signal when the volume is barely audible. The needle points like a bird dog and holds.

Almost an hour to go. We cross Burma's Pat Kai Range, descend into the valley of the Brahmaputra, land in the dark at Dinjan. Our five-thousand-foot strip of India was steamrollered out of a tea plantation that was hacked out of a jungle. Humid air bears its smells.

Parking brakes set. I'm sweating. For the second time of the entire trip I hear Pottschmidt's low-key voice. "You're a captain now."

During the next few trips I glanced at the copilot on my right, at gasoline drums and ammunition in back, to convince myself I was actually commanding a multiengine airliner.

A cram course, the Hump, a crucible. A gaping innocent, I was dazzled by its cruel fury, its grandeur, its solitude. By the time World War II ended, in 1945, I felt like a hoary pilot, although old-timers still called me a junior birdman. Sheer elitism, I thought, until I said good-bye to marvelous Pottschmidt and heard him say, "You're just beginning to find out what this flyin's all about."

I'd also learn something about myself. I didn't know I was a captive of China's spell, although I obviously had flown through *Alice in Wonderland*'s looking glass. Topsy-turvy indeed. Peasants didn't even call it China. They claimed it was Chung-kuo—the Middle Kingdom—because it hovered between heaven and earth, the center of the universe, so to speak.

I couldn't define the feeling, but I indeed sensed an extra dimension. The entire country was mystifying. Like many a Chinese puzzle, it was a teaser that couldn't be solved. Not by a foreigner. That was its fascination.

For three centuries, before the First Crusade, the Tang Dynasty glowed with philosophers, architects, calligraphers, and artists. They enticed travelers from afar and nurtured the infants Korea and Japan.

Despots reigned, like the Chin Dynasty emperor who buried Confucian scholars alive and burned their books.

Enlightened potentates engendered fine literature printing, the compass, and the seismograph.

Between heaven and earth? Its exalted position was justified, but it also hovered below heaven, far below—closer to hell—depending on the swing of history's pendulum.

Ever so slowly, it still swings from brilliance to darkness and back again, this unfathomable place. Deeper south than Cuba, it reaches north past Tibet to the latitude of Labrador, and it spreads west from the Pacific Ocean, farther west than most of India. It once touched Arabia.

Arab mercenaries with *nu-gungs* (crossbows) were employed by China a thousand years ago, and their descendants are still there with names like Wong and Mah although they have big noses and round eyes. Marco Polo was a relative newcomer. We Americans with *fei jees* (airplanes) were a splash in a river of history.

I jumped into that endless river, but I was wiser than those Arabs, I bragged. The Middle Kingdom couldn't seduce me—I'd stay a year and go home.

My reveries ended when the YMCA room boy banged on my door and shouted, *"Di wo."* ("Telephone.") I hurried down the hall to where it hung on the wall. A Daniel Nelson was calling, but he wasn't from Chennault's office. He was a missionary with an airplane in need of a pilot.

"Sure," I answered. "It'll keep me in beans until the general's airline starts."

3

Missionaries

The olive-drab fuselage of the ecclesiastical C-47 was brightened by a red heart with orange flames licking around the edges. Bold lettering underneath announced *Lutheran World Mission*, and the plane's nose read *Saint Paul*.

"As you know from reading your Bible," explained the Reverend Daniel Nelson, "Saint Paul was the first missionary. This is the first missionary airliner."

Next to *Saint Paul* another airliner, *Saint Peter*, minus a propeller, listed on a flat landing-gear strut. "This one's for spare parts," said my temporary employer. "We'll rob Peter to pay Paul." The C-47s—military versions of DC-3s—were offerings from a devout Air Corps supply officer who had declared them war surplus.

Four thousand Bibles for Kunming and a carton of surgical instruments for Chengtu were lashed down. Copilot/flight engineer/radio operator/mechanic Springweiler had attached a telegrapher's key to the arm of his copilot seat. His years in China as flight engineer for Eurasia, a subsidiary of Lufthansa, qualified him for the title "Old China Hand," a distinction he bore with modesty. Medium height, solid physique, dignified, with sophisticated European manners, he had a gentle voice but spoke in a forthright manner common to his German heritage and lapsed into stretches of contented silence. Before his Teutonic-thorough training as a master mechanic, before becoming a Lufthansa/Urasia flight engineer, Springweiler lived in the Black Forest village of Waldkirch. Meticulous, he spent our stopover in dusty Kunming at our right engine, changing spark plugs. Using the back of his hand, he swept a black forelock whenever it drifted from his neat pate.

After he got the engine running smoothly, we took off and headed for Chengtu, the capital of Szechwan Province far to the north, and

landed hungry, but the airport was still occupied by the U.S. Army
Air Corps, which meant we wouldn't find any noodle men.

An opened registry book on a desk at the mess-hall door was monitored by a duty officer who frequently stared at the sky. I recognized the blah look of a pilot saddled with ground duty, wishing he
were up there instead of down here. He didn't even watch when
crewmen in jump suits as wrinkled as mine signed the book and
walked into the officers' mess.

"Springweiler," I said, "American food, probably steaks. The Air
Corps is fanatical about T-bones. Follow me and do what I do; just
sign your name and any old squadron number." I strolled to the
mess-hall door and recorded, "Smith, 124th Troop Carriers." Its
guardian was still sky gazing. Immensely pleased with myself, I
looked back to coach Springweiler and discovered he had outdone
me by scrawling, "Springweiler, Luftwaffe."

With the wrinkles out of our bellies it seemed easier to look for
Dr. Laube, the recipient of the cargo. With time to visit with a fellow
American deep in China, I was fascinated to learn that Laube was a
brain surgeon and the leader of Chengtu's medical school. He had
kept classes in session during the entire war with Japan.

On our second flight we returned families to provinces they'd fled
during the Japanese invasion. With Buddha-like acceptance, villagers sat on the canvas benches along both sides of the *Saint Paul's*
cabin and hung on to their trembling animals. It was their first flight
in a Chung-kuo *fei jee* (Middle Kingdom flying machine), and my
first over the farmlands of central China. It seemed strange to be flying two miles above the earth with bleating, mooing, crowing
sounds and barnyard smells at my back.

Evidence of the eight-year war passed under the *Saint Paul* like a
scroll unrolling. Mouth agape, I looked down on bomb-pocked
roads, rivers clogged with rubble that had once been bridges, train
tracks that jutted and twisted skyward.

On another flight from Shanghai we carried two middle-aged
American women to a mountain strip in Szechwan Province.
Enthusiastic as college kids on a backpacking trip, they were
replacements for their missionary sisters who'd served a year in
some remote village. When Springweiler and I helped our two passengers down the ladder we were watched by a wiry man who
grinned broadly, amused, I supposed, by the female aliens in high
button shoes, long skirts, ballooned denim blouses.

No fashion plate himself, he wore a ragged tank top, black
trousers that barely covered his knees, straw sandals. His face was
similar to the missionaries'—the bronze, weathered complexion,
crow's-feet at his eyes, but the unpinched look of country folks—and
he sat on his heels on the tarmac with a bamboo carrying pole at his

toes, a pot of charcoal at his side. Short-legged stools, tied in a cluster, waited near a wicker cage of small bottles, greens, and goodies.

Springweiler and I invited our two passengers to lunch. The roving chef looked startled for a moment and then laughed while his eyes squeezed shut and he fanned charcoal, clattered utensils, and jabbered with some hangers-on. I picked up a word here and there—*tao-bee-tzas* (big noses) and *quai-lohs* (ghost men)—until he got his second surprise of the day, when the big-breasted ones from Mars returned his banter in his own dialect colored with an American prairie twang. Startled for a moment, the chef recovered his poise and resumed his *walla-walla*.

In moments he had untied his four stools and unrolled a square of bamboo matting on which he placed teacups, teapot, bowls, porcelain spoons, bamboo chopsticks—and a big bowl of steaming noodles with vegetables.

We slurped the noodles and asked the missionary ladies how they'd get to their village.

"On muleback."

"Six days," the other one said. And then she pulled her teeth and swished them in a bowl of tea. "No dentists where we're going." She laughed. "If I break my plate I'll have trouble eatin'."

No doctors, either, I thought, and this was malaria and dysentery country.

Our next trip took us to a steamy southern town called Henyang. "I've been there—it's the end of creation," Springweiler groaned.

We parked off the end of the dirt strip where a jeep waited. Springweiler chuckled. "I spoke too soon." I looked out and realized the driver was a young Caucasian woman.

"I'm Betty Neuman," she said cheerfully. Her vitality and grace more than made up for her lack of rouge or lipstick, her simple cotton frock, her flat shoes. "You're welcome to stay with us." Her smile was like the sun coming out. "My husband is the surgeon at our hospital."

It eventually became apparent that Betty was a registered nurse, attended patients at the mission hospital, ran an adjacent orphanage, was raising two of her own children. When we walked past the courtyard of the orphanage the kids rushed over to press against the fence and stare, wide-eyed. The parents and relatives of most of the kids had died in Japanese air raids.

"Workers steal sacks of rice," Betty said, "and they jab pins into the children to scare them into silence. . . . But there's a worse frustration—clearing medicine through customs." American companies donated drugs, but they spoiled in a hot shed, waiting to clear customs. "Appealing to Madame Chiang Kai-shek doesn't help. It's usually spoiled by the time her orders filter down."

At the hospital, an unpainted wooden building, Betty parted the mosquito netting over a cot and introduced us to the town policeman, who managed a grin. "This lovely man was directing traffic when a truck ran him down," she said. His pay stopped when he hit the ground, nor did he, as a policeman, have medical insurance.

On our way back through the shabby town, which was sapped by war and bureaucratic bungling, and stifling in muggy heat, I doubted that any American family could find contentment here, but Betty must have been a mind reader, because she said, "We're happy here—our work is a joy."

When we got back to Shanghai I stopped at Springweiler's house to be introduced to his wife, Ruth, and their two young, blond daughters. Feminine, slender, with manners that matched her physical beauty, Ruth said she had been Springweiler's classmate since primary school in the Black Forest village; and when she reached her twenties and told her boss at the pharmacy that she was going to China to marry, the pharmacist had exclaimed, "All the way to China? Can't you find a husband closer to home?"

After Springweiler's whiskey limbered my tongue I said, "Those missionaries . . . their tolerance for frustration . . . their unshakable faith in the goodness of man in the face of contrary evidence. . . ."

"How long do you plan to stay in China?" asked Mrs. Springweiler.

"I don't make long-range plans," I answered. "They have a way of getting bashed."

"Sometimes it feels as if we're riding a giant wave we can't control," she said.

"Auch, it's not so mysterious," said Springweiler. "Airline families feel that way because a company can change your base. Barbara was born in Hanoi, Suzy in Shanghai. The crew scheduler flicks his pencil and that determines if a family will be together on Christmas Day."

"A single day is full of changes," I said. "We don't fly miles, we fly through time. Leave a modern city, and hours later stay overnight in someplace that feels as if we're living a thousand years ago. The airplane's a time machine. What's customary in one place could bring a death sentence somewhere else. . . . After a while we're not dogmatic about anything." It was just talk over whiskey at the time, but the coming years would foster the feeling that I was indeed flying through time.

Ruth smiled at Springweiler and said, "Do you think we can adjust to a stable life?" Max smiled.

Turning to me, she said, "We plan to go home after things settle down in Germany."

I won't become an Old China Hand like the Springweilers, I reminded myself. I'll give it a year.

The next morning the director of the mission, Dr. Daniel Nelson, said, "My father, also Daniel—a famous missionary—was murdered by bandits in western China. My brother was buried alive by Communists in the north. I'll also die a violent death—probably in an airplane." And then he laughed.

An intense man in his forties, the Reverend Daniel Nelson apparently had a premonition, or perhaps spoke in heavy-handed jest, I thought. But months later he boarded a Macao Airways flying boat with his wife and two children, unaware that four of their fellow passengers were bandits who coveted the shipment of gold in the cargo hold. Halfway between Macao and Hong Kong the bandits ordered the crew to land on the open sea alongside a junk. The Macao Airways captain refused, and the dumbest of the hijackers, mindless of who'd fly, shot both pilots. The sole survivor of the crash into the sea was one of the bandits.

On one of my last missionary flights we landed at Tientsin in northern China and parked alongside an olive-drab C-47 that belonged to General of the Army—turned statesman—George Marshall. On a diplomatic mission to persuade President Chiang Kai-shek's Nationalists and Mao Tse-tung's Communists to form a coalition government and cooperate in the reconstruction of China, he'd negotiated an uneasy truce, although his idealism seemed futile to Old China Hands, because both sides were intractable, with neither expecting the other to honor pledges.

I was delighted when Marshall's aide, Colonel Barrett, a ruddy-cheeked Old China Hand and General Chennault's friend, walked over to eye our flaming-heart insignia and ask, "Been hornswoggling good Buddhists?"

"Not yet, Colonel. How're you guys doin' in this conversion business?"

Colonel Barrett threw back his head and laughed. "I guess we are missionaries of a sort."

I asked if the Communists were a serious threat.

"Damn good soldiers." He shook his head from side to side, gravely. "All Chinese are—when they trust their officers."

"Fourteen years fighting Japs—the last thing they need is another war."

"It'd be terrible. Marvelous people, nobody like them . . . nowhere else. This could be such a great country."

That night I pondered China's wealth. Tungsten, antimony, magnesite. They were found nowhere else in the world. And there were oil, coal, iron ore, steel mills, locomotive factories, cement plants; and the enterprise of the people themselves—all the ingredients for a prosperous country. But myopic politics—international as well as domestic—was driving them to self-destruction as inexorably as if they were characters in a Greek tragedy.

Marshall's well-meaning truce enabled Communist soldiers in south-central China to escape an encirclement and filter back to north China, where Mao Tse-tung used the breather to distribute Japanese weapons and turn his ragtag guerrillas into an army.

In comparison to the human butchery that would follow, the agonies I saw in Shanghai were mild. In that huge seaport, United Nations food and medicine overflowed wharves while children within walking distance died.

The supplies that were stuck on the docks through bureaucratic bungling were often sabotaged by merchants' goons to keep prices high. One night they dumped forty tons of food. Stuff that found a way off the docks was sold in black markets.

On early morning walks I detoured around corpses on downtown sidewalks. The Shanghai Benevolent Society dumped the bodies into dark green pushcarts. The slamming of lids was a funeral dirge.

On a December morning, after a snowfall, more than three hundred corpses were collected. More than half were children.

Dismayed, I asked the missionaries, "How can you be cheerful in this town?"

"Because we're making a dent. For one thing, we're pipelines to our churches back home. They're applying pressure. We think we're the reason why the United Nations sent a Colonel Olmstead to take charge. He knows China; he and New York's mayor La Guardia persuaded the UN to lend cargo planes to move stuff inland. Chennault's a natural, but he's got to show operating capital—a quarter of a million U.S. dollars. He's looking everywhere."

In mid-December, Chennault's aide caught me at the YMCA. "We're putting you on a plane for Honolulu this afternoon. You'll ferry a C-46 back. Don't give up your room—you'll be back in two days. The planes are ready to go. They're in perfect shape."

Chennault had found his angel.

I was lucky enough to find another pilot for the missionaries after rushing around Shanghai for a couple of hours.

When I said good-bye to Springweiler, he looked disheartened. Shaking my hand, he said, "Auch, you Americans—you change jobs with such optimism."

The staunch German would have been more cheerful had he known we'd fly together again, in that same airplane, on a CIA junket, several years later.

And I would have been the glum one, had I known my optimism would be shattered as soon as I got to Hawaii and saw Chennault's perfect airplanes.

4

CAT's Wings

Winter 1946. The Air Corps' DC-4 left Shanghai with my new boss, Chennault's chief pilot, Dick Rossi, in the adjoining passenger seat. The twenty-hour flight to Hawaii, with a fuel stop at Wake Island, gave him ample time to brief me.

As Rossi's story unfolded, I realized that my neat plan of enjoying the best of both worlds—the excitement of China under the wing of an American company—had gone awry. For the second time in my budding career I found myself in a Chinese airline.

After a year of Chennault's searching in vain for investors, his remaining funds wouldn't last the week. As a last resort, it seemed as if he rubbed Aladdin's lamp and a genie appeared—a tall, courtly gentleman in a blue Mandarin gown.

Poet, inventor, composer of popular songs, he had solved many of the general's problems during the big war when Chennault commanded the Fourteenth Air Force and all the sky over China. He was Wang Wen-san, Doctor of Philosophy.

Whenever strategic war supplies were delayed by broken trains or trucks, leaking junks, or any other form of damaged transport—or damage to the roads, waterways, and rails on which they traveled—Chennault notified China's minister of communications, who tossed the hot potato to Wang Wen-san, even though the Doctor of Philosophy was the director of personnel, whose job description didn't include liaison with foreign military chiefs. But the minister knew that Wang had learned the quirks of foreign devils when he was an exchange student at Columbia.

Far more important, everyone from the minister on down knew that Chennault was an old comrade in arms of Generalissimo Chiang Kai-shek, at whose frown bureaucrats trembled. Should the American general ever carry a complaint on high, heads would roll.

19

Dr. Wang Wen-san therefore became the fixer, the insurer of tenure at the Ministry of Communications.

Rossi and I laughed when he told the story, because we recognized the innovative ways the Chinese accomplish goals. We didn't know it then, but the same spirit would become the soul of our airline.

As the Air Corps' propeller-driven DC-4 droned across the Pacific, headed for the Hawaiian Islands, where our fleet of airplanes waited, Rossi spoke of the genie's most dramatic wartime coup.

It occurred after Chennault advised the ministry he wanted a thousand tons of supplies delivered to a secret airport behind enemy lines, near the village of Chien Ao, on the coast of Fukien Province, and he needed it within forty days.

Wang Wen-san knew the safari's crucial stage would be the crossing of the Canton-Hankow Railroad, which was heavily guarded by sentries. Posing as a merchant in the area, he analyzed the Japanese patrolling pattern and then coached relays of coolies, who hurried double loads through the gaps. Chennault got his supplies in half the allotted time.

Dr. Wang Wen-san himself would recall the conversations years later, when we reminisced, with my cassette recorder beside our teapot on a café table.

"The general said, 'Who pulled this off? I want to meet him.' When Wang Wen-san stood before him, Chennault said, 'Wang! That task was worthy of Hercules. I hope we meet again, after the war.'

'It would be an honor, sir.'"

A year after the war's end, Dr. Wang again stood before Chennault. It was easy to believe the tall gentleman in the blue Mandarin gown was indeed a genie, for he appeared to have a supernatural gift. His number three son wrote of earlier years when China's wartime capital was vulnerable to Japan's warplanes.

"My father had a dream that a bomb would destroy our house in Chungking, and he moved us to the mountains. A week later the house and the whole block was gone. My father had many dreams that came true and saved our lives by moving just in time."

Resourceful as any genie, Wang Wen-san had become manager of the Nanking branch of the Kinchen Bank, while the Fourteenth Air Force commander, in a small Shanghai office, had become a civilian, almost broke.

Chennault revealed his plan for an airline that would fly United Nations medicines, food, clothing, and factory machinery to the interior of China, and return to its seaports with tungsten ore, tin ingots—any dormant commodities inside China that could be sold in world markets to jump-start the economy.

"I persuaded my boss, President C. M. Chow, to invest the bank's money," Wang Wen-san remembered.

"It must be approved by our board of directors," Chow had said, "but these things are perfunctory. Chennault will get the money in two weeks."

Champagne corks popped at Chennault's office, with the first toast to Dr. Wang Wen-san. He had raised twice the amount needed to launch the airline.

Three days later, at the bank's meeting, a board member complained, "The general is a controversial figure. Some say he is a war-monger."

"We'd be treading on political ground," warned another. "It would be bad for the bank."

The bank president said, "Let's shelve it for a while."

"I'll have to resign from the bank," Wang Wen-san replied. "It is the only graceful way out."

"All you exchange students are alike," the president scoffed. "You take these things too seriously. Forget it."

"No, I told the American general we would give him the money. Now I must tell him we will not. The bank's face is at stake. My face is at stake."

Wang wrote his letter of resignation and showed it to his old schoolmate from Columbia, Y. L. Wang, owner of the Tung Kwan Cigarette Company.

"Hold it," said the Cigarette King. "Don't resign. I'll put up the money—under certain circumstances. . . . I must be the chairman of the board. Chennault would be the president, of course. Two of my men must be on the board; another will run the accounting office. But it must be clear, I will be the general's boss."

"Of course, you'll deserve all that if you finance the airline," Wang Wen-san replied. "But why do you emphasize that you want to boss the general?"

"Remember when I started making cigarettes in Sian? The city asked me to donate money for a farewell party for the famous American general. I paid eighty percent of the cost. But when the celebration began, I was denied the honor of meeting the general, because I was only a small merchant. Now I'll spend half a million dollars, I'll be the general's boss. I'll point at those cheapskates and say, 'Look! Who's the greatest now?'"

Chennault and the Cigarette King agreed. The tail of the planes would show the Chinese flag, and the nose would be decorated with the general's talisman—a tiger cub, the peaceable offspring of the Flying Tiger that had emblazoned his warplanes. And the name of the airline would be CAT. Official documents would bear the name

CNRRA Air Transport (CNRRA being the Chinese branch of the United Nations Relief and Rehabilitation Association). Eventually its legal name would become Civil Air Transport. But during its entire existence it would simply be called CAT.

Hawaii

It was noon the next day when the Air Corps DC-4 landed at Honolulu. On our way to a barbershop I said, "Imagine starting an airline with brand new airplanes."

"Most of them didn't fly a hundred hours before the war ended."

After indulging in every tonsorial luxury, I gave the barber a big tip and said, "The dirt and smells of China are off me," and he looked at me quizzically. Rossi and I headed for the interior of Oahu to view our fleet.

When we got to Wheeler Field, we stared at a graveyard where airplanes had gone to die. Our fifteen Curtis C-46s looked like decaying elephants. Brown, bloated, skin-diseased beasts. The engines were missing. Bulging fuselages were splotched with heavy grease. Olive-drab camouflage showed through the gook, giving the hulks a sinister appearance. The Hawaiian sunshine made the scene as stark as a neon-lighted morgue.

"This looks like the answer to what's the use," Rossi said.

"We ought to go get drunk, but who the hell wants to face this through a hangover?"

I had one of those what-am-I-doing-here feelings while scenes of ski slopes and Wisconsin Central Airlines flitted through my head.

We eventually found the dismantled engines, oiled and stored, in a warehouse. The gook on the fuselages was Cosmoline. The reason for the optimistic report we'd received in Shanghai became obvious. The planes were in perfect condition because they'd been pickled.

We stopped at the cable office to advise Shanghai the status of the fleet and then retired to Waikiki Beach.

Rossi stretched on his back, spread suntan lotion over his forehead, and said, "You have to admit, this beats getting stuck in Kweiyang." With a glint in his eye he turned to survey women who lounged in the sand. I'd seen his modus operandi in China, where he endured delays by slinging a hammock under a wing and snoozing. Missionaries pointed to him and said, "That's why Rossi has been able to stay in China so long." When others frantically tried to resolve some Asian frustration, he lounged in the shade of a wing with a book. Perhaps he'd read Rudyard Kipling's admonition:

> It's not good for the Christian health
> To hustle the Asian brown,
> For the Christian riles and the Asian smiles,

And he weareth the Christian down,
And the end of the fight is a tombstone bright,
In the name of the late deceased,
And an epitaph drear, a fool lies here,
Who tried to hustle the East.

Slender without looking frail, immaculate without appearing dapper, Rossi was neatly mustached and debonair. His carefree mien belied his past. He'd been jumped by Japan's Imperial Air Force and threatened by Himalayan granite. After graduating from the Navy's flight school at Pensacola he joined Chennault's American Volunteer Group in China and shot down six Japanese planes after America joined the war. In China National he had flown the Himalayan Hump more than any other pilot on earth. The Air Corps awarded the Air Medal after fifty trips. Rossi made 738.

"I told the Old Man I'd be chief pilot until he got going," Rossi said. "Never be chief—takes the fun out of flying. The best job is line pilot."

I didn't answer. I concentrated on women strolling along the beach. It was a revelation. I had forgotten the friendly, informal manner of American women, their refreshing forthright style.

Rossi hired a pilot named Wingfield whose wife was Hawaiian, and we discovered carefree backyard luaus.

Mechanics arrived, some from the Fourteenth Air Force, a few from China National, others from the U.S. mainland. They unpickled the Pratt & Whitney engines and mounted them with fuel pumps, magnetos, generators. Engines were bolted to airplanes. Airplanes were mounted on jacks while landing gears retracted and extended. Wing flaps cycled down and up. Chennault advised he was sending a demobilized Air Corps engineering officer who'd be project manager, whose duties included the purchase of spare parts.

Rossi and I met him at Wheeler Field. Almost six feet tall, handsome in spite of his bulk, in a neat gray suit, he removed a long cigar from his mouth, and a diamond ring sparkled. I happened to be closest. He gripped my hand and hung on while a commanding voice said, "Colonel Roderich."

"Felix Smith."

"You were in the service, of course, Smith—what was your rank?"

"Private, Air Corps Reserve." He released my hand. I felt as if I had vanished.

Turning to Rossi, he repeated, "Colonel Roderich."

"Dick Rossi, civilian." The colonel's nose twitched as if he detected a foul odor, and he disappeared among the airplanes.

Colonel Roderich spent the following day visiting government warehouses overflowing with parts that had been designated war surplus. At day's end the Hawaiian sunset, seen from the Moana Hotel bar, loosened us all. The colonel fired up an Alhambra Corona, the diamond ring sparkled, and he lamented, "It's no piece of cake, purchasing parts. Waste half my time parking."

My Mai Tai had raised a flush of magnanimity. "I'll drive you around tomorrow, Colonel."

Drive I did and parked his rented Packard while he went inside and ordered gadgets that would make our airplanes go. But after a couple of days with the colonel in the backseat ordering faster, slower, right, left, puffing clouds of Alhambra smoke, and referring to his rank at the slightest opportunity, I said, "When you want someone to fly an airplane, call me. I'll be on the beach."

Rossi got a communiqué the following morning. "Your pilots are undisciplined. Furthermore, you don't look like a chief pilot to me. I am the senior officer present. I therefore assume command of the pilots, effective immediately. You are relieved."

Rossi sat at the desk in the room we shared, composed an answer, and handed it to me for proofreading.

"General Chennault appointed me chief pilot; therefore, only the general can relieve me. Furthermore, you don't look like a colonel to me."

My guffaws were imprimatur enough. Looking immensely pleased with himself, Rossi poked it into a mail slot as we hurried to the beach. We had invited a few nurses from Queen's Medical Center to shoot Waikiki's surf in an outrigger canoe.

The next morning a slim youth from a Colorado mountain town showed up, listing with the weight of a metal toolbox. I was surprised to see, impeccably arranged inside, "Snap-On" tools, the best in the industry. Although he was only in his early twenties, his lower front teeth were false—the legacy of a crashed airplane on which he'd been flight engineer. The colonel scrutinized his cowboy boots and jeans, and frowned. "You're too young to go to China."

"That's all right with me. Soon as I get my year's salary I'll go back to Colorado." From his pocket, he pulled a folded yellow paper. "The way I figure," he drawled, "this here's a contract."

The colonel glared at it. The cablegram from Shanghai to Pueblo offered mechanic Lewis a salary of $550 a month.

"Put Lewis to work," the colonel said, but he got the supervisor of mechanics—Johnny Glass—aside and ordered, "Get rid of him at your first opportunity."

"Don't worry," Glass told Lewis, "you'll disappear, all right. I'm putting you on the first flight to Shanghai. That colonel's been trying to run my job ever since he got here."

As I drove them to Honolulu International, Lewis said, "My father told me, always get a contract."

At Pan Am's gate, Glass advised, "When the Colonel gets to China, stay out of his way, and you'll be okay."

Lewis chuckled and reseated his dentures with his tongue. "I'll take care of myself. When I left home my father told me, 'Always remember—the two most influential people in town are the chief of police and the madam of the whorehouse.'"

But the colonel never returned to China, nor did we see much more of him. While seeking happiness at the Hale Kualani bar, he met a vacationing Californian who sold used parts for trucks, and the purveyor could scarcely contain his excitement when he heard the colonel's tale.

The story began with a U.S. Navy supply officer who had the largest stockpile of aircraft parts in Hawaii. He'd received orders to auction it off in one fell swoop—for junk. The Navy supply officer admired General Chennault and saw an opportunity to benefit the new airline and the U.S. Treasury simultaneously: he'd sell the stockpile to Chennault for a song, but the price would be higher than any junkman's bid. The colonel's tale of the impending purchase made images dance. The Californian watched trucks turn into airplanes; his bank account and social status climbed as high as airplanes fly; he heard his own voice offer half his company to the wassailing colonel.

It was an easy decision for the colonel. Instead of purchasing the Navy's cache of airplane parts for Chennault, he got it for his new partner.

"It was General Chennault's own fault," explained the colonel. "He didn't get the funds to Hawaii on time, and the man from California was there with cash. The naval officer had to get rid of the stuff—he had no choice."

The colonel and the trucker took the spares to California, where their company grew into a large supplier of airplane parts, and CAT was slated to suffer in China with a shortage.

"You can't blame the colonel," I told Rossi. "His introduction to civilian life was traumatic."

"Yeah. His chauffeur abandoned his post and loafed on the beach—the chief pilot refused to stay fired—the despicable cowboy reached China."

"His subordinates were insubordinate."

"He couldn't court-martial anyone."

A new pilot got to Honolulu amid tumult and shouting: Marine captain Bob Buol—two Distinguished Flying Crosses and a citation from Admiral Halsey. A demobilization celebration with his Marine Corps buddies rocked the Niamalu Hotel.

In the morning the conscience of Buol told him his party must have sounded like Pearl Harbor to the unfortunate vacationer in the room below. He dispatched a dozen roses with a note: "May I apologize over lunch?"

She was Sue Pollock, a stunning woman with chestnut hair that hung in waves to her shoulders. A native of Minneapolis and a graduate of the University of New Mexico, she spent the war in the university's physics lab, where the proximity fuse was developed, and then in Washington, D.C., at the first National Academy of Sciences, which had been formed by the Joint Chiefs of Staff and America's leading scientists. At that venerable place Sue had been administrative assistant to Dr. Karl Compton, president of MIT.

"I came to Hawaii to cheer up," she said, and she laughed. Sue's laughter was as soothing as a Hawaiian breeze. "I had such exciting jobs during the war, I just know the rest of my life will seem unbearably dull."

I think Buol fell in love with her the evening she painted black shoe polish on the ankles of Joe Rosbert, a Flying Tiger ace. Invited to a formal celebration for the reopening of the Royal Hawaiian Hotel, the famous ace had dressed himself in a tuxedo, cummerbund, white tie—everything but black socks. There were none to borrow, and it was too late to buy what he had forgotten. The problem didn't baffle Sue.

Buol said, "You're just what we need in China."

"I have no intention of going to China," Sue replied, but the jaunty former Marine dwelled on the mystery of China and got the local manager to offer her a secretarial job in Shanghai's head office.

"I'll take you in my plane," Buol said, grinning. "You'll be safest with me."

The last person to join CAT before we left for China was Natasia, wife of Gene Bradley, one of our station managers. We threw a welcome party outside the Royal Hawaiian Hotel. We didn't go there often, because it was expensive, but we'd heard that Natasia was a Russian princess.

"Bradley met her in Chungking when he was in the Army," Rossi said.

When they arrived I was struck by her beauty. In a white summer dress, her body lithe and supple, she walked confidently, her head high. Good God, she was a princess for sure. Introduced to Buol, she flirted in the way of European women, a custom more social than provocative. Bradley introduced her to me, and I saw a white alabaster face framed by tawny silk hair. The upward tilt of her nose, its high bridge, accented Natasia's patrician appearance. Her blue eyes focused on me, and I felt I was assessed by a cobra.

I had been lucky enough to meet a Marine Corps pilot named Paul Nones who with his friends was starting an interisland airline called

Trans Air Hawaii. They called me "China Smith," took me on flights between the beautiful islands, and offered me a job. The sunshine, the beautiful American women—who knows why I returned to China?

We became increasingly busy with test flights. We monitored oil consumption, logged instrument readings, checked the hand-operated fuel valves on the auxiliary fuel tanks in the cabins—extra tanks that would enable us to make the long jumps between the Pacific islands. Paint remover was sprayed on olive-drab camouflage, slushed off with hoses and replaced with Chinese flags and Ministry of Communications registration numbers. Noses were decorated with the peaceful tiger cub.

A message from Shanghai said five Douglas C-47s, purchased at a military base in the Philippines, were airborne. We had 128 employees, mostly Chinese. Frank Hughes and Doug Smith had flown the inaugural flight from Shanghai to Canton on January 31 with food, medicines, a jeep, and a lone passenger—General Chennault himself. CAT had wings.

The message also said the secretarial job in Shanghai wasn't available after all. Sue's trip was canceled.

"Three hundred dollars I spent for clothes, and now I'm not going," Sue said.

"Never fear," Buol said reassuringly. "Get to Shanghai as best you can. Chennault will take one look at you and grab you."

I was in the first formation of three C-46s to head out from Hawaii, bound for China. Before taking off we said good-bye to the others, knowing they'd soon join us, but it was inconceivable then that most of us would spend the next twenty years together in Asia.

As I walked to the airplane I saw the peaceable tiger cub under the cockpit window and the Chinese flag on the tail. Little did I know what I would learn of civil war, revolution, dictatorship. Or of firm friends that could be won and lost.

Flying the Hump had put me in awe of Mother Nature's ferocity, but her wildest phenomenon is benign compared to human cruelties. And during our brutalities we're tantalized by exhibitions of nobility that flash, in those dark hours, like summer lightning.

Hungjao

"A sign we've reached China," I said when we ran into layers of stratus clouds with heavy rain. Our destination, Canton, waited inside China's south coast, seventy miles up the Pearl River. When gyrations of our radio compass told us we were overhead, we descended in a teardrop pattern to four hundred feet before we ran in and out of ragged bases of clouds and caught intermittent flashes of red mud rice paddies. At three hundred feet we saw the concrete of White Cloud Airport.

Lewis, in cowboy hat and jeans, waited on the tarmac with his team of Chinese mechanics. I said, "How do you like China?"

"It's enough to make a guy stop drinking." Lewis pointed at elephants working on a road project. "When the sun's shining, which ain't often, those critters plaster their hides with mud. After it dries I see pink elephants."

They removed the long-range fuel tanks and performed various inspections, and the next day the three C-46s headed for Shanghai, seven hundred miles north.

Fifty miles out of the big seaport we saw low afternoon sunlight bouncing off the huge hangars at Lunghwa—Shanghai's international airport. It was the home of China National Aviation Corporation, my previous employer. Their DC-3s glittered. The classy airplanes reflected the technical and financial support of Pan American World Airways. Compared to China National—"the Pioneer Airline of the Orient"—CAT was an orphan.

The ham that's in all pilots came out. We closed to a V formation, flew over Lunghwa at a respectable altitude, and then dived to skim the Whangpoo River where it parallels downtown Shanghai before flowing into the mouth of the Yangtze. Mystic eyes, carved into the bows of junks, told me I was really back in China. We pulled up to crisscross Shanghai a few times and then flew twelve miles west to land on a clay strip among vegetable farms. It was Hungjao, an abandoned fighter strip, our home port, courtesy of the Chinese government.

The head of CAT's secretariat, Tom Freeman—son of missionaries—had led a group of volunteer Chinese mechanics in filling potholes, removing sharp stones, and marking the borders of the obsolete strip with rocks. They highlighted the rocks with a mixture of white powder and water from a nearby stream. Freeman said, "I didn't know how big an airport could be until I carried those rocks."

CAT's security chief—former Chinese Army colonel Lee—stood ramrod straight. His was a striking face with bristle-brush eyebrows, stiff black hair, and flashing dark eyes. "If boof-a-low"—water buffalo—"try to cross our runway," he vowed, "I shall arrest and in—in—in"—his eyes squeezed shut and his bristle brows met until the word exploded from his mental dictionary—"*incarcerate* them. When farmers come to claim the beasts I shall in—in—*incarcerate* them also."

When I recalled the night China National's Captain Hall took off from Calcutta, hit a water buffalo, lost half his landing gear, all of his electrical system, and the fuel line to his right engine—and circled on one engine in darkness to crash-land back on the runway—I was delighted to hear our security chief's bombastic declaration.

"This aerodrome is Chinese history," he added. "I brought to a con—con"—eyes shut, brows squeezed—"*conclusion*"—beaming smile—"the Japanese truce. Nine August, nineteen thirty-seven. Jap army officer O—*Omaya* came here with his men. I told him, 'You cannot gain entrance upon sov—*sovereign* Chinese territory.' He ignored my order. They drove the vee—vee—*vee-hickle* through the gate. I told my guards, '*Send them where they belong!*' My men main—*maintained* their fire until the clips in their machine guns were empty." Colonel Lee beamed. "*Aagh*, it was *beautiful*. Japanese guts and blood all over the place. . . . The Japanese high command called it the mass—mass—*massacre*. I was their excuse for starting the war again. Eight years more fighting. They could not *defeat* us."

Hungjao's dirt-and-pebble strip wasn't much; no one else wanted it. To us, it was home. It felt that way after a Russian dressmaker in Shanghai fashioned a wind sock out of yellow silk.

We always found our home in those beginning days, even when clouds hugged the ground and made the view beyond our cockpit windows opaque white or black. We tracked the beacon to Lunghwa until our radio compass swung around and pointed aft. Knowing we were over the international airport, we headed 315 degrees at 115 miles an hour while descending to three hundred feet. In four minutes and fifteen seconds—with adjustments for the estimated wind—we saw the white rocks ahead. At night we saw two rows of flames wavering from coffee cans of sand and rags and crankcase oil.

Chennault

A crew car took us into Shanghai, to 255 Gordon Road, where CAT had rented a three-story Victorian mansion for the pilots, and it was inevitable that some wag would decorate the front veranda with a sign, CAT HOUSE. An amah did laundry while her rascal husband managed the house and squeezed excess profits with fuel and grocery chits.

The enthusiastic inhabitants had been honorably discharged from a Marine Corps detachment in Tsingtao, an Air Corps combat cargo squadron in Peiping (Beijing), a Navy air wing in Shanghai. One had been flying the C-47s while we were in Hawaii, waiting for the C-46s. "After we landed at some places," the C-47 pilot said, "our cargo wound up in town before we did. We found our relief supplies—canned food and stuff—on sale on the black market."

Another one said, "Radio beacons? China National owns them, but won't turn them on for us."

When someone squawked, "This sure is different from the Air Corps—no spare parts," I thought of Colonel Roderich.

"Think of the bright side—no damn regulations."

A group of us walked to Hwang's bar, where we nibbled watermelon seeds and sipped beer with slivers of ice while the jovial barman's son ran to the bank with our per diem checks. We were reimbursed for hotel and food bills outside of Shanghai but had agreed to fly without pay until the airline got into the black. Our postponed salary was eight hundred dollars a month plus overtime, which brought us up to eleven hundred.

The bar boy dragged in sacks of money that reminded me of the burlap sacks I'd stuffed with raked leaves in Wisconsin's autumns. When I flew the missionary plane a U.S. dollar had bought about two thousand dollars of CNC (Chinese National Currency); it had inflated to a quarter of a million and was still rising. We had sent the bar boy because it took the bankers such a long time to count it. They fanned out ten-thousand-dollar bills, flipped through them with deft fingers, and tied them into stacks with paper tape, which they stamped with an ivory seal. We just counted the stacks.

The powwow eventually centered on Chennault and the pilots' meeting he'd attend that night. Paul Holden said, "I heard the general chewed out the ops manager for asking which pilot he wanted for his Nanking trip. The general told him, 'Don't ever ask who I want. All my pilots are good—I'll fly with any of them.'"

Catfish Raine said, "That's the way the Old Man is. He sticks up for his pilots. In the Tigers, we didn't salute. He didn't care what we wore as long as we knew what we were doing in the air. He didn't tolerate sloppy flying."

"A British general asked him to reprimand us after we buzzed Rangoon," Rosbert said. "Chennault called us in and asked if it was a good tight formation."

"His pilots will do anything for him," Rossi said. "It's the brass he rubs the wrong way. He's forthright. Back in the thirties, when the bomber was the king of the air, he wrote an analysis—how pursuit planes could shoot down bombers. Colonel Hap Arnold read it and said, 'Who is this damn fellow Chennault?' Unfortunately for Chennault, Hap Arnold became general of the entire Air Corps."

Bus Loane said, "In 1937 he flunked a physical. The open-cockpit planes had wrecked his hearing. He was discharged. Then China hired him to train its air force. Before America got into the war—before Pearl Harbor—he organized the AVG, the American Volunteer Group, and the USA donated some obsolete P-40s."

"Japan's Zeros were more maneuverable. They turned tighter and climbed faster, but that didn't faze Chennault," Catfish said. "He sat us in a classroom with a chalkboard and itemized the characteristics of both planes and taught us how to exploit our strong points."

"We never got into turning maneuvers. Our P-40s had a wide turning radius compared to the Zeros," Shilling said. "He taught us to dive on them and keep on going. Our heavier weight and those in-line Allison engines made us dive faster than the Zeros, and they couldn't catch us, and we used the excess speed to climb back up."

"Chennault told us, never refuse a head-on pass—our firepower was much stronger," Rossi said.

"By the time we disbanded—just before the U.S. got into the war—our record was two hundred and ninety-four Japanese planes destroyed. We lost just six guys in the air-to-air combat," Catfish said.

"Chennault taught us to fly in pairs," Rosbert said. "The lead man focuses on the attack. His wingman protects him without distraction, because there're no other planes in the formation. In a turn, he just cuts across to the other side. In the old three-plane formation the guy on the outside of the turn had to speed up just to stay in place. It cost fuel."

"When the U.S. got into the war, Chennault became a general," I said. "The brass must have approved him."

"At Chiang Kai-shek's and President Roosevelt's insistence, Chennault was appointed commanding general of the Fourteenth Air Force," Rosbert said. "It galled the brass. When the war was almost won—only a couple of weeks before the Japanese surrendered— General Hap Arnold maneuvered him out of China and into retirement. He wasn't even invited to the surrender ceremony on the *Missouri*, even though he fought Japan longer than any other American—eight years. And the Fourteenth Air Force record was almost a legend."

I asked how Arnold got away with it, since Chennault was a war hero.

"Arnold offered medical retirement at full rank if he resigned quietly—or retirement at his permanent rank if he balked."

"Must be bitter."

"He didn't stay bitter," Catfish said. "He said no one can hurt you but yourself."

I was so absorbed by the Tigers' stories I forgot to drink my beer. It seemed only days and yet aeons ago that I had taught flying in single-engine putt-putts and read of these guys' exploits. I had never imagined I'd meet them someday, let alone drink with them; and flying for Chennault had been beyond my wildest dream. Yet in a couple of hours the pilots' meeting would begin and Chennault would be there.

I walked downstairs to our big dining room ten minutes or so before the meeting was supposed to start and saw a gray felt hat, in need of blocking, on our dining-room sideboard and Chennault at the long table with a few pilots who'd gathered. His robust body was relaxed but erect in an unstylish gray suit with wilting lapels. I was struck by the informality. When Chennault smiled at something a pilot said, his wide tight lips, down at the corners, straightened, cheek muscles tightened, their furrows deepened—and so did the

crow's-feet near his eyes. Not a Hollywood smile. His face looked as
weather-beaten as an airmail pilot's leather jacket. He held a lighted
cigarette between his thumb and forefinger as a maestro holds a
baton. He looked up at me, so I introduced myself.

"You're the China National pilot," he said. His voice was soft,
husky, modulated—a Louisiana drawl. Severe as he looked, he had
warmth in his expression and handshake, and a matter-of-fact, no-
pretense mien that put me at ease instantly, as if he were a fellow
pilot. In spite of his casualness, I sensed I was in the presence of
greatness. I looked integrity in the face and understood, for the first
time, charisma. When his luminous brown eyes turned toward whoever talked, the large eyeballs in their deep sockets moved in a way
that reminded me of an eagle on a pinnacle, surveying his domain;
but I also saw humanity and recalled an event I had read in newspapers. . . .

*Chennault is leaving Chungking two weeks before the end of the war,
unable to taste the fruit of victory. Thousands of Chinese swarm around
his car. The driver shuts off the engine while the people push it to a ceremonial platform. Chennault says he'll never forget his love of China
and the Chinese people. They file past, city people and peasants, take his
hand and shake it the way they had seen Westerners do. Tears trickle
down the cheeks of Old Leatherface.*

The chief pilot's voice brought me back to the here and now when he
opened the meeting. And when he introduced Chennault, the general
said, "I'm a military pilot—I don't know anything about running a
civilian airline. You fellas will have to show me how."

"The radio beacons, General. China National is telling their technicians to keep them off when we're around."

"We're negotiating with the airline to pay for their use. Long-
range, we'll get a good technician from the States and install our
own."

"Why are we impounded up-country, General? A week, sometimes."

"Our planes are new to various authorities. They'll get used to seeing us. If you don't get angry you'll win them over. The Chinese
respect self-control. If you show patience you'll be repaid a thousand
times over."

It wasn't a lecture. He spoke softly, in a matter-of-fact way. "The
country needs us. There's lots to do, apart from the relief supplies
you fellas are flying. Lots of people in Yunnan are out of work. The
tin mines are producing only ten percent of the world's tin. They can
do fifty percent if they have good transportation. People carry tin
ingots on their backs for days. Then sampans and trucks take the tin

to Rangoon or Canton. We can fly it to Haiphong for six cents a pound."

Maybe he wasn't lecturing, but he was as articulate as a professor of geography or economics.

"It'll take coordination with the French. And we'll have to persuade steamship companies to put into Haiphong. In the meantime we'll fly it to a river where junks will carry it to Canton."

At the end of the meeting, Chennault said, "We're going to have a baseball team. There's other teams around Shanghai we're going to beat." Another craggy smile. "Anyone who wants to play, come out tomorrow."

Roger Faye, a new pilot, blurted, "You can umpire, General."

Chennault's eyes got stormy. He grimaced. His inflection was decisive: "I'll pitch!"

A bottle of Jack Daniel's and glasses appeared, and everyone poured a couple of fingers and raised his glass, although nobody stood or mouthed a fancy phrase.

I knew I had made a good decision in sharing my destiny with this outfit.

5

Licking the Wounds

The next morning I was at Hunjao early, checking the weather at Hankow four hundred miles up the Yangtze, where I'd drop off an electrical generator for some factory. We'd take the rest of the cargo much farther west, to Kunming in the province of Yunnan. "From Kunming you'll bring back wolfram," the operations man said. Wolfram was tungsten ore. I walked to my twin-engine C-46 and watched barefoot men in rags use ropes and bamboo poles and hi-ho chants to worry the heavy generator from a flatbed truck to my plane. Inch by inch it moved toward our cargo door; they were going to have trouble clearing it. It'd take many men a long time.

Peering through horn-rimmed spectacles, C. Y Chu, my radio operator, looked like a physics professor. "If have engine trouble cannot throw out."

I nodded. "See they use plenty of rope. We don't want it shifting when we run into weather."

The airplane next to us was taking on sacks of vegetable and cotton seeds for the prairie town of Chengchow, where the planting season had begun.

I strolled over to another plane that was loading sheep. The American captain, six feet tall, lifted and shifted bales of hay as if they weighed nothing, making barriers to keep the animals from bunching up. Stopping to wipe sweat off his forehead, he said, "This kind of flying is new to me." He stuck out his hand, shook mine vigorously, and said, "Rousselot." Tidy hair and neat clothing suggested he liked to do jobs right, and piercing eyes hinted trouble for anyone who kept him from completing whatever he set out to do.

I pointed to pedigree numbers that had been singed into the woolly backs of the sheep. "Donated by New Zealand," he said. "Improve the stock." He cracked a smile, and his voice reminded me of Oklahoma cordiality. "We're callin' this Operation Bo-Peep."

I returned to my airplane to see if they had worried the generator through the door. It was in the cabin, but the loading boss held up the end of a tie-down rope and pointed at empty spaces overhead where tie-down rings had been. "What happened?" I asked.

My brainy radio operator said, "Mr. Winpisinger gets one-dollar bonus for every pound he makes airplane lighter."

"Winpisinger's the new chief engineer," I told our copilot.

"He told the company he can take fifteen hundred pounds off every airplane," the radioman said.

My copilot laughed. "This place ain't changed a bit. Chinese get the scoop before any of us round-eyes."

Although it was the copilot's first flight with CAT, it was his second time in China. He'd been a weather observer—a "balloon-buster," he called himself—with Chennault's Flying Tigers. After they disbanded he had returned to the States, where he learned to fly and got a job with a good airline, but he became bored. "Got an urge to come back," he said.

I threaded the tie-down rope through the lightening holes in the metal beams in the ceiling until the loadmaster got the idea. "The longerons aren't structured for that," I confessed, "but it'll get us to Hankow." Looking dismayed, the copilot shook his head.

We inspected the belly compartment and found an empty space where oxygen bottles had been. "Don't bark at us," an American mechanic said. "Orders from Winpisinger."

"We'll probably need oxygen where we're going," I said, and he got us a couple of walk-around bottles.

While taxiing out, I mumbled, "All the horseshit you gotta go through before you push the throttles up."

The Curtis-Electric four-bladed props snarled when we charged down the runway, and I knew we kicked back a storm of dust and pebbles. Close to the end we broke ground, then retracted the landing gear and relaxed when we felt the wheels drop onto the latches in the wheel wells.

By the time we reached our cruising altitude we were in the multilayered flat stratus clouds that a warm front can bring. As we cruised at 155 miles an hour in heavy rain, water flowed around us as if our streamlined windshield were the bow of a submarine, and I wondered how Pratt & Whitney engineers had managed to design an air-cooled engine that could run submerged. Although it was midmorning the cockpit was as dark as an underwater cave. Water muffled the roar of the engines and cooled them. The cylinder-head temperatures dropped. I pushed the propeller rpm up to 2,100 and was relieved to see the needles settle on 150 degrees centigrade, the manufacturer's recommended minimum.

There weren't any navigation aids on our route, but we'd be passing fifty miles south of Nanking, the peacetime capital of China, and it had a powerful radio beacon. The needle of our radio compass pointed to the right of our nose and swung slowly aft, clinging to Nanking. We got a positive fix with the simple equation that coastwise mariners have been using for decades: the 45/90 bearing. Distance run equals distance off, because both sides of a 45/90 triangle are equal. When our radio compass pointed forty-five degrees off our nose, the copilot jotted the time on our radio log.

The needle slowly worked its way to ninety degrees. Twenty minutes. We had flown fifty miles. That meant Nanking was also fifty miles off our right wing. I had a mental image of China's capital, the bend in the Yangtze, the flat farms, and the single cone shape of Purple Mountain. The airplane's instrument panel painted mental pictures as clearly as black dots conjure sounds for a musician examining a score.

An hour later we ran out of the heavy stuff, but we remained in clouds. The copilot tuned in a radio station, heard the Morse code for HK—dit-dit-dit-dit, dah-dit-dah—and then we were sure it was the Chinese Air Force beacon at Hankow. When the needle of our radio compass swung rapidly from ahead to behind, the copilot picked up his mike and reported overhead. A Chinese accent cleared us for an approach and gave us the altimeter setting, and we leaned forward to adjust our altimeters to the local barometric pressure. I pulled off some power and called, "Half flaps." After descending outbound at a forty-five-degree angle to the runway we turned back toward the beacon and recrossed it at a thousand feet while rain hammered our windshield. We peered ahead for a sight of the runway but didn't see a damn thing except a gray mask that said we were in heavy clouds. "Gear down," I said, while I watched the radio compass and adjusted our heading for wind drift. We hung to the imaginary line that stretched from the beacon behind us to the runway ahead of us. And we continued our descent: nine hundred feet, eight hundred, seven hundred. . . .

I sensed the copilot's eyes bugging out. When a fellow pilot sits alert at the dual controls, he's your Siamese twin and you can read his mind. The Stateside airline had pampered him with sophisticated navigation aides.

At four hundred feet we saw gray concrete ahead. I opened the windshield wiper valve, the copilot breathed a sigh of relief, I called, "Full flaps," and we splashed down.

We stopped at the far end of the concrete, where the water overflowing from a rice paddy was almost knee-deep. A farmer fished.

"Not only is he fishing on the runway," the copilot said, "but damned if he didn't catch one." The fish wriggled at the end of his line.

"They plant baby fish in rice fields," our radioman said. "Grow big enough for eating before the dry season."

Back on the tarmac, standing in the rain, waiting to off-load our generator, laborers wore neatly woven grass capes that shed rain as efficiently as any thatched roof.

We left Hankow in a southwesterly direction, swallowed by clouds soon after we were airborne. Four hours later, still in weather, knowing the winds were unpredictable, I wanted some kind of navigation fix. I turned around and told our radioman, "Ask China National to turn on their Kweiyang beacon."

After a lot of metallic clattering of his telegrapher's key he said, "China National radio operator cannot open beacon for CAT." His boss had ordered it, he said. I showed our radioman a chart and pointed to a 14,500-foot mountain about sixty miles to the right of our course line. That's all I had to do. He was smart enough to know an adverse wind could carry us that far off course. "Monitor all the frequencies," I said. "If you hear a China National plane, ask the captain to call me on a voice frequency."

I heard our radioman broadcast over and over again dah-dit-dah-dit, dah-dit-dah, the code for "Anyone who hears me, please answer." After several minutes with no reply, I pushed the props and throttles up to climb power, and we strapped oxygen masks to our faces. The radioman plugged his oxygen hose into a walk-around bottle while the copilot and I took turns at the other small bottle. Damn Winpisinger, I cursed, while I blessed my old instructors— MacPherson, the canny Scot, and Pottschmidt, the genius who looked like a bookkeeper—for showing me how to be cagey. We leveled off at sixteen thousand feet and then tuned in Kunming and waited to get within range.

For much too long a time, our radio compass wandered aimlessly. It was a phenomenon that had something to do with changes in the ionosphere near sunrise or sunset.

I held a compass heading until the clouds broke up and we saw, still far ahead, a blue lake, twenty miles long, that the Chinese had named "the Pearl on the Plateau."

A chalk-white cliff rising from its western shore looked as familiar as the face of an old friend. Called "Old Baldy" by pilots in the big war, the white cliff marked the beginning of the Hump, the first landmark before crossing the Himalayas to India.

Like Denver, Kunming was a mile high. After we landed, our station manager greeted us. He was Captain Chang, formerly of the Chinese Navy, who had been decorated for pulling Chennault's

Fourteenth Air Force pilots out of the South China Sea during raids on Kong harbor.

"The CAF"—Chinese Air Force—"will ground you, also," said Captain Chang, pointing at another C-46 on the tarmac. "Holden's been here a week."

We found him in the CAT hostel, which was a wooden cabin overlooking mountains and terraced farms. Holden was more handsome than his namesake, the movie star. His hair neatly combed, he wore a pressed Army officer's shirt without insignia. His expression was one of amusement, bordering on surprise. He hunched a shoulder toward an ear and said, "Sharecroppers in Kansas have better shacks than this."

"It ain't the Air Corps barracks, for sure," I said.

"I didn't expect it to be like Uncle Sugar, but I didn't think it'd be this honked up. We're orphans—no nav aids, no runway lights. . . ."

I just grunted. Zany China, I thought. Hailed a democracy amid deeds of autocracy, it was a loose assortment of feudal states. Lousy communications made it so. People were separated by mountain ranges and dialects. They communicated via radio in the dit-dahs of Morse code after translating Chinese into English and then back to Chinese. They wouldn't telegraph their own language—they don't have an alphabet. Provincials mistrusted strangers in the distant central government.

The isolation bred certain kinds of freedom. It made space for colorful idiosyncrasies—like "the Christian General," the late Feng Yu-Shang, who had enthusiastically converted his troops to Christianity and then baptized them en masse with a fire hose. Other generals were free to withhold their soldiers' pay and lend it commercially for personal profit. Chinese Air Force commanders got away with renting combat cargo planes to merchants. Army press-gangs snatched youths off village streets and denied it when parents came searching for missing sons. Provincial governors felt free to levy an import duty on merchandise from other parts of China.

I stopped musing when someone said, "Let's eat," and I told them I remembered a good restaurant from my China National days.

The short walk over dikes between farms, after sunset, was tranquil. Homes of adobe brick with roofs of blue tile exuded cooking smoke from open windows. Six thousand feet high, the air smelled crisp and sweet except for whiffs of pigs and an occasional nostril-jolting stench from a pool of human excrement. Farmers stored feces in open pits until it was time to fertilize the crops. Holden asked, "What's that stink?"

"Shit."

"I know that, for God's sake, but what have they done to it?"

Kunming's multiple gates, weathered and ornately carved, gave an impression that we were walking back in history. Marco Polo had walked through them. The notorious Burma Road ended here. If we continued on through the city and trudged west, we'd eventually cross the deep gorges of the triple rivers, parallel and close to each other, cascading dramatically: the Yangtze, Salween, and Mekong. It's where Chennault's Flying Tigers bombed bridges to bring an abrupt end to the Japanese advance on China in the recent war. In a southerly direction, Lolo tribesmen—headhunters and opium growers—lived in rugged hills that stretched to the Indochina border.

Although Kunming was the capital of Yunnan Province, it looked like a backwater enclave, forgotten by time. Crowds eyed us curiously as if they'd never before seen Westerners; as if the foreign devils who had spent the big war there had left no tracks, as if they had been swallowed by China.

I pushed my way into a restaurant, saying, "We call this the Hoc Shop." Diners spat chicken bones and husks of watermelon seeds on the floor. They laughed and shouted numbers while poking the air with various combinations of fingers in a drinking game that was a more sophisticated version of the paper-scissors-rock game played by American kids. Male patrons had removed their shirts, and a kid with an impending bowel movement was set onto a porcelain cuspidor next to our booth.

Holden twitched a shoulder and appeared to be watching Barnum and Bailey's circus parade through Greenleaf, Kansas. "This is what I call gettin' out among 'em," the Kansan said.

"Fookay," called Chu, and a waiter appeared. In no time we were jabbing our chopsticks at succulent chicken with black bean sauce, garlicky eggplant and red-devil peppers, crispy sweet-sour carp, bright-green crunchy steamed *choi-som*. "Bamboo shoots?" Holden said. "What do you think I am, a termite?"

Walking back, past Kunming's gates, we illuminated our way with flashlights. No lights shone in farmhouses. The countryside was dark and silent.

We were glad when Civil Aviation headquarters approved our return to Shanghai; our planes had been loaded with burlap sacks of tungsten ore. But when Holden and I presented our flight plans to Chinese Air Force operations, the duty officer puffed out his chest and shouted, "Not approved."

Holden looked at me sideways, and I read his mind. Like me, he was recalling Chennault's advice to show patience. We heard a commotion and stepped outside to watch military police herd about a dozen Chinese Air Force enlisted men onto a truck. Even though they were in leg chains and the MPs threatened them with bayonets and long rifles—relics from the First World War—the captives laughed with bravado and waved to wives and girlfriends who stood on the tarmac and wailed. The women were too absorbed in grief to wave back.

"Smuggling opium," Chu said. Grinning, pointing a finger at his head and wiggling his thumb, he said, "Execution, maybe."

Captain Chang, our station manager, hurried over and said, "Go back to the hostel. I'll bring some watermelons."

"He's embarrassed for our country," C. Y. Chu said. "He wants to get you off the airfield."

On the way to the hostel, Holden's copilot said, "They grow opium south of here, in the hills. And lots of it comes across the border, from Indochina."

"The officers are too smart to smuggle opium," Chu said. "They make big money renting airplanes to merchants. We call the CAF the Cumshaw [extra money] Airline."

Captain Chang's driver carried some watermelons into the kitchen, and the cook hacked them open. I used chopsticks to pick up chunks of the bright yellow flesh and slurped it. Holden said, "Damned if you haven't become Chinese." Nobody else spoke.

Eventually, Captain Chang walked in. He didn't mention the arrest of the CAF men; he just said, "The return cargo delayed our departure. The CAF got word from Nanking. They say we're a United Nations relief airline and we can't take out commercial cargo. They don't care if it is tungsten ore."

"An airline that flies empty half the time ain't gonna last," the new copilot said.

"Pan American is behind it," Chang said. "They own twenty percent of China National."

"We're invading their turf," I said.

"China National has been around a long time—they have friends in the Ministry of Communications."

"Back home we call 'em lobbyists," the copilot said.

"Before the war ended," Chang explained, "your Foreign Economics Commission wanted to know the number of planes China would need after the war. Chennault guessed two hundred. Pan American got the contract to run the survey. They came back and said thirty. Thirty happened to be the number of planes in China National's fleet."

"Big business," I said.

"The American administrator was shocked," continued Chang. "Like Chennault, he had estimated about two hundred planes."

I thought of the tungsten ore stacked near the tarmac and of ships leaving Shanghai empty. If stuff didn't get to world markets, China wouldn't get hard currency.

"You probably know the man who was Foreign Economics administrator," Chang said. "His name is Willauer."

"Chennault's partner. We haven't met him."

"You will soon. Willauer isn't one to stick to a chair. President Roosevelt sent him to organize the economy of the Philippines after the war. His uncle was Admiral Whiting, one of the first pilots to fly off a carrier. Willauer is crazy about the Navy. I wouldn't be surprised if CAT got a ship or two."

The next morning a message from Shanghai told us to unload our cargo of tungsten ore and return empty.

"So much for the economy," I said.

Holden hurried toward his airplane, shouting, "Shanghai, here I come. I'm ready for a cold one."

I hollered, "I know just the place."

Earthquake Magoon

The next day I showed Holden the Palace Hotel's café bar, which was a favorite of Shanghai's business hierarchy and where deals were negotiated, and it was one of the few oases that served chilled bottles of Tsingtao beer. Holden hadn't been out of his combat cargo squadron, or out of Greenleaf, long enough to tolerate the warm brew with slivers of dirty ice that you got everywhere else. While we nursed the beer I looked through the café's french doors to the hotel lobby and the grand staircase with its plush red carpet that was held taut on each step by a polished brass rod. Laborers carried up wooden buckets of steaming water. I saw a broad foreign man with a bluff face and a black Vandyke beard. Massive eyebrows, like inverted gull wings, reached around the sides of his forehead. Feet planted on the lobby floor, hands on huge hips, he bent forward and scowled as if he didn't know the working class went barefoot on cold days.

Hustling up the stairs, a laborer banged a bucket against the Victorian balustrade and slopped water onto the plush carpet. Blackbeard let out a belly-shaking laugh and headed for the café with an agility that said his hulk wasn't all fat. He stopped at our table to point at the wet staircase and growl, "I thought this was a high-class joint."

"When the Japs left town," I said, "they stole the plumbing. If you want a hot bath it's fifty cents a bucket, leaves and all."

"Didn't expect to find Yank civilians in Shanghai." His wide eyebrows merged into a theatrical scowl as he leaned forward to say in mock confidence, "I could tell you were Yanks by your haircuts." He sat down and bellowed, "Beer." The baggy-tweed Englishmen at the next table stopped sipping their pink gin and stared.

The Falstaffian character caught me eyeing the Air Corps hardware on his shirt. He pointed toward a window, in the direction of the Whangpoo River. "I'm on the aircraft carrier; liaison between the Chinese Air Force and U.S. Navy. . . . I just told the Chinese colonel, 'You speak English—what's the use of you telling me, and then me telling the skipper? Tell him yourself. I'm going ashore.'"

"You believe in eliminating the middleman," I said.

"Navy told me I couldn't go. Said the last liberty boat was gone. 'I'll show you deck apes how to get ashore,' I said. I gave 'em this." He stuck two fingers in his mouth and whistled one prolonged blast. Patrons turned around. "Bumboat came alongside smartly. Cunning bastard charged me double. Said I was double weight." He laughed more high-pitched toots. By now even the dapper Chinese black marketeers were staring.

I stood up. "Time to shove off." I put about 350,000 Chinese dollars on the table and dropped another 40 Gs, more or less, for a tip.

"Where're you guys headed?" Christ, he was coming along.

"To pick up our checks." The three of us walked out onto Nanking Road and around the corner of the Bund, which was a wide boulevard along the Whangpoo River, where the aircraft carrier and a couple of destroyers tugged at anchor chains; and it was busy, as usual, with deepwater junks with the eyeballs that had been carved into their hulls to prevent collisions at sea. On our right were tall stone buildings of prestigious trading houses and banks.

In a block or two we came upon the *North China Daily News* building, where a hag paced back and forth. Scrawny except for a fat belly, which I guessed was a pillow under her dress, she held a placard: GENERAL CHENNAULT IS THE FATHER OF MY CHILD.

Our huge companion chuckled. "Your boss?"

"Extortion," I said. "They'll do the same for you when you're famous."

"In my case it'll be true." He broke into a bullhorn laugh.

We turned into the *News* building and climbed flights of stairs to our head office.

"Where're you guys flying?"

"All over China," Holden said. "We fly the usual stuff—you know, coal, tungsten ore, hog bristles." He was trying to keep a straight face. "Last flight I turned around and saw two big brown eyes staring me in the face—a cow was trying to come into the cockpit."

I said, "He's Paul and I'm Felix. We're flying relief supplies in and anything out that we can get."

The giant chuckled and put out his hand. "Jim McGovern." And then, gruffly, "Friends call me Earthquake Magoon."

Our offices echoed a staccato clatter of abacuses. Desks held glasses of hot water with sunken tea leaves, vases of brushes, and slabs of dry ink with small water wells.

Henry Yuan, the airline's liaison with the Chinese government, stood in his blue Mandarin gown and shook both his hands before him, Chinese-style, when I introduced McGovern. Jenny Huang smiled easily and gave us our per diem checks.

When Holden and I turned to go, Earthquake Magoon was rooted to the floor, staring into a roomful of secretaries.

Glossy hair flowed neatly over their high-necked cheongsams, but the modesty of the prim, neck-girdling collars was belied by the rest of the tailoring. Skintight, the dresses accentuated beguiling curves, while split skirts flashed glimpses of ivory thighs. Earthquake Magoon was as motionless as a taxidermist's bear. Speared by lust.

"Look at that big clown," Holden whispered. "You could knock his eyeballs off with a stick."

On our way down the stairs I said, "We call Henry Yuan 'Prince Henry.' His father was Yuan Shih-kai, the second-last emperor of China. Once in a while you see his face on coins. And Jenny is the fourteenth daughter of the fifth concubine of the chief customs inspector. He used to be rich."

I don't think he heard me. Earthquake Magoon was uncharacteristically quiet, but when we got outside he said, "How does a guy get a job in this lash-up?"

Shanghai

After Earthquake Magoon returned to his ship, Holden pursued his Russian girlfriend and I wound up in some rowdy nightclub where insensitive sods, mostly Westerners, gabbed and swilled so much they didn't even look when a five-piece orchestra answered the downbeat and a Russian ballerina drifted onto the dance floor. A clanking spotlight turned her tiara of fake gems into a princess's crown, and her dancing made the joint a palace.

My invitation for her to join me at my table, relayed by a waiter, handsomely tipped, was ignored. I saw sadness behind her smile as she danced solos from classic ballets, and I guessed she was one of the Russians whose parents had escaped to China in 1918 after the First World War when the victors of the Bolshevik Revolution rampaged against the rich, the titled, and the Jewish. Refugees fled in Gobi Desert caravans or across the Manchurian border, where the Chinese government declared them stateless. Without a country to call their own or passports for travel, they were stuck in China, vulnerable to any bureaucrat's whim.

Less fortunate Russian refugees became streetwise survivors, like the doorman who wanted to fetch a taxi when I emerged from the Palace Hotel bar. I told him I was just crossing the street. "Then I'll carry you across for an American dollar." His cheerful offer seemed like a good idea to one who'd been overserved by the Palace bartender, so I jumped on the doorman's back and he piggybacked me across Nanking Road to a clip joint in the Sassoon Arcade.

After downing a fake Scotch that tasted like a guarantee for a head-busting hangover, I accompanied my buddies to Avenue Joffre in the French Quarter of Shanghai's former International Settlement. The once-prestigious avenue had become a street of dives where Russian barmaids stood shoulder to shoulder. "Scotch," I said. My voluptuous bartender with half-out bosoms cooed, "You buy me cockstail, no?" I said sure.

She poured an amber fluid into her aperitif glass and a watchful, unsmiling Chinese manager gave her a brass token, which she tossed into her purse. It landed with a clank. Raising her glass, which I guessed held cold tea, she said, "My dalink, I luff you." Moments later her glass was dry. "You buy me 'nother cockstail?" Just for a change, I answered no and she shouted, "You soman-abeetch chip-skate."

The Chinese guy said, "Show starting downstairs, gentlemen. You see good performance?"

"We're not patrons of the arts," I said. We had once seen the raunchy exhibitions where every imaginable sexual aberration was performed on a stage.

Even more depraved, I thought, were various Chinese government potentates who skimmed the cream off millions of U.S. dollars that poured into the nation for its postwar reconstruction. The numbers were published in newspapers. Eighty-two million from the Import-Export Bank on Victory Day; five hundred million several months later; fifty million more in long-term credit. I couldn't comprehend the numbers. Middle-class Chinese lived spartan lives because the local currency inflated daily in great leaps. People with a lot of money bought gold bars. Smaller Chinese bills were converted to American bills at money changers' shops. If local currency was needed for shopping, they'd visit a money changer to convert whatever was needed. More was paid for clean crisp U.S. bills, so families washed and ironed them, and the American money that circulated in Shanghai felt soapy.

The government's inability to adjust salaries for inflation corrupted its officials. Policemen survived economically by arresting motorists for speeding even if they weren't. A bribe paid on the spot was better than spending all night at a police substation, arguing over one's rights. Firemen connected hoses to hydrants near fires and wrestled with the "faulty" valves until the frantic owner of the burning building donated a few gold bars.

One of the pilots, a history buff, said, "The Chinese brag about their ancient wisdom, but I don't see any of it nowadays. Eight hundred years ago they had a prime minister named Wang An-shih who believed in revising the budget and raising salaries to keep bureaucrats honest."

A visiting professor of sociology said, "Shanghai's majority, living on the verge of poverty, seem all the more tragic in light of the lack of compassion or patriotism among the privileged."

Predators from all over the world smelled the money that poured into China. CAT was not immune, although the shark that sampled us was a half-baked con man disguised as an aviation consultant. He produced a letter from a fictitious uncle who asked for the privilege of investing a portion of his fortune in the new and promising Chinese airline. The mythical financier also recommended his nephew, bearer of the letter, who had just returned from Spain, where his expertise had elevated the stature of Iberian Airlines. The letter dazzled CAT's board of directors, who'd been wondering how to meet the next payroll. Nephew Anderson was hired on the spot, and I was assigned to fly him on an inspection tour of our bases. Glib and faceless as any car salesman named Honest John, our consultant watched me wind my twenty-four-hour chronometer and said, "My best friend runs Pan Am's instrument shop at San Francisco International—he'll put that in tip-top shape for you."

My trusting Anderson with my timepiece must have increased his confidence in my gullibility, because he started telling outrageous whoppers. "I flew a DC-4 in Russia during the war. You wouldn't believe the cold in northern Russia, especially at twenty-five thousand feet. . . . All of a sudden the engines stopped—all four engines, all at once, frozen stiff by the cold. . . . I glided down and landed on a frozen lake. You probably read about it—I got a medal."

I pretended to believe him and said I'd be needing my timepiece the next day.

"Darn," he said. "I already sent it to San Francisco."

I locked my camera equipment and ceased feeling like a pigeon after discovering he'd bilked a Russian refugee out of ten thousand U.S. dollars and some CAT employees out of less.

His only professional advice to CAT management: "When I inspected your Canton station I discovered the pilots' house is across the street from the secretaries' house. This is not good. Next thing you know—babies!"

The Foreign Affairs Police gave him twenty-four hours to get out of China.

Two Shanghai institutions rose above the sleaze, like flowers in a swamp. One was the Columbia Country Club, a genteel establishment where a smattering of diplomats hung out with officers of the British and American Tobacco Company and the caliphs of Standard Oil. The other enclave of sanity was the Catholic Church and its Sacred Heart and Zikawei Convent schools, whose students became fluent in French, English, and Chinese. Jesuit priests who were also meteorologists were the best typhoon forecasters in Asia.

The employees of China's three airlines breathed life into a third oasis. Tired of Shanghai's nightclubs with their poisonous booze and exorbitant prices, the rank and file of China's three airlines—unlike our corporate executives, who mistrusted each other—chipped in two hundred dollars each and bought a floundering nightclub that we remodeled and renamed "the Airline Club." We hired a manager and awarded him a share of the receipts, which inspired him to search out a master chef plus a sweet and swinging dance orchestra.

It was a relief to step off the streets of frenetic Shanghai into our club, see white tablecloths, hear our favorite tunes or the murmur of friends, confident the drinks weren't spiked with rotgut, and know we wouldn't get hustled.

I got reacquainted with the pilots and mechanics I had known in China National and met new friends in the Central Air Transport Corporation (CATC). We all engaged in uninhibited laughter, away from the abrasiveness of Shanghai. It was a step into a new world. Pan Am crews and those of Northwest Airlines and British Overseas Airways discovered our hideout and added to the cosmopolitan ambience. The club remained a happy refuge until the Communists kicked us out of China.

An American writer, Hal Du Berrier, who hung out at the Airlines Club, took me to the apartment of a Russian widower who lived on a meager fee from the Shanghai Symphony. His name was Dimitri, and he set out glasses that he filled with vodka that he'd laced with shreds of lemon peel. After toasting us he turned and raised his glass to his bass viol, which leaned against the wall. "One of the family," he said. I asked if it came from Russia. "That instrument is the only thing we carried out. . . . Gangs roamed and shot down anyone that looked Jewish. The hoodlum groups were called pogroms. 'Pogrom' means 'like thunder.' We were afraid to go to our bank. My wife sold her jewels until we had enough to take a ship from Vladivostok to southern Manchuria. We slept on deck, my wife and me and my bass viol; she joked about the ménage à trois."

The door burst open, and Sandra walked happily in, put her books on the table, and hugged her father. Dimitri poured a token drink of vodka for his daughter, and she raised her glass. Slender, ebullient,

Sandra looked at me with oversize brown eyes. Eventually, Sandra told me she attended Aurora College and worked part-time at an insurance office on the Bund. How different she seemed from Shanghai's fast set, how like women back in America's distant Midwest, how uncomplicated and refreshing. I invited Sandra and her father to the club.

After he left for a symphony rehearsal, Sandra headed for her favorite shop to buy stockings, which she needed before reporting for work the next day. I accompanied her down Wuchow Road, where we both were surprised to find the shop jammed full of coffins—a dozen or so. Tong, the hosiery merchant, in between the coffins, still sold pairs of stockings, one after the other. With her fluent Shanghai dialect, Sandra carried on an animated conversation. Tong told her his landlord had tried to evict him so he could lease the shop to a wealthier joss merchant who had offered to pay higher rent. Although Tong's lease had expired, he had a right to remain in the shop, he argued, because he had spent his own money renovating it and had offered to renew his lease. But the landlord had ignored him.

When it was obvious that Tong wouldn't budge, the landlord returned with his concubine and several nasty men who carried coffins into the shop. Legal, the landlord claimed, because the law allowed him to open a new business ten days after a lease expired. Although it was a ploy to discourage Tong's customers, the disinclination to haggle among coffins was overcome by Tong's low prices.

A week or so later, Sandra and I walked over to see how Tong fared. He wasn't there. The joss merchant was in his place. Sandra questioned the purveyor of fans next door. I recognized a word or two amid laughter: "*Guon-chai-pu . . . nil-wu . . . shee . . . yee foo dren. . . .*"

After Sandra and I resumed our stroll, she explained, "The landlord came back again with the nasty men. They had more coffins—it was like a parade with the whole neighborhood watching. They piled the new coffins on top of the others. The landlord's concubine walked in, followed by his mother, who carried a chamber pot full of you know what. She put it on top of the coffins. . . . Poor Tong, he moved out." After some silence, Sandra said, "Coming from America, you must think it's insane."

"A refreshing change," I said, "from lawyers and suing."

On the night Sandra wanted to stay home and study, I dropped into the Airline Club, where I found one of the Catholic priests who had taught us aviation meteorology and typhoon forecasting during my China National days.

"Jesuits invariably know where they can get a good drink," I said.

"A welcome respite from Sin City," he said. "Good as a trip home . . . marvelous for you pilots." After a few sips, he summed up

China's busiest city. "If God doesn't destroy Shanghai, He'll have to apologize to Sodom and Gomorrah."

When I got back to the CAT house I found a message ordering me to General Chennault's office in the morning.

Oil Explorers

On my way downtown in a taxi I wondered why Chennault wanted to see me. I hadn't been in CAT long enough to make a mess of anything . . . had I?

Through an open door I saw a wall map of China, a chalkboard telling when and where airplanes were headed, an army cot where Chennault napped daily from noon to one, and the general himself, at a bare desk, yellow pencil in hand, writing.

I rapped on the doorjamb. He looked up, nodded, motioned to a chair beside him, put out his hand, and said, "I heard you're a good photographer."

"I have a good camera, General."

He walked to the map and laid a finger near the top on the tan part marked *Gobi Desert*. In his soft Louisiana drawl, he said, "Geologists want to explore this." I walked over and saw a dot marked *Chu Chuan*. Chennault moved his finger two inches north.

"Gravel washed down this mountain and leveled off at Chu Chuan. The Chinese Air Force lands there. Photograph it, sketch it, tell me if it's good for our C-47s." We returned to the chairs.

"I want to start an operation in the northwest. Strong Muslims up there—they don't like Communists any better than we do." I said yes sir.

"We'll carry fifty-five-gallon drums of fuel," Chennault said. "I'm thinking of single planes that can land anywhere. We won't be dependent on airstrips—we'll be the glue that holds those leaders together."

My copilot was Doug Smith, only weeks out of a combat cargo squadron. Hwang, our radio operator, sat in his cubicle behind us, sending our position reports and copying weather broadcasts. Four Chinese geologists from the China Petroleum Corporation and three Texas oilmen sat on canvas benches on either side of their crates of equipment, which had been lashed to the C-47's floor. The Chinese leader had pleaded, "Please land softly—our instruments are delicate."

The Texans, representing the United Nations, grinned. One of them said, "These gentlemen are three-quarters of all the geologists in China—the oil explorers, I mean."

In a little over an hour we crossed the Yangtze River and saw cone-shaped Purple Mountain rising out of flat farmlands near Nanking. For the next couple of hours the central plains were obscured by a flat undercast. Our shadow, circled by a rainbow, ran along with us until the clouds broke up over mountains, and we saw a valley of the Yellow River and Sian. Another two hours put us within sight of giant waterwheels near a city of wide streets and rows of poplar trees and an encircling wall that was twenty feet thick and bristled with parapets and watch towers. It was the Muslim city of Lanchow.

Our landing happened to be smooth, and when we walked back to the passenger cabin, the Chinese geologists applauded while their leader patted one of the crates and said, "Thank you."

Jeeps carried us past grayish clay mountains honeycombed with caves where people lived like Pueblo Indians. Ornate doors closed the caves. Outside Lanchow's imposing wall, a stick-and-matting shantytown leaned crookedly against the wall's massive black stones.

We entered the tall gate and drove down streets that were deserted except for an occasional horse-drawn water cart fashioned from a rusty fifty-five-gallon drum that had once held aviation gasoline. The few male pedestrians looked pale, thin, stoic, in white smocks and black skullcaps. A white cap, rarely seen, indicated the wearer had made his pilgrimage to Mecca.

We stopped at a rambling wooden building that was a hotel of spacious rooms around an inner courtyard. The large lobby was colorful with a life-size mural of a Russian winter that seemed alive with Muscovites in colorful coats, black fur hats, and scarves that streamed behind while they raced in horse-drawn sleighs or old-fashioned Hans Brinker ice skates that curled over their toes.

It was close to sunset when Hwang guided Doug and me toward a restaurant, and the streets were so quiet we could hear a twanging of stringed bows in shops where tables were heaped with raw wool. The proprietor gripped a long bamboo bow that had been bent by a single tight string of sheep gut, which he plucked hard enough to get it humming, and then he held it on top of a pile of wool. The vibrating string fluffed up strands, which his wife pulled off and carried to her spinning wheel.

We turned into a restaurant courtyard, where we sat on benches and watched our cooks squat on the ground and barbecue strips of lamb that had been marinated in aromatic tongue-searing oils and spices. We stuffed it in pockets of unleavened, grainy bread coated with toasted sesame seeds. Our tea, brewed from toasted grains of whole wheat, had a pleasant nutty flavor.

It was pitch dark when we finished. The air had turned crisp and the stars shimmered. We walked in companionable silence until we came upon a shop, still open and illuminated by Coleman lamps. "The owner buys things from grave robbers," Hwang said. "He knows foreigners are in town; that's why he's still open."

Doug Smith looked around and haggled over a dirty cylindrical vase covered with cracked mosaic bits, and I wondered why he wanted that piece of junk. I bought two clay pots because they were decorated with ochre-colored zigzag spirals of the American Indian thunder pattern. One of the pots was also encircled with swastikas. "Those swastikas are a Sanskrit symbol of well-being," Hwang said. "Some people believe they have a strong influence for good. . . . Those look like a wheel rotating counterclockwise—that's good. The points of Hitler's swastika pointed in the opposite direction—that's why his evil was powerful."

I brought the clay pots home with me to lend proof that Native Americans had migrated from Asia. However, my hometown museum eventually said they didn't prove anything unknown to archaeologists except they were five thousand years old. Native American infants, I learned, bore a pair of Mongolian spots on their lower backs, and these birthmarks faded away as the babies grew.

Doug Smith's crackled vase, he later discovered, was cloisonné from the Ming Dynasty.

The next morning our exploration flight was delayed while Lanchow police telegraphed Shanghai. Frowning slightly, the leading Chinese geologist said, "We opened the crates, and they were filled with stones."

Turning to Doug and me, a Texan said, "Thieves in Shanghai, I'm not surprised, but I can't believe the philosophical way the Chinese are accepting this."

"Geological instruments," Doug Smith said. "Who'd want them?"

"They'll buy them back at the thieves' market," I said.

"While we wait for word from Shanghai we'll concentrate on aerial photography," the Chinese leader said. "We'll begin tomorrow morning."

Doug and I took the opportunity to see the waterwheels. We were close to the Ani-mah Ching Mountains, where the snow melts and the water tumbles down to form the Yellow River, which flows three thousand miles to the Yellow Sea. Close as Lanchow is to the headwaters, the river is deep and swift enough to turn Lanchow's waterwheels, which are forty feet in diameter and resemble spiderwebs. Buckets on the rims of the wheels scooped up water, rotated over the top, and dumped it into troughs that led to green fields of Wallace melons. The Chinese named them after our secretary of agriculture, who had mentioned during his visit, "Your soil looks like it would grow honeydew," and when Henry Wallace got home he sent the seeds.

Transportation for the ripened melons, raw wool, and combed yarn was interesting. Row upon row of bloated sheepskins, inflated and dried into parchment, were lashed to limbs of trees. The arrangement formed rafts with sufficient buoyancy to float heavy cargo downstream, yet a raft was light enough for one man to carry on his back. We saw the raft men trek homeward after a journey. In the late desert sun, the translucent floats glowed like gold.

In the morning the geologists boarded with huge aerial cameras, and we flew up the Yellow River for an hour or so to Sining and turned north up a deep valley toward Koko Nor, which was a lake 10,500 feet above sea level, the highest on earth. We saw it in the distance, glittering like a sapphire and shaped like a tiger's head, mouth open, swallowing a waterfall. While we were flying toward it, the geologists pointed their cameras out of the sliding side windows of the cockpit and called out angles and azimuths for their cohorts to record. We flew close to a peak that emerged through a jagged crack in a plateau while a Texan yelled, "Look at the horst," and I heard exclamations that sounded like "That fault's showing metamorphic rock . . . igneous formation of the Pliocene stage. . . ." Between takes he said, "No one knows what's here; two-thirds of China has never been surveyed—not with modern geology."

When we flew over the lake our shadow startled gazelles, and they scampered, but yaks—long-haired high-altitude cows—remained placid. Stone buildings on an island in the middle of the lake housed monks who walked once a winter over the frozen lake to a village to get the next year's supplies. On the following day, after departing Lanchow, we flew due north while the engines purred with the reduced power of a long-range cruise. Our destination was Chu Chuan, with the gravel cascade that Chennault had asked me to survey.

Forty-five minutes after leaving Lanchow we flew through a mountain pass and emerged over the Gobi Desert, which was a mile above sea level and appeared to be an endless rocky plateau. We turned northwest to follow the Marco Polo Road, which blended elusively with the reddish-brown and sometimes gray desert. It was also called the Silk Road, traversed by Marco Polo and countless caravans on course from Beijing to Europe.

The Lien Mountain Range, on our left, paralleled our course. On our right, the rocky desert, like a calm gray-brown sea, extended to the horizon. Our charts said Russia lay beyond it. Doug or I occasionally peered through our drift sight to determine what the wind was doing to us. Eventually, we saw the city of Wuwei, our first checkpoint. The sight would have brought joy to Euclid, because the wall around it formed a perfect square.

An hour later we flew alongside a rectangular granite slab that had pushed through the desert floor. It looked like a sheer wall, a mile tall and seventy miles long. A lonely town lay at its far end. "I wonder who lives there and what they do," Doug said. Hwang just shook his head.

Fifty miles before we reached our destination we recognized it by the mountain that had burst and spewed its innards down its side, and the small white stones flowed like water to the wall of Chu Chuan.

After dragging the field—that is, flying a few feet above it to look for obstructions—we circled back, landed, and bumped and rattled to a stop near some officials in jeeps who waited to take the geologists on an exploration. Hwang sat in the shade of our wing while Doug Smith and I walked around and estimated the gradient and dimensions. I enjoyed making sketches and photographs of the future airport for Chennault.

It was a silent place with jagged, rocky, snow-capped peaks to the south. I was as excited as an explorer. It seemed unbelievable. Only months ago I had been a junior birdman with China National. But as soon as I was laid off I had acquired the stature of a China National veteran, and now, trusted by Chennault, I was looking south toward Tibet.

A stroke of luck had brought me here—I happened to be in the path of Canadian pilot Ced Mah as he was leaving China National. Laden with bags and a Speed Graphic camera, he swung the camera toward me and said, "You can take this off my hands for two hundred bucks."

The flight back to Lanchow seemed shorter because the terrain was familiar.

CAT operations scheduled our airplane back to Shanghai, and the oil explorers remained in Lanchow. Doug and Hwang and I had breakfast with them and said good-bye.

On the way to the airport, Doug said, "I don't suppose we'll ever know if they find oil or not."

I said, "My friend who flew a missionary plane with me—a guy named Springweiler—told me pilots see brief episodes of dramas, but seldom the entire play."

The Renaissance Man

We were glad to get back to the Airline Club in Shanghai. Doug and Sandra and I sat at a long table with a few pilots and their guests.

A Flying Tiger ace—Rosbert—took a shine to Lil, the voluptuous daughter of a Soviet Army officer who had fled to Manchuria after getting wind that he might be executed because he lacked enthusiasm for Communism.

"Rousselot threw four billion Chinese dollars overboard when he lost an engine over the mountains," someone said.

Holden, with his surprised, amused expression of a Kansan tourist in Times Square, said, "Imagine a farmer in those terraced hills, not two pennies rubbing together, and he plows up a bale of money."

The conversation drifted to the next day's pilots' meeting, which would be attended by Chennault's partner, Whiting Willauer. None of us knew him, except one who had bumped into him at the Manila Hotel bar when we ferried the C-46s from Hawaii. "Said he was Whitey. I thought he was a pilot until a navigator squawked about sending a shirt to the laundry with his ferry pay still in the pocket. Willauer wrote a personal check for two hundred bucks and handed it to him."

"Pilots are daft, if you ask me," an English blonde said. "Lovely music, lovely ladies, and you talk airplanes." ·

Holden twitched his shoulder and got up to dance. Sandra sat there quieter than her perky self, so Lil asked, "What's all this Slav melancholy?"

The orchestra played "I'd Like to Get You on a Slow Boat to China." I said, "Let's dance."

Moving with the melody, Sandra said, "My father isn't keen about me getting friendly with pilots."

"Smart man."

"You fly away without knowing when you'll come back, and then it's only for a couple of days." Sandra snuggled closer. I felt her warmth and unbelievable softness. I was falling in love with her and was torn. Somehow, conventional stability alarmed me more than the uncertain future of a winged gypsy.

Later in the evening, with everyone else jabbering, Lil turned to me and said, "Now you're the quiet one," and I wanted her to keep out of it.

The next afternoon I found Willauer in our dining room with a few pilots, waiting for the meeting to start. In his mid-forties, wearing an open-collared bush jacket, he looked alert and athletic. Symmetrical features and neatly groomed black hair made him handsome. I must have arrived at the end of some pilot's outrageous yarn, because Willauer tilted his head back, drooped an eyelid, raised a cheek muscle in a half-smile, and stared at the guy. I would see that look often in years to come—the Willauer glare that halted liars in midsentence, squelched pontificators, arrested flatterers.

When the meeting started, Willauer said, "The general and I want to thank you guys for deferring your pay. When all this impounding stops, we'll get out of the red. We'll jump-start merchants out of the feudal age. The stuff you fly out will get textile mills spinning. Tin and tungsten mines will reopen.

"Impounding of our planes up-country—we've got a problem, but we'll solve it. China National pioneered China, they believe it's their turf, they don't want us here."

"We got a franchise," a pilot said.

"And China National has friends in the ministry and in Washington. Pan Am owns twenty percent. Their lobbyists are doing a number on us. Congressman Vursell—right on the floor of the House—said the UN is using taxpayers' money to finance a private airline. We've got a fight on our hands."

"They still shut off their radio beacons," a pilot said. "China "National turned it off when I was halfway through my letdown at Sian. I had to climb back out of those mountains, no bearings."

Willauer looked angry. "I told William Bond if we lost an airplane because they turned off a beacon I'd see him indicted for murder."

I said, "If you need a beacon, call any China National pilot on a voice frequency. Sometimes they're in cruise, miles away, but they'll order it for us, even before we ask."

"Any other problems or suggestions, come in," he said. "The general and I will be in our offices Wednesday and Friday afternoons, ready to listen to anyone, from laborer on up. We're still learning this business."

A new pilot spoke up. "I was grounded in Tientsin waiting for a part from Shanghai that could've been bought at the local thieves' market for fifteen bucks."

Willauer said, "Why didn't you buy it?" Everyone else nodded while the newcomer looked puzzled, and I realized we had acquired an autonomy bred by an absence of regulations. We were free to focus on the job at hand.

"One last thing," Willauer said. "The general and I have been hearing exaggerated complaints about our chief engineer. We investigated Winpisinger thoroughly before we hired him, and we believe we've found a gold mine."

A long silence was broken by Rossi. "You thought you found a mine, but all you're gonna get is the shaft."

We all laughed, except Willauer, who tilted his head back, drooped an eyelid, and raised a corner of his mouth.

Our embezzling houseboy brought glasses and a bottle of bourbon, and the meeting adjourned with a drink.

At four o'clock the next morning at Hungjao Airport I was surprised to see Willauer in a tan leather jacket with a bulge in front and the neck of a fifth of bourbon sticking out. He was talking to a laborer in his limited Shanghai dialect. When he saw me he stuck out his hand and asked, "Mind if I ride copilot?" I knew he had a private pilot's license, and the guys had been letting him fly.

A sleepy traffic clerk said we had a C-46 load of United Nations supplies for Canton, in south China, on the Pearl River, which is navigable and open to the sea.

During our preflight check the number one radio compass was so weak it would barely point to Kiangwan beacon fifteen miles away, but number two responded normally.

Willauer took the copilot's place and the copilot sat in the jump seat behind me, happy because he'd be able to sleep all the way to Canton. When Willauer flew, the regular copilot usually made a bed on top of the cargo.

The night was black, but flare pots framed the runway and our weight was way under maximum, so I told Willauer it was all his. He grabbed the wheel and throttles like a kid on a new scooter and we hurtled down the runway, swerving slightly from side to side because he was overcontrolling the rudder, while I sat with one hand on the throttle quadrant, at the shafts of the throttles, the other hand on my lap an inch under the wheel, and my heels on the floor with the soles of my feet not quite touching the rudder pedals.

He sashayed on up while I opened the cowl flaps wider because the cylinder head temperatures were at 210 degrees centigrade, the maximum allowable. When the temperatures crept above 210 I opened the engines' cowl flaps so wide we felt the airplane tremble with the buffeting of the cowl flaps protruding into the slipstream, so I closed them a crack. "Drop the nose slightly," I said, "and maintain a higher airspeed; it'll take us longer to get to eight thousand feet, but the engines will keep cool."

"Both engines? What's going on?"

"Half the louvers on the sides of the engine cowlings are covered up."

"What for?"

"Reduce drag. Supposed to give a higher cruising speed."

"Whose idea was that?"

I shrugged my shoulders. I knew damn well whose— Winpisinger's. But after the pilots' meeting with Willauer saying he didn't want any more complaints about the guy, I let Willauer figure it out.

"Forty-five minutes after takeoff and we haven't reached eight thousand feet," he said. "Doesn't that take a lot of fuel?"

"Lots more," I said. "But that's not so bad. What'll happen if an engine quits and you have to pull max continuous power on the other one? Then you'll really have an overheat problem." Willauer didn't say anything, but I sensed wheels turning in his head.

After we got to eight thousand feet, Willauer engaged the autopilot and talked. "UN supplies have been sitting on a junk in Canton for a week because China National can't spare a plane, and when the junk gets around to sailing it'll be another couple of weeks before it gets to Liuchow. You'll be flying it in a couple of hours."

"How're you going to jump-start the merchants up-country?" I asked.

"By example. We're buying a small trading company. Buy wool in Lanchow, ship it to Shanghai on CAT. We'll leave the ledgers open where the merchants can see 'em. When they see our profits they'll jump."

Willauer's eyes glowed. "You know the Lanchow merchants' biggest problem? Finding honest raft men. Single-handed, they get the cargo to the coast. First they turn yak hides inside out and inflate them. They're the floats. The raft frames are expensive wooden timbers that can be sold. They pile bales of wool on top and float down the Yellow River for more than a thousand miles."

"I heard they can't get all the way to the coast. The river goes underground or something for a spell."

"That's right. The raft man takes the raft apart, hires a truck to portage all the parts to the place where he can navigate the river again. He assembles the inflated hides and timbers and bales of wool, and when he reaches the China coast he sells the whole shebang."

After Willauer's saga of the Mongolian rafts, his next spiel—about ham—seemed mundane. "Yunnan hams from Kunming bring high prices in overseas Chinese restaurants. When the merchants see the profit we make flying them to Shanghai, they'll catch on. . . . We don't want to be in the trading business. As soon as the merchants take over we'll close down our trading company."

We flew south with the number two radio compass pointing aft to Lunghwa's strong beacon, telling us the wind was drifting us to the east, off course.

After we'd flown south for a couple of hours, Willauer played with our radio compasses and said, "What am I doing wrong? I can't pick up Foochow."

"Too far out," I said. "Number one was weak when we left Shanghai, but number two should come in soon."

By the time we got close to Foochow I picked up the beacons' tone, but the radio compass refused to point, nor could I rotate the loop with its manual control. The radio operator changed fuses and switched indicators, but nothing fixed the problem. We were cruising in bright sunshine, above flat clouds that stretched to the horizon, as if we were lost on a flat expanse of ocean. We didn't know how the winds had drifted us or what lay below the white sea of clouds. Willauer looked at me.

"Turn left," I said. "We'll head for Hong Kong—their radar will pick us up." I looked continuously, knowing that clouds sometimes break up over rivers.

We saw a hole over water and circled it, while remaining above the clouds; and then we spotted a resemblance to a Mississippi River steamer, and we knew it had to be a Pearl River boat. "Half flaps," I ordered, so we could make a tight spiral without brushing the clouds at the edge of the hole. When he got to about three thousand feet we saw a good length of the river and wet green farms. "Lucky it's daylight," I said, but I didn't relax until we saw the concrete of Canton's White Cloud Airport and landed.

We were greeted by CAT's station manager, a retired Chinese Air Force colonel who'd graduated, years before, from the Virginia Military Institute.

Meanwhile, mechanic Lewis, in his cowboy hat and jeans, said, "We don't have a spare radio compass, but I've got a radioman with mean needle-nose pliers and a solderin' iron who can make a silk purse out of a sow's ear."

In the morning the radio compasses were still on the workbench and ops said they'd prepare a C-47 for the river port of Liuchow and then on to Kunming. The copilot said, "I hope they load us soon." I knew what he meant. We saw cumulonimbus clouds boiling angrily in the mountains to the west and knew they'd grow higher and more violent as the day progressed.

The station manager invited us to wait in his office, where we sipped tea, and he spoke cultivated English in a Southern accent, which he'd picked up at VMI, I supposed. My copilot and radio operator, in their innate courtesy, also spoke English in my presence, because I wasn't fluent in Chinese. On the other hand, they weren't too shy to ask questions about Willauer, who had completed his business and returned to Shanghai early that morning. Chinese don't feel it's impolite to display curiosity about people, and they're intrigued by foreigners.

"Willauer loves excitement," the station manager said, "but there's a brilliant mind behind his adventurous spirit. . . . President Roosevelt sent him to the Philippines to restore the economy after MacArthur recaptured it. He wanted to spend the war in the Navy, but a bad shoulder kept him out; dinged it when he was on the lacrosse team at Princeton." I ventured that Willauer had studied the sciences before he attended Harvard Law, but the station manager laughed. "Few people would guess English literature, or that his thesis was something about the influences of Shelley and Keats, or that he graduated with honors before he went on to law school. The British would call him a Renaissance man."

An ops clerk came in and told us our C-47 was ready. We checked the tie-down ropes, because we knew were in for some jolts and bolts.

We climbed out toward the western mountains, where the dark clouds boiled and flashed bolts of lightning. "Try to keep track of the lightning and we'll fly between them," I said. We called it eyeball

radar. It was useless to try to maintain our assigned altitude, and we
assumed, for peace of mind, their other traffic would be riding up
and down in the same vertical air currents. When it got too rough to
read the instruments, my briefcase levitated and hovered upside
down while maps, manuals, navigation gadgets, and stuff I thought
our houseboy had stolen plopped on the floor, and I recalled a sign I
had seen in some Air Corps operations office: "It's better to be down
here wishing you were up there, than up there wishing you were
down here."

The last thunderhead shook us violently, and suddenly we burst
into brilliant sunshine. I went aft to check the cargo and found the
airplane's plywood flooring on top of the cargo, still lashed down. A
dozen men couldn't move the flooring to the top of the cargo, within
the rope lashings, but the turbulence could.

We landed at Liuchow, discharged most of our cargo—the stuff
that would have taken two weeks by junk—and taxied back out. We
hadn't gone more than fifty feet before we heard an explosion and
felt a lurch. "Left tire," I said.

We got out and looked at the gash. "Sun rot," the mechanic said.
"Look how gray the rubber is; probably sat out the war on some
Pacific Island. No spares here—I'll radio Canton."

"Ask for two," I said.

"Why two?"

"After you guys change it I'll taxi ten more feet and the other one
will blow."

Several hours later, someone passed through from Canton and
dropped off two C-47 tires. Our mechanics replaced our bad tire and
kept the other spare. We taxied out again and soon heard another
explosion—this time on the right.

"They'll think you're a fortune-teller," the copilot said. The
mechanics laughed and jabbered among themselves.

The sky was blue the rest of the way and the lush green mountains
of south China eventually gave way to flat, high ground, and then we
saw the long azure lake the Chinese called "the Pearl on the
Plateau," and the red soil of Kunming with its long runway.

We parked alongside a CAT C-46 that had control locks on its tail
and canvas over the windshield. "Looks like someone's stuck," our
radioman said.

The operations clerk drove up in a jeep. "No clearance. You stay,
may be long time."

"Whose C-46 is that?"

"Captain Rousselot's."

The jeep carried us up a hill, still outside the city wall, to our hostel, where we found the black-haired six-footer relaxing in a chair
with his feet on the low windowsill, looking at the mountains. Easily

as he sat, I sensed an aura of latent energy. After standing up and shaking hands all around, he said, "I like it here—it's like a trapper's cabin."

"A country vacation," I said. He lapsed into silence and seemed to find peace in the terraced hills.

Eventually, Rousselot spoke. "Something's in the wind. My radio operator's been monitoring radio traffic. Chennault's in Nanking. Maybe he's seeing his buddies in the Chinese Air Force. A Chinese board member is with him, friend of the minister of communications. . . . I have a feeling they're going to settle this impounding routine once and for all."

Impounded in Kunming with Rousselot, I discovered he'd been raised on a Missouri farm near the Oklahoma border, where he had endured tough times like all farmers in the dust bowl and Depression years. World War II interrupted his premed studies. He flew Corsairs off a baby flattop in the Pacific and then cadged time in Marine Corps transport planes, just for the experience.

Holden flew in with a load of medicines from Shanghai, which made a total of three crews stuck in the far-western city.

We sat around the "trapper's shack" and talked airplanes, but much as we gabbed, no one felt nosy enough to ask Rousselot about throwing four billion Chinese dollars overboard. We sensed it had been a painful experience.

Listening to the shortwave news, we learned that Jackie Robinson, the first black baseball player in the history of the major leagues, had signed with the Brooklyn Dodgers. "Seems like much ado about nothing," someone said. "After living in the Orient, all the skin colors."

Then we heard something about President Truman establishing a central intelligence agency to monitor the Soviets, who were pouring money into Communist factions throughout Europe. "We can relate to that," I said, recalling how the Soviets had betrayed their Chinese allies when they short-circuited Japan's surrendered war material to Mao Tse-tung.

None of us, though, entertained the slightest notion that we'd someday become the major air arm of the CIA.

The next night, on his own, Rousselot talked about his flight. "The money was for Chungking," he explained, speaking quietly. "We were too heavy to go nonstop; we refueled at Liuchow. Climbed out, and the left engine quit, just before we reached cruise. Put max continuous on the good engine, but we drifted down. We were on instruments."

Rousselot gripped the arm of his chair. "The copilot and radio operator wanted to throw out the load, but I told 'em, 'Wait, let's see if this dude will hold. Calm down—I know there are mountains underneath us.'"

The hostel got quiet. Everyone listened.

"Every time we ran into turbulence we drifted down a few hundred feet. I said, 'Get your knives out, get ready to cut the ropes.'

"At the rate we were drifting down it was obvious we weren't going to hold six thousand, and the peaks were that high. 'Throw out half the load,' I said."

Rousselot was quiet for a minute or two and continued, "They wanted to get rid of it all. I told 'em half, dammit." He shifted in his chair, uneasy. And then I realized, the danger hadn't bothered him—it was the four billion Chinese dollars he threw away.

"After about an hour the clouds broke up and we picked up the Liu River valley and worked our way back to Liuchow."

Rousselot shook his head. "Equivalent of half a million U.S. The next day I borrowed a liaison plane from the CAF . . . looked all over those mountains. Actually spotted some bundles. The bank recovered a few."

Rousselot stayed in the hostel with a few guys while the rest of us headed for a restaurant. Walking there, Holden said, "Can you imagine? Save the airplane, then think you have to go back and look for the stuff."

"I can't imagine finding it in those mountains," I said.

"Flying between those peaks with a single-engine putt-putt."

"Rousselot's a guy who doesn't like to lose," I said.

"I heard he left the Marine Corps 'cause it got too lax."

"Jeezus Keerist," I said, "Marines too lax? How would you like him for chief pilot?"

Holden hunched a shoulder. "Wow! Fortunately, we already have a chief."

After the Chinese feast, Holden said, "I got so interested in Rousselot's story, I forgot to give you the scoop from Shanghai. Winpisinger got promoted, so he can't screw around anymore with the airplanes. Willauer built him a shack with a big sign—Long-Range Planning and Development—far away from ops. We got a new maintenance chief, thank God."

"It was the engine-louver fiasco," I said.

"I think the last straw was Winpisinger's rhubarb with a coolie. You know how big and overbearing he is. He found a coolie living in the supply shed. Ordered him out, but the coolie had to load airplanes all day, so he got his father-in-law to pack his stuff, but the next morning some of it was still there, so Winpisinger tossed it out. When the coolie got back from work and found his stuff lying outside, he got in a helluva argument with Winpisinger."

Holden laughed and hunched a shoulder. "Chennault asked Colonel Lee to look into it. You should have seen Lee's report . . .

stuff like 'I proceeded full-chisel into the investigation. . . . Mr. Winpisinger is a zealous go-getter. . . . Was unconsciously rude, but should be forgiven because he can't conceive Chinese customs. . . .'

"Next thing we know," Holden continued, "Winpisinger gets the promotion. Now he sits in his shack, planning for the distant future, while everyone else is running around looking for spark plugs for today."

"Chennault doesn't like to fire anybody," I said.

"Lou Wheate is the new head of engineering."

"Best mechanic we ever had."

"He's so quiet you never know he's around."

"He used to be an inspector at Pan Am," I said, "and before that, in the Air Corps."

When our clearances came through, at last, we left Kunming, one after the other, radio-jabbering to stay awake, and got to Shanghai about eight hours later, at midnight, glad to be home. But the ops clerk told me I was scheduled for Tsingtao in the morning. "Take clothes for two weeks," he said.

It was too late to telephone Sandra, and it'd be too early to call before I left the next morning.

After the crew car dropped me us off at the pilots' house I wrote a note telling her what had happened and asked the houseboy to deliver it in the morning.

I dropped into bed, tired, but couldn't sleep. My note to Sandra could be the last straw, no doubt. How right she was when I last saw her and she said, "Pilots might be smart enough to know if they're coming or going, but they never know when."

China's German City

Tsingtao looked like a European city of red brick. Lying on China's coast, midway between Shanghai and Beijing, it snuggled among green hills and spread to coves that were fringed with short pine trees with zigzag limbs that reached over rocks. It could have been Monterey.

Germany had acquired the land before the turn of the century, after Chinese bandits murdered two German missionaries. The Kaiser's demand for reparations, while two of his warships waited offshore, gained a hundred-year lease for the Germans, who turned the deepwater bay into a naval base.

After losing the First World War, Germany surrendered Tsingtao, but China didn't get it back. Great Britain, France, and Italy—China's allies—handed the seaport to the Japanese, who had bribed Beijing's cabinet officials to pave the way.

America's President Wilson had contributed to the scam by intimating that China would get Tsingtao back after the hostilities—if it declared war on Germany. Subsequently, at the Versailles Peace Conference, the Chinese delegates learned that President Wilson had known all along that Tsingtao had been committed to Japan.

Beijing University students howled, "Chinese humiliation! Warlord traitors! Chinese territory may be conquered, but it cannot be given away!" They distributed leaflets and spoke on streets throughout China. They aroused patriotic fervor that sparked riots and strikes throughout China. The turmoil forced the resignation of the Beijing cabinet. Noting it was the first victory of a people's uprising in China, historians named it the May Fourth Movement. It inspired a young librarian at Beijing University, the son of a peasant family. His name was Mao Tse-tung. Chinese Communism wasn't imported from Russia; it was born in Tsingtao.

We departed Shanghai's Hungjao Airport by the flickering light of coffee-can flares and headed north to the Yellow Sea.

Shanghai and Tsingtao are positioned on China's east coast like New York and Boston, and the Shantung Peninsula sticks out like Cape Cod.

After flying in smooth air for two hours, the horizon off our right wing defined itself, and the sun showed its rim and then rose to illuminate the Shantung Peninsula. By the time we got close enough to see the city, the sun was bouncing light off of Tsingtao's red tile roofs, and we saw two cruisers in the bay.

An American voice in the control tower cleared us to land, and we parked next to a row of Marine Corps fighters. The blue Corsairs with inverted gull wings and the warships in the bay represented the only American force in China except for military attachés at various consulates. Ordered to remain aloof from China's internal affairs, the U.S. Navy and Marines gave moral support to President Chiang Kai-shek, who was edgy. His Soviet allies had betrayed him by giving Chinese Communist guerrillas the stockpile of war supplies from Japan's surrendering army. Guerrillas had captured a few Shantung villages; the capital of the province required strength.

Our operations manager, clipboard in hand, said, "We're adding you to the soldier-cotton shuttle." Hundreds of soldiers stood or sprawled on a grassy area near the tarmac, waiting to be transported two hundred miles inland, to the city of Tsinan. Return flights brought bales of cotton to Tsingtao's textile mills.

Tsinan was strategic. In addition to nesting the provincial capital, it produced huge quantities of raw cotton and was an important Yellow River port. Its railroads ran east to Tsingtao and west to join the long rail line that stretched from Beijing to Hong Kong.

It was also famous for the Tsinan Incident, which occurred at the time of Tsingtao's student uprising. In addition to offering the seaport to Japan, China's so-called allies let Japan take over Germany's special privileges in Tsinan. Japan moved in soldiers to protect its commercial interests. Confronted by Chiang Kai-shek's troops, Japan's soldiers surrounded the office of the national foreign minister, cut off the noses and ears of his sixteen subordinates, and then murdered them.

I recalled these tidbits of history whenever my friends complained about China's xenophobia.

"You got a new copilot," our ops man said. "Fresh from the Air Corps."

I waited for fuel and watched Shorty Tam, our traffic agent, load another C-46. He put a bathroom scale at the foot of the boarding ladder and stood there with his abacus while a single file of soldiers stepped on the scale and climbed up to the cabin. The agent kept flicking the beads until they totaled 48,000 pounds gross weight, and then he shut the cabin door.

I heard someone bellow, "Smees," which is the way many Chinese pronounced my name.

I turned and saw a hulk lumber toward me. "Earthquake Magoon," I said. "They let you off the carrier."

"My CO asked why I wanted a discharge in China. Told 'im who the hell wants to go home in the seventh inning of a ball game? We're supposed to be chasing dollies in Shanghai—what're we doing with soldier-boys?"

"Looks more like a Boy Scout hike to me," I said. Earthquake pursed his lips while we looked at boys who couldn't be older than sixteen. Tin cups, parchment umbrellas, potato-masher grenades hung from their belts. Khaki strips of cloth spiraled their calves, canvas sneakers covered their feet. They looked scared.

An officer barked, and they formed a single file at our boarding ladder, where the traffic agent waited with his abacus. I stepped over the scale, climbed the ladder to the plane's cabin, and looked down to see Earthquake standing on the scale, hands on his belly. After turning slowly around to assess his audience, he leaned over to read the scale and then grimaced, threw up his hands, and shouted something that sounded Chinese but wasn't. And he messed with the beads on the abacus. The soldiers laughed and pointed and jabbered, forgetting, for a few brief moments, the war.

By the time I'd checked the escape hatches in the cabin and the latches on the starboard cargo door, Earthquake Magoon had gone to the cockpit. When I got there he was relaxed, with the seat tilted to its full recline position and hands folded across his belly. His face telegraphed self-satisfaction. I didn't see any tools. No protractor to plot courses, no circular slide rule he could easily have carried in his shirt pocket, no charts. "You oughta buy a ticket," I said, and he broke into toots of laughter.

This guy can manipulate an audience, I thought. I wondered if he could manipulate a C-46 as well. I knew it would feel heavy and unwieldy after the fighters he had been flying. "You fly," I said.

"Whatever's customary," he answered, and he straightened his seat and called for the checklist. After takeoff I just sat there and let him make all the decisions. I figured anyone who had raided Japanese warships in Hong Kong's harbor in the big war and shot down a few Zeros could find Tsinan.

A half hour later we saw our first checkpoint, which was the city of Weihsien, north of course—easy to identify because it was cut in two by a river and huge walls surrounded both halves and made a figure eight. Even though its distinctive appearance made it a perfect landmark, Earthquake Magoon didn't pull a calculator out of his pocket or do anything else to determine our ground speed.

In another hour we saw the long suspension bridge over the Yellow River, and Earthquake descended into Tsinan. We hit hard, bounced down the runway, and stopped at the end. Earthquake growled, "I thought this monster was going to turn on me."

The soldiers disembarked, and laborers unlatched the wide cargo doors of our cabin and swung them open. Each bale of cotton weighing a hundred kilos (220 pounds) was carried on the shoulder of a single laborer, up a steep plank and into the cabin.

Everyone called them coolies, although classy Chinese, respecting another's pride, didn't use the word within earshot of a laborer. Although the word "coolie" was demeaning, it was an accurate job description. The literal translation is "bitter labor."

Renee Lym, my Chinese friend, said, "They believe some day the dark clouds will part and God will notice them." I respected China's coolies more than any other group, because their tortured muscles, their very lives, built China's wonders. An old one was the Grand Canal that connected the Yangtze and Yellow rivers and extended north to Beijing and south to Hangchow, and was banked with stones and reinforced with willow trees to give it beauty as well as utility. It remains the longest man-made waterway in existence.

I recall the time a CAT C-46, on an airport that was almost deserted, got stuck deep in mud and wouldn't budge with full power on both engines. A boss gave some magic signal, and a couple of hundred laborers appeared from nowhere and lifted one side of the C-46 up while they joked about the foreign devil's flying machine that wouldn't work. The workers on the edge of the wing released it before others underneath got free, and they were almost crushed. Told to be careful, the boss said, "Never mind; can get more coolies."

There wasn't a coolie who wouldn't escape his cruel station, given the opportunity, and I abhorred the labor that killed half of them prematurely; but I stood in awe of them because they toiled with an acceptance and cheerfulness that was inexplicable. Harsh as their life was, they maintained a capacity to love the world.

The cotton was loaded in twenty minutes, and a jeep was the last item to go aboard. A driver steered it up the planks, under its own power, but it stalled midway. The incline was too steep. Several men grabbed the bottom end of the planks and lifted them above their heads until they were level, and the jeep drove into our cabin. Earthquake let out a belly-shaking laugh and applauded, and the coolies laughed with him.

After we had shuttled all day—soldiers to Tsinan, cotton to Tsingtao—a company station wagon took us to a castle that Willauer had rented for transient crews. A seaside edifice with ramparts and a watchtower, it had been built by a wealthy Russian for his exotic dragon lady, who subsequently jilted him, and he stopped the pain by leaping off the tower.

Over an after-dinner drink, a pilot said, "When I let Earthquake fly, he carried too much power. I reached up to pull some off. He growled and rapped my knuckles with the flag. I wanted to show anger, but found myself laughing." (We carried a Chinese flag in the cockpit. After landing, the copilot opened the window and stuck the flag into a socket on the roof, and we taxied to the terminals with a little class.)

Buol had written, for Earthquake's personnel file, "This pilot went on a check ride without so much as carrying a map or letdown procedure. By a quirk of luck he flew close enough to Taiyüan to locate the town. I would not call this confidence but stupidity. I assume he flies all the time without standard equipment. He is a very lazy pilot and takes much for granted. He definitely isn't responsible enough to be a good captain, and unless he overcomes this attitude I recommend he be given more copilot time."

Another captain reported, "McGovern [Earthquake] is lazy. Won't do anything unless told."

When Buol asked me, I said, "He can do it if it's important enough. He believes in the conservation of energy."

Transiting pilots told us they weren't impounded up-country anymore and were allowed to carry return cargo. The guys in the Kunming area began an airlift of 300,000 tons of tungsten ore to Liuchow—a river port—for China's Natural Resources Commission. Rousselot's guess was on the mark. Chennault had visited his Chinese Air Force friends in Nanking. And Dr. Wang Wen-san, with the Tobacco King, had confronted the Ministry of Communications. Willauer recorded the essence of the latter meeting: "Look, gentlemen, forty cents of every dollar that you cause us to lose by making this trouble in the airline comes out of our pockets. Now why don't you go and shake down somebody else? This is a truly Chinese-

American outfit. We employ mostly Chinese and we deserve a break."

Willauer's promise to jump-start China's economy came alive. He called us the missing link in an economic chain between Tsinan's raw cotton and nineteen thousand mill workers in Tsingtao. Rousselot flew the first load of cotton to other textile mills in Tientsin and returned to Tsinan with a full load of kerosene. The governor of Shensi Province asked us to carry a thousand tons of cotton per month from Sian.

The value of the exportable stuff we flew to the coast averaged almost a third of a million U.S. dollars a month for export or for local use, which avoided the need for imports. Willauer said this was particularly important because it earned and saved foreign exchange—hard currency—for China.

CAT banned luxury items from its airlifts and offered rates to the Chinese Rehabilitation and Relief Association that were a third less than the other two airlines charged.

China National and Central Air operated their C-46s, wisely, I thought, at a maximum gross weight of 46,000 pounds, which was standard for a civilian operation. However, our chief of flight operations, Buol, with Chennault's approval, set our maximum two thousand pounds higher, which the military called the airplane's wartime gross. It meant we carried two thousand pounds more cargo per trip.

Willauer wrote to his wife, "We have built up an operation which is nearly as big as either of the other two airlines. . . . We are carrying, each month, export cargo amounting to about a quarter of China's exports from the interior. These are the types of cargoes that would otherwise not move. . . . We are running the line with 20 percent of the personnel which the other airlines employ."

While this won accolades from government officials and allowed CAT to retire some of its debt to the United Nations (for the airplanes), it inflamed Bond, the suave, courtly vice president of Pan American who presided over China National.

Pilots from Shanghai brought us copies of the *Shanghai Evening Post and Mercury*. Banner stuff. "CAT—Profiteers Masquerade as Relief Airline."

Days later, Willauer told us, "I asked the newsmen to come to my office and invited them to dip a hand into our files and pull out airplane manifests at random—provided they agreed to report what they found."

Willauer's gamble worked. The reporters kept their word. English-language newspapers listed the items they had found on CAT's manifests: rubber shoes for Canton; generators and tires for Henyang; tractor parts, engine equipment, and gasoline for Kaifeng;

gasoline, lubricating oil, medicine, and engine parts for Kunming; pumps and drilling machines for the development of the Kansu oil fields; cloth and cotton yarn for Linfen; nickel and chrome alloy for the steel mills of Taiyüan; water pumps to restore the coal mines of Weihsien; and wires to restore Weihsien's electrical systems.

After surmounting that crisis, Willauer flew to French Indochina to see if CAT could airlift tin ingots from the mines of Yunnan Province in southwest China to the French seaport of Haiphong, where the tin could be transferred to steamships bound for the USA. I was inspired. Willauer showed such verve in spite of the obstacles: Chinese mine owners had to stabilize prices; French import regulations were difficult; steamship companies didn't yet serve Indochina; approval of three governments was required for a single bill of lading.

Willauer stuck one more thorn in Bond's side: a few mechanics and pilots resigned from China National and joined CAT—until the government decreed that any future transfers would require a written clearance from China National.

China's prestigious airline provided more comfortable quarters and tastier food in cleaner mess halls than we did, and their planes were in better shape because they had better access to spare parts. Even China National's future, with Pan Am's backing, looked rosier. I think the pilots and mechanics switched because CAT was more fun. The morale was better. With fewer employees per plane, and much occurring in many distant places, we made decisions on the spot. Our leaders said go ahead, it's your airline.

We turned to the Marine Corps. The old-timers could be discharged in Tsingtao if they had a job there.

Hugh Marsh, six feet tall, with a burn scar on one side of his face (the legacy of a crash in a Corsair fighter, years before), announced, "We're getting reinforcements—two more Marines got jobs. Let's go see 'em tomorrow morning. Nothing like a welcome aboard. No pedicabs for this occasion—we'll take a taxi."

Tsingtao taxis were usually old open-air touring cars with a crew of two. Marsh, Earthquake, and I squeezed in the backseat. The Corps fascinated me. Its mystery was the way each Marine remained an individualist even though the organization was the most disciplined of all.

We disembarked at a large German house with a huge garden and ornate iron fence and rang the bell.

The Rebel, a jaunty guy in a sport shirt, emerged, followed by a stern-looking man with a bulging forehead. Referring to Marsh's old wound, the Rebel said, "Damned if you aren't the best-looking one-eared pilot I've ever seen." Marsh grinned. The Rebel pointed at his housemate. "We call him 'the Skull.'" I discovered later that the

bulge in the Skull's forehead was a steel plate with which Navy sur-
geons had patched his cranium after a wartime crash in a torpedo
dive-bomber.

Inside their house, the Rebel said, "How about a beer?"

"Too early for me," I said.

"Nothing like a cold one before breakfast. Especially when you've
been up all night." The Rebel swigged. "Aah, nothing like that first
cool sip. . . . Reminds me of my ex-wife, the morning after our wedding. I pulled a beer out of the refrigerator and she said, 'You're not
going to drink that before breakfast, are you?' Right then I knew she
was on her way out."

I heard a brassy wail. The Skull looked at his housemate scornfully and said, "You damn rebel."

Outside, their cook blew air and spit and a screech or two out
of a bugle while their houseboy hoisted an American Civil War
Confederate flag up a pole.

"Happens every morning, the Rebel's standing orders," grumbled
the Skull.

A U.S. Marine Corps jeep stopped outside. Two MPs got out. One
asked, "What's going on?"

"This is the Consulate of the Confederate States of America," the
Rebel said pompously.

"What's that flag?"

"Salute it." The MPs looked at each other. Admiral Badger lived
next door. Foreign consulates abounded. Many strange emblems
fluttered in the neighborhood. One of them saluted; the other looked
embarrassed.

The Rebel said, "Don't you recognize the Stars and Bars?"

"We'd better come in and look around."

Earthquake Magoon, at the gate, belly-bumped an MP. "You'll
have to shoot me first."

The MPs returned to their jeep. "We're going to report this."

"I'm reporting this to Jefferson Davis," the Rebel said.

Back inside, over another beer, Earthquake growled, "Before we
let you in, CAT, we have to detrain you, like the Army does those war
dogs."

Marsh invited me to share the house he rented on German Beach.
After living in CAT's seaside castle where Chinese crewmen gambled
all night, clattering and slamming their mah-jongg tiles, I found
Marsh's offer inviting.

My huge upstairs bedroom with surplus closet space accommodated my Hawaiian aloha shirts, which had been disappearing in the
mysterious way things vanished in China. When Marsh's cook told
me his friend needed a job, I hired him just to keep track of my

prized shirts. "I don't mind you hiring the guy as long as he stays out of the kitchen," Marsh said. "That's my cook's domain."

Cheong, the cook's unemployed friend, stood tall and dignified when I interviewed him. His neat, close-cropped hair enhanced the image of a Prussian general. His starched white tunic with its high collar was fastened with cloth loops and tails called frogs. Cheong held a handful of references, which I ignored, because a hunch told me to hire him on the spot. "All you have to do is keep track of my shirts," I said. His cheek muscles repressed a smile.

"You've got to read Cheong's references," Doug Smith said. "He can cook anything: beautiful cakes, roasts—he worked for a U.S. Navy captain for years. No one in the family had dysentery for the entire time."

Cheong's glowing references admitted him to the kitchen, where Marsh permitted him to make ice cream with his hand-cranked freezer, and Cheong became famous. If Marsh or I unexpectedly remained at a friend's house for dinner, we'd dispatch a note to Cheong, who would come in the passenger seat of a pedicab where he cranked his freezer, looking like he was assisting the locomotion.

Ice cream powder from the U.S. Navy commissary was purchased at the thieves' market. Chocolate was the only flavoring available, until the night area manager Burridge threw a dinner party for some visiting American businessmen. His own cook upstaged the famous Cheong by serving a new kind of ice cream: mint flavor.

"This is marvelous," the guests beamed. "Who'll believe we ate ice cream in China? Mint, of all flavors!"

Burridge summoned his cook, who accepted the accolades with modesty. Asked where he had found the mint flavoring, the cook said, "I use wicks."

"Wicks?"

"Yes, wicks. I show you." He went back to the kitchen and returned holding up a jar of Vicks VapoRub.

With the same day off, Marsh and I sat in front of his fireplace, sipped scotch and soda, looked through the picture window to German Beach. An open-air taxi stopped and discharged two U.S. Navy sailors, who appeared to be seventeen or eighteen years old. The taxi's crewmen were north China giants wearing old-fashioned wide-brim hats, and the grim expression on their faces gave them the appearance of Chicago gangsters of bootlegging days.

After some haggling, the cabbies jumped out, grabbed the young sailors, and shook them. The kids looked scared. I burst out of the front door and ran down the outside steps, and I was halfway down when Marsh flew past me, descending three steps at a time. As he sped past the group, his fist shot out and the taxi copilot sailed horizontally through the air and landed on his back. But his hat didn't travel. It hovered momentarily where the head had been and then plopped to the ground.

I picked it up, dusted it off, and handed it to the ruffian, who picked himself off the ground, held his jaw, and wailed, "Owya, owya," while his buddy was in the taxi, rolling.

The two sailors stared wide-eyed as if we had come from nowhere.

"You might as well come in and have a toddy," Marsh said.

Climbing the steps to our house, one said, "I gave him a tip, but I guess it wasn't enough."

Settled before the fireplace, the other said, "We'll just have juice, if that's okay with you."

"This is our first cruise. . . . You guys really fly airplanes? All over China? Gosh!"

After some conversation, Marsh asked his cook to fetch another taxi. When the sailors were gone, Marsh chuckled, "Kids."

"I saw my former self," I said. "And now I'm wondering where it went."

Days later, Marsh returned from western China. I poured a couple of scotch and sodas while he lit up his fireplace.

"I flew one hundred and thirty-eight baskets of silkworm eggs from Kunming to Shanghai," he said. "Those eggs . . . after they hatch they'll produce a quarter of all the silk that China exports this year."

Marsh talked about flying fifty thousand doses of United Nations serum from Shanghai to Changsha to halt an epidemic of hog cholera.

And then he released the bombshell. "We got a new chief pilot. Chennault and Willauer just appointed Rousselot."

"J. Christ! Rousselot! He left the Marine Corps because it got too lax for him."

Marsh put another log on the fire. "He's just what we need. With rugged individualists like Earthquake Magoon and the Skull and the Rebel, we need a Marine with wooden underwear."

During the months on the soldier-cotton shuttle between Tsingtao and Tsinan, I got better acquainted with radio operator C. Y. Chu, a tall man with a high forehead and the aura of a wise owl. A former radio operator in China's merchant marine, he had a reputation for clairvoyance.

Although Chu was the ship's radio officer, with no knowledge of seamanship, a vague intuition induced him to warn his captain to be careful of the ship's rudder, and days later, while the ship was maneuvering around heavy traffic in Singapore waters, the rudder jammed.

After Chu discovered I wasn't one to laugh at the unknown, he said, "I'm the reincarnation of Genghis Khan." He seemed to accept his present low status philosophically, saying, "It's my karma. It's my punishment for the cruel things I did in my last life."

I'll always remember the day I landed behind Hughes and Bushbaum and parked beside them. They stood on the tarmac, shielded their eyes, and looked up at the nose of their bird. "We got shot over Tsinan," Hughes said. I looked up and saw a neat hole through the peaceable tiger cub below the cockpit window. "Right through the tiger's ass," Bushbaum said.

Chu climbed up on an engine stand to inspect the hole closely. Shaking his head gravely, he said, "It's an omen. No more peaceful tiger."

Chu shook his head knowingly when we got a radiogram from the governor of Honan, the province that's called China's breadbasket. The governor wanted five airplanes for an emergency airlift.

Chu was right. No more peaceful tiger. It was autumn 1947, and China's civil war accelerated.

6

China's Civil War

"China's Sorrow" was the name given the Yellow River, but China's sorrow to me was the province of Honan. For centuries its abundance was interrupted by famines, and its flat and fertile fields were parched by drought, flooded by the Yellow River, and stained with peasant blood.

Similar in size to Missouri, Honan belongs to the plains of north-central China. Missouri and Honan are intimate with rivers that flow the same distance, the same silt brown.

Honan's governor asked us to evacuate thousands of bales of cotton from the beleaguered city of Anyang to the safety of Chengchow, which is near Kaifeng, the capital of the sad province.

Although Anyang and Chengchow are only ninety miles apart and lie on the same railroad—the main line that runs twelve hundred miles due south, from Beijing to Hong Kong—they were isolated from each other because Communist guerrillas stole sections of train track at night and blocked the roads.

Even though the Reds had sufficient strength to capture Anyang and grab the stockpile of cotton, they waited. They wanted the ripening millet also. They waited for the farmers to do the work of the harvest.

We were based at Chengchow, the largest city in Honan. While our station manager searched for accommodations, Canadian missionaries took us in. A few had been in China for twenty years and were fluent in the local dialects. The peasants trusted them.

Missionary Rodney McLeod said, "The small skirmishes stopped. I suppose the Reds have long-range plans, guided by the Soviets. Waiting for the harvest is a new strategy."

"The cotton is the least of my worries," missionary Walter Boudreau complained. "Anyang sits on the capital of the Shang

72

Dynasty—four-thousand-year-old buildings—the ruins are still there."

"Four thousand years ago they cast bronze, and the technique has never been improved," McLeod said. "Bronze jugs with delicate spouts . . . mirror frames decorated with images of dragons . . . jade fish. . . ."

"They did the first Chinese calligraphy—on bones—claimed to be dragon bones—oxen, probably. Oracles used them for their predictions," Boudreau said. "Before some diggers ran into the wall there were scholars who denied the Shangs ever existed."

"Those things are safe in museums," McLeod said. "It's the remains of the buildings that worry us. They're archaeological treasures."

The next morning my C-46 jumped into the air because the cabin was empty and we carried little fuel. The thirty-five-minute trip north seemed like flying from Chicago to Milwaukee—the prominent north-south railroad and the same flat pattern of green-and-brown farms. Millet made waves with the wind, and I saw fields of barley, soybeans, and winter wheat. It could have been southern Wisconsin, except my home state had more trees, and no one stole train tracks.

Horse-drawn wagons brought the cotton to our planes, and skinny laborers carried almost double their body weight. Their timing and balance—gracefully shifting a hundred-kilo bale from the wagon to their shoulders, hustling up an inclined plank to our cabin, maintaining rhythm by singing—turned bitter labor into a performing art.

After we got the cotton to Chengchow we waited while our mechanics transferred gasoline from fifty-five-gallon drums to our wings with hand pumps. When we asked the Chinese Air Force base commander if we could use his motorized pump to speed our refueling, he answered, "You are welcome, for one thousand U.S. dollars a day, payable in gold bars." We stuck to our wobble pumps.

On the second day the base commander's men searched the cotton for contraband. Before severing the baling wires they rolled the huge bales behind our planes, and the scattering cotton resembled a snowstorm when we started our engines for the next mission. Even though contraband wasn't found, the sabotage continued for our entire mission.

"The base commander is angry," my radioman said, "We spoiled his business. Before we came he made plenty of money with his C-47s."

A missionary I flew into Chengchow watched, dumbfounded, while the base commander's men hacked open our bales with meat choppers. "The cotton's for soldiers' uniforms," I said. "Designated strategic war material by Chiang Kai-shek himself."

That night at the missionary compound I grumbled, "This place is the same as three thousand years ago." They all looked at me. "The Shangs you mentioned—their bronze, their calligraphy—weren't the Shangs followed by the Chou Dynasty? Didn't the Chous ignore their emperor? Their corruption spilt China into feudal states, and they warred on each other!"

"Don't be tough on these people," Boudreau said. "If you're going to judge the Chinese, include the Tang Dynasty. For centuries, it enlightened the world."

I shut my mouth but recalled the Chin emperor who buried Confucian scholars alive.

The following day some missionaries I evacuated from Anyang said, "Nothing is organized. They send you empty to Anyang; you could carry food. Hundreds of children have starved to death since the siege started."

Upon reading, years later, the letters I sent home, I wondered how children could starve in that fertile province and why I didn't ask about it at the time. Most of us, it seemed, lapsed into accepting paradoxes without question. The more foreigners asked, the less we knew. Often, it seemed, the Chinese answers to foreigners' questions only added mystery to obscurity.

Our station manager eventually set up two large army tents and canvas cots at Chengchow's airport and produced an enthusiastic cook whose only utensils were a huge wok, long chopsticks, and a dish towel that doubled as a sweat rag, which he wore around his neck. Since vegetables and eggs were abundant in Chengchow, Davenport taught our chef to make Spanish omelettes. Whenever we called "Mexico," our runny-nosed chef laughed and went into his act.

At the end of our campfire meals the cook's large dishpan was full of dirty dishes, greasy water, and floating beer labels. Leery of dysentery, we drank weak, warm Tsingtao beer.

The night of a rainstorm one of the tents blew down. We cursed our way out from under the canvas and sat in an airplane and grumbled until dawn, when there was a rush to depart. The first couple of planes to get airborne could escape the bottleneck of refueling and fly more trips. Gene Bable was so fast he preflighted the wrong airplane. Its pilot watched in silence and then said, "Thanks for preflighting my bird," and took the airplane.

We raced simply to inject fun into a miserable project. I took off behind Bable and flew formation in his blind spot, a thousand feet above so I'd descend into Anyang in a steeper, faster gradient. I pushed the nose down and zoomed past Bable, who radioed, "You son of a bitch, you're burning up the engines."

We asked our missionary friends what would happen after the Communists captured Anyang. Those who'd seen villages change hands back and forth said, "The Communists split the land into units of approximately three-quarters of an acre and distributed them equally. But merchants and craftsmen and teachers didn't know how to farm, so the land deteriorated. Some villagers preferred the Japanese, because they brought some form of order. They were strict but efficient. If they wanted to do away with someone they simply killed him. But the Communists resort to torture. And some of the farmers say whoever comes it's all the same."

A week later a cold front moved in from the northwest. When we got back over Chengchow the ceiling was a thousand feet with a visibility of a couple of miles—an easy instrument approach. I descended through six thousand feet, still in heavy clouds.

Hearing our engines overhead, the base commander barks an order: "Shut off the beacon." His radio technician hesitates. The commander shouts, "That is my order."

My earphones are silent. I don't hear the beacon's reassuring identification tone, and my radio compass wanders aimlessly. Turning to our radio operator, I say, "The beacon went off. Find out when they expect it to come back on." In the meantime, Mao, our station manager, hurries to the Chinese Air Force radio room. Their radio technician guesses why Mao has appeared and says with alarm, "My commander ordered me to close the beacon."

Mao runs to the base commander's office. "Please open the beacon. Five of our planes are coming."

"Your planes are not my concern. It takes gasoline to run my generator; I have no gas."

"I'll give you one of our drums."

"Ten drums."

CAT laborers roll ten fifty-five-gallon drums of aviation fuel to the Chinese Air Force area while Mao radios, "Beacon come on soon."

The other planes are arriving from Anyang, so I broadcast, "I'm holding five thousand."

"Bable's holding six."

"Davenport at seven. What happened to the beacon?"

We circle and wait. Without a beacon to orient us, we guess at the wind. Thirty minutes pass.

Station manager Mao hurries back to the commander, who barks, "It takes many radio parts to run a beacon. Many tubes burn out. No tubes."

"I'll fetch a carton of tubes."

My radio operator twists in his chair again. "Chengchow says only five or ten minutes more, beacon come back."

An hour creeps by. The clouds are thick, the cockpit is dark, rain hammers the windshield. "Black Christmas" lurks in a recess of my mind. It happened last year. China National and Central Air lost three planes when fog enveloped Shanghai and the pilots waited for it to lift. "You can always get into Shanghai" was the maxim. "It's flatter than piss on a platter. One airport has military radar; the other, a long runway with a strong beacon." Those planes got to Shanghai with sufficient fuel to return to Hankow, but the Black Christmas pilots spent it waiting over Shanghai. The fog didn't lift, the radar developed a blind spot, they crashed.

My radioman speaks again: "Not much longer, very soon." But time passed at an agonizing pace. We got to Chengchow with enough fuel to hightail it to Süchow, where the weather is good, but we thought the interruption of the beacon was temporary—a frequent occurrence in China. But we're still circling and no longer have the fuel to get to the fair-weather airport. I call myself a fool for getting suckered into the oldest trap in aviation. I feel dumb and scared.

Minutes before sunset, station manager Mao turns the dial of CAT's safe and takes all of the money to the base commander's office. Our compass needles swing around and point steadily. The identification is loud. "Smith leaving five thousand," I broadcast.

"Bable leaving six."

"Davenport leaving seven," and then two more planes announce their descent.

My altimeter shows two hundred feet when I bust through the ragged cloud base and see Chengchow's concrete. "Smith's clear of the runway, two hundred and one, with moderate rain." The other planes follow, one by one.

I see Mao. I probably look irate, because he says, "Don't blame me," and then he tells what happened on the ground while we were circling overhead. The other pilots, dark circles under their eyes, gather around and listen. Mao is saying, "First I'm afraid for our airplanes. But now I'm afraid for myself; for what company do to me. I give away valuable company supplies, money."

"Don't worry, you did the right thing—you got us down," I say.

Bable says, "You're a good man. We'll talk to your boss."

Davenport says, "Mao, we're proud of you."

Chennault thanked Mao and told our meteorologist to train our ground radio operators in Chengchow to be weather observers. It was a crash course.

I got a scare soon after the last weather episode. Returning from Anyang with a full load of cotton, I got the startling news. The latest Chengchow weather report: ceiling zero, visibility zero. Nowhere else to go. I had carried minimum fuel out of Chengchow so I could carry more cotton out of Anyang. I sighed with relief when I saw Chengchow's runway lights ten miles ahead.

After the easy approach and landing, I walked over to the radio shack alongside the operations building and asked our newly trained double-threat radioman/weather observer to come outside. Stars shined overhead; lights glowed from distant buildings. "What made you think it was zero-zero?"

"I can't see anything. It's dark outside."

I pointed at the sky. "See the stars? No clouds." I pointed at various buildings. "See the lights? You can guess the visibility. Just guess the distance of the light farthest away."

The next night he reported, "Dark night, starlight, visibility invisible on account of darkness."

Grossly inaccurate wind reports aroused Doug Smith's curiosity, so he asked another radioman how he measured wind direction and velocity. The graduate picked a wooden profile of a rooster off his desk. It swiveled on a stick while celluloid tail feathers waited to spin in the wind. Still sitting at his desk, he stuck it out his open window, into the narrow corridor between the two buildings.

Eventually, the Chinese Air Force base commander kicked us out of Chengchow. "The airfield is required for military purposes," he said. Our Chinese crewmen told us he wanted to resume his rent-a-plane scam.

After my last takeoff I saw peasants digging moats around their villages. A cultural lag from medieval days. Something to confound and delay the enemy. I knew that Red troops would soon be using the same forced labor to shovel Honan's rich soil back into the ditches.

Whipsawed peasants became a familiar sight. The Nationalist Army believed in moats; the Reds didn't. As the villages of Honan switched sides in seesaw fights for the fertile plains, the villagers labored again and again at the same moats, digging them out or filling them in, according to the affiliation of their soldier-supervisors.

For months, flying over that sad province we saw ragged circles of peasants on the perimeters of their villages, toiling at the moats.

A Militia Leader

By the time crew scheduling returned me to Tsingtao, a nearby city had fallen.

Because of its history, it was my favorite. Weihsien showed China's age. The wall was added in the twelfth century to fend off Genghis Khan's marauders, but even then the city was old, because it had grown from the kingdom of Wei. Only weeks before my arrival, Mao Tse-tung's soldiers had clamored at the wall, shouted through bullhorns, promised annihilation.

Within Weihsien's wall, buildings of dark stone faced each other to form the familiar honeycombs of Chinese courtyards. A newer munitions plant, school, and athletic field stuck out like strangers.

Outside the wall, tobacco and peanut fields were interrupted by a religious mission and a landing strip for warplanes. The one had been built by foreign devils who called themselves Presbyterians, the other by invaders who called themselves Nihon-Jin and laid their runway over an ancient graveyard.

At the big war's end, Japan surrendered the city and released the American Presbyterian missionaries, who immediately asked Admiral Cook at Tsingtao to send medicines. The request was bucked to a Marine colonel, who bucked it to a young captain, who flew in with elixirs and splints.

What followed became a legend among China pilots. According to the yarn, the Marine captain was greeted warmly by Weihsien's city fathers and missionaries.

After the medical supplies were unloaded, he shook hands all around and taxied out. He turned his airplane onto the runway, and the well-wishers gaped in disbelief as his right wheel plunged through the runway into a grave and stopped on the bones of a subject of the king of Wei.

When the colonel got the message he shouted, "Those missionaries wrecked my plane," and he dispatched three Grumman F7F fighters to circle low and assess the damage.

While other Marines debated how they'd send in a heavy crane to lift their plane out of the grave, the young captain shoved the plane's inflatable life raft under the right wing and yanked the lanyard. The raft's CO_2 bottle released its compressed gas and the tough neoprene rubber made thubbing noises while it unfolded and ballooned. The plane rose from the grave and the lieutenant took off. The missionaries called it Weihsien's Easter.

I never expected to meet Lew Burridge, the hero of the episode, because I assumed the young Marine with his ingenuity had had the wit to leave China and become a general or a captain of industry; but he joined CAT instead. He was a slim, casual man; Hollywood wouldn't cast him as a Marine. No macho glint in his eyes, he appeared to be carefree and reflective, as if he followed a desideratum I had seen in some church somewhere: *Go placidly amid the noise and haste. . . . Speak your truth quietly and clearly. . . . In the noisy confusion of life keep peace with your soul.*

After CAT had been flying into Tsingtao for several months, Chennault summoned Burridge. "You flew into Weihsien?"

"Yes, General, when I was in the Marine Corps."

Chennault showed him a radiogram, a poignant request from the city. Although a railroad ran the eighty miles from Tsingtao to Weihsien and continued for 350 more to Beijing via Tsinan and Tientsin, guerrillas had stolen sections of track and blocked the roads. The city was besieged.

"We could parachute supplies," Chennault said, "but if nothing's exported it'll die an economic death."

Burridge knew the value of Weihsien. Although it was only the size of Racine, Wisconsin, its munitions plant, machine shops, and produce gave it importance; and its hogs sprouted bristles that were sought in overseas markets because they were flat and held large quantities of paint that wouldn't streak. Chennault said, "I don't suppose there's any way we can help these people."

"It's only eighty miles from Tsingtao," Burridge replied. "We could shuttle with our fuel tanks practically empty—reduce the cabin weight if necessary. I could fly in first with buckets of paint and mark the weak spots."

Burridge came back to the castle and told us, "It's just like Chennault. Throws us a problem, says it can't be solved, waits for us to show him. He baits us."

The runway held up. A parade of C-47s flew machine parts, money, medical equipment in; and peanut oil, tobacco, hog bristles out; merchants and politicians both ways.

The commissioner of Shantung Province wrote,"Weihsien's prices halved. Without CAT, the city would be without electricity or coal, and the mission hospital would have to close. . . . Thirty-five tons of mail arrived in the last ten days. Four hundred students for Tsingtao's university were flown out."

Pilots worked so enthusiastically that Tsingtao's accountants pleaded, "Stop flying until we catch up with the paperwork." We jeered, "Get more abacuses," and kept flying. Promoted to area manager, Burridge never seemed to work or worry, but his bailiwick ran without a hitch—except for paperwork, which earned him a summons to the comptroller's office in Shanghai, where he explained why it lagged so far behind the airplanes.

I enjoyed the small-town bustle of Weihsien's airport. Courtly peanut salesmen in black gowns and skullcaps squatted on their heels and puffed long bamboo pipes. They weighed the peanuts by suspending bamboo sticks on threads. The black-lacquered sticks were graduated with delicate lines of inlaid brass.

Sometimes we were greeted by the town's militia leader, General Chang Tsien-tso. He didn't wear a uniform—he didn't need one. His black suit, fedora, big cigar, and boisterous confidence were distinction enough. He had become a hero to the peasants during World War II when Japanese solders ruled the Shantung Peninsula. Any rumor that Chang Tsien-tso's guerrillas were in the area would turn Japanese arrogance into fear.

After the Japanese surrender, Chang became general of the Weihsien militia. His citizen army was reinforced with a contingent of Nationalist soldiers under the command of a pompous General

Ching, who looked upon Chang with the disdain of a West Pointer for a National Guardsman. The peasants were proud of their militia, but they detested the Nationalist soldiers, because they stole chickens and ripped doors off hinges so they wouldn't have to sleep in mud. The morale of the Nationalist soldiers was low because they had been transplanted from the south to this alien province, where strangers spoke an unintelligible dialect.

"The Nationalists are losing," a Marine colonel told us, "because they don't send out patrols to keep track of enemy positions. They believe in sitting the enemy to death. The Commies practically own the countryside."

"Get us out of here," our Weihsien staff pleaded.

"Stop acting jittery," Burridge answered. He flew to Weihsien with his assistant, John Plank (another former Marine), and they remained overnight to prove its safety.

"General Ching is the ranking Nationalist general here," Burridge soothed. "He assured me the city is safe. If it was in jeopardy he'd be screaming for reinforcements."

On the following morning, Burridge and Plank, the two optimists, accompanied their subordinates to the airport to greet CAT's first arrival. They watched the C-47, piloted by Earthquake Magoon, touch down while explosions of mortar shells followed the plane throughout its landing roll. Earthquake ground looped and took off in the opposite direction.

Burridge and his men hurried to the Presbyterian mission, hid in the attic, and listened to sounds of battle until a violent thunderstorm interrupted the firefight. A militia man took advantage of the interruption to spirit the CAT people back to the city. Inside the gates they met the militia leader, General Chang, who took the cigar out of his mouth to say, "You're in much danger."

"General Ching assured us it was safe," Burridge said.

"General Ching likes to save face. He should have asked for reinforcements. I knew the city was in danger; your men knew it was in danger."

Burridge radioed Tsingtao: "Athletic field four hundred feet long; okay for light plane."

Willauer radioed back, "Take it easy. We'll provide twenty-four-hour coverage while we arrange to get you out."

Willauer asked the Chinese Air Force squadron at Tsingtao for help. The commander replied, "We can't help—our planes are needed somewhere else." But his B-25s sat on the ground all night.

The next afternoon, Roger Faye putt-putted over in a sixty-five-horsepower Piper Cub with two five-gallon cans of gas in the front seat for refueling after he landed at Weihsien. But gusts of wind eddied around the buildings on the perimeter of the athletic field and tossed the plane violently while Faye blasted at full power, climbed away, and hit a building on the way up. It tore away the tip of a wing. Faye kept flying, headed back toward Tsingtao, and solved his refueling problem by landing on the bank of a small river. He poured a can of gas into his tank, keeping one eye on a Communist soldier on the opposite bank who was busily mounting a machine gun on a tripod. "I spilled some," Faye told us, "and then I spun the prop by hand. The engine started on the first try. I was so fast the guys in the C-46 overhead who escorted me didn't know I made the pit stop."

That night, Red artillery killed thousands of defenders in the fields outside of Weihsien while CAT's C-47s dropped flares to illuminate the approaches to the wall. Noting the lack of air support by the Chinese Air Force, a military observer called it a disgraceful exhibition of air power.

Willauer asked Admiral Badger to lend him a Marine Corps L-5, a liaison plane capable of landing on Weihsien's athletic field.

Standing orders prohibited America's military forces from engaging in China's internal affairs. Nevertheless, Admiral Badger presented the dilemma to the U.S. consul in Tsingtao. Consul General Strong knew us, and he was a kindred spirit. He was a familiar sight, often running toward a departing plane at the last minute, clutching his rolled-up black umbrella, hanging on to his homburg hat, and shouting, "Wait for me—what's happening?"

After he heard Admiral Badger's plea, the consul general said, "If you let CAT borrow your airplane, I'm prepared to say I approved it. I'll say it went on a mission to rescue American citizens who went to Weihsien on a peaceful journey of commerce. If the worst happens— if it crashes—I'll share the blame with you."

Receiving orders to release his plane with as little fanfare as possible, the Marine Corps commandant told CAT's chief mechanic, "The Corps has lost discipline. I can't even trust my sentries. My liaison plane sits outside our hangar, unguarded. Anyone could steal it and I'd never know who."

CAT's mechanics checked the small plane's fuel tanks. They were full. A can of gray paint and a spray gun lay under a wing. CAT mechanics painted out the military insignia and identification numbers. A former Marine, Dick Kruske, flew the eighty miles to Weihsien, circled the school's athletic field, saw people sitting on rooftops and walls, waiting for the show. He performed a spectacular, tight-turning aircraft carrier approach, touched down, and stopped in front of the school-yard wall. A green-uniformed postal employee bicycled up and handed Kruske a sack of outbound mail.

The guys decided that Burridge should go first. He climbed in with the mail. Kruske's sixty-five-horsepower takeoff roll seemed painfully slow. He got airborne but hit a rooftop and crashed to the ground. Burridge and Kruske extricated themselves from the wreckage while the people applauded and laughed. Burridge radioed Tsingtao, "Send a fourth for bridge."

That night they watched the sky glow red from burning neighboring villages. Militia leader Chang gave them pistols and said, "If you're captured you'll know what to do."

"I haven't had the honor of meeting Mr. Strong, your consul in Tsingtao," General Chang said. "My people tell me he's a fine man. . . . If you escape alive, please present this with my compliments." He handed his lacquer cigarette case to Burridge. And then everyone dined on boiled peanuts.

Burridge led the mechanics to the crashed plane. They recovered its landing lights and battery and improvised a portable searchlight, which was strapped to a militiaman who roamed Weihsien's wall, looking for enemy soldiers who might attempt a climb.

Communist loudspeakers blatted, "Brother must not fight brother! Open the gates! No one will be hurt! We will shoot only the Americans who are using Chinese people as tools for their war with the Russians!"

Militia general Chang, silhouetted against the sky, with his fedora and cigar, strutted along the wall and shouted, "Go to the devil, miserable bandits! Shoot me if you can!" His men cheered. Wounded soldiers, carrying others on their backs or dragging their dead, were admitted through the city gates.

In Shanghai that night, mechanics dismantled a CAT liaison plane and loaded it into the cabin of a C-46. It got to Tsingtao early in the morning. Faye flew it into the old city's athletic field and made a successful takeoff with Kruske and Burridge in the passenger seat, while Plank remained behind with CAT's local employees.

The next few days resembled musical chairs with light planes crash-landing and others extricating CAT people, one or two at a time. At night the stranded ones heard the loudspeakers. They didn't understand the dialect, but they recognized their names. Communist bullhorns shouted, "Send out Marshall Stayner; send out John Plank; send out Edwin Trout. We will shoot them. Then you will be free. . . . We shall kill the American devils and General Ching and General Chang. We shall kill your bank presidents and city officials. The rest of you will be unhurt."

Nationalist general Ching, grabbing a bullhorn, shouted back, "The flares you see dropping are only warnings. Next time, five-pound atomic bombs will be dropped. Surrender!"

The Communists answered, "We give proof that you are our brothers. We have captured your electric generator outside the wall.

We can put your city in darkness. But we will keep it lighted as a symbol of our good intentions."

Militia general Chang patrolled the wall, shouted defiance, encouraged his militia. CAT pilots circled and dropped flares. About 250,000 Communist soldiers surrounded the city.

Louise Willauer, private pilot, said, "I'll fly a rescue plane."

Husband Willauer replied, "Don't be crazy. If you're captured, the Commies would demand the whole airline for ransom, and I, being a gentleman, would have to give it to them."

Chief pilot Rousselot, the last foreigner in Weihsien, was rescued after spending a night in a dugout with the two generals, Ching and Chang.

For the first time, the Chinese Air Force flew support missions, and newspapers proclaimed a Nationalist victory.

After nightfall, the Reds pulled their artillery pieces close to the wall and blew holes through it. Nationalist general Ching surrendered, but militia general Chang kept fighting while CAT's employees, disguised as merchants, walked eighty miles to Tsingtao. The last they saw of General Chang, he was with his officers, rallying his men.

When the Communists mopped up Weihsien they counted 4,500 Nationalist dead. General Chang's body, riddled with about seventy holes, lay near the wall.

The Fall of Tsinan

Rural China was dotted with countless walled villages whose inhabitants retired with the sun. No electricity, no streetlights, no traffic on the roads. Except for moonlit nights that made rivers glow, we flew over a sea of black. Sparse cities illuminated by electricity were navigators' friends.

Weihsien had been a nighttime landmark, north of course, on our way to and from Tsinan. But now it blacked out when its "liberators" heard our engines. Far away, we saw the lights disappear suddenly, as if the Reds had pulled a main switch. We assumed we'd be executed if we crash-landed in rural Shantung.

Months before, a China National plane had been hijacked. The American captain and crew were invited, at gunpoint, to the passenger cabin while a Communist pilot took over the controls. It quickly became obvious that he didn't know a C-46. After he had made many hair-raising passes at the runway at excessive speed, out of control, the China National captain told his captors, for God's sake, let him land the plane and then he'd give it back. His offer was accepted. After the easy landing, the Reds released the China National crew and they got back to Tsingtao via donkey cart and on foot.

After the battle of Weihsien, the crews of all three airlines knew the Reds wouldn't be that friendly.

I was glad to have Rossi for a copilot on the Tsingtao–Tsinan cotton shuttle. This unlikely position for the Flying Tiger ace, the veteran of more than seven hundred crossings of the Himalayan Hump, had come about because he had resigned from CAT to fly for his friend Moon Chen, who had founded Central Air. Some insignificant difference between the two strong personalities grated against Rossi's independent spirit, so he switched back to CAT. Avoiding favoritism, chief pilot Rousselot put Rossi on the bottom of the seniority list, like any new hire.

Rossi discovered he liked the copilot's seat. Flying with his old friends, he enjoyed the vacation from work and responsibility.

On a takeoff from Tsinan with a full load of cotton, it was obvious we wouldn't get airborne before we ran out of runway. I called, "Quarter flap," which Rossi promptly executed, and we leaped into the air. We had proper lift, but the added drag slowed our climb.

"We're overloaded," I said.

"How can you tell?" A typical Rossi jest, but I didn't laugh. Hugging the ground as if we were plowing the cotton fields, we maintained takeoff power and avoided turns, which rob lift. After we hedge-hopped hamlets that were probbably guerrilla hangouts, our airspeed gradually increased. It seemed an eternity before we reached our zero-flap minimum speed. And then Rossi milked up the flaps, inch by inch, to preclude sinking into the ground. Only then could we retard the throttles to maximum continuous power. The cylinder heads cooled, and we climbed high enough to reach Tsingtao.

After landing we counted the bales and discovered the scam. The shipper's airport staff had developed their own business, loading extra bales from the stockpile, which their cohorts in Tsingtao sold.

On our next trip together, as we waited at Tsinan for the cotton, Chu handed us a radiogram from chief pilot Rousselot. "Effective immediately, Rossi promoted to captain."

Lounging in the copilot seat, Rossi said, "I don't want to be captain. I'm enjoying this." He was the only copilot I ever knew who didn't want to be a captain. Happy as he was, with a strong inner balance, nothing to prove, respected by everyone, he didn't need the prestige or the work. He radiogrammed, "Suggest I remain copilot, need more experience."

Rousselot's reply: "You're a captain or out."

Chennault had happened to notice the low status of his Tiger ace and had ordered the promotion.

By then, fortunately, Rousselot needed more captains, and Chennault's order gave him a clear conscience in jumping the veteran ahead of some less experienced guys.

Tud Tarbet, another new captain, switched from China National. Knowing I had been a China National pilot, Rousselot asked for an opinion. "Don't worry about Tud," I said. "He's so short and good-looking, he appears to be immature, but he isn't. He's a good pilot, and he's congenial."

I had known Tarbet since the day the Army Air Corps flew us to Calcutta for training at Dum-Dum Aerodrome. Tarbet carried an Army-issue canteen at his hip, which contained scotch and led me to believe he was a man who understood priorities; and he was a good poker player. So all the China National pilots were happy for him when he met someone who suited him. A spontaneous American beauty, she was a Red Cross volunteer named Mary Margaret. We called her Chouta-peg, which sounds like the Hindustani word for "short drink."

They matched so perfectly, they soon married and waltzed happily together through the war in the Far East, with Tarbet flying the Hump and Chouta-peg entertaining troops. They were so exuberant in their happiness that I recalled the Bible's warning, "Rejoice with trembling," and immediately admonished myself for worrying.

The Marines also liked Tarbet. A cocky, affable guy, he was like many of them. With many Marines receiving discharges in Tsingtao to join CAT, and others remaining in the Corps—and none of us wearing uniforms off duty—strangers couldn't tell us apart.

We watched their Corsair fighters chase each other in the night sky, and when they practiced aircraft carrier landings within the short rectangle they had painted on Tsingtao's long concrete strip, their LSO (landing signal officer) maneuvered his paddle for us as we landed a big C-46 in the same space. When the airport socked in with fog or rain, and only CAT flew, their team of experts hurried to the GCA (ground controlled approach) shack to talk us down, and then the control tower guys invited us up for coffee.

For months, various operations had been overlapping, and we took them in stride: our soldier-cotton shuttle; supplies to embattled Manchuria and another northern industrial city called Taiyüan; scheduled passenger flights, wool flights from the northwest, tin flights from the southwest. But in midsummer 1948, the crisis mushroomed. A radiogram from Dr. Ernest Struthers, dean of the College of Medicine at Cheeloo University at Tsinan, sounded laudatory. Between the lines, it was ominous: "Ever since February, railway service from Tsingtao has been suspended. Without air service we should have found it impossible to continue. It is our hope that CAT will continue to render such service and that the company will have a long and useful history in China. We feel that the service which CAT is giving is not only a great help to the missions, but to China as well." And troop movements to the Shantung capital increased.

I remember watching Tarbet's C-46 on its takeoff roll. He had a top-notch crew; I knew them well. Copilot H. S. Har had recently transferred from China National, and the radioman, W. K. Chan, had been a radio officer on British merchant ships during the war and a radio operator for the United Press in Hong Kong afterward.

Tarbet's plane accelerated to takeoff speed and started a normal climb until it reached a hundred feet. Its nose pitched up abruptly and hung there, shuddering for a horrifying moment. Then it pitched down and plunged into the runway and exploded in an orange ball of flame.

A Marine pilot, at a Corsair on the tarmac, shouted, "Who got it?"

Earthquake Magoon shouted back, "You damned ghoul," and the Marine looked ashamed.

The Marine Corps fire truck couldn't get close, because the live ammunition of the soldier-passengers continued to explode for more than an hour afterward, and by then the fire had burned itself out and everyone was dead.

It was our first crash. We had begun to think we were invincible, and now we knew we weren't. If it could happen to Tarbet it could happen to any of us, we knew.

General Chennault ordered an autopsy to determine if Tarbet had been accidentally killed by one of his passengers. The soldiers had boarded fully armed, including grenades that hung from their belts, and the soldiers themselves were new.

The autopsy didn't occur, because one of our drivers said he had seen Tarbet taxi past with the control locks still on the tail surfaces. Captain Plank, first on the scene after the wreckage cooled down, said he found the elevator locks on the ground near the tail. With this evidence, an accident board decided the crash had been caused by the failure of the crew to remove the control locks and by Tarbet's failure to check the flight controls for freedom of movement before he took off.

Unfair, I thought, to hang the accident on the crew, because our C-46s had been painted recently with the locks in place. The locks were two flat boards held firm by elastic bungee cords. Clamped onto the rudder and elevators, they prevented the wind from slamming the controls back and forth when a plane was parked. When the boards were removed from the freshly painted tail surfaces, the unpainted portion that had been under the boards had the same shape and dirty appearance as the boards themselves. The inexperienced driver may have mistaken the "holidays" for the boards themselves. As for finding them near the tail after the crash, there were many items near the tail that weren't there when Tarbet took off, and the control locks, when not in use, were stored in the rear belly compartment, which was near the tail. It occurred to me that pilots, unlike lawyers and doctors, don't stick together. Some pilots are quick to ascribe blame to a colleague in an accident. I believe it is a defense mechanism. An admission that a similar fate could befall the critic would be too heavy to bear. But a belief that the accident was caused by some mistake—an error that the critic himself would never make—is reassuring.

The families of Tarbet's crewmen arranged Chinese funerals, while a number of American pilots visited a Protestant church in Tsingtao to plan a memorial service for Tarbet. "Not only will I conduct a service in honor of your departed friend," the pastor said, "a brass plaque in his memory will be attached to one of our pews. . . . May I suggest a donation to our parish in his memory? A few hundred American dollars, perhaps?" In our grief we acceded, but after the conference, the Skull said, "Damned if I didn't feel like I was in a used-car lot."

After the crash, when lined up on the runway, ready for takeoff, and the last item on the checklist was called, "Flight controls—free and easy," most of the pilots moved the airplane's controls through their full range of movement while saying, "This one's for Tarbet," although I never said those words because I didn't want to hang that on him on such flimsy evidence.

My rudder would jam after departing Peiping and the cause wouldn't be a forgotten control lock.

By early autumn, there was another radiogram from Shantung's capital, typically Chinese in its grace and subtlety. The director of the Tsinan Power Supply Company was asking for more help. "Your pilots did indeed an an excellent piece of work bringing important materials to Tsinan. It enables us to make vital repairs, and thus secure against a breakdown of the electric current and water supply for the city. We express our thanks, and the same also in the name of the inhabitants."

I was flying sacks of flour to the besieged capital of Manchuria when Richardson, Burridge, and Carleton flew sacks of rice to Shantung's capital. When they descended toward Tsinan they saw soldiers fighting a mile from the airport, and they knew it would be CAT's last trip.

As they parked, troops of the garrison command ran up, shouting, "The Reds are here!" Bullets whined. The entire CAT staff had gathered at the airport, and they clambered aboard. Richardson and Carleton taxied out while Burridge and others at the open cabin door tossed off bags of rice and pulled in refugees who clung to the plane.

Burridge told us later, "I'm so thankful everyone got out. I didn't want a repeat of the Weihsien thriller."

Peiping

On CAT's first birthday, in December 1947, the wooden beads on our abacus told us we had flown almost two million miles and were one of the largest cargo lines in the world—in ton miles flown.

We repaid the United Nations loan for the planes, plus 10 percent interest. With the China National Rehabilitation and Relief Association contract completed, China gave us a franchise to fly with the official name "Civil Air Transport."

The quarter of a million dollars invested by the Tobacco King had mushroomed.

Sharing a pot of tea with me, Dr. Wang Wen-san, manager, Nanking branch of the Kinchen Bank, recalled his conversations with his boss.

"'This airline of your friend Chennault's—it's prosperous— where's your loyalty? Why doesn't our bank own shares?'

"'Little more than a year ago, you promised Chennault money. The board vetoed it and you shelved it, remember?'"

"'Never mind that. Ask the owner of the tobacco company to sell us his shares. He'll listen to you—you're his schoolmate.'"

"'He risked his capital when the future was uncertain. He'll want a profit.'"

"'You exchange students are all alike—all you think about is money.'"

Dr. Wang carried the message to his old schoolmate, and the Tobacco King replied, "Your president is foxy. I took the risk and now he wants my shares dollar for dollar. I wasn't born yesterday. He thinks I'll do it because you and I are good friends, and so we are. The shares are worth more than double, but I'll sell them to your bank for only fifty percent profit." China's Kinchen Bank became CAT's principal stockholder.

At the end of that year, 1947, Chennault remarried. As China's lure captured the general, America's ties held his first wife back home, and they had divorced.

Chennault had known the family of his new wife, Anna, ever since her father, Y. W. Chan, a Chinese consul in San Francisco, had ushered the Flying Tigers to China. Subsequently a correspondent for the China News Agency, Anna had maintained a vital interest in the career of the American general.

Elegantly feminine like many sophisticated Chinese women, Anna's modesty masked a brilliant mind and a perky kind of courage. No stranger could guess that petite, gentle Anna had fended off Japanese soldiers and Chinese bandits. She and her five sisters were in Hong Kong in 1941 when their genteel world collapsed. Their mother had just died of cancer and their father was overseas on a diplomatic mission when the Japanese invaded the crown colony. Anna led her youthful sisters on a horrendous odyssey to freedom, selling her mother's jewels for food along the way, walking, hitching rides on wagons and local trains. They became separated for weeks and found each other again. After the better part of a year they reached Kunming, deep in western China. That was Anna.

After the marriage, Anna remained in the background although she lent her professional skill to CAT's monthly bulletin. Through her feature articles, which were devoid of CAT's affairs, she acquainted us in depth with China itself. Anna walked gracefully in both cultures, fathoming and liking both. She took their foibles in stride. With generosity of spirit she overlooked our unwitting violations of Chinese customs.

In January 1948, China's National Resources Commission asked us to move families of the government's employees from the capital of Manchuria to the safety of Peiping. The historic city's old name— Peking (Northern Capital)—became Peiping (Northern Peace) in 1928, after the nationalist government shifted the capital to Nanking. In the year to come—1949—the Communist government would return the capital to the original site and its name would again be Peking, although contemporary spelling would translate to Beijing.

A tired taxi rattled us from South Field, past the brown stubble of winter wheat, to Peiping's high granite wall, where bored sentries waved us through huge wooden gates.

I knew it was the terminus of the ancient Silk Road to Persia and Europe and had been China's cultural capital for centuries, but I was unprepared for such a grand city. I gaped at wide, tree-lined boulevards and thick, red archways that separated neighborhoods. The city itself was a monument to China's past glories and a testament to the skill and discipline of countless laborers and artisans: the blue-tiled Temple of Heaven; spacious Tiananmen Square; the Forbidden City, with its glistening roofs of orange tile; the Summer Palace on a hill above a frozen lake with a marble boat; the alabaster white Winter Palace on another lake on which families in knitted hats and scarves pushed kids on sleds or darted past on old-fashioned curly nosed skates, looking as if they had burst out of a Grandma Moses painting.

An aged serenity permeated Peiping. Its people spoke Mandarin with a charming twang, and they were unfailingly polite. Even the rickshaw pullers were courtly.

Wandering with my camera, I saw a camel train disappearing around a corner. I jumped into a rickshaw and the puller jogged down the street, passing men who sat on their heels and called what sounded like *"Tar shur mu yuan?"* ("Who's he?") and *"Yo ben tshu?"* ("Where are you going?"), and my rickshaw man, without breaking stride, yelled, *"Lour tu nor nay lei?"* ("Where are the camels?") and

"Yun shee gee." ("Camera.") Laughter and pointing. *"Yu ben tshu."* ("Turn that way.") We found the camels resting on their bellies on a sidewalk in front of a bar where rice whiskey was served, and I assumed the driver was slaking a Gobi Desert thirst.

Back-alley markets sold endless varieties of silk. Yards of the heavier fabric were hand embroidered with multicolored images of birds and flowers.

A thieves' market was a central clearing place where missing possessions could be reclaimed for a modest price.

I saw more bread than rice in the north—crispy spirals that shattered with the first bite into a thousand morsels, soft whole-wheat sesame buns, scallion pancakes, and steamed buns, round and white as snowballs stuffed with meats and spices. Down a mud alley, a duck restaurant with broken steps leading to a second floor had been in the same family for more than four hundred years.

The Wagon Lits Hotel sheltered young Americans from Ivy League universities whose woolen sweaters with a huge letter H or Y or P certified athletic excellence. Recently hired by Standard Oil or the British American Tobacco Company, they studied Mandarin, the dialect of culture, at Peiping University.

"We weren't warned outright," Wesley Riley confided, "but the company intimated we'd ruin our careers if we married an Oriental." An Occidental wife, a suitable appendage for the country clubs, tennis courts, and bowling greens that coddled Western socialites in Asia, would ensure a journey up the corporate ladder. Even more than Asia's bizarre sights, this vestige of Yankee colonialism astonished me.

I was refreshed and delighted to see CAT's own princess, Natasia, in the grand city of Peiping because she jolted its peacock society. She threw dinner parties, the only times the elite didn't gossip: "She's not a Russian princess; she's a common Pole."

"I heard she was a concubine of a Chinese general during the war. In Chungking, of all places."

"He dumped her."

Raised eyebrows. "How did she support herself?"

Natasia sat at the head of her fine dinner table and cooed at the guests until the conversation turned to the fine fabrics of China. "The rarest of all," a guest pronounced, "is woven from the wool of unborn lambs. It's called astrakhan."

"They couldn't produce much yarn that way," said another.

Natasia laughed. "Hell, maybe they have abortions."

After another bottle of champagne, the name of an absent socialite came up. "That bitch," Natasia crowed. "She called me a Chinese whore, but anybody can tell by looking at me I'm not Chinese."

At the other end of the table, her husband, Bradley, our station manager, repeatedly held his champagne glass before the comely

Miss Brown, the freelance writer beside him, and he talked to no one else. Natasia's blue eyes looked like chips off a glacier as she summoned her houseboy and whispered something. Minutes later Natasia announced, "Miss Brown, your taxi is here."

Natasia's jousts with Peiping's Western society diminished as her interest in CAT's adventures grew. When we evacuated two hundred orphans from the Sisters of Charity mission in Shihkiachwang Natasia met the airplanes and mothered the children until they were safe within Peiping's walls. After we rescued Trappist monks from the same long-named place, Natasia befriended them. It became obvious that she knew many dialects. "They say the other brothers were dragged off by Communists," she said. "They were tortured and buried in shallow graves."

She visited them often during their week's stay in Peiping. On the eve of their departure for Europe they held a ceremony in her honor and gave her a tapestry of silk that had been embroidered with the image of a Chinese Virgin and Child. The brothers had seen compassion where I had seen ice chips, and my slow brain suggested Natasia had endured untold hardships in a strange, harsh land and had survived with her beauty and love of life intact.

I stayed in Peiping for the entire year and shuttled to Mukden (Shenyang), the capital of Manchuria. Besieged by Communist troops, the city saw its prices skyrocket. One egg cost twenty-five cents and Elephant Brand cigarettes were several dollars a pack. More alarming than inflation, the battle for Manchuria brewed, and seven thousand dependents of government employees wanted to get out while the airlines still flew.

The Head of the Giant

Manchuria protrudes from China's northeast like Maine from the United States. Larger than New England plus Texas and California, it stretches north from Korea's Yalu River to Russia's Amur and east from Shanhaiguan, 150 miles east of Beijing—to the outskirts of Vladivostok on the Sea of Japan. Fertile prairies, forests thick with timber, coal and iron mines, huge dams, hydroelectric generators, and steel mills make Manchuria an economic jewel. Its capital was called "the Chicago of China." Railroads converged on Mukden and fanned out again. The Pin Han Railroad tied Manchuria to the body of China via a long, level stretch that squeezed between northern mountains and the Yellow Sea. The flat corridor was called "the Jugular Vein," while Manchuria itself was "the Head of the Giant."

It was nurtured by an enemy and destroyed by an ally.

Japan grabbed Manchuria in 1931 and spent six years turning it into an industrial colossus for warring on the rest of China.

In the summer of 1945, at the close of World War II, Russian troops entered Manchuria, ostensibly to accept Japan's surrender and then guard public and private property until Chinese troops arrived. That was Uncle Joe Stalin's pledge at the Yalta Conference. Instead, the Russians ripped heavy machinery from Manchuria's factories, looted gold from its banks, and shipped it all to Russia. The outrageous betrayal of China's ally gutted the place that was crucial to the reconstruction of China.

Moreover, the Russians gave Chinese Communist rebels vast caches of supplies that had been surrendered by Japan's powerful Kwantung Army: one thousand artillery pieces, 366 tanks, 300,000 rifles, 4,836 machine guns, 2,300 motor vehicles, and ammunition for half a million soldiers. Enough to give Mao Tse-tung's ragtag guerrillas a foundation for a formidable army.

The devastating effect of the Soviet betrayal was compounded when America's idealistic secretary of state, General George Marshall, sought the cooperation of Chinese Communists and Nationalists to rebuild their country. The fruitless negotiations for a coalition government gave Mao Tse-tung time to train his rebels and gave Communist troops that were encircled in central China time to break out and filter back to Manchuria.

Chiang Kai-shek himself increased his burden by ignoring advice to enlist 300,000 soldiers who were on the spot and unemployed and who might otherwise drift into the Communist camp. They were Manchurians who had been drafted into Japan's army. Intimate with the terrain, the dialect, the peasants, they could find a place under the banner of Nationalist China. But their previous service in the enemy's army stuck in Chiang Kai-shek's craw.

Even more difficult to accept, the dynamic leader who could rally them—"the Young Marshal"—was a North China warlord. The mention of his name—Chang Hseuh-liang—raised the hackles of China's president. His ire sprang from his loss of face in the Sian Incident nine years earlier.

It occurred in the winter of 1936, when Chiang Kai-shek journeyed north to review the Young Marshal's troops. Serving China with distinction, they had fended off invaders from Japan.

In the evening, while relaxing at a hot springs resort, Chiang Kai-shek was abruptly arrested by the Young Marshal's bodyguards and intimidated into focusing less on Chinese Communists and more on Japan.

Chiang Kai-shek was incensed. A brilliant tactician, he didn't resist Japan's invasion of Manchuria because his army then was no match for the Japanese empire. He planned to build his forces before resisting the Japanese. But first he aimed to unify China by resolving its internal conflict.

Enraged by the brash subordinate who challenged his master plan; humiliated when he escaped out a window, only to be recaptured; shivering in his nightshirt in the winter night without his false teeth, Chiang Kai-shek thundered, "Shoot me and finish it all," but Captain Sun, the Young Marshal's bodyguard, replied, "We only ask you to lead our country against Japan."

After extracting the agreement, the Young Marshal escorted Chiang Kai-shek back to the capital—into the lion's den. Dr. Wang Wen-san told me the Young Marshal's gesture expressed Chinese nobility. It meant, "I did what I thought best for China, and now I stand before you—do with me what you will."

Unmollified, Chiang Kai-shek detained the Young Marshal and placed him under house arrest. Interestingly, Chiang Kai-shek didn't hold a grudge against the entire family. The Young Marshal's brother spent his career as a CAT captain. I once asked him to speak of his father and brother—two of the most colorful characters in Chinese history—but was disappointed by his silence.

When I got to Manchuria in January 1948, I heard the popular adage "China will survive or perish with the Northeast." With crucial battles in the wind, we began to evacuate government dependents out of Manchuria's capital.

My first trip began before daylight at the end of a rope with copilot Norwich on the other end. After flinging it over our C-46's wings and sawing off the crusted snow, we huddled and shivered in the cockpit, trying in vain to start the engines. Cowboy Lewis climbed an engine stand to remove a spark plug. "Look at this," he said. A glaze of ice covered the points. "No spark's gonna arc between these. When the engines cooled after yesterday's flight, moisture in the cylinders condensed and froze."

Lewis and his mechanics removed their heavy gloves to reach into the narrow spaces to change the plugs. They had to stop intermittently, come down the ladders, turn their backs to the north wind, and jump up and down while they warmed their hands in their armpits. It was still dark when we got into the air.

When I turned on course I couldn't move the rudder. "It was free and clear on the preflight check," I said. Norwich helped me push on the rudder pedal, but it wouldn't budge. Loss of rudder control wasn't immediately dangerous, because an airplane, like a bicycle, turns by banking. But we'd need it for Mukden's blustery crosswind. And a failure of an engine would compound the problem, because all of our power would be on one side. Engineers called it asymmetric thrust. To us it meant we'd be condemned to fly in circles, because there'd be no rudder to counteract the yaw. We asked the tower for clearance to land.

When we extended our wheels the rudder freed itself, so we aborted our approach, raised the wheels, and headed for Mukden again; but as soon as the gear came up the rudder jammed again. We went back into Peiping.

I knew if anyone could fix it, Lewis could. After all, he had outsmarted the pompous colonel in Hawaii. After I described the mystery of the jammed rudder he mulled it over for a brief moment and then crawled under the tail. He reached up inside the tail wheel well and unzipped its canvas lining. Several crushed cases of Elephant Brand cigarettes dropped to the top of the tail wheel and fell into the snow. They were crushed when we retracted the landing gear after takeoff. The tail wheel, with twelve hundred pounds of hydraulic pressure, had retracted into its well and jammed the cigarettes against the rudder cables. When we extended the wheels before landing, the cables had room to move again.

Copilot Eddie Norwich, a former Marine Corps sergeant, grumbled, "Give me some of those damn cigarettes." We both stuffed our pockets with the packs and took off again and climbed east across the frozen farms of north China. By the time we reached eight thousand feet the reduced air pressure had sucked some of our cargo of flour through the mesh of the cotton sacks. It filled the airplane like fog and settled on us. We looked like ghosts.

We intercepted the Pin Han Railroad at dawn and looked down at the end of the Great Wall, and we watched the early sunlight bounce off the snowy mountains on our left and chunks of ice in the sea to our right. A couple of hours after we got over Manchuria's plains we saw smokestacks standing tall and stark in the crisp air, although there wasn't any smoke, nor did we see trains on the converging railways. Wary of guerrilla small-arms fire from farmlands, we didn't descend below five thousand feet until we were over Mukden, and then we spiraled down and landed on a short strip where our radio technicians had installed a communications radio in an abandoned bus. A welding torch and the ingenuity of our Chinese mechanics turned the bus into a control tower, and when the last plane departed, it transported the ground crew to their homes before the curfew hour.

Laborers carried our sacks of flour to rickety flatbed trucks while the families of government officials stood in line on the tarmac and stomped their feet against Manchuria's subzero ground. They looked roly-poly in many layers of quilted clothing, and they wore black fur hats that covered their ears. One old man wore an aviator's helmet and goggles. "Someone told him he was going for an airplane ride," Norwich said. "He came prepared."

Outside the airplane, Norwich and I strolled back to the tail, where mechanics, on their backs, were looking up into the wheel well. "What're you looking for?" I asked. They didn't answer. After a long silence, Norwich and I pulled the Elephant Brand cigarettes from our pockets and lit up. And then we passed out many packs. One or two of the mechanics looked uncomfortable, but the others would have made good poker players.

"Did you see the look on those bastards' faces?" Norwich said. "How's that for the death of a thousand cuts?"

Our outbound passengers were sitting on the canvas benches that lined both sides of the cabin, and their bundles were tied down the middle and crisscrossed with rope. An old lady braced her elbows on her knees and clutched her head. A slim woman clutched her throat and rolled her eyes until only the whites showed. Infants suckled. One passenger puked, and then everyone puked. We hadn't even begun to taxi. When we landed at Peiping we climbed out the cockpit window, walked down the top of the airplane to the tail, and jumped off. It was our way of avoiding the stench and the vomit-covered floor.

I got hold of Lewis and we gathered his mechanics around. I told them, "We pilots aren't policemen. We don't care if you're carrying on a cigarette business. Put them in the baggage compartment. Don't jam them in the guts of the controls."

A couple of days later while preflighting the airplane I saw a screwdriver on the floor of the empty belly compartment. I climbed in and unscrewed the inspection plate on the aft bulkhead. I saw cartons of cigarettes stuffed below the elevator cables. If we ran into turbulence they'd be tossed around and perhaps jam the elevator cables. We could lose our up-down control. We'd be helpless while the airplane pitched up to a stall or down into the ground. Perhaps this had happened to Tarbet and his crew, who were dead, while colleagues and historians called them careless. Colonel Lee, our security chief, flew up from Shanghai to say, "I shall apprehend the criminals." But other pilots found cigarettes similarly hidden, and we added one more item to our preflight checklist: "Check vulnerable places for cigarettes." When we found them we threw them away. After the smugglers lost their business investment a few times they abandoned the practice.

Lewis rode our jump seat to Mukden, explaining, "Tire change. They got a jack, but it won't lift the airplane."

After we landed we parked alongside the C-46 with the flat tire. The local mechanics had done everything right; they had tied the landing-gear strut with a chain. A landing gear smooths out the jolts of landings and rough runways with a strut that slides in and out of a sleeve. There's hydraulic oil in the sleeve and a small hole through which the oil escapes when pressure is applied. It's a hydraulic shock absorber. Before a wheel is changed, the strut is chained up to prevent it from sliding out to its full length when the plane is lifted.

"Can't find anything wrong with the jack," the mechanics said. "But it won't lift the airplane."

Lewis checked the jack's hydraulic fluid and fixtures. "Looks okay." After standing around for a minute or so, he said, "Get a can of oil."

Lewis built a small fire around the bottom of the flat tire. "Bet ya it's frozen to the ground," he said. By the time my plane had been off-loaded and reloaded, we saw Lewis and his men raise the grounded plane.

On my second trip I was surprised to find Lewis still working on the ground-loving plane. "Got the tire changed," he said, "but can't budge the engines. The oil has the viscosity of Vaseline. Removed the bottom of the oil tanks and scooped it out. Took it to a stove in the hangar and warmed it up; poured it into the top of the tank, and pulled out more congealed oil. Been working seven hours."

The pilot, huddled against the cold, emerged from the warmth of the passenger shack. "When the hell is it gonna be ready?"

"You dang fool," Lewis snapped. "If you'da diluted the engines before you shut 'em down you'd be outta here." (When we stopped the engines for more than a couple of hours in subzero temperatures we toggled a switch to an electric motor that squirted gasoline into the oil tank to preclude congealing.)

"Had I known they'd screw around that long with a tire change I'd have diluted it."

"When they couldn't jack it up," Lewis said, "some bright guy should have restarted the engines and diluted 'em. Now quit bugging me. I'm pissed off and freezing my ass."

By early spring, all government dependents were out of Mukden, and the One-Eyed Dragon (Communist Liu Po-cheng) straddled the Jugular Vein (the Pin Han Railroad), thus severing the Head of the Giant.

General Barr, the American military attaché, advised the Nationalists to abandon Manchuria and consolidate their armies in the body of China, but Chiang Kai-shek couldn't bring himself to hand China's gem to the Communists.

Other Western military observers predicted the fall of Manchuria because the Nationalists believed in "sitting the enemy to death." They defended strategic cities from corner pillboxes while Communists roved the countryside and severed supply lines. The Reds captured Fushun and its coal mines; Anshan and its factory, which could build three locomotives and a hundred railroad cars a month; Changchun, only 150 miles north of Mukden. The Communists defeated the Sixtieth Army, which then joined the Reds and took part in the destruction of the New Seventh Army. And the captured American equipment was assembled for the coming battle for Mukden.

Landlords and business owners fled, because they were primary targets, and students left because they abhorred the Red system of education.

One of my passengers—Mukden manager of the British American Tobacco Company—said, "I drove my Mercedes-Benz to the airport, handed the keys to my car and house to my houseboy, and said, 'They're all yours.' A tobacco company limousine met him at Peiping's airport. The other refugees climbed atop their bundles on a truck and were driven into the city, where they sold their gold bars and jewelry. A few would beg on the streets and eat the steamed bread that was distributed by the Social Welfare Bureau.

Displaced college students fared according to the leadership ability of their professors. I saw students camping in parks, barbecuing stray dogs. Those lucky enough to have enterprising professors slept on canvas cots in temples, formed food-scrounging teams, and attended classes.

One of the professors said, "The students get an allowance for three months. If they complain after that they're told to join the army."

Manchurian students, less fearful, demanded access to Peiping's universities without taking entrance exams. "Clerks in the admissions office sell the questions," they complained. After a rally they marched to the home of the president of the municipal council, and some were shot down by men in armored cars.

The Wagon Lits lounge was somber that night. A Standard Oil trainee, with Harvard's letter still on his college sweater, asked, "How could they shoot unarmed students?"

"The May Fourth Movement thirty years ago," a professor explained. "Every government official knows that date. Students rallied against the selling of Tsingtao. The fervor spread. It precipitated strikes throughout China. Government officials were impeached. The power of students has been feared ever since."

In the summer of 1948 I still shuttled to Mukden: food, ammunition, green troops in; refugees out. Copilot Howard Brooks, new to CAT, but an old-time captain from the California-based Flying Tiger Line, looked down on Manchurian farms and saw clods of earth kicked high by exploding 75mm shells. He blurted, "My God, what's that?"

"Exactly what you think it is," I said.

That night I thought of his startled reaction. A revelation, it confirmed that battles seemed normal to me. I had lost perspective. And I was relieved when the return trip took us to Tsingtao, where I slept in my home on German Beach for a change, and Cheong cooked my favorite—pork shreds with bean sprouts and garlic.

With the wrinkles out of my belly I was ripe for reflection. On the other side of the world, a Communist coup had taken over Czechoslovakia. Soviets blocked roads and railroads leading to West Berlin; a U.S. Air Force emergency airlift delivered food. A U.S. State Department functionary, Alger Hiss, was accused of selling secrets; Wisconsin's senator McCarthy enjoyed the heydays of witch-hunts. He slapped a never-opened briefcase and claimed it held evidence of numerous Reds in our State Department. The House Un-American Activities Committee produced a blacklist of subversive writers and actors in Hollywood. China was but a hot section of the same Cold War.

The next day, Earthquake flew with me. I was glad. It was like a vacation. Events lost gravity in his presence. During our drive to the airport we saw a Chinese Army corporal lead three scared youths he had roped around their necks.

"They got one helluva draft board in this town," Earthquake said.

"The wrong street at the wrong time," I answered, and I thought it was medieval until I recalled modern history. Less than a hundred years ago, Royal Navy press-gangs had snatched villagers off England's streets.

The grass field near Tsingtao's tarmac was thick with boyish soldiers who were jammed onto one airplane after another until it was too late to reach Mukden before nightfall. Those remaining slept all night on the grass, guarded by military police with fixed bayonets.

After we got to Mukden and the kids disembarked, we saw flatbed trucks of wounded. Some had the blue tinge of death. Others bore the special silence of pain. The stillness was eerie; no muttering, no moaning, they lay quietly. Some lay in their own excrement, some caked in blood. Earthquake walked in between the youths and made comforting sounds that sounded Chinese, and I sensed he was touched and wanted to help in some way. I recalled words I had read somewhere or other: "ambassador to the human race." That was the fighter pilot from New Jersey. He was blind to the barriers that separate us, and I knew then that I had been blind to his compassionate heart—a giant heart that ached at the sights. I liked him better every time I flew with him.

We didn't speak much on the way back. A smell of death, the stench of gangrene, permeated the cockpit.

At Tsingtao I filled out a flight plan for our next flight, but the Chinese Air Force meteorologist was absent and we needed his signature before we could go. "We just got back from Mukden," I said. "The weather is clear all the way. Can you release us?"

The CAF duty officer barked, "You must follow rules."

"We have a load of soldiers waiting to go to Mukden. When do you expect the meteorologist back?"

"Not your business."

The meteorologist returned two hours later. It meant we'd only have time for half a trip. We'd have to stay overnight in Mukden.

Climbing north out of Tsingtao, we looked to our right and saw the tip of the Liaotung Peninsula sticking out of Manchuria near the North Korean border. We could barely see the contour of Port Arthur. It had been a Chinese seaport, but now it was a Russian naval base. How easily Stalin had stolen it; how easily America and Britain had let him take it.

Pointing to the peninsula, I said, "We foreign devils wonder why the Chinese call us 'foreign devils.'"

Earthquake said, "Right about here is where Buol and I got jumped by the Rooskies. Two P-39s with big red stars on their tails signaled for us to follow them. Buol said, 'Do you want to go to Port Arthur?' I said, 'Hell no, I'd sooner get shot down.' One of the bastards stuck his wing tip damn near in the cockpit. Buol showed him his mike and pointed at Tsingtao—just to let him know we'd alerted the base. They buggered off."

Fifty miles from Mukden we saw the railroads converging and stands of huge smokeless smokestacks and started our descent. We got our parachutes out of the cabin and placed them on our seats to shield us from small-arms fire. Earthquake made a production of it and growled, "Confucius say one hole in ass is sufficient." Kwan, our radioman, laughed and said, "You studied Chinese literature."

Mukden's ground crew was in a hurry to meet the curfew. They took us to the Railroad Hotel. On the way we sped down wide boulevards that were deserted and saw modern buildings of cream-colored glazed brick. Some were roofless because the local people had stolen the tiles to resell them. The empty city square displayed a Soviet tank atop a fifty-foot stone column.

The once-elegant hotel put chamber pots under the beds because the Russian troops had stolen the toilets and bathtubs. I tossed in my bed, and visions of the war raced through my head.

I heard an intermittent rumble of far-off artillery and a continuous rumble of Earthquake snoring in the next bed. He had immediately fallen sound asleep as if he didn't have a care in the world. I guessed what made him tick. The world is so illogical, he seemed to believe, that only a fool would take it seriously.

There was a strange undefinable stir in the air. The gutted city, the sound of big guns, the reality of death we had seen. I saw, for the first time, the stark reality of my own life. I hadn't cared when Sandra dumped me, because it left me free to follow my adventures in flying, I thought. But it was a lie. Unconsciously I had been believing the unreality that I would marry the special one I knew before I left America. Her entire being was beautiful beyond reality. We met by sheer chance. Lovers in a previous life, it seemed, but this time we were like autumn leaves, joined momentarily by the wind. The situation was untenable; she was already married and loyal. With infinite wisdom she said, in parting, "A brief encounter and it haunts you for the rest of your life." The painful echo lingered in my heart. There in bleak Manchuria, about to fall.

A few miserable trips later we learned that two Nationalist armies had broken out of Mukden and fought toward the Yellow Sea until they ran into General Lin Piao's troops and were all but annihilated.

Only two Nationalist armies remained in Mukden. China National and Central Air withdrew. Our mechanics and traffic people were jumpy. "A Chinese Air Force plane took out a load of Russian bar girls," they said.

"A sure sign," Norwich said.

The next day the mechanics repeated a rumor that Generals Tu and Wei, abandoning their troops, had flown out on a Chinese Air Force plane.

It was time to take our own people out, October's last day. All of Manchuria, the jewel of China, belonged to the Communists.

A Warlord and His City

After Mukden fell we focused on China's second-largest industrial center, which was Taiyüan in the province of Shansi. It was surrounded by the Communist Eighth Army.

It didn't seem like a besieged city. A steel mill went full blast; clanging noises came from a locomotive factory; lathes in precision machine shops turned; an arsenal made guns and ammunition. Even a cigarette factory hustled.

If Mukden was the Chicago of China, then Taiyüan was its Pittsburgh.

An unlikely home for industry, Taiyüan sat isolated north of the Yellow River, where the land rises to a bleak plateau and spreads farther north, beyond two mountain ranges, to the Great Wall.

The beeline from Peiping to Taiyüan was only 250 miles, but the terrain made it remote. We got there by flying southwest from Peiping, across a sea of farms that skirted the Wutai mountains on our right. Eventually we turned right and crossed over them to look down upon an eroded gray plateau with gorges and caves. And when we saw dirty haze on the horizon, we knew Taiyüan waited underneath and it would be the first sizable city we'd see since leaving Peiping almost two hours before. The industrial center was easy to identify. Smokestacks stuck up and belched yellow clouds that testified to enormous drafts of air fanning a steel smelter.

Taiyüan was the materialized dream of Governor Yen Hsi-shan, who personified the province that bore him. Its harsh land and climate made the people diligent, persistent, shrewd, avaricious. Its history—the backbone of the Kingdom of Wei, nurturer of Buddhism in north China—made them proud.

Governor Yen Hsi-shan appeared to be frail. Although he was self-effacing, he smiled like a poker player who's sweeping up your chips. He suffered from diabetes. His Sun Yat-sen blouse (a high-necked jacket with four flap pockets) drooped on his body as if his shoulders were a coat hanger. But a glint in his eyes spoke of a will of steel. He was flexible, like the bows of his steel-rimmed spectacles. He was a graduate of Japan's Imperial Military Academy. One of his secretaries had been an Oxford scholar. He employed German and Japanese technicians. If he decided to wear his long blue Mandarin gown and show courtly manners, he could be the epitome of north China charm.

Burridge said he was the George Washington of China. I said, "Bullshit," but would change my mind after the battle. Most historians called him a warlord. Some said he was "the Beneficial Governor." Visiting American congressmen, charmed by his wit, gushed, "Statesman." Of those who cried, "Despot," Governor Yen scoffed, "All that Americans know about China was learned from missionaries and compradors."

The verdict depended upon one's reaction to various events. Leaders of a peasant uprising were chained together through holes punched in their collar bones. When disciples of a bizarre religious sect claimed they were impervious to bullets, Governor Yen demonstrated the fallacy of their belief by having a few of them shot. Family heads were responsible for relatives' crimes; landlords were liable for tenants' misdeeds; spies were encouraged to report idle wives to their husbands; members of the Early Morning Rising Society knocked on doors and reported those in bed after 6:00 A.M. Mothers who persisted in binding their daughters' feet for beauty's sake were sentenced to hard labor in the governor's factories. (Although the practice kept feet small, they looked like clenched bird claws and made walking difficult.)

I learned most of this from the reporting of a scholarly American, A. Doak Barnett. Unlike newsmen who interviewed each other, Barnett, with the heart of a scholar, spent months in a place until he satisfied himself that he understood its people and the situation, and then he moved on. His book *China on the Eve of Communist Takeover* fascinated me and gave me perspective. Hoodwinked less and less by stereotypes, I began to look beyond unfamiliar faces and skin and titles and clothes and to realize what I should have understood years before—we're captives of our history and our land. We do what we must to survive.

Yen Hsi-shan made Shansi Province an industrial-military complex that furnished half of China's coal. There were mines that gave iron, irrigation systems, thousands of trees, schools, a cement factory, a printing press, machine shops, a steel smelter, a locomotive factory, and an arsenal that produced, monthly, three thousand rifles, eight 75mm field guns, sixty heavy and three hundred light machine guns, two thousand mortars, and innumerable bayonets, swords, grenades, cartridges. Surrounding farms grew cotton, sorghum, kaoliang, and winter wheat.

Warlord or governor, Yen Hsi-shan was too powerful to be controlled by Generalissimo Chiang Kai-shek, so the president of China honored him with the title of marshal. In return, Yen paid the Nationalist government lip service and actually supported it when their interests coincided. China's civil war was one of the times. Yen agreed with Chiang, who said, "Japan is a disease of the skin, but Communism is a disease of the heart."

By the autumn of 1948, rural Shansi wasn't entirely Yen's anymore. His sycophants didn't warn him that his peasants were furious with his tax collectors. If the hated functionaries failed to squeeze taxes out of a poor farmer, a wealthier neighbor had to cough up the difference.

When Mao's guerrillas filtered into the province with promises of a new deal, the peasants fed the bearers of such good news and then hid them from Yen's soldiers.

By the time we supplied Taiyüan, Yen's empire had become an island fringed by a reef of nine thousand pillboxes, seven hundred artillery pieces, and a wall forty feet thick. Outlying areas were guarded by stone sentry boxes nine feet tall with names like Old Tiger, Plum Blossom, Autumn Wind. When I stepped inside one of the pillboxes, the old stones—older than China itself—breathed durability. They were quiet inside, silent as a church. Any wind outside sounded like a seashell held to an ear. Seen through the slits, the countryside seemed tranquil, although my head told me that Yen's remarkable city would go the way of Mukden.

We had been supplying Taiyüan for almost a year. However, the loss of Manchuria enabled all three of China's airlines to concentrate on the last free industrial city.

Twelve CAT C-46s, ten of China National's, eight of Central Air's made an aerial parade. Taiyüan's survival hung on two hundred tons a day: rice, ingots of metal alloys, oil, tobacco.

The ongoing Berlin Airlift was a move in Europe's chess game; this was Asia's. Our fracas may have been hotter than Europe's, but it was the same Cold War.

I remember vividly an early flight to the besieged city because of the misery of the cold drizzle in pitch-black Peiping—our point of departure. At 4:00 A.M. two taxis picked up two crews at the Wagon Lits Hotel and rattled through deserted streets, nevertheless honking their horns until we got to the closed gates of Peiping's wall.

The great portal was abandoned; its sentries snoozed in a hut, out of the miserable drizzle.

"Yesterday the weather was good," I squawked, "and they stuck rifles in our faces."

Davenport, the other captain, reached over and beeped the horn. A sentry appeared in a doorway. *"Mayo. . . . Kung shen ching. . . . Chi den, Kuo-ye."*

"We need a curfew pass," copilot Wang said. "Or wait for seven o'clock."

"Never needed one before," Davenport said. "Ask to use his phone; Bradley will send a pass."

After much *walla-walla* with the sentry and telephone, Wong said, "Mr. Bradley's sleeping. His houseboy's supposed to wake him at eight."

Davenport jumped out of the taxi. "Give me the phone. . . . *Wei— Wei*—Call Mr. Bradley. . . . Emergency! Call Bradley, dammit!"

A defeated Davenport returned to his taxi, grumbling, "Bradley's got his houseboy terrified."

We half-dozed in the taxis until seven, when I beeped the horn. A sentry came out of the shack, and I held up my wrist and pointed to my self-winding Omega. The sentry put the butt of his rifle on the ground, propped the muzzle against his chest, and put a finger on a big timepiece on his wrist. It was ten minutes slow. I told the crews, "The gates will open at seven—his time."

A half-dozen sleepy sentries eventually emerged to shift various timbers and push against Peiping's gates while the forty-foot-high relics creaked and groaned and slowly parted.

Our airplanes were full of sacks of rice, ready to go. Mechanics had slept at the airport. A radio operator handed us bad tidings of clouds sitting on the ground at Tientsin and Tsingtao, which were our alternates in case Taiyüan or Peiping were socked in. Taiyüan reported a fifteen-hundred-foot ceiling, visibility two miles, and rain, and the remarks said, "Radio beacon inoperative due no fuel." Peiping forecast a lowering ceiling to eight hundred feet, visibility one mile in rain.

"That's why China National and Central Air aren't flying," Davenport said.

"Smart guys."

"China National's radio beacon won't be on."

"We'll have to let down on the commercial station."

"I suppose this tower's gonna have a taxi drill."

"Might as well. Everything else is screwed up."

I was the first to move out, and sure enough, we endured the antics of a taxi drill. "Cleared to runway one-eight," the tower said. After we got there, copilot Wong announced ready for takeoff, and the tower replied, "Negative, proceed to runway two-two," and when we got there the tower commanded, arrogantly, "Go to runway zero-four."

"Wong," I said, "I'm not curious about that nut in the tower—you find screwballs everywhere—but why does his commander tolerate such stuff?" Wong shrugged.

Chu said, "He wouldn't do that in Yen's province." Chu was our radio operator. He had been with Burridge when they overnighted at Taiyüan and found empty tanks in the morning. Fuel had also been stolen from two other CAT planes. They drained residue from two and added it to the first plane, which got it back to Peiping. Another plane carried drums of fuel to the two grounded ones. The caper delayed the Taiyüan airlift half a day.

Yen Hsi-shan caught the thieves and hanged them by their necks. The next morning, three corpses twisted over the entrance to the airport. Chu was impressed.

Peiping's ding-a-ling control tower got tired of its game and cleared us for takeoff.

After we climbed through seven hundred feet, clouds wrapped around and cuddled us in the smooth wet blankets that come with a loitering warm front, and we didn't see a bit of China for the next two hours. We followed our magnetic compass until we heard a radio station playing "Rainbow Clouds"—Westernized Chinese jazz—and then our radio compass pointed. Since it was the only broadcasting station within a couple of hundred miles we felt safe in following the pointer; and when we got over the station we descended in a teardrop pattern until the music stopped and the radio compass wandered aimlessly. "J. Christ," I said. "It went off the air."

Ordinarily the situation demanded maximum continuous power and a maximum-angle climb, but we were in a warm-front calm with no wind to drift us into the surrounding hills. "We'll descend to two thousand feet," I said. "We'll be well above the smokestacks."

We dropped out of the clouds at 2,500 feet. Yellow smoke pushed against the flat bottoms of the clouds and spread out, obscuring the scenery, but we could see straight down if we looked out of our side windows. I clung to two thousand feet and flew a wide circle to the left. Davenport's voice, coming through my earphones, said, "The damn station went off the air."

"Ain't it the shits," I replied. "We broke out at twenty-five hundred, visibility a mile or two. We're circling, looking for the stacks."

"Sounds like fun."

We saw the shadowy forms and I knew it was safe to drop down on the heading to the airport.

As soon as we parked I stood up and stuck my torso out of the side window and heard a C-46 overhead.

Davenport radioed, "My clock says I should be over the city."

"Diddle your pitch," I said, and I heard props on a couple of R-2800 engines snarl. "I hear you—you're over the field."

After Davenport landed and parked, General Mah drove up in his jeep and shook both his hands before him, saying, *"Howla, howla,"* and we conversed in broken English and Chinese until artillery boomed not far away, and he grasped his hands before him and shook them a little, Chinese-style, and left.

Soldiers tossed bags of rice off my plane and off Davenport's. "Did you see the spread in *Life* magazine," he asked, "of Yen and his men around a table piled with cyanide capsules they're gonna swallow if this place falls?"

"Yeah? We'll be flying 'em out before that."

We radio-jabbered all the way back to Peiping. "Did your radio operator get Peiping's temperature and dew point?" Davenport wanted to know.

"Yeah, they're merging."

"It's going to fog in."

I got over Peiping first—an hour and three-quarters after leaving Taiyüan. "We're starting our descent," I announced.

"Let me know when you see home sweet home."

It took concentration to stay on the imaginary path from the radio station to the airport. The radio compass pointed aft, which meant our corrections for wind drift increased the deviation of the needle. It gave the illusion that we were turning the wrong way. After about four minutes of making small heading corrections opposite to the backward-pointing needle; scanning airspeed, rate of descent, and altitude; and snatching glimpses out of a windshield that revealed nothing but opaque gray, we descended through six hundred feet and came upon a beautiful sight: the airport. It was off to our left. My shoulders dropped to their normal position. I told Davenport, "Six hundred and three," and then I heard him begin his approach.

As I expected, station manager Bradley stood on the tarmac with the collar of his raincoat turned up, but not enough to hide a red silk tie. His black hair, parted in the middle, flowed back and glistened with Vitalis and raindrops. He sounded as smooth as a Wisconsin lightning-rod salesman. "You'll be ready to go again in forty minutes."

"There'll be no second trip."

"I can't believe it's you talking. Taiyüan needs two hundred tons a day to stay alive."

"Tsingtao and Tientsin are socked in; no runway lights at Taiyüan. If we can't get back in here there'll be no place to land."

"The weather'll improve," Bradley said.

Davenport walked into our conversation, and Bradley gave him the same pitch. "You talk like you fell out of a tree," Davenport said.

"You too? This is no peacetime operation."

"I'll tell ya what," I said. "It's not difficult to get us airborne. All you got to do is tell us where to land if this place fogs in."

"You guys know how changeable the weather is."

"Yeah, it can get worse."

Bradley sent a radiogram to the vice president of operations plus all hands and the cook: "Smith and Davenport refuse to fly."

I radiogrammed, "We are guilty of poor airmanship by flying the past several days in marginal weather without alternates or beacons, playing tag with Taiyüan's smokestacks. Barometric pressure dropping, temperature and dew point merging, we canceled. When the day arrives that planes are flown from a station manager's desk I'll leave China voluntarily."

On the way back to the Wagon Lits Hotel, Davenport said, "Why waste your time arguing with Bradley?"

"Yeah, I'm mad at myself for getting mad at him."

"Rousselot's our boss—the only boss we've got."

"Yeah. Iron-ass as he is, he never questions our judgment." I was glad to have a good friend confirm my decision.

On the following day, Natasia puttered around the operations office at the airport. Turning saucy eyes my way, she purred, "Your radiogram was naughty."

"You folks fly the desk, I'll fly the airplane." She repressed a smile. Her lips were provocative; how could I remain hostile? I tolerated Natasia's backseat driving more than Bradley's because she said what she thought to everyone, including Peiping's snooty society.

More pilots arrived and Natasia displayed a radiogram from CAT's headquarters in Shanghai: "Taiyüan closed. Expect fog for next few days. Governor Yen Hsi-shan requests we drop supplies from our instrument altitude. MOC [minister of communications] ordered China National operate beacon continuously."

"Dropping stuff on instruments is a good theory," Marsh said, "but they didn't consider the zone of ambiguity." He was referring to the antics of a radio compass when a plane passes over a beacon. The pointer switches from dead ahead to dead astern, but it meanders before changing directions. In the meantime the airplane traverses several miles and the pilot doesn't know the exact moment he's overhead.

My C-46 was loaded with brass ingots the size and shape of fence posts—for the manufacture of shell casings by Taiyüan's arsenal, I guessed. And there were alloys for the steel mill.

In a parade of airplanes in clouds, invisible to each other, we spaced ourselves at thousand-foot intervals and maintained a listening watch with our voice radios. The lowest guy in the stack, upon reaching the beacon, jettisoned his load and left the area on an easterly heading before heading back to Peiping for another load.

When my turn came I radioed, "CAT eight-four-eight descending to one thousand." The needle of my radio compass switched 180 degrees, and I threw a toggle switch that rang the bell in the cabin and twisted around to watch. Used to seeing bags of rice shoved out toward a landmark, I thought it was weird. Soldiers dumped brass cylinders and other stuff into the clouds.

On the next two trips we carried rice that had been double-bagged. The impact with the ground burst open the inner bag, but the loose outer bag retained the rice. I think China National invented the technique during the big war when it supplied construction laborers on the Burma Road.

After a few days of dropping on instruments, Taiyüan authorities advised the operation was a great success, but when I flew overhead on the first clear day I was dismayed to see houses with jagged holes in their roofs where they'd been hit by rice bags, brass cylinders, and tungsten ingots.

I landed and parked, and General Mah met us with his usual cordiality. "General," I said, "we don't want to drop on instruments anymore. I saw the damaged houses—we must have killed some people."

Mah replied jovially, "Never mind get killed; not so many people to eat rice."

All three airlines and the minister of communications agreed: there'd be no more drops via radio compass. By that time, clear weather had set in and we were able to land.

We heard the rumble of artillery, and Mah told us 150,000 enemy troops encircled Taiyüan. Mortar shells exploded on the perimeter of the airport. A soldier who looked young enough to be in elementary school said, *"Bow-loos boo-hao."* ("Eighth Army no good.")

Back at Peiping's airport mess tent we ran into Burridge. We all looked at the *Life* magazine photo of Marshal Yen Hsi-shan with his cyanide capsules.

Someone asked, "Do you think he's serious about swallowing that stuff?"

"He's one of the grand old men of China, and Taiyüan is his life. If it falls, he'll want to die with it."

When mortar shells landed on Taiyüan's airport, we abandoned it, and Yen's soldiers, assisted by civilians, scraped a strip closer to the city. Its single taxi strip was a bottleneck, so Yen Hsi-shan asked us to resume airdrops around the clock whenever the weather was clear.

The other two airlines refused outright to drop at night, but the CAT pilots talked it over.

"Nationalists draw back to the city every night. . . . Commie gunners would have free reign. . . . Exhaust flames make a good target. . . . Crash-land in the dark, don't stand a chance."

Chief pilot Rousselot asked if I'd go with him. "The other guys think you're an old-timer. If you're willing, they'll feel better about it."

"Sure," I said. Severe as he was, I liked him. Marine Corps strict, yeah, but he didn't boss us from some paneled office. Whatever he asked, he did first. And he was smart enough to be diplomatic when he wanted to be. Actually, it wasn't the first night trip. Wingfield had paved the way, but he was a cowboy—he'd do anything. We had seen him relax under a tree while his delighted copilot soloed to Taiyüan with no one else in the cockpit of the big C-46. On the subsequent trip his copilot sat under the tree while Wingfield soloed. We kept it mighty quiet, and Rousselot didn't find out, but he knew Wingfield. It wouldn't mean anything if the cavalier guy made a night drop on Taiyüan. However, Smith? He was conservative.

Rousselot flew while I rode the copilot seat. Without lighted cities to measure our progress over the ground and no sun to generate vertical currents of air, it felt as if we were suspended, just below the stars. Rousselot engaged the autopilot and leaned forward with his arms on the glare shield and his chin on his arms and watched the stars. I had seen him at house parties slip outside for ten or fifteen minutes to watch some trees or the sky and return refreshed. A rumor said he was part Cherokee Indian, although no one was so bold as to ask. His natural dignity and blood-and-thunder expression when aroused gave the myth credence. Some of the guys, behind his back, called him "BB Eyes." Sloppy airmanship, rudeness to cargo handlers, failure to ensure that signatures penetrated all copies of a fuel chit could precipitate a storm. But it was bearable. He imposed the same discipline on himself. I recalled news stories of farmers holding their families together during the dust bowl years of the Great Depression. My boss had been a boy then, old enough to share the work, old enough to worry.

"It's bright tonight," Rousselot said. "Like harvest time on the farm." He sat back and spoke affectionately of his older brother and kid sister.

Mysterious, I thought, how a pilot's personality changes in the air. A cohort who is carefree on the ground can become a terror in the cockpit. But Rousselot, a notorious ass chewer, invariably became a relaxed pal.

Our radioman behind us cast a light on his logbook. "Careful with that," Rousselot warned. "Don't ruin our night vision. . . . We'll drop the stuff from five thousand feet; we'll be above the range of their forty-five-caliber stuff. . . . I'll approach on a curve and straighten out over the DZ [drop zone]."

I recalled an RAF pilot describing how he changed heading often in flak zones to complicate the aim of antiaircraft gunners. He called it waltzing.

"The Commies will see our exhaust flames," Rousselot said. "Nothing we can do about that, but why help 'em with these?" He reached up and cut off the navigation lights.

We saw the ghostly white of the concrete runway in the dark. From there it was easy to pick out the cloth white panels on the DZ.

"Open the cockpit door," Rousselot said, "and watch the kickers." Our radioman got out of his seat. "When all the rice is gone, sing out, and we'll hightail it out of here."

Below-zero air burbled through the open door, and the roar of our engines joined the *whoosh* of the slipstream. The sound of a New York subway express shooting past a local station.

It took several passes to get all the rice out. Red golf balls—machine-gun tracers—curved below us. "Forty-five-caliber, it looks like," Rousselot shouted. "They're comin' up in a beeline. Our forward motion makes it look curved. Every fifth one's a tracer—for every one you see, there's four you don't."

When we got back to Peiping I told the other guys, "Not much to it if you keep above the range of the guns."

"The crew schedule will be simple," Rousselot told us. "After two trips you'll go to the bottom of the list, and your name will work its way to the top."

After grabbing a stand-up meal in our mess tent at Peiping's airport, a few of us walked past the wooden dining hall that China National had built for its pilots, and we looked inside to see comfortable chairs and white tablecloths. We walked past China National's polished airplanes, and when we got to our tired C-46s we saw Lewis cannibalizing one plane to make another one go, and our mechanics bitched about the shortage of spare parts.

"CAT expects a lot from us," a pilot said. "Look at China National's luxury. And the pay is higher."

"And they don't drop at night," said a new CAT pilot.

"Don't underestimate their pilots," I said. "China National is a legend. Those guys made it. All through the war with Japan, their guys were shot down. They pioneered the Hump, died in mountain passes, landed seaplanes on the Yangtze at night, rescued people. They crashed a DC-3 in a Burma jungle. Their mechanics hacked their way there, carrying a DC-2 wing, bolted it on, and got the plane out. It's become famous, their DC-two-and-a-half."

I didn't realize I was that angry with China National's high-handed management. I heard myself saying, "After the war, China National fired a lot of their old-timers so they could hire new guys cheaper . . . fired guys like Rossi who'd crossed the Hump more than seven hundred times without scratching an airplane, and Shilling, another ex–Flying Tiger who crossed the Hump damn near that many times. Fired the guys with transparent excuses. . . . The *Shanghai Evening Post and Mercury* lambasted it."

"Chinese," someone said.

"Chinese, hell, it was a Yankee, Pan American vice president and general manager of China National—Bill Bond—a legend himself. Rode a jungle train into Burma to start a runway. I guess he got parsimonious after the war. He took the magic out of it. Now it's just a job."

"CAT's still a religion," Davenport said. "Chennault and Willauer got us flying half-ass airplanes with lousy living conditions and loving it."

A couple of weeks later, CAT put twelve C-46s on the Taiyüan project and moved the staging area to the city of Tientsin, which was less congested and only thirty miles farther to Taiyüan. We slept in an abandoned hangar with World War II shell holes in the roof and cobwebs. Not enough bunks for everyone. We'd come back exhausted and wait until someone abandoned his cot; no change of sheets. At 2:00 A.M. a voice loudly said, "Slaves in the deepest South lived better than this."

I hadn't been in my cot more than a few hours since my last flight when Hughes shook me awake. It didn't take long to get ready, because I'd been sleeping in my clothes. "The Commies moved in some big guns, thirty-seven millimeter, I think. We're dropping from ten thousand feet."

I'm airborne with half a dozen soldiers in the cabin, waiting to shove bags of rice out the door. "We'll be dropping from ten thousand feet," I say. "What've you guys heard about the big guns?" Not much, they say.

A returning pilot announced his approach.

"What's cooking?" I ask.

"Stick close to the city."

An hour and forty-five minutes to think about it. . . .

Glowing balls streaking in a curve, one after the other. Four invisible ones in between. Close in I see ghostly silver C-46s circling. I have a protective mechanism: denial. "Commies are piss-poor shots," I say, while I space myself in the ring-around-the-rosy and roll the wings level over the white X and ding the bell. The nose pitches forward, which tells me the batch near the door is out. Quick bank and around for another pass. The red, glowing stuff streaks ahead of us, missing by a mile. Suddenly I see a C-46, big as the *Queen Mary* in front of my nose. I can even see the pilot, that's how close we are. Instinctively, I pull up and pass over it.

Back at Tientsin, we discuss the near miss. The other guy was Bigony. Commies can see our exhaust flames, we agree; we might as well illuminate our navigation lights.

After Tientsin was threatened by Red troops we flew out of Tsingtao, 450 miles from the besieged city. I was glad to get back to the house on German Beach that old Cheong had turned into a home.

Awakened by impatient honking of the crew car, I squinted at my watch; I had slept four hours.

The company driver carried a curfew pass, but guards at Tsingtao's roadblocks waved us through without looking—they knew CAT's station wagon.

At the airport, six soldiers wearing padded clothing and caps with long earflaps loaded bags of rice. Eight tons. My crew and I wore parkas, Russian fur caps, and mittens. I saw dark circles under their eyes. "You guys look like I feel," I said. "No use trying to fool each other, we'll be dozing off, but our sinking spells won't come at the same time. If you feel yourself dropping off, let the other guys know so at least one's awake."

At six thousand feet we engaged the autopilot. The cockpit heaters didn't work, because there was a shortage of glow plugs, so we draped ourselves in blankets like fans at a December football game in Wisconsin.

"I'm not sleepy," I said. "You guys sleep if you feel like it." The copilot tilted his seat back and tipped his hat over his eyes, but the radio operator's seat wouldn't tilt, so he folded his arms on his desk and cradled his head.

A clear night, but ground pitch-black, with an occasional light from a village. Communist country. Six hours to Taiyüan and back. So cold I couldn't bend my fingers.

An hour later we passed over Tsinan, the capital of Shantung Province. Blacked out, but we could see its shape along the curving, spooky flat Yellow River.

My circular plastic slide rule said we were making 150 miles an hour—not much of a head wind.

I recalled a few nights ago, when Scotty Wilson, CAT's ex-RAF copilot, flying with some other captain, fell asleep after takeoff.

Scotty slept all the way to Taiyüan; incredibly, he slept through the noise and jolts of the airdrop. When he awoke, on the way back, over that Tsinan checkpoint, he looked at the lights, manipulated his slide rule, and exclaimed, "Jesus, what a head wind!"—thinking he was outbound although he actually was inbound. His mathematics said his ground speed was thirty-five miles an hour, and he believed it.

I felt the wave of sleep swallowing me, so I tapped Tang's shoulder and said, "My turn." He yawned, shook his head, straightened his seat.

I thought I'd slept a minute or two when the copilot shook me, but he said, "Ten minutes from Taiyüan, Captain."

I put on my earphones. No one knew who started the custom, but we used names of famous radio stars of the forties.

"The Green Hornet, over the DZ, ten thousand." That was Holden.

"Lone Ranger, five minutes behind you."

"Fibber McGee, headed for home. Where are you, Shadow?"

"Only the shadow knows, heh, heh, heh."

"Jack Armstrong, Jack Armstrong, the aawwl-American boy, ten minutes out."

"What's that red stuff comming up?"

Over the DZ. I looked back and saw my kickers on the floor, hanging on to ropes, shoving their feet against stacks of rice. Burlap bags vanished into darkness. The red stuff streaked in a curve far to our left. "Lousy gunners," I jeered loudly.

Relieved to be heading back to Tsingtao in one piece, I was suddenly cold again.

After landing at Tsingtao we got hot tea in the operations shack, and by then our airplane was loaded with the double-bagged rice and we took off again.

Headed for Taiyüan, we were almost over Tsinan with its few remaining lights, our first checkpoint, when our right engine went *blam blam blam blam* and stopped with a jolt. I threw off my blanket and straightened my seat at the first *blam*, disengaged the autopilot, retarded the throttle, cut the mixture control. Then we tried to restart it. It was dead. I pushed the red feathering button, which told an electric motor to twist the prop blades to a streamlined position, and I heard my radioman's key clicking and knew he was on top of the situation—I didn't have to tell him to send an operational message.

Fifteen or twenty minutes later our so-called good engine on our left side ran rough and misfired intermittently. I tripped the switch on the signal bell so the soldiers in back would kick out the rice, and I tried all kinds of fuel-mixture and rpm combinations.

"It'll run smooth with reduced power," I said. "See that they get the rice out." The radio operator looked into the cabin while the copilot leaned forward with his chin on the glare shield and watched for the lights of Tsingtao.

Light in weight, we held our altitude with reduced power on our remaining engine, but every few minutes it ranted off on another series of explosions, and we drifted toward the ground. "Jack Armstrong headed for home on half an engine."

"Throw out the damn load," someone called.

"It's out. Didn't waste it. Someone will eat it. . . . Every time the damn engine poops out we loose another five hundred feet." I wondered if the coffee-can flares at Tsingtao were half burned out. "How are the runway lights?"

"Not bad," Richardson said. He was on the ground at Tsingtao. "I'll stand by with my landing lights."

We had drifted down to four thousand feet by the time we saw the few wavering flames from the coffee cans that hadn't yet burned out. And Richardson pointed his nose at the threshold of the runway and depressed his landing lights so it sparkled like a jewel.

After touchdown I let our plane roll to the end and coasted onto the taxi strip and waited for a tow. A C-46 won't taxi straight on one engine.

On the ground I had time to ponder what the Communists would've done with us if we'd been farther out when the trouble started, had we survived a belly landing at night.

The next night, after dropping supplies into Taiyüan, I saw headlights of a long convoy of trucks headed for the besieged city, and I knew it was a Communist parade, on the main road from Shihkiachwang. They weren't blacked out.

After landing at Tsingtao I hurried, chart in hand, to the Chinese Air Force operations office. Even at fifty miles an hour it would be hours before the convoy of Communist reinforcements reached Taiyüan, but it couldn't be traveling that fast. Plenty of time to stop the convoy. Chinese Air Force B-25s were parked outside.

After a few polite words I put my chart on the base commander's desk, showed him the position of the convoy, and waited for him to bark orders, waited to hear the cacophony of B-25 engines, waited to watch them scramble.

Instead, the commander gave me a go-to-hell look and said, "Not your business." I departed without another word from either of us. The B-25s remained parked.

I was curious. The Nationalists had the air to themselves but didn't use it. Why didn't the Chinese Air Force support the ground forces? I'd seen the same lack of action during the siege of Weihsien. Was it Chiang Kai-shek's way of ridding himself of a powerful warlord? Perhaps the Chinese Air Force, with complete control of the air, didn't want to kill fellow Chinese.

The Chinese Air Force had been good before the civil war; it had been trained by Chennault in 1937 and equipped by the United States in the big war. Its ability and spirit were praised by American pilots. I recalled the story of Art Chin, whom I flew with after he got out of the Chinese Air Force. A legend said he was shot down, but he pulled the machine gun out of the wreckage and carried it to operations to ask, "Can I get another airplane for my gun?" Wounded in another air battle, he was recovering at home when Japanese bombers flew overhead. Protecting him with her body, his wife was killed; and Chin lived to fight again. . . . Somehow, that Chinese Air Force had disappeared.

After New Year's Day 1949, Governor Yen offered a hundred U.S. dollars a landing if we'd fly into his new strips close to the city. CAT left it to us to volunteer. I kept my mouth shut. I was willing to drop stuff from the air, but I didn't feel like landing under mortar fire when the loss of Taiyüan seemed inevitable. With Communist convoys converging on Taiyüan with impunity, headlights boldly lit, knowing the Chinese Air Force wouldn't protest, it seemed obvious—Taiyüan was doomed.

One of the gung-ho guys told the rest of us, "Three mortar shells landed within a hundred and fifty yards of me."

Another one said, "After I landed I turned around and watched two shells bracket me. Another one exploded a hundred feet behind. I didn't wait for the fourth."

Willauer said, "I'll confer with Yen Hsi-shan. I have a plan. Rousselot will take me in, and we'll land in the dark."

His C-46 was loaded with tons of dynamite and separate boxes of fuse caps, and Willauer waited for the first clear night.

Willauer's wife got wind of it and wrote, "You won't do any good to Marshal Yen if you kill yourself trying to help him. . . . And you certainly will let your shareholders down, not to mention all the other airline employees and omitting your wife and kids. Cut out the heroics, you damn fool."

But Willauer had this thing about personal honor and talking face to face.

It was only a quarter moon. Rousselot and Willauer couldn't find the runway in the darkness. "We'll have to land in daylight," Willauer said. Rousselot agreed.

They carried enough explosives to blow up Taiyüan's factories, including its steel mill and arsenal. Willauer said with a wry smile, "One shot in the wrong place will blow us to smithereens."

Richardson followed with a C-46 load of black powder.

They landed under shell fire and taxied under a cliff. Richardson off-loaded the black powder and returned safely to Tsingtao. Rousselot waited in his plane while Willauer sped toward the city in Yen Hsi-shan's station wagon.

Willauer and Yen, alone in the governor's headquarters, stood facing each other.

"We'll get you and your people out," Willauer said. "Blow up your factories. Use your best troops to break out. Head northwest through the mountain passes. Get to Paotow. CAT will drop supplies along the way. We'll evacuate everyone from the airfield at Paotow."

They stood in silence together. Willauer sensed the turmoil within Yen. Destroy the smelter? The arsenal? The grenade launchers invented by my people? The locomotive factory? The arsenal? Three hundred machine guns a month. Blow it up? Yet here was salvation: break out; reach Paotow. With my Taiyüan in ruins there'd be no Communist victory. . . .

Yen Hsi-shan was silent.

"I saw nobility," Willauer told us, "and I knew he wouldn't leave his people."

Willauer returned to the airplane, and Rousselot took off while mortar shells exploded. After they landed at Tsingtao we examined the fuselage and found more than fifty shrapnel holes.

CAT added four more airplanes, and we flew as many as twenty-eight airdrops a day. Every time a C-46 flew over the besieged city, eight tons of supplies rained down.

We were airborne eighteen hours a day. Richardson broke the record by flying twenty-one hours and forty-five minutes in a twenty-four-hour period.

Earthquake Magoon's engine got sick and died near Taiyüan. Faced with the choice—a long flight back over enemy territory with a dead engine or land at Taiyüan—he chose the latter. Assistant chief pilot John Plank brought him a good airplane. After landing at Taiyüan, Plank said, "Fly the good bird out—take your crew and bugger off. I'll stay here with your piece of junk."

At Tsingtao I said, "You gotta admire Plank—he feels responsible for his men."

Rousselot stiffened his back and growled, "He's a Marine, ain't he?"

The next morning, Schwartz brought a good engine and a team of mechanics. Four hours later, everyone got out.

By February the Nationalist government owed the airlines more than a hundred million gold yuan. The company refueled on credit and we deferred our pay. After Willauer thanked us at a pilots' meeting, he tilted his head back, drooped an eyelid, and said disgustedly, "If it weren't for old Marshal Yen we'd stop the operation."

It stopped anyway. Tsingtao ran out of fuel. I crawled into my bed at the house on German Beach and slept for fourteen hours.

A CAT plane flew Yen to Nanking to ask the Nationalists for help. "I'll get food," he had told his people, "or I'll come back to die with you." He persuaded the government to transfer Chinese Air Force fuel from Shanghai to Tsingtao and make it available to China's three airlines, and to pay the money it owned the airlines. "CAT pilots have been flying without pay," he said.

Willauer wrote his wife: "Hard-boiled as I sometimes seem, I am caught with the real sense of the dramatic by that old marshal flying out to do battle with all the vagaries of the present chaos of the Chinese government in order to hold on to his world and the people he rules."

After Tsingtao fell, we flew from Shanghai. Six hours a trip. The days and nights that followed were a blur of zombie-like fatigue, numbing cold when the heaters wouldn't work, and dozing in a crew car or circling the drop zone and radio-chattering to stay awake on the way back—and watching the red balls get closer. The gunners were learning to bracket us. I saw the first red streak to the left, then the second to the right, and the third curved up in line with me, but a hundred yards or so ahead or behind. "The flak is so thick you can walk on it" became a cliché.

A China National plane was shot down, but the crew crash-landed within Yen's perimeter. "Lucky," I said. "At night they'd never have made it."

The next morning Yen's artillery set up a counter-barrage while another China National plane flew in and got the crew.

We decided to suck oxygen and drop from fifteen thousand feet. I was leaving the house with my oxygen mask and flight kit when Marsh emerged from the crew car to say, "Go back to bed. Rosbert stopped the flights . . . he thinks the Commies are withholding their fire to suck us in. I think he's right."

It was over. We had kept the besieged city alive for more than a year. It was spring 1949. Christmas had passed without notice. Chiang Kai-shek had resigned the presidency of China. Senator McCarthy still fought Communism by recklessly accusing his fellow Americans. Russia manufactured an atom bomb. The Berlin Airlift continued.

I was too numb to care. After a long sleep I joined Marsh, Earthquake, Plank, and the others in drinking too much whiskey.

"Yen and I were in Nanking when the news came in," Burridge eventually told us. "An American reporter, covering the fall, intimated to Yen's face that he had left his people, he had bugged out; and he taunted Yen about his vow to swallow the cyanide and otherwise painted Yen with the broad brush that covered all of China's incompetent generals. Yen showed class—he ignored him.

"Later, when we were alone, he begged me for a plane to fly him back into Taiyüan.

"'I'll buy the airplane,' Yen pleaded.

"'We can't risk a crew.'

"'I'll parachute out.'

"I told him we couldn't do it," Burridge said. "I didn't want him to die."

News of Taiyüan's last day eventually got to us. Outnumbering Yen's soldiers three to one, Communists breached the wall and fought hand to hand on Taiyüan's streets. Yen's son-in-law and the chief of gendarmerie were last seen trudging down the street at the end of a rope. More than four hundred men, including Yen's nephew, swallowed the cyanide capsules, and their bodies were cremated by their friends.

It wasn't the last we'd hear of the doughty warlord.

The Battle of Hwai-Hai

It was "the battle of Hwai-Hai" to historians because the site stretched across vast plains, from the Lunghai Railroad to the Hwai River. On the other hand, CAT called it "the battle of Süchow," because Süchow (or Hsü-chou, or in modern spelling Xuzhou) was the principal city, the home of almost a third of a million people, at the junction of important north-south and east-west railroads, midway between the capital of Shantung Province and the national capital. In short, Süchow lay 175 miles south of Tsinan and 175 miles north-northwest of Nanking. It was the center of the flat, wide-open rice fields of eastern China.

Whatever its name, the battle was one of the greatest in modern history. It was particularly brutal because it was a battle of annihilation. Winter weather and primitive medical care compounded the horror.

It was a war to end the war.

More than half a million Nationalist soldiers faced three times that number of Communists.

Chiang Kai-shek himself chose the site. The flat plains gave full scope to his tanks and field pieces. His treasured artillery was commanded by his number two son, Chiang Wei-kuo. The Nationalists' mastery of the air was an advantage over the Reds, who customarily fought guerrilla-style. The Chinese Air Force and China's three airlines could supply ammunition, reinforcements, and food from Nanking, only 175 miles away—a one-hour flight.

General Li Mi's 13th Group Army took defensive positions in the city itself, while the armies of Generals Huang, Sun, and Chin deployed east, south, and west. Chiang Kai-shek masterminded the battle, via telephone, from Nanking.

It started on November 7 with a Communist attack on Huang's army, east of Süchow. Two of his generals and about 23,000 soldiers—a quarter of his army—defected to the enemy. With his remaining troops, General Huang fought westward toward Süchow while a relief column came out of the city.

After eleven days of dropping supplies to General Huang or flying supplies to Süchow, one of the CAT pilots, Roy Watts, made this report: "About 50 miles east of Süchow, General Wang's [Huang's] army of 40,000 is encircled. There is another Nationalist column driving eastward toward this fighting and they have now reached the halfway point, having progressed approximately 25 miles in two days.

"The city of Süchow is completely surrounded within a radius of 10 to 15 miles on all sides—except the north, where the troops are about 20 to 25 miles away."

The report was unusually clear. Most of the time we were too busy to find out which army fought or too tired to ask; or we saw only flashes of artillery in the night.

The Reds shot a China National plane full of holes, but the crew got it back to Nanking.

All airlines flew around the clock. The night missions came out of Shanghai, two hours away. In the early stages of the battle we carried crates of mortar shells and grenades and rice to Süchow's airport, and returned with wounded soldiers.

It seemed like a nightmare out of Manchuria. We crammed stretchers on the plane's cabin floor—seventy-five in a C-46—without taking time to tie them down. Boy-soldiers without blankets, in pain, shivering, died in their own blood and excrement. I landed at Shanghai sometime after midnight, hoping for but not expecting military ambulances. There were none. Our laborers carried the laden stretchers to a grassy field beside our Hungjao tarmac, where our own doctors and nurses, with flashlights, tended then. A cargo building became a temporary hospital.

In the operations building, our meteorologist, John Fogg—his real name—said, "Those westerly winds are increasing."

An angry Willauer at the next desk used our dispatcher to interpret: "Call another hospital! Get 'em to send doctors and nurses—and ambulances." He saw me. "We ran out of opiates. Some of these guys are dying just from shock—they could be saved."

I walked toward my C-46. The operations dispatcher caught up with me, as if he wanted to talk to someone—anyone. A careless flashlight illuminated his breath. "Jesus, how'd you like to be a private in the Chinese Army? Willauer has been here all night, trying to get help from civilian hospitals. Chennault is phoning from the down-town office. He's goading army headquarters into doing something."

Soldiers on the ground moaned. Some called for water; others were silent, which seemed even worse. "Good iron is not used for nails, or good men for soldiers," I recited, with passion. "They really believe their fucking proverb."

"These poor bastards can't fight anymore, so they're garbage."

Fogg had warned me about the wind. It increased even more than he had forecast. We got back over Süchow eleven minutes later than our flight plan's estimated time of arrival.

"You can't land!" the tower screamed. "You lied about your ETA."

"Sorry, tower, strong head winds."

"Go back to Shanghai."

"We have rice and ammunition."

"Go back to Shanghai. Landing is forbidden. You lied to us. Permission to land cannot be granted."

We circled in the dark, above flashes of gunfire, while my copilot spoke to the tower controller in his own dialect. "Its no use—he's angry because we gave him a bad ETA."

"Does he know we have food and ammo, for God's sake? We can carry the wounded out."

"He doesn't care. He said punishment for lying."

When the enemy lobbed mortar shells onto Süchow's airport, our crews fended off refugees with poles before we could taxi out. Deserters brandished their weapons to force their way onto our planes, claiming priority over the wounded.

A panic-crazed solder wandered into a C-46 propeller, which became a giant Mixmaster and flung body parts over the tarmac. It was a repeat of Chengchow.

On subsequent flights we circled the city and parachuted mortar shells and crates of grenades out of our main cabin doors and shoved out rice in double bags. We circled the diminishing drop zone at two thousand feet for accuracy, while the Chinese Air Force circled at five thousand feet for safety and dropped their stuff through our formations. I feared we'd fly into their stuff, but couldn't do anything about it, so I dismissed it from my mind.

After the fall of the city, on the 1st or 2nd of December, General Tu led his armies sixty miles west, where they made a perimeter of foxholes and trenches and placed their tanks and artillery in the center to lay down protective fire. Also within the perimeter, government officials, families of soldiers, students, and other civilians huddled against the cold.

The low-altitude aerial deliveries stopped after the Communists brought in Soviet antiaircraft guns. And then a miserable cold front moved in. Snow and sleet obscured the battle zone.

A Christmas Day message from General Tu to the Chinese Air Force, copy to CAT: "Our troops have been surrounded for more than ten days without any airdrops. The officers and soldiers are so hungry and cold that they have killed the horses and cows, ate the barks and roots of grasses, and burned the houses, furniture, and clothes for fuel use. Under such hungry-stricken conditions, there is no way to encourage the esprit de corps of the troops. In recent days, the soldiers are gradually deserting, and there is no means to get hold of the main force. . . ."

The weather improved a few days after Christmas. Howard Brooks and Eddie Simms, CAT pilots, lost an engine when fragments from an antiaircraft shell struck the carburetor. On one engine, they completed the drop and then flew back to Nanking. Fuel poured out shrapnel holes in their engine and wing. The Chinese commended them for the accuracy of the drop.

Chiang Kai-shek's son was evacuated by air. General Li Mi, disguised as a merchant, was pushed through enemy lines in a wheelbarrow. (He would turn up in Burma.) General Tu, disguised as a soldier of low rank, pretended he was a prisoner of his bodyguards, but the Communists recognized him.

Little more than two weeks after Christmas, two months plus four days after the battle began, more than half a million soldiers had been lost. A message from Nanking was poignant in its simplicity. It advised us to cancel all airdrops, "because there is no longer such need now."

We pilots didn't know much of what happened because we seldom had the luxury of continuity.

While the battle of Süchow raged, besieged Taiyüan maintained its need for supplies; and Tientsin, only sixty-five miles from Peiping, fought for its freedom. Scheduled passenger flights throughout China continued while tin and tungsten ore came out of the west and wool from the north. The exigencies of crew scheduling scattered us.

After we had time to talk to each other and read the reports of military observers, this is what we read and heard:

The Nationalists lost Süchow by maintaining a defensive posture, whereas the Reds were aggressive.

Conducting the battle from Nanking via telephone, Chiang Kaishek was unmindful of last-minute developments.

Communist officers forced civilians ahead of their troops, thus disconcerting the Nationalist soldiers.

Poor leadership, missed paydays, and infrequent meals eroded the morale of the troops. Many responded to the bullhorn invitations of Communists who offered steamed bread, bowls of rice, and employment in the people's army.

We didn't need military observers to tell us—all that existed between the Communist strongholds in the north and the capital of Nanking was the army of Nationalist general Fu Tso-yi.

The Agrarian General

Fu Tso-yi was one of Yen Hsi-shan's lieutenants before he became general of eleven Nationalist armies. The two warriors remained close friends.

We called him "the Agrarian General" because he wore a simple uniform, ate and slept with his men, paid them on time. His troops were well fed, disciplined, respectful of civilians. Even the Communists respected General Fu and his men. "We know we can beat them in battle," the Reds said, "but we'd sooner not try."

Fu bivouacked southwest of Peiping, in the hills, where he made ammunition for small arms. Whenever he moved his soldiers, he also moved their families, close enough to stay in touch, without courting danger. Eleven armies sounded impressive, but three were short of arms and four had no equipment.

In the summer of 1948, Chiang Kai-shek moved Fu's armies east, to an area seventy miles southwest of Peiping—near Tientsin, which had access to the Yellow Sea. Were he properly equipped, he could open up a corridor to Manchuria.

Fu was reluctant to leave his soldiers' families and the familiar hills until Chiang Kai-shek promised to supply him with arms and ammunition. America's aid officials recommended a sixteen-million-dollar shipment of supplies direct to General Fu Tso-yi, and the U.S. Joint Chiefs of Staff concurred.

A Marine attaché with the U.S. Navy claimed that three supply ships had been dispatched from America's West Coast, only to be recalled three days later. Rumors said the State Department had convinced President Truman that he was chasing a lost cause and he had ordered the recall.

Whatever the reason, General Fu's resolve weakened. A Catholic missionary—Father Day—journeyed from Tsingtao to Fu's bivouac outside Tientsin to bolster him.

A shipment eventually arrived, long after the summer had passed. It was the end of November, almost a month after Mukden fell. Moreover, the supplies were useless—they lacked vital parts. The fiasco contributed to the loss of Tientsin.

John Plank said, "The Commies had the airport, so I landed on the racecourse. Walt Koenig [Tientsin's station manager] ran into town to get his girlfriend. All our people were aboard except Walt. The Commies began mortaring the racecourse, so I took off." Unable to get back in time, Koenig made the best of it by radiogramming, "I volunteered to remain as a test case."

Tientsin's fall—three days after the battle of Süchow, January 14, 1949—left Peiping without access to the sea.

General Fu Tso-yi regrouped his soldiers behind Peiping's wall. His old friend Governor Yen Hsi-shan of besieged Taiyüan radiogrammed six times: "Sacrifice and struggle, giving up any idea of survival."

Outside Peiping's gates, the Red general was reluctant to damage China's architectural heritage—its Forbidden City, the Summer Palace on the hills, the Winter Palace on the lake, the azure Temple of Heaven, Tiananmen Square—so he lobbed a shell over the wall occasionally to get Fu Tso-yi's attention.

Chief pilot Rousselot, rescuing our staff, flew through twenty or thirty bursts of antiaircraft shells before he landed safely on a street near the Temple of Heaven.

Peiping's business community pleaded with Fu to do nothing rash. The municipal assembly asked him to preserve the historic capital. A northwestern warlord—Teng Pao-shang, the father-in-law of Fu's daughter—concurred. And the Reds offered him a high post in their future government.

General Fu asked for a temporary truce.

After a series of conferences, both sides acknowledged that the people wanted peace. If the wishes of all people were honored, no one would lose face. Although Fu Tso-yi's soldiers would have died for him, the fight was over, and the honor of both sides was preserved. It was January 21, 1949.

An example of the Chinese at their best, I thought. When so inclined, they're masters in the art of compromise.

General Barr, an adviser with the AMG (American Military Group), stated that the morale and efficiency of CAT were so good he didn't see how it was possible in view of the state of emergency that had existed over the past two years.

Kind as General Barr's words were, the many hours we had flown, day and night, and the lack of spare parts worried the pilots and frustrated the mechanics. I saw our engineering people, with little credit for an operation, endure bitter cold to change an airplane part, which sometimes required bare hands, only to find it defective.

Airplane tires that got retreads in a truck garage in Canton flung the tread during high-speed takeoffs. The flying rubber whacked the wing and left a dent.

Brongersma's right carburetor blew its seal and the engine died suddenly. Ten minutes after he got a rebuilt carburetor, the other engine blew a cylinder head and stopped. He had come within ten minutes of flying an aluminum glider.

The conditions affected different guys in different ways.

Master mechanic Johnny Glass tried to surmount the situation by laboring outside on the ground at Tsingtao because he had no where else to work. He opened the guts of engines and adjused the backlash of gears. It was precision work, normally performed in engine overhaul shops.

"I get Tsingtao's planes in top shape," he grumbled, "and Shanghai takes them away and sends us more dogs."

"Hollywood" handled the situation differently. He refused to worry about a situation he couldn't control. He relaxed. He showed up for work in a white cashmere sport jacket, tailored in Hong Kong. He grinned and said, "Your bird's ready to fly." I looked at the electric power line that led from a coughing gas-powered generator to the belly of my C-46. I hadn't seen Hollywood so prepared in months.

When I got to the cockpit I stuck my head out the window. "Hollywood, pull the power cart."

"You're supposed to start the engines first."

"Pull it now—I'm going to check the battery." He pulled the plug and the ammeter over my head dropped to zero. "You're sending me out with a dead battery."

"No spares." He was still grinning.

"Next time tell me."

It affected Buol in still another way, even though he seemed to be as cocky and debonair as I had first seen him in Honolulu after he and his Marine Corps buddies kept half the Niamalu Hotel awake. He had become CAT's chief of operations, which meant he scheduled the airplanes so they'd turn up in Shanghai when their overhauls were due. When Jones refused to fly until a magneto was replaced—the engine backfired on one of its twin magnetos—Buol strolled out of his office, boarded the plane, and flew it to its destination. "A helluva way to run an airline," Jones said.

An unwritten rule said a pilot won't fly what another turned down. It precluded a subtle danger. In general, confident pilots tended to say, "Hell no, I won't go; fix it," whereas a timid pilot, unsure of his employment, would accept it. If the sick airplane deteriorated into an emergency, statistics indicated the old-timer was on the ground and the timid pilot was in the cockpit. Whatever the theory, one pilot wouldn't take a plane another had turned down. But Buol would.

By sheer bad luck, Brongersma won the prize for the number of engines lost. Four in three days.

The series of sick engines began when he shut down his right engine because it had lost oil pressure. He landed and found a broken oil line. Ten minutes after it was replaced, the other engine backfired and shook violently. He landed again, and a torn carburetor seal was replaced. After he took off for the third time, his right engine failed again. Three days later, in early morning darkness and rain, he climbed in clouds for five minutes and his left engine gave up, forcing him to make an instrument approach on one engine with a fully loaded airplane. He didn't see runway lights until he got down to eight hundred feet.

When my turn came I was lucky enough to have Bob Snoddy with me.

Bob Snoddy

He was a new pilot, fresh from Hawaiian Airlines. A slender American from Oregon, with a nose that turned up at the end, he moved in a way that was calm and precise. In the U.S. Navy's Seventh Fleet in the big war, he earned the Navy Air Medal several times over, plus four Battle Stars and a Purple Heart.

He returned to Oregon State to study aeronautical engineering, but he missed flying and got a dream job with Hawaiian. He still missed excitement and transferred to CAT.

I met Snoddy at 4:00 A.M. in Hungjao's operations shack. He was my copilot. I sized him up and said, "Pretend you're a captain—I'll watch from the right seat."

Snoddy pulled a flashlight from his flight kit and checked the C-46 as if he knew what he was doing, and I knew he wouldn't be a copilot very long.

When we got on the flight deck he picked up the C-46's big logbook with its aluminum covers, turned a page, and said, "This logbook is brand-new."

"It's telling us something," I replied. "We have one or two mechanics who'll put a new logbook in the airplane if they aren't able to fix something—so we can't see the previous squawks." Snoddy nodded. "I talked to the pilot who brought this in," I said. "The right engine has been backfiring intermittently."

I walked over to the American mechanic and asked, "How's the airplane?"

"Perfect shape. I'd fly anywhere in it myself."

"The last pilot told me the right engine was farting."

"Carburetor. Changed it myself. I guarantee it."

Snoddy settled into the left seat, fastened his belt, called for the checklist, turned down the cockpit lights. After he got us started and taxied to the end of the runway he set the brakes and checked the engines. They were smooth on each magneto. He eased the manifold pressure up to fifty-two inches of mercury, which was full power, and released the brakes. With our full load of cargo we accelerated slowly. Flames from coffee cans defined the edges of the strip and accentuated the darkness. Beyond the flames it was pitch-black, but I knew trees were there.

Our speed reached ninety-five. Snoddy eased the control column back. At that moment the right engine exploded. My peripheral vision told me it was on fire—I didn't have to look. I pulled the fire handle and pushed the red feathering button.

Snoddy used enough rudder pressure to keep us flying in a straight line. The altimeter didn't leave zero, although we had climbed slightly—enough to clear the trees that our landing lights illuminated.

Without talking, we confirmed that the other guy knew the situation: I laid a finger on the altimeter, which still showed zero, while Snoddy touched the airspeed instrument, which showed ninety-five. We both knew it. We could run into tall trees, but if we tried to climb, we'd stall. We were trapped between altitude and airspeed.

I angled the landing lights down; Snoddy avoided tall trees. The leaves looked huge and dirty green. Flames on my right said the fire extinguisher didn't work, nor did the fuel shut-off valve on the fire wall.

Snoddy raised the wing on the dead side a few degrees, which meant he wouldn't have to use as much rudder to counteract the yaw, and that meant less drag. His every action was perfect, by the book. The smartest thing I could do was to stay off his back. He nursed the plane up until the altimeter needle rose off its peg.

Ten long minutes later, at fifty feet, we saw the runway lights of Shanghai International and landed in the dark. We got out to inspect the engine and found glowing clinkers in a gutted engine.

"You saved us," I said. "I'd never have made it with a run-of-the-mill copilot."

"You saved us," Snoddy said. "I'd have flown into the trees if you hadn't tilted the landing lights."

On the way back to Hungjao in a taxi I said, "Let's not tell them we gained altitude. If the bastards find out we got up to fifty feet they'll increase the maximum gross to fifty thousand. We're already operating two thousand pounds heavier than China National and Central Air." Snoddy nodded.

When the taxi dropped us off at our home airport, we saw Buol, the cocky Marine with the debonair grin. He was in the operations station wagon with a copilot. "We're going to pick up your bird," he said, and drove off.

Snoddy looked astonished. "He thinks he can take off on one engine? Who the hell's that?"

"Chief of flight operations," I said. "When a pilot turns down a plane it upsets his schedule. He flies it."

"He didn't even ask its condition or what happened."

"That's Buol. Go on home," I said. "I'll wait here."

Buol returned—via his station wagon. I said, "Where's the air-plane, smart-ass?" I was damn mad.

Buol just stood there with his go-to-hell grin.

"If Snoddy and I can fly it with a full load, on fire, at night, we sure as hell can fly it back empty in daylight—if it's flyable."

Buol glared at me for a few seconds and walked off.

The operations clerk came out to hand me a message from Sue Buol. General Chennault wanted to see me in the morning with a full report.

I walked to the shack that was called the engineering library. I knew they wouldn't release the airplane logbooks, so I stole an arm-ful, took them to the pilots' house, and sat up the entire night, mark-ing various pages with paper tabs. The next morning, with Chennault, Willauer, Rousselot, the chief engineer, and Snoddy all at a long table, I answered questions, and Snoddy, when answering, didn't peep a word about gaining fifty feet. The group looked sur-prised when I stacked the aluminum-covered logbooks on the con-ference table and said, "These engines have been giving plenty of warning before they quit." I opened logbooks at my markers and read, "'Right engine backfiring. Write-off: water in fuel, drained sumps.' Next flight: 'Right engine still backfiring.' Write-off: 'Spark plugs fouled; engine run at takeoff power for one minute, checks okay.' Next flight: 'Right engine failed during climb-out.'"

Picking logbooks off the pile, I read page after page, aloud, until a clerk came in to chalk a message on Chennault's status board: "A/C 804 returning to Sian. Right engine inoperative. Kaffenberger."

I pointed at it. "We all know the mountains around Sian are high-er than his single-engine ceiling, don't we?" Silence. "We don't know if Kaffenberger and his crew will make it, do we?" More silence.

Willauer said, "You don't have to show us any more logbooks, Felix."

A few days later, Rousselot told us the maintenance department had agreed to leave the old logbook in the cockpit, for reference, after a new one was introduced.

A representative of Pacific Airmotive arrived from Los Angeles. They overhauled our engines. He said, "You need more spare parts." Willauer nodded; he knew it only too well. The rep added, "I can recommend the best supplier of aviation parts on the West Coast"—and he recited the names of the California trucker and the pompous colonel we had last seen in Hawaii, it seemed like a hundred years ago. At the sound of the names, Willauer blanched and bit his lip.

I was glad to get the hell out of Shanghai, back to Tsingtao and the fireplace in the house on German Beach, where Marsh and I had lined a wall with cases of scotch that the Marine Corps club had sold at suicide prices. The U.S. Navy and Marine Corps were shipping out.

On my approach to the old German seaport, I saw an American troop ship and two aircraft carriers that had come to evacuate American citizens. And I knew that the seaside city of red bricks and ceramic tiles was next on Mao Tse-tung's list.

The Fall of Tsingtao

The CAT driver honked his horn and waited in the darkness outside our house on German Beach. Marsh and I had been assigned to the first two flights of the day.

The route to the airport was obstructed with more roadblocks than usual. Sentries usually saw the Chinese Air Force sticker on our windshield and waved us on, but this time a soldier pointed his rifle at us while his partner inspected our curfew pass.

Low clouds reflected flames. The U.S. Navy warehouse at the airport burned. Perhaps the Reds' Eighth Army had arrived. They had lobbed mortar shells close to the south end of the runway the night before, and our staff had heard rifle shots.

The U.S. Marine guard at the airport gate said the Navy building had just caught fire, but otherwise the airport itself was peaceful. A contingent of Nationalist soldiers outside the airport had turned their caps upside down, thus signifying their switch to Chairman Mao Tse-tung.

Our airplane logbooks were not on the operations counter, nor were Chinese mechanics at the planes. The mechanics were in the company dining room, and when we looked in the door one of them shouted, "Strike!"

Soha, our crew chief, stormed in. "I caught four mechs disconnecting the carburetor linkage and screwing around with the fuel lines. I almost got clobbered on the back of the head with a wrench, but Chase hollered just in time." Marsh popped open his flight kit, pulled out his .45, and tucked it in the armpit of his parka.

"Are the radio operators striking?" I asked.

"The entire Chinese ground staff, including Shanghai."

Radiograms littered the floor of the radio shack, and the six chairs were empty except for a lone operator who pounded dit-dahs on his brass telegraph key. I said, "What's the Shanghai weather?"

"I don't know."

"If he isn't working the weather," Marsh said, "he's talking to his cohorts in Shanghai." He lifted the earphones from the operator's head and said, "If you're not working the weather you might as well leave."

A gang of Chinese mechanics crowded at the open door of the radio room, although Marsh couldn't see them because his back was turned. They advanced through the door. I shouted. Marsh wheeled around and opened his parka fast enough for the zipper to zing. It revealed the butt end of his .45. The mechanics reared back, and the radioman followed. They muttered to each other outside.

Marsh and I were slower than the pros, but we knew Morse code and tried to raise Shanghai. Minutes later we lost power.

"They shut down the generators," I said.

We found Wong, our traffic manager, at the generator shed, where the strikers had gathered. "No planes received damages," he said. "Only taken apart."

Ops manager Chase said, "Get them off the airport." They hesitated.

"Wong," I said, "if they're telling the truth—if they don't want to damage anything—they can now prove it by leaving the airport."

"They want money."

"No money at the airport," Marsh said. "It's downtown." After a long discussion among themselves, they left.

"Every pilot and American mechanic must come and inspect the planes," Chase said. "My phone is dead. Go back to town and round them up."

"I'll take the crew car," I said.

"I'll go with you," Marsh said. I was glad of his offer, because I knew he had another .45 in the house.

On our way to the airport gate we stopped to ask the Marine Corps duty officer, "Do you think our squabble has anything to do with the fire in the Navy building?"

"Don't think so," he said. "But we'll double the guard on our planes."

When we got to our house on German Beach I tried to rouse the guys at the CAT castle, but their phone was dead. I got through to our downtown office. Burridge said, "Our cars disappeared, including mine."

"I'll ride the crew car to the castle," I said.

"Wait," Marsh said. He held out his spare .45. "Try a few practice squeezes. Don't pull the trigger. Squeeze your fingers against your thumb and the piece will stay on target." He knew his subject. I had seen his marksmanship medal the day he got decked out for a celebration of the sacred Marine Corps birthday.

The "piece," as he called it, was heavier than I expected. I turned it over and over in my hand curiously. It seemed benign, beautifully machined, a work of art, even though I had seen a camper fire one in a forest. It went *blam* and half a tree stump disappeared. I didn't want to shoot anyone, but the weapon gave me a secure feeling.

After getting the hang of it I shoved a clip of cartridges into its butt and stuck it into a shoulder holster under my parka.

Marsh stayed at the house to pack his valuables while the loyal driver of the crew car took me to the castle, almost. I saw the missing CAT cars in the courtyard and didn't want their drivers to draft mine, so I told him to continue on to the house where Norwich and Earthquake Magoon stayed. They drove Norwich's car to the airport. Like Paul Revere, I continued on to other houses to sound the alarm. I picked up Marsh and we returned to the airport.

Like peasants in a revolution, pilots arrived with clubs, old canes, Samurai swords, and a few .45s and .38s. The crew chief said, "So far, all I found were deflated landing-gear struts, missing carburetor parts, and run-down batteries. But I'm wondering if there's sand in the oil or in the hydraulic systems. When you guys nose around, look for particles of sand around the filler necks."

"When I flew for China National," I said, "a saboteur altered the indicator on an elevator trip tab. When it showed neutral the control was in the maximum nose-up position."

Earthquake, Norwich, and I formed a team. We found flat landing-gear struts, broken cockpit lights, a loose nut on an elevator trim tab, and some jammed fuel shut-off valves.

When most of the planes were ready for test flights I suggested we fly with parachutes plus a striking mechanic with none. If he knew of some hidden defect he'd sing like a mockingbird before we took off. But Burridge led us to believe it'd be best to keep the strikers off the airport.

General Leong shouted, "I shall draft you into the army immediately." That ended the strike.

Norwich said, "I'm not worried about the planes right now. I'm worried about twenty hours from now when stuff they loosened drops off, or when battery acid eats away the control cables."

Indeed, the next few days of flying had us edgy, but after flying for a week without encountering problems and discovering the purpose of the strike had been a salary increase, not political, we relaxed.

None of us resented the strike for more pay—they were getting little enough—but balking when the Commies were on our doorstep was something else. Old Flying Tiger Bus Loane said, "In China there's no such thing as treason."

"Marsh," I asked, "were you going to fire your forty-five when those guys moved toward you?"

"You bet. I had no intention of falling into their hands, maybe turned over to the Commies. I'd have shot and flown a C-46 to Okinawa."

In a couple of weeks, mortar shells fell regularly on the perimeter of the field, and the last of the Marines and the Chinese Air Force, with its unused B-25s, left. All except Colonel Chow, the base commander. "I'll leave with CAT," he said.

The fall of Tsingtao was imminent. We knew the pattern: first the CAF, then Central Air and China National. Finally, the Russian barmaids.

They waited on the tarmac, unafraid. Lilly (Lilly of the Alley). Snow (Snow White). Tamara (Mascara). Tanya (Piana). She had been Piana ever since she wheedled two hundred dollars out of Kruske for a new piano for the bar that never showed up. It was a festive gathering. At least a dozen fair-skinned bantering women. How cheerful they were, how they trusted CAT.

Boarding my C-46, one of them cooed, "Look at our handsome pilot. He looks like a nice Ukrainian boy."

"Maybe he's a virgin, ho ha ha ha, cackle cackle."

"He looks sexy."

I stood at the cockpit door and announced, "Ladies, on this flight we're serving cold tea in brandy snifters. We know that's what you like best." More laughter and shrieks.

By the time I returned from Shanghai, Tsingtao's staff had stowed file cabinets and a desk in the cabin of a C-46. The radio operator became message center chief. Electricity came from a putt-putt (the C-46's auxiliary power unit). The airplane was our customary fly-away office from which we directed our evacuation flights.

Each night, our mechanics ran the engines for fifteen minutes to keep spark plugs from fouling, and wing flaps were cycled to keep hydraulic seals moist. We didn't want any hitches when the Eighth Army mortar shells started to fall.

In town, I stopped at the Fiat automobile agency to see McCann, the American manager. "Come with us," I said. "This is your last chance."

"I've been here thirty years. I've seen governments come and go, but the Chinese people always stay the same."

"This time it's different."

"I'll be okay. I have many friends here."

On one of our last nights, during the ritual of running the engines on our standby plane, Colonel Chow stormed out of a Quonset hut, brandished his .45, and yelled, "You woke me up! You make too much noise!" He fired at our plane. *Blam, blam, blam.* An engine oil line and a couple of hydraulic lines spewed oil. The Chinese Air Force base commander had destroyed the means of his escape— until our mechanics, working all night, repaired the severed lines.

The mortar shells arrived a couple of nights later, and we flew away.

CAT's Navy

When Tsingtao fell, we lost the heavy maintenance equipment— whatever we couldn't squeeze through the C-46 cargo doors. The Reds got our nose hangars, cranes, engine stands, trucks.

Willauer said, "There'll be no more donations." Our best mainte-nance equipment was in Shanghai, and the Communist Eighth Army was only twenty miles north. He leased a World War II LST (Landing Ship, Tank) from the China Merchants Steam Navigation Company. It was 327 feet in length and had been designed to run aground on a hostile beach, drop its flat bow, and discharge a mechanized force.

It was large enough to carry our oversize equipment to the safety of south China. Willauer said, "There's four thousand square feet of space belowdecks—enough for a machine shop, propeller shop, a dust-free air-conditioned instrument shop. It'll be the only mobile airline maintenance base in the world. There's even room for a medical clinic."

I asked for temporary assignment to the ship to wet my U.S. Merchant Marine third mate's license, which would otherwise expire. The request seemed reasonable to sea-minded Willauer, who then assigned me the responsibility of keeping inventory of everything it carried to Canton.

Lewis wanted to come along and tried to make himself indispensable by pickling the deck cargo of C-47 wings with Cosmoline while I inventoried incoming cargo.

"This is no time for a pleasure cruise," groused the chief of maintenance, so Lewis disembarked, leaving me a fifth of Canadian Club.

The steamship company furnished a crew to get the LST to Canton, and then CAT would hire its own. I'd be the only foreigner— down the Whangpoo River to the mouth of the Yangtze, south, along the China coast, past Hong Kong, and seventy-five miles up the Pearl River to Canton.

The chief steward graciously offered to stock Western food, but I replied, "I like Chinese food better." My reckless statement came from memories of Shanghai's Sun Ya Restaurant, which served succulent morsels while a Chinese nightingale sang Shanghai jazz.

Sailing through heavy traffic in the mouth of the Yangtze, I was suprised to see the chief engineer up from the depths of his mechanical world. It was standby time when most chiefs would hover close to the engine-room telegraph. Our chief's top half was nattily attired in a traditional navy-blue jacket with brass buttons and sleeves with four gold stripes. More gold glistened from the long bill of a cap that perched at a jaunty angle. The chief's bottom half was clothed in greasy once-white pants tied at the ankles with rope yarn that would keep them from snagging in machinery. He leaned into the freshening breeze and saluted, waved, smiled at passing steamers, junks, coal barges, sampans.

On the bridge, a guest of the captain, I was surprised to hear him give orders in English: "Right rudder. . . . Ease your helm. . . . Steady as you go. . . . Half speed." No one in the crew spoke conversational English, but he obviously had been trained by the Chinese Navy, which in turn had been trained by the U.S. Navy to sail the sophisticated LST. Save for the flamboyant chief engineer, the crew appeared to be disciplined. I wasn't surprised, for I knew that China for centuries had been a seagoing nation.

By the time we were on the open sea with the China coast off our starboard beam, I was hungry. I followed off-duty officers to their dining salon, anticipating food similar to Sun Ya's. I didn't expect a sexy vocalist or quality food. As a matter of fact, the most ordinary Chinese fare made me drool. Bean sprouts, for example, were common, but Cheong maintained the crunchiness while sautéing them with garlic and tiny morsels of pork plus slivers of ginger. And he shredded bell peppers and beef in a matter of minutes. It tasted better than prime rib.

Instead of any of these simple home-style dishes, the ship's waiter emerged from the galley with platters of fish heads. Eyes stared out of gooey brown sauce. The pièce de résistance happened to be fermented bean curd that stank worse than Wisconsin's infamous Limburger cheese.

I asked for steamed rice and two boiled eggs in their shells, which I cracked over the rice and decorated with soy sauce. The captain leaned toward me and asked, "You say you like Chinese chow?"

On the bridge, I discovered that Chinese mariners didn't use aviation navigational aids (the radio beacons that happened to be on the coast). But this was no different from American practice. Mariners and aviators didn't utilize each other's aids.

I penciled the label of Lewis's Canadian Club with graduations to fit the five days we'd be at sea. It stood at attention on my desk. But the skipper dropped the anchor to wait for fog to dissipate and I ran dry by the time we passed Hong Kong.

We turned up the Pearl River and the skipper posted a double lookout for mines. It was a routine precaution. Pirates booby-trapped the narrows and extracted tribute from shipowners.

As we traveled farther upriver where the water was fresher, we saw more and more lush green farms along the riverbank, and when we arrived at the river port of Canton we saw men and women workers with their bamboo carrying poles, waiting to unload the ship.

The port captain assigned a low dock where we lowered the hinged bow. After thanking the skipper for his hospitality, I stood on the dock, clipboard in hand, checking the stuff while men and women carried it off with bamboo shoulder poles and hi-ho working chants.

Across the Yangtze

When I got back to Shanghai, Willauer said, "We can't get any information from the government—we have to find out for ourselves—but how much time do we have? When do we evacuate Shanghai? When the Commies cross the Yangtze, Shanghai will go in a couple of days."

Chiang Kai-shek had vowed the Communists would never cross the famous river. His troops would make a life-or-death stand at the Yangtze, near Nanking. They would shield China's capital.

"Fly up the river and report what you see," Rousselot said, and he assigned to the right seat Captain Lampard, who had been a fighter pilot in the Royal Air Force. Chu, one of our best radio operators, sat behind us.

It was late afternoon and the sky was clear when we headed north to intercept the Yangtze and then turned west and followed it inland, where the river was two miles wide, and we saw soldiers gathering in orderly groups.

"Estimate ten thousand troops massing on north bank, fifty miles east of Nanking," we radioed. "About fifty junks and barges in the river. No troops south of the river."

The soldiers of the Communist Eighth Army didn't look up, although they must have heard us overhead. They appeared to be unconcerned, unhurried, and unopposed.

We flew along the Yangtze until nightfall. When we landed back at Hungjao, Rousselot was waiting for us, and he said, "Thanks." It was at times like that when I knew Rousselot. Strict as he was over small discrepancies—which earned him the monikers Iron-Ass and BB Eyes—he was understanding in important matters. Like Chennault and Willauer, Rousselot had an innate respect for pilots.

"We won't be in Shanghai much longer," he said quietly.

The Fall of Shanghai

It played like a broken record: the last-minute dashes into town. (A pilot said, "When I got my stuff out of the CAT house I looked in the attic. It looked like a haberdashery. T-shirts and shorts stacked in rows—all the stuff our houseboy had stolen over the past two years.") The head office and message center moved into the cabin of a C-46 and chalked the crew schedule on the fuselage. Russian barmaids, magnificent survivors when confusion reigned, claimed to be wives of airline employees and demanded passage south. Their grapevine revealed that CAT employed three Smiths, China National several, Central Air one or two. Earthquake ribbed me, howling, "You have many wives!"

Chiang Kai-shek bolstered the defenders with several armies and predicted "total victory within three years."

Police seized those suspected of spying or black marketeering and shot them on the street.

Laborers dug a moat around China's largest city and erected a bamboo palisade.

Nationalist general Tang En-po boasted, "Shanghai will be a second Stalingrad!"

Chou Tso-min of the Kinchen Bank, negotiating secretly with Communist general Chen Yi, asked him not to destroy Shanghai. Roots of their friendship reached back to the previous war. Under the nose of Japan's Imperial Army, which occupied Shanghai, the banker found a way to supply Chen's Fourth Army with medicine and money.

Other tycoons, with the banker, asked Nationalist general Tang not to make a last-ditch Stalingrad stand. They offered him gold bars.

History doesn't judge the weight of the negotiations. It only records the departure of General Tang with half of his troops, and the entry, almost unopposed, of General Chen. He took 100,000 prisoners.

The only bright spot left was China's northwest.

Northwest Warlords

Five single-engine planes followed a C-46 like chicks trailing a mother hen. Chennault's long-awaited project was at hand. We were on our way to the provinces that butt against Inner Mongolia and Tibet.

On that same day, in Washington, D.C., Chennault told Congress that China's northwest could remain free with very little aid because its people were Muslim—tall, strong people with round eyes and large noses. Only recently had they defeated a Communist army that invaded their turf. Hatred of Peiping's godless regime bonded the warlords. CAT's aerial taxis would be their means of communication.

Chennault intended to launch his project whether or not Congress put up the money. He told us, "We'll make expenses by flying light-weight, high-value things. Musk oil, mail, herbs, furs, currency, small machines."

Kansu, the middle province, was the economic base. It nurtured Lanchow, the northwest's largest city. Its sinister black wall loomed over the Yellow River, which was navigable and ran three thousand miles to the Yellow Sea. Powerful and swift, the river drove huge waterwheels that irrigated the desert. Governor Kuo was a pussycat compared to the warlords on his flanks.

Tsinghai Province, on the west, resembled the Rocky Mountains and was ruled by Ma Pu-fang. A Hollywood stereotype of a warlord, he was a direct descendant of an Arab mercenary who had fought in the Tang Dynasty's army more than a thousand years ago. His son was general of the army.

The military tradition assured that each family gave one son to military service. Although they were conscripted for life, morale was excellent, because the warrior class commanded respect. And families with only one son could donate a horse instead.

The warlord's cousin, Ma Hung-kwei, ruled Ningsia, the province to the east. It reminded me of the wide desert sweep of Nevada. Unlike his hearty cousin, Ma Hung-kwei had a smile that could scare a kid. His army performed at the drop of any military observer's cap. Cavalry charged at full gallop across a field while riders leaned over to snatch prizes off the ground. Infantrymen shimmied to the tops of telegraph poles to perform headstands before pushing off in an arc to land on their feet.

Labrang—a city across Tsinghai's swiftest river and beyond its highest mountain range—perched on a mountain two miles high. Several thousand Tibetan lamas sat in a complex ruling hierarchy. It was also headquarters for the wise General Hwang, the grand negotiator among Buddhists, Muslims, and Chiang Kai-shek. The entire northwest held endless fascination for me.

Our five Cessna 195s, with three-hundred-horsepower engines, got to Hong Kong in the hold of a ship. After mechanics uncrated and assembled them I test-hopped two and gained an impression that they were designed for America's smooth runways and sophisticated navigational aids. The rigid landing gear didn't suit China's dirt-and-pebble strips, although I was more concerned with the radio direction finder, which we rotated by hand. And it wouldn't detect China's weaker beacons until we were close. Had pilots been asked, we probably would have suggested the De Havilland Beaver used by Canadian bush pilots.

We radio-chattered all the way from Hong Kong.

"Funny how much steeper mountains look from a single-engine putt-putt."

"We oughta return 'em to Sears Roebuck."

"Who the hell bought these toys?"

"Not difficult to figure out—Taylor owns a Cessna agency and he's on our board of directors."

My Jacobs engine faltered for a moment, ran awhile, and missed a few beats again. I switched fuel tanks and played with the mixture control, but the problem persisted.

"My engine's misfiring," I radioed.

"Which one?"

"Smart-ass—one minus one is zero."

"We'll be within gliding distance of Peishi soon."

Peishi, in the mountains near Chungking, was our fuel stop. After I landed behind mother-hen Johnson, his C-46's lone passenger strolled over to my ailing Cessna. He was Winpisinger, who by now was business assistant to our board of directors. He grabbed my wing tip, rocked the little plane, said, "Little water in the gas," and returned to the mother plane.

Water, my ass, I thought, but held my tongue. I wanted Winpisinger and me to become better strangers. Besides, the intermittent misfiring had been going on for so long, instinct told me it was a minor ignition fault, and I wanted to keep up with the pack. Nevertheless I was happy to see the Yellow River and the giant waterwheels that told me Lanchow's grass airport lay within gliding distance.

I landed and rolled to a stop on the clay tarmac and saw Bradley and Natasia, former station managers of Peiping, alongside a huge man in a black. He had to be Governor Kuo.

Schoolgirls with long hair, braided into pigtails, and wearing blue denim dresses with sailor collars stood at attention. Their arms pressed tight against their sides, and they sang. We listened attentively. And then Bradley introduced the pilots to the governor while Lewis stood in the background, waiting to trouble shoot my Cessna.

Citizens in pointed Tibetan hats patted the planes curiously, moved the tail surfaces up and down and back and forth, and jabbered until soldiers prodded them with rifles.

"We know something important is beginning," I told Lewis, "because big-ass Winpisinger is here."

"Yeah, and I get a kick out of Natasia," he said. "She's in her glory, yakking with all the wheels in their own dialect, buddy-buddy-like. She even told the Panchen Lama she'd let him fly our C-46."

Velvet-tonsil Bradley walked over. "You'll fly to Sining tomorrow—first airmail to Upper Tibet, first in the history of China." Upper Tibet was the name before the Manchus stole it and renamed it Tsinghai. The old name sounded more exotic.

"Take your flyswatter," Lewis said.

"That bad?"

"There's hardly a damn fly left. Governor Ma put a quota on 'em. Everyone's running around with flyswatters, trying to get their minimum. There's a black market on the critters: fifty thousand Chinese bucks per hundred. I'm thinking of starting a fly farm."

The next morning, on the way to the airport, Bradley steered us to Lanchow's post office, where a photographer recorded the governor handing me a small sack of mail. I wondered if the letter I had written to myself was inside.

With the sack on the backseat, I followed the Yellow River for a quarter of an hour and then turned up a tributary for another twenty minutes and turned again, up a broad parched valley that soon became light green. Poplar and willow trees lined irrigation canals. More trees framed farms and wide streets within small, walled villages. Even the foothills that towered above us displayed symmetrical patterns of trees.

After almost an hour's flight up the valley we saw a larger city with boulevards and knew it had to be Sining, which was the capital of Tsinghai Province. I bounced down a landing strip that was seven thousand feet above sea level.

Bradley and Natasia, having passed me in a C-47, were there to greet me. They waited with Governor Ma Pu-fang, whom I liked immediately. As huge and robust as a pro wrestler, dressed in a black Sun Yat-sen blouse and a wide-brim black fedora, he had a swarthy Occidental face with almond eyes and a drooping Fu Manchu mustache. He sported a beard of a few long, sparse hairs. When Natasia introduced us his face became animated. I handed him the green sack of mail, and he shook my hand graciously, Western-style. I recalled that Chennault had told us we could trust him.

Schoolgirls, like those in Lanchow, sang, and Natasia spoke to them. Catching a word now and then, I knew she was introducing me in glowing terms. She turned and said, "The schools in Tsinghai are the best in China. These lovely girls are honor students—they can even speak Arabic." Then she said something to Governor Mah Pu-feng that made him smile broadly, which didn't surprise me, because I knew Natasia could charm any man on earth. Reveling in the pageantry, intimate with the languages and customs, loving life, she was at her best. I felt vicarious joy and knew that Natasia, princess or not, had more substance than any ten grand dames in Peiping's Western clique.

That afternoon Lewis and I sat on the bench of an outdoor tea shop with station manager Eddie Ma, who'd been an interpreter with the Chinese Expeditionary Forces in Burma. Tsinghai was green with sixty million trees, he said, because every citizen of the province spent one week a year planting shoots. It was a civic duty. Willows lined irrigation canals and poplars bordered boulevards or served as windbreaks for the relentless west wind that swept sand from the desert.

We also learned that Tsinghai was the birthplace of Tibet's Dalai Lama. After his elders determined he was old enough to go to Lhasa, Governor Ma Pu-fang refused to let him leave until he donated a third of a million silver dollars to the province. After a year of fruitless negotiating, some transiting Muslim merchants, en route to Lhasa on horseback, paid the ransom and carried the boy to his throne. The Tibetan government repaid the Good Samaritan Muslims.

Two women in black dresses and hoods passed the tea shop. We watched them walk down the tree-lined street. Ma pointed in that direction. "Right up the valley is where Tsong Khapa was born. He was the reformer of Tibetan Buddhism."

"A Buddhist Martin Luther."

"He was born in a nomad's tent. A tree grew on the spot. The veins of the leaves were shaped like Tibetan words. They built a temple over it—you probably saw the roof."

"We saw a gold roof from the air."

That night in a hotel I slept on a *kong*, which is a clay fireplace with a bed on top.

In the morning, waiting an interminable time for the mail, I sat in a chair outside the airport shack and dozed, or looked through half-mast eyelids at the tree-green valley, the mountains, and a smattering of people—some in Tibetan garb, others draped with sheepskins—all of them stoic in some mystic way; and the strains of Borodin's "On the Steppes of Central Asia," eerie and memorable, drifted through my head.

A mail truck rattled and backfired, waking me up. The real music of wind whistled through trees, sand stung my face, and people shielded their eyes with spectacles of flat plate glass and hand-wrought brass frames that would turn a Gucci designer green with envy.

A week or so later, on the anniversary of the Sunning of the Buddha, I flew five honor students from Lanchow to Tsinghai. The trip was their prize.

The ceremony occurred when the abbots of Kumbum's monastery unrolled a huge scroll of Buddha's scriptures to be cleansed by the sun. I landed the girls at Sining, and they continued to Kumbum by bus. Lewis borrowed a maintenance jeep and we followed. We smelled the city far off. The wind carried an odor of rancid butter. Huge images of yaks and temples, sculpted from butter, decorated Kumbum.

We couldn't see the scrolls for the crowd, but we got into the gold-roofed temple and stood silently until our eyes adapted to the dark. Flames from wicks in bowls of melted butter cast flickering light on portraits of Buddhist scholars. In the center of the room a silver cone glowed softly with rubies and emeralds. It covered the tree of ten thousand images, no doubt. I had a fleeting sense of floating in space with no past and no future, and that instant was eternity.

After we got outside and inhaled fresh air I recalled something a psychiatrist had written—something about Tibetans and their uncanny ability to design a temple's interior to evoke a predetermined emotional response, a response strong enough to influence an encephalograph.

I mentioned it to Lewis. "Yeah," he said. "I sort of felt suspended in time, but I was afraid if I mentioned it you'd think I was nuts."

On the Cessna flight from Sining to Lanchow with Governor Ma's aide, the wind kicked up dust. By the time we got to Lanchow the fine-grained windblown stuff of the Gobi Desert obliterated the view. I looked straight down and hugged the Yellow River. We were close to Lanchow, but the Cessna's toy radio compass didn't pick up the beacon. The dust acted like snow static. It seemed a long time before I spotted the black wall of Lanchow and picked up the heading to the grass airport.

After a few dust-storm scares, CAT built a meteorology station sixty-five miles north, at a growing village. Sarkasian and Hill had erected a carpet factory. They hailed from Pueblo, Colorado, and knew Lewis's mother. Acting as contractors for us, they scraped a runway long enough for a C-47. It cost thirty-seven silver dollars. Lewis drawled, "Cheapest airport ever built."

The two carpet men, our best customers, commuted to Lanchow daily for nine dollars, round trip—half the cost of a rough trip in a jeep.

Our meteorologist—John Fogg—eventually told Lewis and me what happened the night he and his technicians arrived with their supplies. "I had just climbed on the hotel bed—that damn carpet nailed to a wooden table—when I heard the commotion. Soldiers herded a dozen or so teenage girls into the courtyard. They were cowering and sobbing. My guys interpreted for me. The girls were just unlucky. They happened to be walking down the street."

The sergeant said, "Your girls for tonight. Pick one or two." Fogg told him to take the girls home. The sergeant shrugged his shoulders and sent them home.

"This is Kansu Province," I said. "Governor Ma wouldn't allow that in Tsinghai."

"His cousin in Ningsia would," said Lewis. "I wish I had known how mean the bastard is." I realized Lewis had been uncharacteristically depressed. "I feel like I killed some guys," he said.

"I drove to the Ningsia airport with my mechanics," Lewis continued. "We stopped and picked up some hitchhiking soldiers. They climbed on the back of our truck and shouted and pounded on the roof over my head all the way to the airport. I got pissed off. I walked into the colonel's office and told him we'd give his soldiers a ride anytime, but tell them to behave. I thought that was the end of it.

"Next thing I knew the colonel had lined up his soldiers, and they counted off. The colonel shouted something, and every fourth man took one step forward. They had a desperate look in their eyes, like an animal caught in a trap.

"The colonel shouted again and they followed him behind the barracks. They looked more than scared. I heard shots. I was afraid to ask what happened, but I did. Those guys were executed." Lewis stared at the floor. "I wish I had known how brutal Ma Hung-kwei is. I would never have squawked."

Unlike his hearty cousin in Tsinghai, Ma Hung-kwei ruled by fear. Executions in his province averaged one a day. In my eyes he resembled a Hollywood cliché of a fat Nazi concentration camp commandant. The resemblance faded when he spoke of his seven wives and his penchant for ice cream. He mentioned this to Rousselot. Undaunted by anyone on earth, Rousselot rejoined, "I have a pilot named Smith who'll challenge you to an ice-cream-eating contest." The notion didn't sound like fun.

Lewis recovered from his depression after he got busy with CAT's airmail service to remote Labrang, where Nationalist general Hwang sat with thousands of Tibetan lamas. He wanted communication with the outside world, something quicker than horseback.

A Cessna could land on a huge meadow near Labrang, but its altitude—eleven thousand feet—would hold the plane there forever. Thin air would rob lift from the wings and power from the engine. Lewis suggested we drop mail and snatch outbound stuff from a line between two poles. He rigged a hook and line at Lanchow, and permanent Cessna pilot Eddie Norwich practiced until he snagged a sack on every pass.

Over a drink at Lanchow's hotel, Lewis said, "Guess what? Bradley chose me to take the rig to Labrang. I'm the only guy who can ride a horse, outside of Rousselot and Willauer's wife."

Every CAT person in Lanchow watched Lewis start on his trek— 150 miles with Lewis, General Hwang's cook, the cook's wife. More cheerful than I had seen him since the execution of the soldiers, he said, "I got orders to stop every three hours so the cook can suck his opium pipe—that's his maximum endurance." The trio perched high on top of supplies on their horses' backs while two yaks for the general's butter and cheese followed on a tether.

He returned a month later with tales of crossing raging rivers on rafts pulled by ropes, shivering above tree lines, and seeing village mothers unafraid even though their children played near precipices.

Colonel Poston, a U.S. Army intelligence officer, with two American consular officers, came to Lanchow to interview him.

"It was a short interview," Lewis laughed. Colonel Poston asked how many soldiers accompanied him. "Just me and the cook and the cook's wife," Lewis said. Asked how he got back, Lewis said, "With three Muhammadan traders." They asked, Colonel Poston explained, because they had received news of an explorer, looking for a mountain higher than Everest, who took ten thousand soldiers to fight off hostile forces.

On my next trip to Sining, Natasia photographed an eleven-year-old boy near our C-46. Dressed in red robes, he smiled shyly while seven or eight abbots waited in the background. Two of them watched the boy's every move. Natasia said they were his teacher and political adviser, and he was the Panchen Lama.

Unlike the famous Dalai Lama—the Tibetan spiritual leader—the Panchen Lama presided over secular affairs. His political adviser was sensitive to Chinese government politics.

The boy had arrived from his ride in the copilot seat. Wingfield, grinning, said he helped the kid fly the plane. Clark, the debonair explorer, remained in the northwest; he hadn't given up on the mountain.

"Amne Machin is a jinx," Clark said. "Bandits once caught an early French explorer, sewed him into a leather sack, and tossed him into a river, where he drowned, and other explorers died here."

"Undoubtedly those fellows were amateurs," Natasia soothed. "I believe you'll find your mountain." Was Natasia a stronger attraction than the mountain? I wondered.

Due for three months' home leave, which we got every three years, I wound up in Hong Kong. Chennault often encouraged us to spend the interval in America, "to regain your perspective," he said. Good advice, I knew, but the attraction of China's northwest was strong, especially when Etta Bowen and Mary Hayhurst, two of CAT's head office secretaries—Sue Buol's colleagues—said they wanted to see the place.

Etta, with liquid brown eyes, could charm anyone just by standing in silence. In Etta I saw a captivating alchemy of humility and confidence and heard a soothing voice that expressed gentle wit. From Maine, she had been a secretary in the graves registration branch of the U.S. Army Quartermaster Corps and found herself, at the end of World War II, in Shanghai, a captive of China's mysteries.

Mary, a striking brunette with a cheery, doughty personality and an accent that contained all of England, had served her country in India. How she got to China at the end of the war I never knew.

A genius at rationalization, I told myself a jaunt with two Western women would be tantamount to a vacation in the USA. I found myself deadheading northwest in the cabin of a cargo C-46, with another pilot and the two attractive women.

Educated, intelligent, and trustworthy with CAT's corporate secrets, Etta and Mary cadged a ride whenever a CAT plane flew to some outlandish spot. Their excursions may have elevated the blood pressure of a conventional executive, but Willauer and

Chennault knew their star secretaries were captives of China's spell. Without the excitement, China's dirt, smells, and frustrations would remain. The women would return to the comfortable West, and the head office would never again find such jewels.

The base of our travels was Lanchow's rambling hotel, where the other pilot and I tried to entice the ladies to bed, but they gracefully advised us that sex wasn't in their itinerary, and we settled into platonic excursions with spirited companions.

Even before we got past Lanchow's hotel lobby, Etta and Mary were fascinated. Modern nomads checked into the hotel. Pete, a Turk in a white Chinese high-necked jacket with cloth loops instead of buttons, was an amiable, unassuming, gentle man. His tranquil demeanor suggested he loved northwest China. An agent of Sears Roebuck, he'd been purchasing rugs for the company for years without a contract other than mutual trust. And we saw the roving Swedish merchant Gus Soderbaum, who wore a Western suit.

We introduced them to a young American woman, an artist who'd come on a U.S AID program to advise rug manufacturers about the colors and designs that would appeal to American customers.

And we met Felicity Titus, a German student of Chinese art whose lone hitchhiking on dilapidated truck caravans seemed extraordinary because she was a slender woman, almost frail, stunningly beautiful, with waist-length red hair, and mysterious because she seldom spoke.

In spite of all those people, our travel companions were most interested in Natasia. "A spellbinder," Etta said, "in a dangerous sort of way. . . . Look at her eyes flash. . . ."

"She exposes her thighs accidentally on purpose," Mary said. "Bradley's still enchanted, even though they've been married for years."

We showed our friends the huge waterwheels that irrigated melon farms, sheepskin cargo rafts, outdoor shashlik restaurants, and shops that fenced the loot of grave robbers. And when we walked along the poplar-lined streets of Outer Tibet's Hsining, it seemed as if half the town followed us at a respectable distance, grinning and whispering among themselves.

Before we left Lanchow, Cessna pilot Norwich laughed, "You're on home leave and you came up here? You've gone Asiatic!" I recalled my vow at Springweiler's house in my days of flying the missionary plane. "I won't become an Old China Hand," I had bragged.

"I have two months left," I said. "I'll take Pan Am home."

"If you really go," Norwich said, "make a reservation for me—I'll tag along." Those were his last words to me.

I had met Norwich two years before, in Tsingtao, after the Marine Corps discharged him. He was a navigator who wanted to be a pilot.

His Marine buddies had let him bootleg flying time, so he was a good copilot by the time he joined CAT. Rousselot had said, "He's a Marine, isn't he? He'll make it."

Impressed with Norwich's skill, I asked operations to assign him to me permanently. He flew from the captain's seat while I coached him. Weeks later, after a busy day, I cut off the automatic pitch control of the Curtis electric propellers. He had to control them with manual toggle switches while he approached the runway on instruments. He performed perfectly.

After his landing I said, "A little more experience and you'll be a C-46 captain." We were interrupted by the operations clerk, who brought radiograms. Among other messages, Norwich was scheduled to fly as captain to Tientsin. We looked at each other and laughed. It was the mistake of an overworked scheduler.

"All we gotta do is keep our mouths shut and follow orders and you're checked out," I said. I was on the verge of urging him to become an instant captain. But I said, "You ought to get a little more experience." I'd regret the advice.

After Etta and Mary returned to work I reserved a Pan Am seat. I wanted to go alone, without a guy who hung on my every word, as if I were Lindbergh, when I knew I wasn't.

After two weeks' play in Hong Kong I decided it was time to board Pan Am to America. I stopped at Gingle's on the way. Lewis sat in the inner sanctum.

"It happened in the afternoon," he said. "One of those dust storms that made it dark as night, even though it was day. . . . We heard a Cessna engine and knew Norwich was looking for the airport. He flew over us and kept right on going. . . . The Lanchow beacon was on, but I suppose he couldn't pick it up with that half-ass radio compass. . . .

"An hour later our Chinese staff telephoned villages all over the place until one said yes, a silver plane with two people tried to land and hit the rising terrace of a farm. They were dead."

I put down my drink, because I couldn't swallow. Lewis went on, "There was a rumor about Norwich hesitating to depart Ningsia because of the dust storm, and General Chang insisted on his aide reaching Lanchow for a military powwow. A rumor says the general faked a weather report to make it look good."

When I got to America I headed for New Jersey to see Norwich's sister, and we cried when she brought out portraits of her brother in his Marine Corps uniform. She gave me one and asked, "Why didn't he come home? He told me he was coming home."

"I don't know," I fudged. I knew it would hurt even more if she knew her brother had almost got there, with me. I was relieved in a cowardly way—I had such a good excuse for not telling the entire story. And I took further refuge in telling myself operations might have held him in Lanchow anyway.

I rode the subway back to New York, twisted on the seat, trying to shrink away from myself, and I asked for a room at an apartment hotel where I'd be able to entertain friends in whom I'd find solace, although I sensed I wouldn't have the honesty to tell what gnawed me.

"We're full up," the manager said. "Unless you're willing to take an apartment that's just been painted."

I couldn't believe its cleanliness, and when I saw the living room's parquet floor I told myself I knew luxury when I saw it—until my friends arrived from Connecticut.

"Whatever happened to this room?" Marcia asked.

"What's wrong with it?" I asked.

Wesley said, "If you don't know, we're not telling."

The next day various movers came with carpets, floor lamps, a couple of easy chairs. By late afternoon, when pictures were hung, I began to understand. I had lived in China so long I was accustomed to sparsely furnished rooms.

I got to Wisconsin, convinced I was a dingdong for dallying in China when I could have come home a month sooner. I had been away so long I had forgotten how clean and green and peaceful a place could be.

A letter from China said the northwest had all but fallen, and the Bradleys were transferred to south China and rented a big house in Canton's swank residential district where the diplomats lived. A day before my home leave expired, a subsequent letter said Bradley had been murdered.

Bradley's Death

"I heard the shots but thought it was an automobile backfiring," Rosbert said. "Hours later I found Bradley at my front door, holding his belly. Blood covered his hands."

A European doctor next door, with Rosbert's help, placed Bradley on the backseat of his automobile. Natasia ran from her house and cradled Bradley's head on her lap, and they sped to the hospital.

The police found the servants cowering under the dining-room table. Bradley's English friend lay dead, facedown on a bed. His wounds and three bullets embedded in the blood-spattered wall indicated he had been standing when the bullets struck. Clark, the explorer, lay on the floor, moaning. He fingered a bullet hole in his chest.

The police asked, "Who shot you?

"Don't know." His empty pistol lay on a table nearby. Smudges indicated the fingerprints had been wiped off. Bloody sheets had been bundled and dropped on the floor. Half-filled suitcases littered the room, as if someone had packed in haste.

The first Civil Air Transport (CAT) C-46s, from Hawaii, arrive over Shanghai.

The author with one of the *Saint Paul*'s young guards. "Saint Paul was the first missionary," explained the Reverend Daniel Nelson, "and this is the first missionary airliner."

Author with Claire L. Chennault, the cofounder of CAT and before that the leader of the American Volunteer Group, better known as the Flying Tigers. The CATC airliner in the background is one of the 71 planes Chennault bought with his personal I.O.U. to deny them to Red forces who needed transport for paratroops. A U.S. Senator called it, "One of the first Allied victories of the Cold War."

Bob Rousselot, CAT's chief pilot and eventually vice president of operations, who believed the Marine Corps was too lax. He helped mold a collection of rugged individualists into a disciplined group.

Paul Holden (left) was wounded in the battle of Dien Bien Phu. French Air Force doctors wanted to amputate his arm, but Holden remained awake all night to fend them off. Like a number of CAT pilots, Erik Shilling (right) served during World War II in Chennault's Flying Tigers.

Legendary CAT pilot and bon vivant James McGovern, also known as Earthquake Magoon. In the 75th Fighter ("Tiger Shark") Squadron, 23rd Fighter Group, of Chennault's Fourteenth Air Force during World War II, he shot down two Japanese planes and was credited with seven probables. After crash-landing a CAT plane on a riverbed in Communist China, he was imprisoned and subsequently released, only to die while flying supplies to the besieged French forces at Dien Bien Phu.

Nationalist troops boarding the author's C-46 en route to the fighting in Manchuria. Some looked no older than Boy Scouts.

Author with Norman Schwartz (left) who, with Bob Snoddy, was shot down while attempting to snatch a spy out of Manchuria during the Korean War. He was awarded (posthumously) the Distinguished Intelligence Cross.

A CAT C-46 flies over a walled village during a bleak northern China winter.

Bob Snoddy (left) and John Dexheimer. Betrayed by a double agent in the Korean War, Snoddy was shot down and died while attempting to snatch a spy out of Manchuria.

Nationalist troops and curious villagers on the Gobi Desert.

The author in Lanchow with Governor Ma Pu-fang, who is accepting the first air mail from Hsining (Xining). Warlord Ma was a direct descendent of Arab mercenaries who had come to China with crossbows more than a thousand years earlier.

CAT pilot Bob Buol and his wife, Sue, before his imprisonment in Communist China. Piece by piece, over several months, Buol stole colored yarn from his captors' wash lines and secretly knitted an American flag. Sue battled five years for his release. He died eight months after he left prison. *Courtesy of Sue (Buol) Hacker*

The author with Walter Morse, the Rebel Monk. Upon reaching retirement age, the Episcopal medical missionary refused to return to America. He remained in Taiwan where laborers, without pay, built him a cabin on land donated by Catholics. Presbyterians let him use their church, and a Tao priest relinquished part of his temple for the monk's soup kitchen and clinic. Madame Chiang Kai-shek supplied funds from her Methodist church.

The author in a DC-4, 1955.

Hugh Hicks, CAT's assistant chief pilot, and son. Although he was a trainee on CAT's latest jet and Taipei's instrument landing system was faulty, he unnecessarily shouldered the entire blame for CAT's last crash. With uncommon nobility, he stuck to the code of aviation's pioneers. *Courtesy of the Hicks Family*

The servants said the deceased Englishman, Bradley's best friend, had been en route to Hong Kong. And Clark had been a houseguest for weeks, writing an account of his search for the highest mountain.

Maya said, "I don't know what happened. It was our wedding anniversary, and I drank too much." Asked whom she suspected, she said, "I think our gardener did it. He's a very unreliable fellow."

The police put Clark in jail. Interviewed by newsman Spencer Moosa, he said only, "Bradley pulled a jealous act."

Conscious for brief periods, Bradley lay in the Feng Pin Hospital with two bullet wounds in his intestines. When Spencer Moosa asked who shot him, Bradley didn't answer. Tears welled in his eyes. He died.

The European doctor said, "I knew Bradley during the war, in Chungking, when I was in the Fourteenth Air Force and he was a supply officer—a good man.

"And I knew Natasia, even before she met Bradley. Her father was a wealthy merchant in Warsaw until the Russians kicked them out of Poland—exiled them to Siberia.

"Natasia's mother and father died there. Her brother got out of the internment camp by joining the Soviet Army. Natasia was alone."

The doctor looked torn, but he continued. "Somehow, Natasia got to Manchuria, found a job in a Russian nightclub in Port Arthur. She made her way to Chungking, where she met Bradley. . . ." It was the most anyone heard.

At Bradley's funeral, Natasia, in a black dress and veil, kissed the coffin and swooned onto the floor of the church, and when smelling salts revived her she called his name.

Only a few days later, in Kunming, I attended Maya's party at the Metropole Hotel. Paper lanterns swung above long tables in the courtyard. Gorgeous in a flowery dress, Natasia greeted me cordially. Rosbert and Lil and Buol were there, with Chinese and American crews; and Jawbert, our Costa Rican mechanic; Braga, our Portuguese traffic manager; Russian barmaids who had migrated from Mukden to Peiping, Tsingtao, Shanghai, Canton, Kunming; demure American wives, fresh from the USA; Peppi Paunzen, our Austrian public relations manager. We had taken Peppi's mother— recently arrived from Vienna—into our pilots' hostel because she had nowhere to stay, and now we plotted for some humane way to evict Mama Paunzen, because her snoring rattled the thin walls.

As platters of food and carafes of wine passed up and down the tables, the cacophony became deafening. Natasia stood up, rapped her spoon against a wineglass, and called, "Quiet, everybody, I want to propose a toast." Holding her glass aloft, she said shrilly, "Here's to the biggest crook in China—Bradley."

There was a moment of silent surprise. Even the Russian barmaids were stunned, but not for long. The bash got raucous again.

The biggest crook in China? It was not a defamation; it was a joking, shrill cry of bravado, I thought. Her eyes told me so. A shield
against her world. Warsaw, Siberia, Port Arthur, Chungking, and
the air raids. I sensed loneliness within a gregarious cloak. Visions
of Benedictine monks befriended. Orphans mothered. Warlords captivated by the banter of an enigmatic charmer. Suddenly, the party
didn't seem like fun anymore. I looked around and remembered a
story from long ago, "The Outcasts of Poker Flat."

When the Communists reached Canton's doorstep, American consular officials persuaded the police to release Clark, who hightailed
it to the USA and never again saw Natasia.

Natasia, the survivor, found a government job in Washington.

"On home leave," Lewis said, "I visited Natasia in her apartment.
She's with the Department of Agriculture, I think. Maybe advising
farmers how to grow Lanchow melons. She's beautiful as ever. . . .
We talked, some, of the northwest."

We lost track of Natasia. What a splash she'd make at our
reunions! Forever, she'd remain a fascinating mystery.

The morning after Maya's party, Rousselot summoned me to
Hong Kong. What had I done wrong? The tasteless party? A summons from the chief had a way of inducing that reaction.

My boss surprised me by asking, "How'd you like to be Hong
Kong's station manager?

"If it's temporary. I like flying."

"Until we get the bullion out. We've got a contract to move all the
silver out of China. We'll fly it to Hong Kong. We need someone who
can get along with the Brits."

7

Hong Kong Capers

A few miles off the South China coast a mountain poked its summit out of the sea, grew a coat of shrubbery and vines, and acquired a name—Hong Kong. It means Fragrant Harbor. A prize of the Opium War, it enlarged the British Empire by thirty-two square miles. The precipitating incident had some resemblance to the Boston Tea Party.

Little more than a hundred years before I first saw the island, silk and tea flowed into Britain while the empire's silver flowed out in payment. To reverse the imbalance, merchant ships of King George IV inundated China with India's opium. Calling it "foreign mud," the Manchu emperor dispatched Commissioner Lin to south China to confront the English merchants. "How dare you bring your vile opium into China, cheating and harming our people," he harangued, while his men destroyed six million dollars' worth of opium.

King George responded with warships that bombarded China's coastal cities until the Manchu emperor signed the Treaty of Nanking, which awarded the British Empire, among other things, the island of Hong Kong.

English and Scottish engineers blasted its granite and bossed Chinese laborers who built freshwater reservoirs, docks, roads, trading houses, banks, churches, bowling greens, a racetrack, and a courthouse.

The British established a ferry service to the mainland, leased 360 square miles of the Chinese continent, and called it "the New Territories" and "Kowloon." Mountains on its shore were dynamited flat and became Kaitak Airport.

Decades later, the airport's authorities leased an operations office to CAT.

I stood on the balcony of my airport office and looked a mile north, inland, at Lion Head Mountain, while the same cumulus

147

cloud danced around the head, changed form, vanished, and regenerated.

To the south, Hong Kong harbor was different every time I looked. An aircraft carrier or nest of destroyers, anchored in deep water, replaced a rusty freighter or white cruise ship. High-pooped junks with cinnamon-colored sails tacked in between. Water taxis hustled.

Beyond the frenetic harbor I saw the island of Hong Kong with its typhoon shelter, modern office buildings, and aged warehouses that once stored tea. Halfway up the mountain, grand villas overlooked the harbor. Rising above it all, Victoria Peak stood proud as the British Empire, green as jade.

The energy and ingenuity of the Chinese, along with the integrity of the British police and the stability of the courts, made the British colony prosperous. I seldom met anyone who didn't like this best of two worlds.

Immaculate ferryboats provided a pleasant interlude for businessmen who commuted between Hong Kong and Kowloon. Predominantly Chinese, interspersed with traders from the rest of the world, most of them wore seersucker suits, carried briefcases, and looked purposeful, although no one appeared to be under pressure.

Willauer bought a PT boat that had been converted from a high-speed submarine chaser to a luxurious yacht, and he hired a Chinese crew "to evacuate the Hong Kong staff in case the Commies take over." He kept the crew proficient by operating open-house cruises on Sundays. On weekdays any employee could use the yacht and sign chits for refreshments from the galley or bar, although the company seldom billed us.

Earthquake and I spent a therapeutic morning on deck, sleeping our hangovers away while the Chinese skipper circumnavigated Hong Kong. I suppose he was miffed because his only two passengers didn't ooh and ah at the sights his skills provided. Sue Buol, Chennault's secretary, telephoned the next day. "The captain reported you. He was too angry to speak coherently—what did you guys do?"

"More peaceful passengers he's never seen."

"Oh yeah? We know you and Earthquake!"

I got off the hook after I became the hero of a news item invented by our director of public relations. "The Brits are nuts about sagas of the sea," he gloated. His press release, publicizing CAT's navy, began with the first voyage of the LST that carried our heavy maintenance equipment from Shanghai to Canton: "CAT pilot navigates LST, snatches supplies from Communists. . . ."

"I didn't," I objected.

Our public relations chief scolded, "What kind of loyalty is this? Don't you care about CAT's image? We need all the exposure we can get. Don't be so damn naive."

After going along with the scam I discovered I had only to keep mum while recanters magnified and distorted the tale. I began to enjoy them, and eventually I believed them; and then I knew how pretenders evolve.

Even General Chennault wanted to believe it. When Poop Deck Gordon, a former lieutenant in the Royal Navy, said, "Your pilot didn't know what he was doing when he brought the vessel down the China Coast," Chennault replied, "He got it here, didn't he?"

Poop Deck Gordon was a salty, swarthy martinet of Captain Bligh's ilk who had been hired to command our ship. Months later he became the hero of a more dramatic saga that occurred after he resigned from CAT's navy. He found more lucrative employment skippering Red China's freighters up and down the China coast.

Chiang Kai-shek's navy captured his ship and herded it to Taiwan, where the Chinese crew was imprisoned. Captain Poop Deck Gordon and his Scottish chief engineer, however, were allowed to remain aboard the freighter, under house arrest, so to speak.

A few nights later, they stole their ship and sailed it to Hong Kong. Only the sea-minded British could appreciate the feat. The chief engineer ran the engine room single-handed, while Poop Deck threw off the mooring hawsers and manned the wheel and navigated the several-day trip to Hong Kong.

Lloyd's of London, the ship's insurer, gave the pair a generous bonus and made Captain Gordon a nautical surveyor. The bonus financed Captain Gordon's parties at the fashionable Peninsula Hotel, which I usually attended. Twenty or more of Hong Kong's bons vivants gathered to feast and drink and toast "Captain Gordon" and sing "For He's a Jolly Good Fellow," until the big spender's money ran out, and then he was Poop Deck again.

Hong Kong seemed more stable after I brought Cheong, my house manager, and his twelve-year-old son and amah to the seaport. Cheong endured a spell of culture shock. He looked disdainfully at tradesmen who appeared and spoke their staccato dialect. "South China people talk too loud, argue too much, no talk Mandarin," Cheong complained.

I also saw a cultural difference when an English resident warned, "Caucasian women will ostracize you if you're seen with Orientals." To me, one of the colony's beautiful sights was the sophisticated Chinese women in finely tailored, form-fitting cheongsams, with split skirts. They walked with a supple grace; straight postures contributed to their elegance; and when I saw Mei Ling at a party I asked someone to introduce us.

Mei Ling had a way of smiling demurely, and then abandoning shyness briefly to look straight into my eyes, boldly, it seemed; and then she'd cast her eyes down again. Her musical voice carried a soft burr that accompanies those who speak Mandarin. Even in blue jeans she looked exotic. We visited a shipyard where junks were built with the same techniques used centuries ago. Timbers were hand-shaped with an adze. Other tools, more complicated but age-old, such as stringed bows that would drill holes, were still used. Chinese are innately sociable, and it amused Mei Ling to interpret when I talked with the shipwrights.

In the evening she was enchanting in her jade-green dress, with thighs like satin showing through the peekaboo skirt. We'd walk to the Star Ferry landing and ride a *walla-walla* (water taxi) to Hong Kong Island to be ushered up stone steps to a seaside cabaret, or go farther to a picturesque cove called Aberdeen, where ornate floating restaurants mingled with oceangoing junks. Aboard a lavish restaurant, we leaned over a varnished rail, watched live fish in a huge trap, and pointed to the one we wanted. It was netted, steamed, and soon appeared on a platter with scallions and fresh ginger.

Before long I worked continuously, dispatched planes and crews, accepted silver bullion brought from China, conferred with British police and customs. Without time for a social life, I lost Mei Ling to the very Englishman who had advised me to shun Chinese women. Instead of loss, I felt liberated. As in my last day in Manchuria, I faced myself squarely and realized I still wanted freedom to visit the keepsake in a chamber of my heart as if it were a shrine. The unique woman I had known before I came to China—the eternity in the moment we shared—was it a magic-carpet flight to unreality or a journey to sanity? Would it haunt me forever? I wondered.

In addition to bringing silver to Hong Kong, pilots flew our precious maintenance equipment and spare parts to the safety of Hainan Island, which lies between south China's Luichow Peninsula and Vietnam's Gulf of Tonkin. The size of Vermont and Massachusetts combined, the island had been a Japanese submarine base during the big war.

Every department had its pressures. Hainan Island's makeshift coffee-can flares didn't flame long enough for the all-night operation. "Send flare pots," they radiogrammed.

"Buy good runway flare pots," I told supply.

"They weren't budgeted. Besides that, we're broke. We'll have them made locally." A couple of days later the supply chief showed me a sample pot. "How many shall we order?"

"None. I'll test this first."

"You're a pain in the ass."

During a hurried lunch I lit the wick. The heat melted the solder on the seams, and it fell apart. Carrying the pieces to supply, I said, "Order good ones, dammit."

Although I was steeped in work, I missed Mei Ling's cheerful company. A minor compensation was the excitement of being in a position to observe the workings of intrigue. . . .

While CAT carried silver bullion to Hong Kong, the Chinese Air Force and Navy moved China's gold to Taiwan.

Chiang Kai-shek made Taiwan the seat of the Kuomintang Party, which he continued to rule even though he had resigned the presidency of China.

Vice President Li Tsung-jen remained on the mainland with a new title—acting president of China. Grand as the title was, the money wasn't. Chiang Kai-shek didn't leave enough to run the government.

The acting president couldn't even pay the soldiers who were expected to defend the Nationalist's turf. My Chinese friends said, "We feel sorry for Li. We call it *wu shi wu ming* (responsibility without power)."

Disheartened, and fearing that Chiang might have him murdered, Li resigned and emigrated to the USA.

The Executive Yuan elected Governor Yen Hsi-shan prime minister. CAT's old warlord friend now headed China, although Chiang Kai-shek continued to pull the strings.

CAT's headquarters, now in Hong Kong, didn't have direct contact with its airplanes. The British government ruled that operational messages must filter through its system. All other messages, including passenger and cargo reservations, were transmitted via a commercial company, Cable and Wireless, Ltd. Willauer grumbled, "It's easier to cope with the disarray of China than the red tape of England." We thought of installing a radio station on a junk in international waters and motorboating messages to the airport.

My staff, in place before I arrived, included a cargo and passenger manager, a message center chief, a New Zealand secretary, a young errand boy, and an operations manager with two assistants.

Ramsey, the operations manager, was an energetic, skinny American with a sheaf of blond hair that stuck forward. His nose was sharp. Even his chin was pointed. John "the Heimer" Dexheimer called him "Ratchet Head," and Ramsey retorted in a brassy voice. He believed pilots were his adversaries. He even shouted into the wind at Royal Air Force Spitfire pilots while they fought against ground loops in gusty crosswinds on Hong Kong's runways. He himself never had flown an airplane. I occasionally caught Ratchet Head, like a used-car salesman, pressuring pilots who balked at an overload or engine malfunction, or if a thunder-head threatened a runway. "Don't ever pressure a pilot," I warned.

Astonished, he said, "You mean I'm supposed to say, 'There's the airplane, take it or leave it, whichever you want'?"

"That's it exactly. Don't manipulate a pilot's judgment. It's fragile. When he appraises a situation, his brain integrates past experience even though he's forgotten it. Call it sixth sense or whatever you like, but don't tamper with it. Pilots don't hang back without a reason. They more often bust the minimums."

Ramsey shook his head in disbelief.

I should have fired him, but we were short of help, so I decided to monitor our departures.

After a couple of months there came a rare time when our last plane left at noon, and the few inbounds were slated to remain overnight. I went home and slept all afternoon and most of the night.

It was a rest I'd regret.

Earthquake Missing

When I got to Kaitak Airport in the morning, Ramsey said, "Bad news. Earthquake is down."

"Where?" My guts cramped.

"Nobody knows. Departed for Kunming at five P.M. yesterday."

"Nothing was scheduled yesterday afternoon."

"Yeah, but he got in from Kunming about four, and immigration wouldn't admit his passenger. Had to fly her back to Kunming."

"You dispatched a crew that'd been flying all day? To Kunming? Five hours over Communist territory? At night? No nav aids, a weak beacon at Kunming—you sent him out?"

"Immigration said we had to take her back immediately. What else could I do?"

"Tell them the airplane was sick, anything, refuse to dispatch it. They'd detain the passenger in quarantine."

"She had a Hong Kong visa, issued in Kunming."

"Why wouldn't they admit her?"

"Wouldn't tell. She's White Russian, wife of Central Air's Liuchow station manager. Her baby was with her."

"Her baby? How the hell could they send a mother and baby back into Kunming? Goddammit, they know it's going to fall. If they'd—"

The Teletype clattered. I leaped across the room. XT-812 LANDED ON BEACH NEAR HAIKOW 0340, RADIO COMPASS OUT. IN AIR 9 HOURS.

Cockrell was boarding our DC-4, going to Kunming.

"Wait," I hollered.

Cockrell watched me walk my dividers across a chart. Haikow, a fishing village on Hainan Island, lay ninety miles south of his course to Kunming. "Twenty-seven minutes' extra flying," Cockrell said. I nodded. That's all he needed.

The Teletype clattered again. ALERT AIR TRAFFIC CONTROL AND ALL SHIPS NEAR HAINAN ISLAND. XT-812 LANDED ON SANDBAR NEAR COAST NEAR HAINAN ISLAND BUT POSSIBLY ON CHINA COAST. RELAY ANY INFORMATION.

I ran the message to the chief of air traffic control, a stern, stiff-backed man with a Hitler mustache. His name was Hewson. Eyeing me coldly, he clipped, "I'll handle it."

Back at my office, I told Ramsey, "Hewson will launch a search. Keep your eye on the RAF flying boats."

I hurried to Hong Kong's air traffic control center, where a civilian and a Royal Air Force flight leader sat at a lofty desk high above a massive table that depicted the South China Sea and all its coastlines and islands. Model ships and planes, pushed by clerks with croupier sticks, progressed across the table, according to their position reports. A box stored other models, including replicas of Royal Air Force Sunderland flying boats. Nobody put a flying boat on the table.

I returned to Hewson's office. He looked annoyed, but he always looked annoyed. I asked, "What happened to the search?"

"I must refer this to our DCA [director of civil aviation]."

"When?"

Looking as if he had just stepped in a glob of dog dung, Hewson replied, "In due course."

I said, "We've declared an emergency!" His Hitler mustache twitched.

I gave him thirty more minutes and returned; he was out.

I hurried back to the air traffic control center, where the toy ships and planes plied across the table. The search-and-rescue planes were still in the box.

Looking up at the civilian and the RAF duty officer, I said, "A few weeks ago one of our planes landed with a bad radio and didn't send an arrival message. You gentlemen complained—you said you had almost dispatched a search-and-rescue unit."

The pair stared at me.

"What search and rescue did you have in mind?"

The civilian controller tilted his nose while his eyes remained on my face. "Exactly where is your aircraft, this eight-one-two?"

"If I knew exactly, I wouldn't be asking for a search."

"If you don't know where your aircraft is, how do you know it's in our FIR [flight information region]?"

"We have reason to believe it. The SOS states it's near Hainan Island."

"We aren't allowed to cover inland China."

I lost my peripheral vision. I saw only the two men. "Hainan Island is not inland. Cathay Pacific flies over it every day on its way to Bangkok and Saigon. The SOS indicates it might be on the coast; that's within your FIR. You signed the agreement at the ICAO Conference in Montreal." I felt the hairs at the back of my neck rise. "You've played some kind of game long enough," I shouted. "There's a lost plane out there! I demand a search!"

Calmly turning to the RAF officer, the controller said, "Do you chaps know anything about this?

"We have a Sunderland boat ready to go, but it was my understanding that CAT's DC-4 was searching."

"If our plane searches," I said, "does that relieve you of your responsibility?"

"How do you know we won't be fired upon by the Nationalists?"

That was it. He'd tipped his hand. Britain had recognized China's new regime. It was the Nationalists they feared. In their haste to recognize Red China they had overlooked their search-and-rescue obligation. They hadn't resolved it with either regime.

I sent, urgently, to our liaison with the CAF: NEED ASSURANCE THAT RAF SUNDERLAND FLYING BOAT CAN SEARCH HAINAN ISLAND AND CHINA COAST UNMOLESTED.

As if the balky Brits weren't trouble enough, CAT's chief of flight operations walked in. This time Buol didn't have his debonair grin. "What the idea of sending a four-engine airplane on a search mission?"

"Not strictly a search mission," I said. "It's going to Kunming. Hell, it's only twenty-seven minutes out of the way. We fly farther than that around thunderstorms."

Buol frowned, shook his head, and walked out. Twenty minutes later he telephoned from Chennault's house. His voice was abrupt. "There will be no more search missions with CAT planes," Buol said. *Bang*, he hung up.

I needed fresh air; I wanted the company of pilots. I walked to the airport's Dairy Farm Restaurant. Many of our pilots gathered.

"The bastards wouldn't donate twenty-seven minutes' flying time to a passenger with a baby," I said.

"One of us goes down and they don't give a damn."

"All the dough CAT made by us getting shot at, and they won't even look for us."

"Aw, hell," Plank said. "Calm down. Everybody knows this is a blood-money outfit."

Almost unobserved, our flight surgeon listened. I turned to him and said, "How can we ask these guys to fly if we don't even look?"

He stood. "Don't go away," he said. His six-foot-two frame disappeared beyond the restaurant door.

Our flight surgeon had been Chennault's comrade in arms during the rough days of the Flying Tigers and then chief medic for the Fourteenth Air Force. In CAT, he was the epitome of a retired colonel. Dignified, with courtly drawing-room manners and a gentle bass voice with a Texas drawl, he purred to bejeweled women at lofty social affairs. Even his name was patrician. It was Thomas Gentry.

He was back within the hour. "Dispatch two C-47s on a search. List me on the manifest, and get me a parachute."

I didn't have to ask what had happened; I knew. Doc Gentry had gone to Chennault's house to say, in his calm drawl, "So what if a search is fruitless? What about the morale?"

Doc Gentry and I walked in silence to the RAF hangar. The officers seemed relieved to hear we'd operate our own search. They gave us all the rescue equipment we wanted.

The enlisted men were more congenial than the adenoidal fops in the air traffic control center. "Here's a special canister for your surgeon's medical kit. . . . We filled others with supplies. . . . Here's the inventory, sir. . . ." I read sleeping bags, mosquito nets, insect repellent, signal mirrors, fishing tackle, electric torches, gauze bandages, splints, morphine. . . . The young Englishmen rigged each canister with a parachute and helped us load them on our two C-47s while our cargo handlers stowed bundles of leaflets from a local printer: *Reward—gold bars—for information about silver airplane number XT-812 and crew.* It was printed in Chinese, Burmese, and Thai.

It wasn't difficult to find crewmen for the search, because off-duty pilots had gathered at the airport. During the refueling delay, Doc Gentry and I walked to the Dairy Farm Restaurant. The other guys came along, and more gathered.

Quiet, as in church, the gang sat around our table. There's a special time, waiting for a friend to depart on a dangerous trip, when you feel close and companionable without either of you speaking a word. The special silence of the pilots was a tribute to the Texas doctor. We were seeing, for the first time, the real Gentry. Until now we had assumed he was a social lion who belonged to the head office. But now that the chips were down, he showed up in a bush jacket, ready to bail out of a C-47, anywhere, to patch up Earthquake and his passengers and crew.

Buol somehow wound up on the other side of him, and I pretended not to listen when Gentry quietly told him, "The guys think you're harsh. You've got your reasons, but they're entitled to their feelings. . . . This airline won't last forever. When it's over, you'll want some friends." I looked out the tail of my eye and saw Buol nod. By God, I thought, there's hope for the cocky guy yet.

When the planes were ready and the crews boarded, Doc Gentry grinned, stuck out his hand. "See ya," he said.

The planes returned late that night after searching all the way to the French Indochina border. "No luck," they said. We printed extra leaflets, in all the languages of Southeast Asia. The crews shoved them out during their Kunming trips.

I couldn't sleep . . . take a nap and Earthquake goes down. Had I been at the airport he wouldn't have left Hong Kong. Mrs. Liu and her baby and Earthquake and Chang and Lay wouldn't be injured or dead or captured, or whatever happened to them. . . .

A week later, copilot Tang gave me a wad of paper the size of my thumbnail. "A stranger gave me this," he said. "He made me promise not to tell where I saw him or what he looked like." A page from a small notebook, it was penciled with the number of Earthquake's plane and a latitude and longitude. Tang and I looked at the chart on my wall. The coordinates put it eighty-five miles north of the coast, near a village called Yulin.

Brongensur and his crew, scheduled for Kunming, dog-legged over Yulin. An hour and a half later we got their message: XT-812 ON BELLY ON SANDBAR. NO APPARENT DAMAGE. NO SIGN OF PASSENGERS OR CREW.

Several days later I found another wad of paper on my desk. A note in Earthquake's writing. *Sorry about the plane. ADF [radio compass] out. Landed on sandbar near Yulin. Everybody safe. Reds released Mrs. Liu and baby. Lay and Chang escaped. Reds moving me.*

The Pirate

The sign over the cafe near Hong Kong's Star Ferry announced "E. F. Gingle, Proprietor." Rattan chairs at tables with white cloths were occupied by homesick American tourists and English families who liked the American lettuce and celery that had somehow found a way from the galleys of American President Lines ships, and they savored the chili made by Gingle himself.

An archway marked PRIVATE led to a back room that was a gallery of photographs of Gingle in his U.S. Navy chief's uniform; Hong Kong water policemen standing at their deck guns; CAT pilots at their airplanes; a framed prayer, "Oh Lord, help me keep my damn nose out of other people's business." The room was furnished with a conference table and captain's chairs. An oversized teak chair at the head of the table was Gingle's throne.

I had learned why Gingle weighed three hundred pounds when I saw the gnome-headed giant, on many an occasion, grasp a beer with a hand so big it hid the can. He tilted his skinhead back, opened his mouth like a newly hatched sparrow, and dumped the entire contents down his throat without gulping.

His courtiers were Tiny Tommy, toothless beer nurser and spitting image of Snow White's dwarf, Grumpy, with a fouled anchor tattooed on the back of his hand; blissful Red Sammon, with a permanent foggy smile, sparse hair that matched his name, and Popeye forearms bearing the indelible USN; and Art Herick, a taciturn master sergeant, U.S. Marine Corps, retired. No others were admitted to the inner sanctum except water policemen, CAT pilots, and mechanics.

Gingle pounded his cane on the floor and raised his beer toward the portrait of Earthquake—a photograph as large as a poster. It hung above all the other pictures. From the exalted place, Earthquake's image scowled out of its frame. The mustache and goatee were prominent, but nothing like the black eyebrows that spread across his forehead like inverted gull wings and reached the sides of his head, which was topped with a leather helmet and goggles.

Beer can aloft, Gingle bellowed, "Here's to Jim McGovern, may he walk in here damn soon."

"To Earthquake Magoon," said the CAT guys.

"Hear hear," said the water policemen.

I remained silent, wrapped in memory, reliving the instant I had snapped the photograph—the day Earthquake Magoon moved into our house in Tsingtao, where he emptied his footlocker and found his old fighter pilot helmet and goggles, and I held up my camera and said, "Make like you're looking for Japs."

And now that scowl was on Gingle's wall; Earthquake's C-46 was on its belly, out of fuel on a sandbar in some Chinese river; and his indestructible hulk was undoubtedly alive and kicking, albeit imprisoned somewhere in Red China.

Water policeman Dudman beckoned me to the isolated end of the table. "I believe I can help you get your friend out," he said. "I happen to know the chief of the pirates in these waters. His organization has wireless contact with the entire bloody mainland. If anyone can find your friend, he can. Can get 'im out, too. The kind of bloke who'll dynamite a prison wall if the price is right."

"I'm ready. Right now."

"May I suggest a go-between? . . . I know a Jesuit priest, Father Zeller, a Belgian. . . . We'll be here tomorrow."

Gingle stopped me at the door to Nathan Road and gave me a brown envelope. "Take this," he said. "Use it all if you have to. Just get Jim out."

When I got home I sat in our red leather chair and opened Gingle's envelope and found a letter of credit for sixty thousand dollars—half a million in today's buying power—everything he had, I guessed. Gingle had put his entire fortune into my hands. I recalled the day Gingle hobbled into the inner sanctum, after his heart attack, when his cane was brand-new:

Everyone's eyes focus on that damn walking stick. It symbolizes Gingle's infirmity. He eases painfully onto his teakwood throne and slams the cane on the table—*bam*. Head down, he stares at the floor.

Earthquake leaps up, snatches the cane, turns it into a billiard cue. Pursing his lips, he jabs at an imaginary ball, circles the table, shoves us out of the way to take aim. Yelps, grunts, curses with theatrical gestures, conjures images of flubs, near misses, successes. Gingle's belly shakes. We jabber again.

I'm in the Nathan Hotel bar, where we had agreed to meet. I look out the window. Earthquake is outside, talking to a beggar. Gesturing flamboyantly, they're oblivious to pedestrians' stares. Earthquake presses a wad of money into the beggar's hand, walks in, bellies up to the bar.

"One of your buddies?"

"When the Japs took Hong Kong, he wouldn't tell 'em where the Limey artillery was. They cut out his tongue."

"What was all the conversation?"

"I told him to get over to Mohan the tailor man for the second fitting of his suit."

We're in our living room, clowning around like a couple of school kids. Television hasn't reached Hong Kong, but Earthquake calls our windows a TV. He puts a flagon of cognac and a quart of milk at his end of the table, a fifth of scotch at my end. "Come on, it's time to watch TV." We lean on the windowsill and gawk at pickpockets and cops. Two old women push a cart that's stacked high with bamboo baskets of squealing pigs. Younger women wear clinging cheongsams.

"Absolutely beeeyootiful."

"Those split skirts."

"I can almost see Honolulu."

"New Jersey was never like this."

"Wisconsin either."

The street scenes lull. We give our attention to the Wan Fook Construction Company across the street, where bamboo scaffolding surrounds a budding high-rise. Baskets of bricks and mortar rise to the top with ropes and pulleys. Woman after woman scampers up the jackstraw scaffolding to grab a rope and step into space while the weight of her body, in its descent, hoists the building supplies. Earthquake growls, "Wait till they send up an empty basket."

Two or three hours have passed. Much of his cognac is gone, but my scotch is barely below the Plimsoll mark.

Next morning, I'm holding my head and yowling, "Cheong, bring the aspirin."

Earthquake's shouting, "I do the drinking and Smith gets the hangovers."

Cheong came into the living room and drew the curtains—his nightly ritual. I must have dozed off. Gingle's sixty-thousand-dollar document, the stuff that'd break Earthquake out of prison, was on the floor. Cheong picked it up. "Are you all right, master?"

"Yes, Cheong, go to bed."

The next night, in Gingle's, water policeman Dudman told me, "The pirate chief is reluctant to meet you. Thinks Yanks are too nosy about Hong Kong and China."

I understood. America had induced the British to join an embargo on Red China, but Britain's Asian colony silently reneged. Its economy depended on trade with Red China. Its water reservoirs dried up during droughts; water was piped from Canton. It was unwise to annoy the Red Dragon. Although British customs officers guarded Hong Kong's overt borders assiduously, they ignored smugglers who plied its inlets and bays and sailed up the Pearl River to Canton; and the British further ensured the flow of commerce by siccing their water police onto renegade hijackers who plundered the bona fide smugglers.

"I have no interest in politics or police," I said. "I just want to get Earthquake out."

A couple of nights later I walked into Gingle's inner sanctum and found Dudman and the Belgian priest sipping scotch and water. We talked about China. "I loved to see the snow lee-o-pards," said Father Zeller. He dug through a white cassock underneath his black cape and pulled out a watch. "We shall go now."

In silence, we walked a few blocks to a room at the Miramar Hotel, and Father Zeller knocked. Never had a door opened so slowly.

I was astonished. My eyes swept from the man's impeccably groomed hair, past his dour face, starched shirt, paisley tie, and pinstriped blue suit to gleaming black shoes. Maybe I expected a swashbuckler in sea boots or someone out of an Errol Flynn movie. The fastidious man before me looked like the president of a bank.

Although he asked us to sit down, he omitted the customary tea. I saw no baggage. He waited for me to speak.

"I have long admired the Chinese respect for friendship," I said and waited for Father Zeller to translate it. The pirate chief sat stiff. His face was a mask. "I want to see my friend safe in Hong Kong. I have no other interest."

The chief maintained stoic silence. I've seen poker players, I thought, but this dude is a master par excellence. Without moving a muscle of his face or shedding a drop of sweat, he could signal his men to cut a throat or blast a prison wall.

I looked at his silk tie, at the pleats on the window drapes, at the fold on the bedspread, at Father Zeller.

It was I who broke the silence. "Please excuse me for mentioning money. But you will bear expenses. It is only right that I reimburse you." More silence. "You would be doing me a kindness if you could advise the approximate cost. I must make plans to gather the money."

The chief finally spoke. I caught a few words, but Father Zeller's translation made it clear. "It depends upon the circumstances. If your friend is under house arrest, the cost would be low. Ten thousand American dollars, perhaps. But if he is in a proper prison it will be considerably higher." I nodded and waited. "I will discover the whereabouts of your friend. I will let you know."

I thanked him. Father Zeller stood, and so did I. With no further comment, his face still stony, the gentleman pirate closed the door quietly.

A short cab ride later I was outside Chennault's house near the airport. When I walked up to his door my new shoes were weightless. I was almost airborne. I wouldn't mention Gingle's money. Escape funds should be on the company.

Chennault listened intently while his expressive brown eyes, deep in their sockets, reacted to everything I said. When I finished my tale of the water policeman, the missionary go-between, and the dour pirate, Chennault answered in a voice more gentle than I'd ever heard from him.

"Felix, it's best if we wait. There're no secrets in China, as you know. We'll eventually find out where he is. The smugglers can free him. They'll hide him under the floorboards of a river boat, but if a Communist patrol boat comes their way they'll stick a knife between his ribs and throw him overboard—destroy the evidence—like American slavers years ago when they saw revenue cutters on the horizon." Chennault again seemed like a teacher. "McGovern is safe where he is. The Chinese will let him go, eventually."

I left Chennault's house in shoes that weighed twenty pounds. Oblivious to traffic, I quickly walked street after dark street toward our Cameron Road flat, cursing out loud, "Cheap-ass company . . . Big business . . . Who the hell needs a history lesson? . . . Blood-money outfit . . . Another pilot written off . . . We're expendable." I reached in my pocket, felt Gingle's letter of credit. "Our ace in the hole, Earthquake."

The hour's walk in the night cooled my head. By the time I got home my faith had returned. Chennault's knowledge of China was damn near mystic, I admitted.

I returned Gingle's letter of credit.

The Defection

I fidgeted on the deck of the Star Ferry while it maneuvered like a water bug at its own speed through harbor traffic. It was slow, and Hong Kong harbor had lost its beauty. These crossings usually dazzled me with the panorama of Victoria Peak, lush green, rising out of blue water, and the white luxury liners and junks with cinnamon sails. But this time I had tunnel vision. I saw only tramp steamers, outbound, with the five-star flag of Red China snapping in the wind.

I had found out less than an hour ago, after a taxi dropped me at the airport gate. Groups of people talked earnestly. *Time* magazine's John Mecklin strode over to ask, "What's going on?"

"I don't know. I just got here."

"Bullshit."

I dashed to my operations office, wondering what next. Mao Tse-tung's Communists had captured everything north of the Yangtze, plus Shanghai and then some. Southern cities were falling, one by one.

I heard the telex clattering before I got through the door. It said our own airplanes were operating normally, but twelve belonging to China's other two airlines—China National and Central Air—were making a beeline for Peiping, the Communist capital, now once again Peking (Beijing). They were rubbing it in by openly broadcasting their estimated arrival times and the names of the company officers on board.

I looked out the window and saw mechanics swarming over the remaining planes, preparing them for flight. The combined fleets of the defecting airlines totaled eighty-three planes. Twelve were airborne, headed for Red China, and the remaining seventy-one still on the ground—Convair 440s, DC-4s, DC-3s, C-46s—were going to follow.

The telephone jangled, and Sue told me to come to Chennault's office on Hong Kong Island.

It took some elbowing, but I was the first passenger off the Star Ferry.

As soon as I walked into the head office I saw Sue, charming as ever. She ushered me into Chennault's office.

"We have to find a way to keep the rest of those planes grounded," he said. "What's happening at the airport?"

"Their mechanics are preparing them for flight."

"The Communists have been training paratroops. They asked the Russians for transports but didn't get them. Twelve planes won't do 'em much good, but eighty will. Taiwan is vulnerable. The Chinese consul canceled the registration certificates. The planes can't fly legally. Let me know if any leave."

A couple of CAT lawyers walked in with sheaves of papers. As I walked out, Chennault said, "Set up a flight for tomorrow morning—I'm going to Taipei."

On my way back to the Star Ferry I thought of the things we had accomplished in the last three years with a lean staff and shoestring financing. China National, supported by Pan American, was the elite airline, with plush planes and prime passenger routes. The second airline, Central Air, was backed by wealthy businessmen. And now these two venerable ones turned their backs on Chiang Kai-shek, while CAT, the orphan, remained loyal.

William Bond, the father of China National, wrote to Pan Am, "I had not the least suspicion that this defection was planned, but I dislike to be even close to such a double cross. As you know, I am convinced that the Nationalist government is finished and should be. I have served them to the best of my ability and I owe them nothing. But I would not have been a party to this defection. . . ."

When I eventually read Bond's words—"the Nationalist government is finished *and should be*"—I believed I saw the key to CAT's exceptional morale during the past difficult days. We had absorbed the enthusiasm of Willauer and Chennault, whereas Bond's jaundiced view had trickled down through the ranks.

Back at the airport I stopped at the Dairy Farm Restaurant, where I ran into the American pilots of the defecting airlines. I sat beside Catfish Raine, one of Chennault's original Flying Tigers, who had flown for CAT before some obscure tiff with Rosbert drove him to Central Air.

"Looks like yours is the only airline left," Catfish said. "We got a hint yesterday that this might happen, after two Americans said they had been removed from the schedule. We discovered that every American scheduled to fly had been replaced with certain Chinese pilots who had always seemed sympathetic to the Commies."

Catfish sipped his beer and continued, "I told our guys to stand by until I had time to get advice from Chennault." Catfish was always so casual and relaxed; I felt like prodding him, I wanted to know what Chennault said. "Sue shortstopped me outside his office. 'You can't go in now,' she said. 'You pilots are always dropping in—how do you expect him to get his work done?' I said, well, then, the hell with it, and went back to the house. . . . All the Americans in Central Air had gathered to plan an action. But a couple of guys had bottles. And by the time the party ended it was morning, and the twelve planes were gone."

"Jesus, you might have stopped the defection," I said. "Why didn't you just barge into Chennault's office?"

"I wish I had."

"The rest of the planes are grounded," I said. "Chiang Kai-shek canceled the certificates."

Someone brought the evening paper to operations. Mao Tse-tung's protest was on the front page: *The planes are the sacred property of the people of China. They must be released.*

Another item quoted Hong Kong's director of civil aviation: *The planes will remain grounded until the question of ownership is resolved.*

I put the paper down and watched. Mechanics were still preparing the turncoat airplanes for flight. Willauer showed up. "Spread the word in all the honky-tonks: any China National or Central Air plane that tries to take off will find a truck in its path." Hickler, our supply manager, led us to his supply shed, where we chose weapons. I chose a section of hydraulic hose that had a brass fitting at each end. Willauer selected a big wrench. Other pilots picked out other wrenches or hammers. The Communist mechanics had gone home for the night. We walked around the seventy-one planes unhampered and let air out of tires. Airport policemen saw us, but we pretended we were checking the planes, and they didn't intercede.

The next morning, Rousselot and I stood among our own planes, waiting for Chennault and Willauer to show up for their trip to Taiwan. A few mechanics of JAMCO—Jardine's Aircraft Maintenance Company—hung around Chennault's plane and gabbed the way mechanics do while waiting for a pilot to take a plane off their hands. The scene was so familiar I didn't pay attention. Talking to Rousselot, I said, "It's uncanny the way Chinese find out what's going on. Everyone on the airport knows Chennault and Willauer are going to Taipei for—"

Suddenly, hawk-eyed Rousselot ran the hundred yards to Chennault's plane, grabbed a JAMCO mechanic around the neck, and pulled plier-like cutters from his hand. "Tried to cut the brake line," he said.

The airport police whisked the offender away. Chennault and Willauer arrived. The pilot hurried to the cockpit and started the engines. Willauer called from the cabin door, "See that he's charged with attempted murder."

An hour later, Rousselot and I were subpoenaed. At 3:00 P.M. on that same day we sat in a British court and saw the silvery pliers on a table. The JAMCO mechanic wore his jacket inside out. "Trying to confuse the witnesses," Rousselot whispered.

In the witness box, Rousselot described the hazards of operating an airplane with a failed brake. I testified that I had seen him take the cutters from the defendant's hand.

The English judge peered under the fringe of a white wig and intoned, "The court considers the attempt at malicious damage serious because it would have endangered the passengers." Raising his voice, he almost shouted, "It makes no difference who the passengers were."

"He wants the Chinese to know he's not kowtowing to Chennault," I whispered.

Sentenced to four years at hard labor, the mechanic was hoisted out of the dock in a caged elevator. I looked at my watch. Less than eight hours had elapsed since he tried to sever the brake line.

"I've heard of swift British justice, but I didn't know it was this swift," Rousselot said.

Willauer got back a couple of days later and told us what happened in Taipei.

General Chow, commander of the Chinese Air Force, told Chennault, "Perhaps the generalissimo will cashier me; the managers who defected are ex–air force officers."

Chennault said, "The issue is this: how do we keep the planes out of Communist hands? If they're sold to a neutral country—this month—before the British recognize Red China—the planes won't be in Hong Kong."

General Chow replied, "I suggest you see the generalissimo immediately. Don't wait for tomorrow morning."

That afternoon, at Nationalist headquarters, Chiang Kai-shek said he wanted Chennault to buy the planes.

Chennault replied, "It would be better if they were purchased by some other company—one without any previous connection with China—some company outside of the Orient."

"You're the only foreigner I trust," Chiang said.

Chiang's advisers said the price should be substantial lest it looked trumped up, and payment should be a promissory note signed by General Chennault.

Pan American balked at making its share of China's major airline available to CAT. Delightfully, I fantasized Vice President Bond at the board meeting in New York. "Sell out to CAT? That cavalier outfit? Those cowboys take over China National? Unthinkable!"

I knew Pan American's potentates were conceited, but unpatriotic they weren't. After some pressure from the U.S. State Department, China National's fine airliners plus all of its real estate—and all of Central Air's—became the property of CAT's new American sister, CATI (CAT Incorporated), registered in Delaware. The price: $4.75 million, U.S. currency, paid with an IOU signed by Chennault. By gentleman's agreement, it was a paper sale. CAT was in no position to utilize the planes. The purpose of the "sale" was to keep the planes out of the Communists' hands—to deny them the capability of dropping paratroopers onto Taiwan.

Chennault said, "It was scary stuff. We didn't have any money, not since we converted our U.S. funds to gold yuan."

A few days later, Chennault asked me to meet an arriving U.S. CAA inspector. He opened his briefcase and I gaped at stacks of registration and airworthiness certificates tumbling onto my desk.

Although many of the C-46s—those with hydraulic flight controls—were illegal under the U.S. flag, the entire menagerie, without any inspection whatsoever, had been certified airworthy by heady names in the CAA.

Grinning, as if happy to be out of Washington, the FAA inspector accompanied me to the airplanes while a safari followed with stencils of Old Glory and buckets of red, white, and blue paint.

An English official, flanked by two policemen, announced imperiously, "You are barred from this aerodrome."

Our ally held out his certificate of identification. "I'm a U.S. Federal Aviation official, on an international airport, inspecting American planes. If you bar me you're violating International Civil Air Regulations."

The official clipped, "Our courts will decide that."

A policeman's cockney voice barked, "Disperse your men."

We retreated to my office, where our ally said, "In all my years with the FAA, I've never been barred from an airport."

"Britain doesn't want to antagonize Chairman Mao," I said. "They know the Commies can swallow Hong Kong anytime they like."

The First Trial

I sat in the Hong Kong courtroom where the question of ownership would be decided. Barrister Sir Walter Monkton, later to be minister of labor, spoke for CAT. A slender, courtly man with a voice that was mellow yet precise, he jousted with Red China's barrister over the issues of sovereign rights and whether or not a new government is bound by contracts of the old.

When it ended, Sir Walter described the honor it had been to plead before such a learned court. The judge replied that it had been a delight to listen to an astute barrister. Naive me announced, "We won, hands down—it was an affair of love between Sir Walter and the judge."

The morning newspaper announced, "Communists awarded seventy-one planes." That same morning I watched, disheartened, while painters decorated the tail fins with five gold stars on red.

Sir Walter kept the planes on the ground by filing an appeal, while Willauer told Senator Knowland, "The British decision is a blow to the free world."

Knowland told a Senate session, "It should be made clear that Britain will get no help stopping Communism in Europe if it accelerates its spread in Asia with seventy-one airplanes."

The planes and parts were supposed to remain static until the appeal ran its course. Although the seventy-one planes remained grounded, I saw hundreds of tons of airplane parts crated and shipped to Red China despite the court's order.

After the excitement of the defection, the operations office seemed quiet. But when you fly a desk it can be too quiet—like the alarming silence of the Teletype when a plane's position report is due.

The End of the Southwest

Jones left the mining town of Mengtsz with a C-47 full of tin ingots for Haiphong, but his first position report didn't come in.

I sent messages to everyone: "Attempt contact XT-805 and advise."

When clocks said Jones's fuel tanks were dry, I advised everyone to watch for the downed plane. Nobody sighted a wreck, but a couple of days later, copilot M. H. Kung, guided by friendly natives, walked out of the jungle.

"The right engine was on fire," he told us. "The extinguisher didn't put it out. I think the fire walls shut-off valve didn't work. It kept burning. Captain Jones told us to jump out. I ran back with Chin, but we couldn't push the door against the slipstream. Jones came and pushed us out. My parachute opened and swung one time and I hit the ground. Jones didn't have time to get out, I think."

When I saw Kung's equanimity after the fire, bail out, and jungle trek, I recalled stories of Chinese merchant seamen who had been torpedoed during the big war and drifted alone on a raft for more than a month without suffering psychologically. Western researchers said their stability came from growing up in a Chinese rural community where they enjoyed the security of extended families.

The terrain where Kung and Chin landed was rugged, and we guessed Kung had landed on the lucky side of a mountain and Chin on the other. Lolo tribes roamed the area, and some of them still hunted heads.

Buol, in Kunming, managing the tin shuttle, said he'd hunt for Jones and asked Governor Lu Han for soldiers.

Marsh was in my office when Buol's announcement arrived. "I misjudged Buol," I confessed. "I thought he was a cocky, one-way guy, but he's going after Jones. He didn't even ask Chennault or Willauer."

"He mellowed."

"Maybe Doc Gentry did some good, talking to him when he didn't want to send a plane to look for Earthquake."

"It's Sue," Marsh said. "Buol's been mellowing more and more since they married."

"I was in Hawaii when they met—when we picked up the C-46s at Wheeler Field." Only three years ago, but it seemed a lifetime. "She thought the rest of her life would be boring. 'Unbearably dull' were her words."

Marsh left Hong Kong early in the morning, but instead of proceeding on home leave—his original intention—he went back to Yunnan Province, saying, "Buol can't have all the fun." Jawbert, the Costa Rican mechanic, accompanied them.

We got small pieces of information until Marsh got back to Hong Kong. When the expedition—Buol, Marsh, Jawbert, and a squad of Lu Han's soldiers—reached Lolo territory, the soldiers rounded up a village chief's children and made them hostages to ensure a safe passage.

Rumors said Lolos had chopped off Chin's head. As the party penetrated deeper in the bush, the rumors grew. A soldier—the interpreter—believed it was true.

They found the crashed C-47 with Jones's body inside, beginning to rot. Buol decided to cremate the remains; at least they could carry the ashes back. Soldiers cut logs, which Jawbert crisscrossed into a funeral pyre, and he took photographs for evidence. When they all got back to Kunming they put the ashes into a pewter urn.

When Marsh landed at Hong Kong he told me, "You'd have been proud of Buol. Ran the expedition like a Marine. Rugged mountains, nasty natives, he didn't let it throw him. . . . By the way, I brought Jones's ashes. I left the urn in the cockpit—I'm worried that customs will fool with it."

Doc Gentry said, "Leave it to me," and in a few minutes he'd talked his way through customs. He put the urn on top of my filing cabinet.

The next pilot came in and said, "That's awful, putting it up there. Don't you have any respect for the dead?"

The Rebel said, "We're not going to file him; we're just waiting for someone to pick him up."

Jones's girlfriend came in, crying. She said, "I'll take it to his parents," and we got her passage to America.

Kunming didn't last much longer. The signs were there: the curfew, extra roadblocks, baggage inspection by military police, secret police, one after the other, while soldiers picked whatever they wanted from passengers' bags.

Green, one of our vice presidents—a former Marine and CAT pilot—said, "We'll evacuate the heavy equipment."

Governor Lu Han threw a feast in honor of the American consul and the CAT staff. In a gracious mood, he paid tribute to our station manager, whose father had been Lu Han's instructor at Kunming Military Academy years before.

Lu Han said CAT's evacuation was a wise move.

"It should have alerted me," Green said. "Besides that, he walked out of the room, leaving us to talk among ourselves. I saw a screen in a corner and thought it might hide someone listening. . . . But after all, he had told Chennault he guaranteed our safety."

Fogg, our meteorologist, reported, "Some time after midnight, Buol and I were sleeping in the operations shack. Soldiers poured through the windows and doors and told us to go outside. Buol thought they were joking. He shoved a soldier aside and told him to get lost . . . I was afraid he'd get shot. The soldier prodded him with his rifle and Buol got the message. Outside, we saw machine guns on tripods. The soldiers wore blue uniforms, but their caps were inside out, on top of their heads. An officer said Governor Lu Han had also joined the Communists."

Green explained courteously that Governor Lu Han had guaranteed their freedom, but the officer shook his head. Inbound planes couldn't be warned, because turncoat soldiers guarded the radio room. A clever officer maintained the operation of the radio beacon. My nightfall, four CAT planes were in Red hands: a DC-4, two C-46s, a C-47. A captured CAF C-46 was parked nearby.

CAT's ground staff and flight crews were held at the compound without food. It was a cold night.

"I'm afraid I won't spend Christmas with my wife," a mechanic said.

"Right now I'm worried about running out of cigarettes," the Rebel said.

"So much for Lu Han's promise," Marsh said. "He was Chennault's buddy when we fought Japan."

"This is a Chinese legend," Fogg said. "Before the warlord chops off our heads, he throws a feast."

At dawn, a pilot looked out the window and exclaimed, "The soldiers are gone." Fifty-seven CAT employees ran to the planes, except Marsh, who started the refueling truck, and Fogg, who jumped on his motor scooter and headed for Kunming to get the other employees. A guard stopped him. The DC-4 took off.

After starting his engines, a C-46 pilot couldn't see through his windshield. After he defrosted it he saw soldiers pointing rifles at him.

Angered by the escape of the DC-4, an officer herded everyone into a small room while his soldiers pumped fuel out of the remaining planes.

That night, after the guard changed, Green asked to see the commanding officer. More friendly than his predecessor, he said Governor Lu Han would keep his promise; the planes could be refueled, and CAT's cars could fetch the employees in Kunming, along with the American consul and his staff. The commanding officer warned, "Don't come back. Next time the governor won't let you go."

One C-46, with insufficient fuel for Hong Kong, flew to Hainan Island. After it parked, seven CAF stowaways jumped out of the belly compartment.

I watched the other planes come into Hong Kong. When the Rebel parked, he waved his red cap and yelled, "I almost joined 'em."

By the time our C-47 arrived, wives had gathered at the airport. Some cried. Sue hugged Buol, who grinned as if the fall of Kunming had been a lark.

With Kunming gone, CAT was completely off the mainland. We were left with only three bases: Hong Kong plus the islands of Taiwan and Hainan.

There was a cheerful note, however. No more capture, no more imprisonment—so we thought.

Before we caught our breaths, the Nationalists asked us to return and snatch a stockpile of tin.

The Tin Heist

Barely a month had passed since Governor Lu Han warned, "Don't come back—next time I won't let you go." And we were supposed to go back and tweak his nose?

The operation began on Hainan Island in the South China Sea. The island sprawled like a turtle guarding south China and Vietnam. Its tail pointed northeast to Hong Kong, its head southwest to Hue. Its right foot pointed across the Gulf of Tonkin to Haiphong.

Semitropical, 150 miles long, 120 miles wide, the island was rich with lakes, rice paddies, mountains, coal mines. Its northern seaport, Hoihow, looked across fourteen miles of water to China's mainland. Its southern port, Sanya, or Sama, nestled Japanese submarines during World War II, but now it harbored an old ferryboat—a retired flat-bottomed veteran of the Hong Kong–Macao run. CAT had chartered it for emergency shelter for employees who had fled the mainland. The vessel was overcrowded, because a new personnel manager, fresh from the USA, had announced that everyone's family would be accommodated. In his innocence he thought a family was a husband plus one wife and their kids, but he got stuck with siblings, cousins, parents, grandparents, and good friends.

It was berthed near a white sand beach with palm trees and a red-dirt runway with a fringe of olive-drab tents that sheltered pilots, mechanics, and airplane parts.

We had been one of the largest cargo carriers in the world, but now we were an airline with nowhere to go. Our only route led from Hainan Island to the British colony of Hong Kong and on to another island called Taiwan.

The entire mainland belonged to the Reds except for a city in a green valley in western China, one hundred miles south of Kunming.

Old, walled, it lay at the foot of a nine-thousand-foot mountain near twin lakes that sparkled blue. It was Mengtsz.

It looked idyllic from the air, but the ground was marred—not so much by the scars of tin mines as by the sight of miners who crawled down small holes to fetch the ore. Some were nine years old, and all were orphans who'd be dead before they got out of their teens. A green tinge on the kids' parchment faces said so. It was the signature of arsenic from the ore.

Heaps of tin ingots lay alongside smelting furnaces. Chips of tin-filled rusty drums that had once held aviation gasoline. The mine owners' tally sticks said the entire stockpile weighed 472 tons.

An economic plum, it was guarded by two Nationalist armies. Garrison troops protected the airport.

On the other side of the mountain, fifteen thousand soldiers of the People's Liberation Army assembled.

We could transfer the stockpile to Hainan Island in two weeks if we ran an all-weather operation, but we'd need a radio beacon to guide us when clouds played tag with the runway. The beacon required a gasoline-powered electrical generator. Our ground radio operators had been trained to measure cloud heights, visibility, wind. Mechanics would accompany them, technicians equipped with replacements for the small stuff that can break down and ground an airplane: spark plugs, tires, carburetors, magnetos.

Our assurance that we'd get airborne in the face of an attack was a sun-darkened Chinese–Costa Rican who led the team of mechanics. A taciturn man, he had a quietness that was born of Chinese whispers, "Half-caste." He also had an air of confidence that induced a feeling of security in the pilots who took the airplanes he fixed.

Buol said, "I'll fly the guys in and haggle for space. There's bound to be some wheel who'll say we can't use the hangars near the runway. Bureaucrats are bureaucrats, even in a crisis." A casual grin raised both ends of his mouth. Buol could admit to the hazards of functionaries, but nothing else. All of us except Buol were skittish about returning to China's mainland. Earthquake and his crew still languished in a Communist prison somewhere, and the memory of the Kunming incident was fresh in our minds. Everyone from Chennault on down agreed that no one would remain in Mengtsz overnight. Mechanics and radiomen would fly into Mengtsz on the first flight of the day and out on the last.

We began the tin lift hours after we got the Chinese government's request, before we had time to ferret the beacon and generators and spares from the crates that had been packed for our move to Taiwan.

As Hong Kong's station manager, I got copies of operational messages. I had flown enough evacuations to read between the lines of the terse messages. I flew vicariously even though I was trapped in my airport office, and the pilots filled me in when they came in to gab.

Rousselot assigned Harry Cockrell to temporary duty as chief pilot, Hainan Island. A wise selection, because Cockrell was a master at getting along with touchy CAF officers, who seemed to gain arrogance with every defeat. Their operations shack was close to the short runway.

The CAF officers respected Cockrell. He understood the subtle courtesies better than most foreign devils, because his wife came from a good Mandarin family. Cockrell was also a gentleman by our own standards. If the end of some mission left us disheveled and sweaty, he remained impeccably neat. "A tai chi discipline," he once told me. "Stay calm, don't resist the heat; let it pass through your body and away." Although he lived a saint's life, he didn't censure his wilder pals. As evil didn't exist in him, he didn't perceive it in others. As for his flying—watching Cockrell fly was discouraging. A rare natural pilot, he flew with the smoothness and precision that pilots seek, but seldom attain. After watching him fly I wondered if I should seek some other line of work. Cockrell said he'd transport the beacon, spare parts, mechanics, and radiomen—and Buol, the project manager—into Mengtsz.

The other pilot, Fred Walker, was in his tent packing as if he'd be gone for a week. A cagey pilot, he'd seen many a quick round-trip turn into an odyssey. He was on the trip because he was due for his six-month proficiency check. He'd fly while check airman Cockrell sat in the copilot seat with a clipboard on his lap and graded Walker's preflight check, crew coordination, precision, judgment, navigation, fuel management—the standard stuff of airlines. Anyone from a distance recognized Walker, because he was a six-foot-four redhead. He came from Maine, and his great-great-grandfather, General Frye, was a hero of the Revolutionary War. Walker's integrity was as steadfast as Cockrell's, although the Yankee's was more of a bluff, rural honesty, tempered with Down East skepticism. Walker's wariness extended to machinery. I remember arriving at many an airport to see size twelve feet atop the wheel of a C-46, and knowing without looking that they and the rest of the body— enveloped by the dark wheel well—belonged to the hearty New Englander, and that he was inspecting every hydraulic, fuel, and oil line and all the cables and latches.

After flying off Hainan Island's red-dirt strip, checkee Walker turned the C-46 toward Tin City while Cockrell sat on his right with the clipboard on his lap, and Buol relaxed in the jump seat. Mechanics and radiomen sprawled on canvas benches alongside their equipment in the cabin.

An hour and a half across the placid Gulf of Tonkin put them in sight of the French seaport of Haiphong. Fifteen minutes later they looked down on Hanoi. In the next hour they flew over the jungles of North Vietnam to the Chinese border and descended into the green valley, where they saw blue lakes at the foot of a mountain. And Mengtsz's strip of concrete showed up.

After landing and rolling to a stop, the crew noticed trucks with drums of tin chips. Laborers lolled on the ground, and three generals looked up at the cockpit.

Walker stayed aboard to supervise the loading while Cockrell and Buol introduced themselves to the generals. After a few minutes of polite conversation, Cockrell asked the crucial question: "What's the military situation?"

"We can defend the airport until the end of this month," said General Yao. "But in any event you would get at least twenty-four hours' notice before a bandit attack."

Buol nodded. Cockrell smiled and said, "General, we're concerned because we've been surprised before, not far from here," and he pointed toward Kunming, barely one hundred miles north.

General Yao said, "The bandits don't have airplanes—they will march across open fields. The airport will be safe."

General Li said, "This valley is flat. No trees. No cover to hide an enemy advance. We can give you many warnings."

General Wu said, "The bandits cannot move quickly—they have no motor transport."

"They must use donkeys," scoffed General Yao, and all the generals laughed.

Their unblinking pledges—and Buol's chutzpah—made the decision inevitable. "We'll stay overnight," Buol said. "Who needs a four-hour commute? My guys can spend that time working. We'll have the beacon working by noon tomorrow."

The flight back to Hainan Island seemed uneventful until Walker parked the plane, opened the cockpit door, and saw General Yao and his aide. Walker quickly closed the door and asked Cockrell, "When did those guys get on?"

"At the last minute—General Yao wanted to shop."

"Shopping? With that situation in Mengtsz? That guy's running. Mengtsz's going to fall."

"Relax. He also came for a conference."

"Conference, my foot."

General Yao and his aide took a jeep to town while Cockrell walked to the radio tent to check messages. Walker went swimming.

When the last flight got back to Hainan, the pilot said, "Buol insisted on staying overnight. He'll send a weather report in the morning." Shaking his head gravely, he added, "The CAF flew all its airplanes out—all except a C-46 with a bad magneto."

During supper a radioman hurried into the mess tent to announce, "Mengtsz radio just went dead."

Walker muttered, "I'm glad I'm not with Buol—all night—no airplane."

"You worry too much," someone said.

Cockrell tossed in his sleep, heard a plane land, thought he was dreaming. Someone shook his arm. The CAF base commander whispered, "Don't go to Mengtsz."

Cockrell jumped up, but the base commander had vanished. Cockrell pulled on his pants and hurried into the communications tent, where a radio operator slumped in his chair. He straightened, rubbed his eyes, and said, "Mengtsz is still dead, but around midnight a CAF plane landed with two passengers. Someone said they were generals."

Cockrell doubted the CAF would admit the situation at Mengtsz, but if he filed a flight plan they might.

The operations officer initialed the flight plan and stared at Cockrell with stony silence.

Cockrell returned to his tent and tore his bedsheets into wide strips. Laid flat on the ground, they'd be visible from the air. He wrote a note: "Display a V if okay to land. Display an X if not okay. If you decide to walk out, display an arrow indicating your direction." He stuffed the note and bedsheet signal panels into a cloth bag and weighted it with a rock. A couple of hours later he awakened Walker and radio operator Yu. They took off by the light of coffee-can flares. By sunrise they were circling Mengtsz.

They were familiar with the city's typical honeycombed compounds, yet it wasn't typical. The streets were deserted. No kids, no dogs— nothing. Just a lone stream of smoke from a cookstove. They circled the airport. The abandoned CAF C-46 was the only plane in sight.

Walker took the weighted bag of signal panels in back and waited for Cockrell's signal. After the drop, they pulled up sharply, to the north, and saw a column of soldiers marching toward the city. At the sight of the plane they scattered, which meant they were Communists. Another column, advancing from the east, also scattered. But soldiers marching toward Laos waved. They were Nationalists.

Heading back to the airport to see if the signal panels had been displayed, the crew saw soldiers four deep in the shadow of the wall. Their column was half a mile long, and they saw pack mules.

Cockrell, Walker, and Chu heard a *ping*, like a milk pail banged on the floor. The sound was familiar. It was the strike of a rifle bullet. "I guess he shot at the cockpit without leading his aim and hit the cabin," Walker said.

Circling back over the airport, they didn't see the panels they dropped, but they saw soldiers setting up .50-caliber machine guns at the ends of the runway.

Chu handed Cockrell a message and warned, "This wasn't sent by our man—not his fist."

URGENTLY PLEASE. SEND PLANE RIGHT AWAY SO WE MAY GET OUT. IF SO LATER WE CANNOT GET OUT BUT NOT SEND A/C XT-130.

"That's not Buol's grammar," Walker said.

"They're mad at our plane for buzzing them," Cockrell said. "We can't go back.

The same dubious message came through the telex in my Hong Kong office and into Hainan Island, where off-duty pilots played cards.

"Sounds phony," a cardplayer said. "But someone's got to go."

"Low man goes."

The dealer fanned the deck of cards onto the table. The first captain to draw turned up the king of hearts. Someone else drew a ten. Welk drew the four of spades and chuckled, "Looks like I volunteered."

Davis, our jaunty English pilot, didn't even draw. He just said, "Screw it, I'll go.

Radio operator Chu said, "Me too."

In the meantime, at Mengtsz, Jawbert told Buol, "I'll pretend to join the Commies, and I'll repair the magneto on the CAF plane. When I test the engine, you and the guys jump in."

Jawbert told the Reds he'd repair the plane, but he'd have to taxi to some trees near the end of the runway where he could hide it with branches.

An officer agreed. After the repair, Jawbert discovered a .38-caliber revolver under the pilot's seat cushion. He told Buol he'd shoot the guard in the cabin if necessary during takeoff. But the other guys weren't near the plane. Buol wouldn't leave them behind to suffer the wrath of the Reds.

As the rescue plane headed for Mengtsz, nobody talked much. When they got within sight of the airport, Davis exclaimed, "That's Mengtsz?" The runway was scarred with three bomb craters. The CAF plane was missing. Wu's key clattered. He said, "That was the CAF. They said they bombed their airplane; they didn't want the Communists to get it."

"That heap must be what's left of it," Welk said.

"The runway is kaput," Davis said.

Welk flew low. Jawbert sat near the runway, next to a man in a Mandarin gown. He looked like the man who usually tallied the tin. Unseen by the crew, a soldier in the operations office braced his rifle on the windowsill and aimed at the plane. A second soldier drew a bead on Jawbert.

Welk said, "If I touch down at the edge of the last crater I can stop at the end. What do you guys say?" Davis and Chu held up their thumbs.

Welk said, "Chu, go in back. As soon as we land, put out the ladder. Hook it up while we're still rolling. When the last guy boards, I'll ram the power up. Don't try to pull the ladder back in."

He approached the remnant of runway a couple of knots above stalling speed and touched down at the edge of the last crater. A soldier ran out of a ditch, aimed at the cockpit, and fired. An explosive cartridge hit the ceiling of the cockpit. The flash blinded the crew. They smelled cordite. Davis yelled, "I'm hit." Welk rammed the throttles full open, and the plane lurched forward. Wu was hooking up the ladder. He was thrown halfway out and saved himself by grabbing the doorjamb. Welk skimmed the ground, aiming the plane at a machine-gun crew at the end of the runway. They abandoned the weapon and flattened themselves against the ground.

Welk notified Hong Kong: *Davis hit above ankle. Proceeding to Haiphong for medical assistance.*

I swore, "Goddam, if that isn't just like Buol." I saw and heard him, like a movie in my head. His devil-may-care grin. Cajoling the timid. Jeering, "Screw the Commies, they're not coming." But I couldn't remain angry for long. No phony posturer, Buol was authentic. Fearless or crazily optimistic, I didn't know which. But I saw why Admiral Bull Halsey had bedecked Buol's chest with medals. "Damn him, he thinks CAT is an air wing of the United States Marine Corps."

Rousselot gave the radiogram to Chennault, while Sue, at her desk, watched his expression.

"You might as well show this to Sue now," he said. Rousselot walked over and handed it to her in silence. His eyes showed compassion.

Without looking at it, Sue said, "It can't be him."

Rousselot said softly, "I'm afraid it is."

"But he told me he wouldn't stay overnight in Mengtsz. It just can't be him."

No one spoke. Sue finally glanced at the radiogram. The word BUOL jumped out from all the others. She sobbed.

Chennault walked over to put his hand on her shoulder. "Be patient, Sue. At worst, he'll have a rough trip home. You'll see him again. But not for a long time."

Sue wrote, "Although Chennault's words struck fear and loneliness in my heart, they also built courage to hope, for if he felt I'd see my husband again I felt sure I would. In my despair on that awful day I didn't see where I'd gather strength to live alone in the Orient, but I resolved to remain as close to him as the geography of the free world would allow."

Chennault cabled Governor Lu Han: "CAT has always served your excellency and the people of Yunnan. I prevented the Japanese destruction of Kunming and saved lives of many people. In appreciation of our service to Chinese people I respectfully request your approval of CAT plane flying Mengtsz under safe conduct to return CAT personnel."

Lu Han replied: "It is quite true that you and CAT loyally served the people of Yunnan. That is why I arranged to let your men safely leave Kunming before and after December 9, 1949. Why Buol go to Mengtsz to take such risk? Your request is therefore not what I can help."

Chennault responded: "Our men at Mengtsz were working under orders from the head office and not personally responsible for any actions of airline. Your release of these men will be considered an act of justice."

Hong Kong Cable and Wireless, Ltd., reported, "Delivered at 1800 hours." There was no answer.

In his schoolteacher penmanship, Chennault wrote:

His Excellency
Marshal Yen Hsi-shan
Premier of the Republic of China
Taipei
Your Excellency:
General Yao Cheng-chin, Commander of the Mengtsz Garrison, promised to give us a minimum of one day's notice before any Communist attack would occur. On the afternoon of January 15th, General Yao flew from Mengtsz to Hainan in a CAT plane. During the night of January 15th and early morning of January 16th, Communist troops occupied both the city of Mengtsz and the airfield and took prisoner CAT personnel whose names are listed below:

Captain L. R. Buol
Mr. Lincoln Sun
Mr. P. H. Chu
Mr. Y. S. Woo
Mr. Jose Jawbert
Mr. K. N. Mai
Mr. C. Liu
Mr. C. L. Wong

Neither before his departure from Mengtsz nor after his arrival at

Hainan did General Yao give any warning to CAT personnel that Communist troops were approaching Mengtsz.

Later it was learned that General Li Mi, Commander of the 8th Army, and General Yu Ching-yuan, Commander of the 26th Army, were also safely in Hainan with General Yao.

This would indicate that all of these generals had evacuated Mengtsz exactly at the right time to escape capture by the Communists and therefore must have had some knowledge of the approach of the Communist forces. As the result of the failure to warn CAT we have lost eight valuable men and three sets of valuable radio equipment. This loss has produced a very bad morale effect on CAT personnel.

All of our men at Mengtsz volunteered for this duty because of their confidence and faith in the promise of the Chinese officials that they would be warned in ample time to evacuate in the case of a Communist approach.

I am sure you will realize that CAT must have the cooperation and confidence in the Chinese military leaders if they are to continue to operate in threatened areas.

With assurances of my highest regards, I am

Most sincerely yours,
C. L. Chennault

Sue typed it and sent it to Taipei. As the wife of an imprisoned employee she got Buol's pay, which she deposited in their bank and lived off her secretary's salary. "I'll keep working," she said. "General Chennault is considerate of my feelings. He's a very kind man. And when the good news comes, I'll be first to know."

Davis hobbled everywhere to recount his tale of the last mainland city to fall, and he peeled back his bandage to display torn flesh and laugh, "It's nothing."

Earthquake Returns

We got word that Earthquake's passengers, Mrs. Liu and her baby, were safe in Hong Kong. A few days later, copilot Lay's subdued voice on the phone said he also was in Hong Kong and he wanted to meet me in a room at the Miramar Hotel, where we could talk without interruption.

After their belly landing on the moon-lit sandbank on the river, Lay explained, two villagers had come to the airplane. "Where are we?" he asked. They were in Lung-Sen Gahi, a village in Kwangsi Province, liberated by the Reds just two days before.

More villagers gathered. "Don't worry, we're civilian fliers," Lay said. "Please help us hide our big friend."

After much discussion among themselves, one of the villagers said, "If the Communists catch us hiding a foreigner, they'll kill us. Too many bandits. The Communists reward them for information."

Communist soldiers arrived and took the captives to a schoolhouse, where they waited two days for an officer. "We know about General Chennault," he said. "CAT has many bombers and fighters."

"CAT is a small airline, only twenty transport planes," Lay explained. "We are simple working men. Our captain isn't like other foreign devils; he comes from a family of laborers."

"I cannot settle your case," the officer replied. "You must come to Nanming."

The three crewmen walked ahead of the officer, who rode a horse. Mrs. Liu and her baby were carried in a sedan chair.

Several miles later, Earthquake sat under a tree, removed his shoes, and massaged his feet.

The officer ordered, *"Kwai dee"* ("Hurry"), but Earthquake kept massaging his feet. The officer drew a pistol.

"Go ahead, shoot," Earthquake said. "You're going to shoot me anyway when we get to wherever the hell we're going; you might as well shoot me now."

The officer walked while Earthquake rode the horse.

They were imprisoned in a small hotel with barred windows. Indoctrinators came daily to teach the virtues of Communism. They promised Chang and Lay good jobs with the new people's airline if they joined the Party.

Eventually, the guards became bored. Villagers came to the window. Lay spoke their dialect. "We hear rumors that Mrs. Liu and her baby will be released because she is an innocent passenger," they said. "We'll bring clothes for you and Chang, and you can escape, but the foreign devil is too big."

"We won't leave you," said Lay and Chang, and Earthquake replied, "Go, you guys, go back to your wives and kids. I'll be okay."

Chang decided to stay, taking a chance that he'd eventually be transferred to some northern province where Mandarin was spoken, where he'd have a better chance of passing for a merchant. Lay peeled the photograph from his CAT identity card and gave it to a villager, who returned a few days later with a certificate identifying him as a merchant. And they brought clothes. Earthquake stood at the front door talking to the guards while Lay fled out the back.

A guard brought breakfast in the morning. Shocked, he exclaimed in English, "Where go?"

Earthquake replied, "How the hell should I know? You're the guard."

Lay hid in a farmhouse for three days, waiting for an eastbound truck. "A few villagers came to see me. They said the people in Kwangsi and Kwangtung turned against the Communists because of the heavy taxes," Lay said. "They buried guns and bullets. They are waiting for the right time. Right now there are too many soldiers. The Communists said the conditions would improve, but it's too late. Everyone knows they lie."

I told Lay to take another break, and we drank more tea.

"A truck took me a long way toward Hong Kong," he continued. "There were many inspections along the road. I always said I was a merchant on my way to Canton to buy goods, but I got nervous and decided to travel the rest of the way on junks. Boats moved at night because they feared the Chinese Air Force; they thought they'd get bombed. . . . At Canton I dressed like a coolie and took a train to Hong Kong. My heart was light after I crossed the bridge."

He said Earthquake had lost much weight and suffered a skin disease. He was prepared to overpower his guard and escape. "Send a plane for me," Earthquake said, "If you fly over the town and run the prop speed up and down I'll know it's a flying boat and head for the river. If you don't change the pitch I'll know it's a land plane and run to the airport."

Chennault decided against it.

Days after Lay told his story, I heard that Mrs. Liu, with her baby, had been in Hong Kong for a few weeks but was afraid to notify anyone.

Another couple of weeks passed and Chang walked into Hong Kong operations. The Communists had released him because he was an innocent employee. A month later, Lewis phoned to say, "Earthquake is here—he's trapped in Gingle's."

I found Earthquake in the inner sanctum, sitting on Gingle's throne, slurping lima beans and melted butter while Gingle stood over him with a maudlin grin and wiped his eyes with a huge handkerchief.

Earthquake glanced up, grinned, and returned to his beans. He looked like a scarecrow on Gingle's throne. Not even two hundred pounds. Ragged khakis hung from sticks, it seemed. An unruly beard stuck out in all directions. His feet were clad in bulky cloth shoes.

A newsman pushed his way inside to say, annoyed, "I saw you crossing the border. I thought you were a missionary. Why didn't you say who you were?"

"You didn't ask."

Sue was ecstatic. His release meant Buol would follow.

After Earthquake got home and took a bath and got some clean clothes, we headed up Nathan Road to the Paramount Ballroom, where he jabbered with a flock of dance hostesses. His Chinese had improved in prison.

In a rare serious moment he leveled his gaze and said, "The Communists are rotten. They break people's spirits, make them afraid."

Jovial again, he said, "Soldiers gave me wine on my birthday. With their damn diet, it didn't take much to get me loaded. I sang their songs, denounced their lousy system. What a hangover in the morning. The guards told me, 'No more wine, you say too many bad things.'"

"What made them let you go?"

"I shamed them into it. Chinese hate to be caught lying. I asked, 'Why believe your lessons? You keep telling me you'll release me but you don't. That makes you liars.'"

Chief pilot Rousselot said Earthquake needed rest in New Jersey with his parents and brother, but no one could budge him out of Hong Kong—not until the night he accompanied some pilots and an English doctor to the Peninsula Hotel and tore down a Red flag. After a few Pims Number Ones they wielded someone's diamond ring to cut the window of a travel agency and seized the model of a Communist airliner.

A constable herded them into a cell. A friendly English police inspector telephoned and ordered their release. But when the barred door opened, Earthquake clung to his cell and crowed, "I'm not leaving." His cohorts pulled and shoved, but he didn't budge. The English doctor pleaded, "Don't make more trouble. We don't want our names in the newspapers."

"I want my name in the paper," Earthquake roared. A few policemen helped shove him out the door. He pointed at the relieved constable and shouted, "I'll have your badge. You're letting these drunks escape."

In the morning, Rousselot's eyes narrowed until the pupils looked like BB shot. "You're going back to the USA. Three months' home leave—or else."

Bored in New Jersey, he traveled to Wisconsin to visit my parents and sister. Her kids knew only the Earthquake Magoon in the funny papers, the bearded black-haired giant who shook the earth when he walked. They were sure their favorite cartoon character had come alive when my friend walked through the door.

Celebrating with dinner, the kids stared in awe as he consumed great quantities of my mother's cooking. "What did you eat in that Chinese jail, Mr. Earthquake?"

Their hero swooped imaginary insects from mid-flight, scrutinized them, plucked their wings and legs, gulped them down, and burped like thunder. He leaned back with a satisfied expression and held his belly.

His young audience shrieked, my father laughed until his old ribs ached, my mother spilled her tea.

My father wrote, in his wisdom, "Your friend McGovern is a man."

When his forced vacation expired, he made a beeline for Gingle's. "Got in a fight in a Jersey bar," he growled. "Cops stuck me in the poky. I told 'em it was pure luxury, I'd just got out of a Chinese jail. They didn't believe me."

Day after day, after the head office closed, Sue rode the Star Ferry to Kowloon to be jostled by railroad station crowds while she watched passengers arrive from Canton.

My happy glow faded when a hundred motorized junks carried General Lin Piao's infantrymen across fourteen miles of water to Hainan Island. Sanya Airport was the last battleground. Cockrell landed in Hong Kong, saying, "Mortars landed near the runway."

The lush island's coconut trees and white sand beaches, its mountains with iron and coal, were in Communist hands.

CAT wives and kids, like weary gypsies, disembarked at Hong Kong with bedrolls and wicker luggage, which was opened by British customs officers. Cooking pots, jewelry, clothing, and a pistol or two tumbled onto the inspection counter. Pilots and mechanics in sweaty khakis waited out the inspection while immaculate Pan American and British Overseas Airways crews did double takes. A haughty customs inspector turned to me and scoffed, "Looks like your firm's had it."

"Not yet," I said. This dour man didn't know CAT.

We scheduled our planes ninety miles east to the island of Taiwan, where the Nationalists had established their exile government.

American pilots ran their preflight checks while Chinese pilots and radio operators gathered in Hong Kong's operations office and mumbled uncomfortably among themselves. One of them came over to me, looking more dejected than anytime during our mainland hassles. "We're not going," he said. "It's no use."

I nodded, asked them to wait, and telephoned Chennault's house. "I'll be right over," he said.

When the general got to operations he emanated respect for the crewmen. These were the guys who had flown CAT's rescue flights, worked without heaters, got shot at, buried friends, and now they faced a harsh choice: follow the losers to an island, or return home at long last, make peace with the new regime, and accept jobs with the mainland airline. Only a few days previously a Red agent, promising a bright future, had lured four crewmen.

I wanted to go into the conference room with Chennault, but sensed I'd be an intruder. He began his Southern drawl before I could get the door closed.

The meeting didn't last more than ten minutes. The Chinese airmen came out of the room, still somber, but they flew on to Taiwan.

Their wives, kids, parents, and cousins followed later with misshapen cloth bundles and wicker suitcases, without a hint of self-pity. I sensed a dichotomy of Confucian acceptance and optimism, and I knew they'd be okay on the island, because the Chinese are the most adaptable people on earth; but I also knew their hearts held the hope of returning home, someday, where the spirits of their ancestors lingered.

You come from my village? Tell me quickly all the things
That have happened there since I left.
Your plum tree has blossomed, and a goat ate the little bamboo
Which you planted at the edge of the pool.
                                        —LIN PO, TANG DYNASTY

8

Free China

Shaped like an elm leaf, Taiwan looked as if an ill wind had blown it from a tree and left it floating on the South China Sea. A steep mountainous spine, reaching thirteen thousand feet in various places, ran the 240-mile length of the island and separated its dramatic eastern gorges and narrow farms from the western plains of rice, pineapple, sugarcane, bananas, tea.

It had been governed for half a century by Japan. After the Second World War it was returned to China with a United Nations pledge that the freely expressed wishes of its people would be honored. Taiwanese assumed they'd vote for leaders to represent them in the central government of China. Instead, General Chen, in 1947, shot some demonstrators and imprisoned their leaders while his soldiers looted the island.

In the autumn of 1949, reformed, ethical Nationalists established their headquarters on the northern tip of Taiwan and called their new home the Republic of China, or Free China. It was a humid fixer-upper.

Flat, treeless dots of satellite islands off Taiwan's southwest coast were shelled by Red China's artillery, every other day, on schedule, as if the new rulers of the mainland were saying, "We can grab you at our convenience."

America's hands-off policy made the threat real. More than 100,000 Red troops gathered on the mainland coast facing Taiwan. The exiled Nationalists patrolled the sea with old destroyers and the air with the remnants of their air force.

With the exodus from the mainland at its end, my temporary duty in Hong Kong ended. I was a pilot again.

We were broke. We had been wealthy only a year ago, with surplus assets in U.S. dollars—until Chennault converted it to China's new gold yuan. The board of directors opposed the conversion until Chennault persuaded them to demonstrate CAT's loyalty to Chiang Kai-shek. Moreover, it was Nationalist law. In a matter of months, inflation had made our mountain of gold yuan worthless.

The Standard Oil Company granted us credit for our daily flight around the island—a five-hundred-mile junket with stops at abandoned military runways and grass airfields. They were deserted, with nothing to load or unload.

When Chennault came to his office in a green plaid shirt I said, "General, you look more like a duck hunter than an airline president," and he grinned. Somehow I sensed he'd prefer the former.

We waste fuel by landing at deserted fields, I said; perhaps we could invent a system of flag stops.

"Keep landing," Chennault replied. "The people will get used to our coming at the same time every day. They'll start to depend on us. Buzz the town before you land—let them know we're here."

In a couple of weeks we had a contract to deliver the *China Daily News* around the island, and we flew newly hatched grass carp from Hong Kong to farm towns, where they were set free to swim and grow in rice paddies. A fourth of an inch long and frisky, in huge wooden vats, they were hard to count. Counting was necessary because we were paid for the number that arrived alive. Upon arrival, a canny Chinese divided a vat with a board. One half was divided again and then again and again until we looked into one sixteenth of a vat. The fish were counted and the sum was multiplied by sixteen.

We acquired a championship record for delivering fish alive. During an entire flight our laborers had stirred the vats of water to keep the fish from crowding together and dying for lack of oxygen. And then someone though of sticking a pipe into the slipstream to scoop air into the vats.

Sue rented a Japanese house near Chennault's office, acquired a dog named Rags, and watched for news of Buol.

I found a Japanese house near a market that hawked edible snakes. Distinctive cries or shouts or melodic flutes advertised the products of itinerant vendors. My favorite was the artilleryman. A creaking cart bore his cast-iron cannon, and I heard the excited jabbering of children. I walked outside to watch neighbors give the cannoneer rice, which he loaded into his piece. The cannon roared and the kids shrieked delightedly while a wire mesh around the muzzle caught puffed rice.

Sometimes a roving sculptor knocked gently on my door and a few coins would entitle me to watch him stand outside and deftly mold soft wax into miniature giraffes and tigers, dragons and horses. For a few extra coins I could keep his works of art.

With time on my hands I followed rumors of a missionary from Wisconsin who hung out in some Chinese temple or other. A hero of the big war, the legend said, he confronted marauding Japanese soldiers when they pounded rifle butts on the gates of a mission where Americans hid. Frail as he was, he kept them at bay.

Curious, I hired a pedicab and searched for him.

The Rebel Monk

I found the Episcopal priest in a shack in the Tao temple courtyard. He was frail and slightly stooped, and his beard seemed extra-white against his black Mandarin gown as he peered down the throat of a boy on a stool beside a shoeshine box. Shelves held a miscellaneous assortment of Western capsules, Chinese herbs, and dried sea horses.

"Come in—I'm Walter Morse." A strong voice belied his appearance. Blue eyes sparkled with a child's merriment, but he reminded me of Moses. After a short conversation we discovered we both had been choirboys at St. James's Church in Milwaukee, although he had preceded me by twenty-five years.

Through the door to the courtyard, in the shade of the great temple with its blue-tiled roof and glaring idols, I saw men stirring a cauldron of bean stew while street urchins and derelicts and war veteran amputees with tree-branch crutches gathered. The priest walked out, said a short prayer, pushed up his sleeve, ladled the slumgullion.

"I don't proselytize them," he explained. "I'm not a salesman. They have pride; coming here is difficult enough. We patch them up and feed them and don't ask questions." Ragamuffins jostled, tried to touch him, tugged at his gown. If they got too aggressive he cuffed them and they smiled shyly, as if blessed.

"I give them shoeshine boxes, tell them to make a living as best they can, but I have no illusions—the larger boys beat them up and take away their boxes."

We left the courtyard together and walked past the temple with its swooping eaves and scent of joss to the street, where pedicab drivers haggled over who would pedal him home. Tough as they were, none would let him pay.

Visiting the world of Father Morse was a refreshing change for me. In our frequent conversations in his makeshift clinic or outside in the courtyard with me stirring the slumgullion, I was more gripped by the tales that unfolded, bit by bit, of the missionary's past than by the wildest boom-boom adventure yarns of any sailor or pilot I had known. Although I was an Episcopalian, schooled in the church, confirmed by a bishop, I didn't know that my denomination had a sect of monks who vowed to live a life of poverty and chastity

and went overseas as missionaries. They were called Cowley
Fathers. Father Morse was one. The church had sent him to China,
where he was stunned by the wretchedness.

"I could not believe God intended His people to suffer," Morse
said. "I decided to follow the footsteps of Saint Luke, the healer." He
returned to Boston, where he applied for a job as an orderly at the
Massachusetts General Hospital and several others, but was rejected
until the curious chief of a small Catholic hospital asked the young
man with the beard and the cassock why he wanted to work there.
"To learn healing," Morse replied. He was told he didn't have to
work, he'd have the run of the hospital, and the doctors would help.

"I'm a beggar by profession," Morse said. "After about six months
at the hospital, I found a ship's captain who would give me a free
ride back to China, and he agreed to take the crates of medicine I
got from a few drug companies."

He roved the interior of China for forty years, tending the poor
and the sick. "The first time bandits stopped me," he said, "I told
them I understood their profession, they'd have to take my pack, and
I offered it to them; but instead of robbing me, they escorted me to
the next village, and word was passed on, and I got a safe escort
everywhere I went." I looked at the frail man, barely five and a half
feet tall, with his air of humility and gentle humor, and I asked how
he had defied the Japanese soldiers. "By the force of will," he said. "I
just told them they would not enter the mission."

Soon after he got to Taiwan he reached retirement age. His supe-
riors ordered him to report to the home for retired Cowley Fathers
in Cambridge, Massachusetts. "I wouldn't go," he said. "I'll never go,
I want to die here. The Chinese are my only friends."

The Chinese may have seen a saint, but Episcopal headquarters
saw a rebel. They cut off his allowance.

"The Chinese bishop told me I couldn't hold services at Taipei's
Episcopal church," Morse said, "and he asked the colonel at the
American military chapel to stop inviting me. . . . I used to give a
sermon there every month or so."

My monk friend told me this without rancor. As a matter of fact,
he was slightly amused, and I recalled a yoga teacher in India saying, "Don't take events personally—leave it to God. Detach your
mind from your body, retain your upper level of awareness."

In their machinations to get their monk home, the Episcopal
hierarchy forgot the force of simple friendship. Here he is in
Taipei, I thought, and everyone is helping him—coolies, Taoists,
Presbyterians, Catholics, the United Christian Organization—
everyone but the Episcopalians.

Pedicab drivers built a shanty for him on the bank of the Tanshui
River where they themselves lived; the Goddess of the Sea Temple

gave him a room for his medical clinic and let him feed his constituents in its courtyard; the United Christian Organization opened the back door of its warehouse to supply the food; he held Episcopal services in the Presbyterian church.

Weeks later, Taipei's mayor, K. C. Woo, visited Father Morse at his new home on the bank of the river, where the pedicab drivers jabbered and laughed about the mayor of Taipei visiting their neighborhood, and they were held at a respectable distance by the mayor's bodyguards.

"Father Morse," said Mayor Woo, "you could become mayor of Taipei on the pedicab vote alone. You are revered in China, but you're setting a bad example—it's illegal to squat on the riverbank."

When news of the eviction reached Father McGrath—a missionary from Ireland—he told Morse, "I'm afraid the Tao priest will convert you; it's time you moved close to good Catholics." He donated a plot of Catholic land on the top of Ya Ming Mountain, where the pedicab men built another cabin; and every morning Father Morse rode the bus down the mountain to his clinic and soup kitchen at the Tao temple; and every Sunday he rode halfway down the mountain for his Episcopal ceremony at the Presbyterian church.

His only departure from poverty was an indulgence in German cologne with the label 4711, which I brought from Hong Kong.

He always said, "Thank you, I want nothing else," until the day he remarked, "I'm hungry for an American hamburger—the kind I used to get at the White Tower in Milwaukee."

"Say no more. CAT built a club for our maintenance guys down south; they let the Air Force in, and we use theirs up here."

We sat at a table near the officers' club bar and ordered hamburgers "with everything" and milk shakes. Morse looked up at a poster of a nude woman above the bar and said, "I can't imagine why on earth they'd have a picture like that in place like this." I kept my mouth shut and watched him open his hamburger to remove the lettuce, which he folded in a napkin and stowed in his pocket. "For my canary," he said.

I removed my lettuce and gave it to him, saying, "Give my regards to the canary."

"You're such a good man, so generous."

Big deal, a piece of lettuce, I thought.

His eyes sparkled and he told a tale. "Two black limousines stopped at the temple. Six men in black suits leaped out of the first one and searched the grounds and the rooms. My constituents fled; they didn't wait for their meal. A bodyguard opened the door of the second limousine. Madame Chiang Kai-shek and several matrons stepped out.

"Madame Chiang said she'd come to visit my clinic. I was very nervous when she sat on my rickety stool."

"Father Morse," said Madame Chiang, "you have done much for China. It's time China did something for you. Which bank do you use?"

"Madame, I've never used a bank."

"You shall have one now. We ladies have brought some money from the church so you can continue your work." Turning to the matron whose husband was president of the Bank of China, Madame Chiang said, "Please ask your husband to open an account for Father Morse at the *best* rate of interest."

The street people returned to peek through the window.

The First Lady of Free China walked outside to where the soup was bubbling and lifted the ladle.

The bank's high rate of interest enabled Father Morse to buy better food, more medicines, and to give special help.

News of Madame Chiang's visit circulated Taipei. His Sunday congregation at the Presbyterian church grew, while that of the Episcopal church downtown diminished. Many families of the U.S. Army Advisory Group abandoned their chapel near the officers' club and drove their cars half way up Ya Ming Mountain to the old stone Presbyterian church, which had a pulpit of Philippine mahogany. The church where the frail Episcopal priest with the white beard and Mandarin gown paced the aisles between the pews to be among the people. And during baptisms he invited children in the congregation to gather around the font, "because this is a child's ceremony."

Affluent parishioners brought gifts, but he gave them away except for the German 4711 I brought from Hong Kong. He kept warm with a wood stove, because neither of us was permitted to buy oil. It was rationed. So I delivered wood every week while the military parishioners said, "Who is this civilian who bought a stove? Why didn't he buy an oil stove? Why does he miss church half the time?"

Eventually the Chinese bishop prohibited the newspaper listing of the Morse service. "It's just as well," Father Morse said. "God didn't intend for me to minister to middle-class Americans."

His spartan years in China took a toll. He suffered with increasing frequency from various degenerative diseases. When doctors advised him to go to Tokyo for treatment, he suspected a ruse to get him back to Cambridge and refused to board an airplane unless I was the pilot. After one bout he regained consciousness and discovered he'd been carried aboard a ship scheduled for the USA. He jumped ship and hid in a U.S. Navy captain's house.

During my home leave in America I met, by chance, a thin-faced bishop of some Western diocese and remarked, "I had the privilege of meeting your missionary in Taiwan."

"Oh yes," replied the bishop. "Morse—we call him the Hollywood Priest—he thinks he has a direct pipeline to God."

"Perhaps he does," I said.

"Perhaps he does," parroted the bishop, mockingly, I thought.

On my return to Taipei I found my friend in his narrow bed, barely conscious. Madame Chiang Kai-shek had sent her personal physician, who had made a diagnosis of congenital heart disease.

On the following day I brought a bottle of 4711. After a whiff he sat up and dangled his feet toward the floor. "I'm ready to start working," he said.

It was then we discovered the Chinese bishop had opened Father Morse's desk and taken his ivory seal and checkbook. Using red ink to imprint the checks with the monk's personal seal, the bishop had paid off and dispersed the cooks and pot washers of the soup kitchen, and they melted into the countryside. Still wielding the seal, he had transferred the monk's remaining funds to the Episcopal Church's account. It was the money Madame Chiang had given him, the capital that had funded his work, and now it was gone. The account was zero.

With the hairs on the back of my neck rising, I said, "I'll see the bishop. I'll get your money back."

"Please don't," pleaded Father Morse. "Consider the poor man's embarrassment when he finds out I didn't die."

He planted his feet on the floor and stood, wavering. When he spread his arms for balance I saw an angel poised for flight. His eyes glowed with childlike joy, but he spoke with authority. "I will start over again."

I hugged him and felt a gown of loose bones.

The Korean Trade Mission

The world of Father Morse was a refreshing diversion from the uncertainties of our island operation and from the political news. America's Congress indulged in bombastic arguments over who, among our statesmen, had lost China. Plank said, "Did you ever notice how clever the Chinese are? They're masters at diversionary tactics. If they pull a boo-boo they deliberately confuse the issues and manipulate one American into blaming another. And while we fight among ourselves they laugh and joke about how dumb we are. . . . They're right, we're dumb."

With CAT sinking deeper into debt, Cockrell suggested we lend our personal savings to the company, but Chennault told us to hang on to them. He put everyone on leave of absence without pay, except for a skeleton staff and ten flight crews. Those who stayed offered to work without pay. Chennault and Willauer said, "Thanks—it's just postponed."

Our around-the-island schedules and fish charters barely supported us. Chennault sent Burridge to Korea to confer with President

Rhee's financial adviser in hopes of drumming up business, and the optimist returned as casually as if exiled airlines got contracts at the drop of a hat.

Burridge had agreed, on behalf of CAT, to fly a collection of Korean manufacturers on a trade mission throughout Asia. An erudite adviser, a commercial attaché from the U.S. State Department, would accompany them.

Rousselot assigned Cockrell and me to the junket. We spread out our charts and plotted courses from Korea to Taiwan, the Philippines, Thailand, Indochina, Burma, India, Ceylon, Indonesia, Australia, New Zealand, and back to Korea.

Fifteen merchants and manufacturers would display their products at chambers of commerce meetings—tennis shoes, textiles, ginseng root, cigarettes. The goods would be carried in the aft belly compartment, while the forward compartment would hold everything we might need for a long time away from our maintenance base: tires, spark plugs, magnetos, instruments. Burridge suggested we furnish the soundproof cabin with a desk and typewriter so passengers could write reports en route.

Etta Bowen, to her delight, was appointed secretary/stewardess, and a good mechanic became our flight engineer. After we were airborne, radio operator Chu became our flight nurse. Whenever Etta came forward to report, "A passenger is on the verge of throwing up," Chu, who looked like a dignified schoolteacher in horn-rimmed glasses, peered owlishly at the pale one and scolded in Oxford English, "Come now, sophisticated travelers never get airsick," and the proud Korean, too stubborn to lose face before a Chinese, stiffened and sat tight-lipped until his color returned. No one vomited, not even during our rough flight over India's Sind Desert, which is notorious for turbulence.

Chu also became a gourmet guide. No matter where we landed, he found a great-uncle, second cousin, or brother-in-law who owned a Chinese restaurant in town.

Chennault had told us, "When you overnight at Rangoon, get a guard for the airplane. Lots of Communists in Burma."

The American ambassador met us at Rangoon's airport and asked how he could help. Advised we needed a guard, he replied, "I don't know of any guards. Sleep in the airplane."

Smelling Burma's lush vegetation, I knew mosquitoes would scramble at sunset, and Jawbert had described the agonies of Burma's malaria. The Standard Oil agent said, "Guard? I know the chief of police." Thirty minutes later a grinning Burmese policeman, bearing a sword, appeared.

The crew checked into Rangoon's rambling Victorian hotel. A prim Burmese desk clerk looked sternly at lovely Etta and her four male colleagues and warned, in clipped English diction, "We shall tolerate no funny business in this hotel."

"Calm yourself, my good man," I said. "I was a missionary pilot."

Although the hotel was almost deserted, he assigned Etta to a room in some distant wing.

Chennault had also told us, "The Air Force attaché will meet you at New Delhi. I asked him to give you any help."

He was a captain who met us with a scowl. "You civilians out making a fast buck?"

"This is the Korean trade mission," Cockrell said.

"Carpetbaggers."

"Go screw yourself," I wanted to say, but thought of Chennault and bit my tongue.

Our Koreans, at various trade shows, got mail from home, shook their heads gravely, and said, "We're worried about war."

By the time we got to Sydney, Dr. Oh, their spokesman—a tall, dignified gentleman who'd received his Ph.D. from Princeton—said, "We don't want to continue on to New Zealand. We want to get home before the war begins."

The American economic adviser scoffed, "Nonsense. We'll follow the itinerary."

"There'll be a war," said Dr. Oh. "When a line is drawn through the middle of a country and the separate halves go to opposing ideologies, it makes a powder keg."

The economic adviser didn't appear to be convinced.

Dr. Oh remained courteous, but his eyes showed anger. "All people yearn for a unified homeland. When you defeated Japan, you liberated us from fifty years of cruel occupation, and we were grateful. But you cut us in two. You made a powder keg. There will be a war."

The adviser gave some soothing answer, although in private he told Cockrell and me, "I understand Dr. Oh's feelings. . . . We protect Japan, but Korea is beyond our defense perimeter, out in the cold. They visualize a hundred thousand Communist soldiers shuffling their sneakers, raring to charge across the border."

Turning to me, Cockrell asked, "What do you think?"

"The Koreans chartered the plane—it's their money—they have a right to go where they like."

"I agree," Cockrell said. The adviser nodded.

Our decision surprised the Koreans, who'd assumed we'd back our fellow American. We landed in Seoul eleven days ahead of schedule, and the Koreans threw a farewell party in a lavish garden setting. "Thank you for caring for our safety," they announced. "You even tasted the gasoline each day." Apparently they had watched us drain the fuel sumps and blow on a sample in the palm of a hand to evaporate the fuel and watch for a telltale residue of water.

We left Korea in a cloudless sky. White tendrils of ground fog lingered in green valleys, and we knew why Korea was called the Land of the Morning Calm.

Two days later, North Koreans crossed the border in Russian T-34 tanks. It was Sunday, June 25, 1950. Many South Korean troops had been given leave to work the rice paddies of their home villages. And their officers celebrated the opening of a military club.

I was in Hong Kong, eating Cheong's rice *congee* for breakfast, when the news came. President Truman ordered American forces to defend South Korea's airports while American civilians were evacuated.

Snoddy came over and grumbled, "We practically invited the Commies when Dulles announced to all hands and the cook that Korea lay outside our defense perimeter."

He flew Rosbert and Burridge to Tokyo that afternoon. At FEAMCOM (Far East Air Material Command) headquarters, they offered CAT's fleet to the U.S. Air Force. Rosbert said ten C-46s and crews could be airborne in a matter of hours. We could recall furloughed crews from the States and put five more C-46s in the air within the week, and get still more planes from the Chinese Air Force.

"General Stratemeyer looked surprised," Burridge said.

"We can't spare forklifts—your planes won't get loaded."

"We'll use our cargo men like we've always used."

"How will you refuel? We're short of refueling trucks."

"Hand pumps out of fifty-five-gallon drums, like we did in China."

General Stratemeyer said, "We'll advise you of our decision."

Impatient, Burridge jumped into a C-46, and Snoddy flew him to Seoul to see how it compared to our China experience. "Seoul was in flames," Snoddy told me. "A voice on the radio said Kimpo Airport was under attack, but the L-5 strip near the city was open.

"We landed on the strip. American and Korean soldiers were blowing up equipment. They were surprised to see a civilian airplane but were too busy to squawk. Artillery boomed. Refugees hurried down a road. The soldiers said they had orders to abandon Seoul before sunrise. . . . We took off. On climb out we saw bumper-to-bumper convoys moving south. We smelled the city burning. . . . It was China all over again."

The South Korean Army packed explosive charges in the bridge over the Han River and waited for its troops to cross, but the nervous deputy minister of defense ordered its immediate destruction. The Korean Army's chief of staff argued against it, and the American military adviser reminded him of a previous agreement to withhold its destruction until enemy tanks got close to the Korean Army's headquarters. During the discussion someone blew the bridge without warning. Everyone on the bridge went up with it.

We waited in Taipei, ready to go. General Stratemeyer didn't call, even though the UN Security Council decided to defend South Korea, and the Air Force had only one transport outfit near Korea—the 374th Troop Carrier Wing in Japan. The weight of its four-engine DC-4s restricted them to Korea's better runways. Smaller C-46s and C-47s were needed to get ammunition in and the wounded out of small airfields. It would be at least a week before they could put a C-47 squadron into the area.

"General Stratemeyer isn't ignoring us," Burridge said. "He just doesn't think we can do it. He doesn't know our record in China. He thought Rosbert and I were hot air."

The Newcomers

After the excitement of China's civil war and a new one in Korea, it didn't feel normal to fly baby fish out of Hong Kong. I sensed that would change when a newcomer acquired a lofty title we'd never heard before: chief executive officer. A relaxed, unassuming American with a wrestler's physique, he was a soft-voiced, gentle man, economical with words. A hint of sadness in his eyes and a sensitive mouth made me think he had seen much and understood more than most men. A Phi Beta Kappa key didn't hang on his vest, although he had one from Lehigh University, where he had graduated with honors. A gold football didn't dangle from a watch chain, although he had been captain of the varsity team. Nor was there any bravura about him, even though a French general had pinned the Croix de Guerre on his chest, next to his American medals. A volunteer in the OSS (Office of Strategic Services—the antecedent of the Central Intelligence Agency), he had parachuted behind enemy lines in the recent world war to join a French resistance group that blew up bridges and power lines and ambushed Nazi columns before the Allied invasion; and he had gone on to Asia to organize Chinese airborne commando units for the continuing war with Japan. His name was Alfred Cox.

Another grand title—special assistant to the president—was pinned on a second newcomer, named John Mason. He had been regimental commander in the 90th Infantry Division during the big war in Europe, where he earned the Distinguished Service Cross, two Silver Stars, three Bronze Stars, two Purple Hearts. A tall, dignified man, he won my heart when he told me about his retreat during a battle with the Germans. "A Texas congressman happened to be visiting our headquarters when I ordered the retreat. He asked what the people of the great state of Texas would think if they knew their men retreated. I told him I didn't give a damn what the people from Texas thought—right now I was worried about losing my men."

A couple of weeks later I was landing in Hong Kong when chief pilot Rousselot was taking off, and he radioed, "Go to the head office."

I walked into our Hong Kong headquarters and saw a third new-comer with a sign on his desk: director of traffic. And a new American secretary directed me to the office of a fourth newcomer who didn't have a title. He didn't need one. Six-foot-two and corpu-lent, he had a poker face that spelled *cop*. Without introducing him-self, and before I could sit down, he shoved a slip of paper in front of me and ordered, "Sign." Typed words said something about a feder-al penitentiary if I talked.

I didn't sign or talk. I wheeled around and strode into the office of Cox, whom I trusted even though I hadn't known him long. I asked, "Who the hell's the giant?"

"He's okay."

I went back and signed. The giant was Jones, a former FBI agent—an amiable gourmet who rapidly acquired a taste for Chinese food.

At an informal gathering of pilots we indulged in the age-old flier's obsession for blasting inhabitants of paneled offices.

"For an airline that's broke, we're sure hiring a lot of wheels."

Referring to our Cox's background as a paratrooper, someone carped, "A guy who'd jump out of 'em can't be expected to run 'em."

"The new director of sales doesn't know a damn thing about an airline. Three-piece suit, feet on the desk, he wears jump boots."

Earthquake growled, "It doesn't take a gypsy fortune-teller with a piss pot full of tea leaves to tell us it's the CIA."

Rousselot dropped in and listened until his eyes got stormy, and he scowled like a Cherokee chief about to raid a wagon train. "I don't want to hear you guys say 'CIA.' Not ever again. Not even to each other. If you have to refer to the organization, just call them *our customers*. You'll have me to reckon with."

I got an overseas phone call from friends in Michigan's Upper Peninsula, where I worked before coming to China. "The FBI's been asking questions about you. What've you done?"

"Nothing." I couldn't tell them it was a security check. I had signed the chit.

"Listen, don't try to kid your friends. You're in some kind of trouble."

The FBI appeared at the door of my devout, gentle, former land-lady. She cried hysterically, "All I can say, Felix was always a perfect gentleman." A bigger lie was never told. Her darkest corruption had been bingo at the Catholic church, but now she told a whopper to protect the errant pilot who had lived in her boardinghouse with copper miners. I loved her like a second mother.

The CIA agents were able to rove the Orient and gather information without becoming conspicuous because it's normal for airline employees to move around the system.

Pilots were returned to full salary and CAT got full operating expenses, although Chennault still owed the Chinese Nationalist government, on paper, almost five million U.S. dollars.

We discovered that our new executives were aware of our exploits in China. After our enduring Chinese Air Force animosity and British officialdom's disdain, the newfound respect from high-caliber professionals was refreshing.

The CIA, like CAT, was young. On parallel courses, we grew up together, and the bond of mutual respect grew stronger.

9

A Foot in Both Wars: Korea and Indochina

Late summer 1950. By the time CAT got invited to war, the Communists held most of Korea. Using gallows humor to ease his dismay, an American general remarked, "If they look organized, shoot 'em—they aren't ours."

Caught with a small defense force, the U.S. Army sent cooks and clerks to battle, some from its occupation force in Japan. When we learned that North Korean soldiers dragged wounded Americans behind vehicles until they died or buried them alive, we were shocked and knew this would be another brutal war for the guys on the ground.

Pushed close to the southeast end of Korea's peninsula, Americans and South Koreans made a stand at a line called the Pusan Perimeter. We flew into its landing strip, which had been reinforced with PSP (pierced steel planks). The steel was slippery in the rain.

Air Force B-26s, light attack bombers, shared the tarmac. "Low-level," a lieutenant said, "we shoot anything that moves at night. . . . Flying up these valleys in the dark, your old bunghole puckers—you never know when you're going up a blind alley. We're losing guys." The space under his cockpit window, where pilots paint enemy flags—one for each victory—was decorated with a pine tree with its top knocked off. The inscription: *Lt. Kelly's only confirmed victory.*

Most of the warriors were reservists, because much of the Air Force and Navy had been mothballed. Home from the Second World War, feeling they had done their duty, they had had just enough time—five years—to establish a civilian career and a family before the recall. They lamented, "We caught a horrible disease: gone-to-Korea."

A convincing sign appeared at the exit of a military base near Seoul: *Drive carefully. The life you save may be that of your replacement.*

The 315th Air Division (Combat Cargo) adopted us, and it was Taiyüan again—the same hot-bunk system—thirty cots in a warehouse at Japan's Tachikawa Air Base. When we returned from a mission our names went to the bottom of a roster, and when it reached the top we went out again. After seventeen hours' work I got to the warehouse at 2:00 A.M. and saw an operations clerk prod Calhoun awake. He rubbed his eyes, squinted at a watch, and moaned, "I just got in three hours ago."

"It's your turn—there's no one else."

Someone prodded me to duty a few hours later and said Calhoun had crashed at Iwakuni and the crew had escaped unhurt. He touched down at the Marine Corps base, reached over to push the cowl flap lever, and pushed one of the throttles by mistake. The burst of power on one side veered the plane into a ditch.

The investigation revealed he had flown more in the past two weeks than a pilot normally flies in a month, and he had had only three hours' sleep in a noisy warehouse before the trip. Calhoun showed us a transcript of the accident report. Data showing his excessive flying time and insufficient rest had been crossed out, with the notation, "Deleted for the protection of the company."

"The company had no choice," Calhoun said. "It needed protection, and I went along with it." Even though our friend had had an impeccable record in China, we also agreed it was right to sacrifice a career for the good of CAT.

After reading the sanitized report, the Chinese Civil Aviation Authority revoked his license, which meant he couldn't fly CAT's planes, because they flew the Nationalist Chinese flag, but his American license was still valid. He left for the USA to look for work. "Leaving CAT is like leaving home," he said.

My first passengers of the war were airborne troops returning from a respite in Japan. Their exuberant company commander, riding in the cockpit, pulled my leg, I suppose. "We like hand-to-hand fighting the best," the young captain said. "Got our bayonets replated in Tokyo—they got dull again. Our company is notorious. Before we charge we wave our bayonets so the nickel plating flashes in the sun. Scares the hell out of 'em. Most of the time the gooks run."

On our approach into Taejon he said, "I'll join my men in back. I don't want to watch the landing—it scares me. We airborne guys would sooner jump. Most crashes occur on landing. A parachute is safer."

A CAT C-47 arrived with a new coat of camouflage. A previous design—a flaming heart—tried to shine through the olive-drab paint. I recognized the logo of the Lutheran World Mission. The lanky pilot with the grin and carelessly placed cap was Bill Dudding, the pilot who had replaced me the day I joined CAT. When the mainland fell, the mission had given the crew the *Saint Paul* in lieu of pay. "CAT leased it and hired us too," Dudding said. "Springweiler is in Taipei."

Dudding became an object lesson on restricting passengers from the flight deck. He invited an Air Force legal officer to the jump seat. In the course of the conversation, Dudding remarked, "I own the airplane." He might have escaped with that. New to the area, however, he followed Fukuoka's instrument approach pattern instead of flying straight in. There wasn't a cloud in the sky, and the runway had been visible for the last fifty miles. Yet it was prudent that a newcomer acquire a mental image of the leeway that was provided over and around hills near airports. The complicated instrument pattern gave an appearance that he was searching for an airport yet unseen. The observer thought Dudding was off his rocker. A USAF complaint noted, "Pilot lost: had difficulty finding destination. Claimed he owned the airplane."

Believing dramatic action would protect CAT's hard-won contract, Willauer fired Dudding.

News correspondents were less fussy about regulations. They liked to fly with us because of our safety record. "You guys made all your mistakes in China," one said. "You're like mongrel dogs who know how to cross the street without getting an ass full of fender."

I took them out of Korea and set them down at Tokyo's Haneda Airport, where I was supposed to rest overnight. The passengers said, "We'll put you up at the press club."

A redbrick building in Shimbum Alley displayed a brass plate: "Foreign Correspondents Club of Japan." It was two o'clock in the morning, yet the bar was still open. After a couple of nightcaps, someone said, "Let's sign him up." In no time I was a member.

"Where's your book of rules?" I said. "Such a prestigious club—you have rules, no doubt."

"No rules. These damn guys wouldn't follow 'em anyway. The bar closes when the last drunk crawls out on his hands and knees, and opens when some poor son of a bitch wants a cure for his hangover."

One morning I walked into Shimbum Alley, headed for the redbrick building, and saw an empty U.S. Army bus waiting to take correspondents to the airport. A famous photographer from *Life* magazine test-focused his Leica on various buildings. Zenier, the Warner-Pathé newsreel cameraman, came outside, looking grave. Many others emerged, jabbering, with drinks still in their hands. An excited correspondent exclaimed, "The tide!" I guessed they had just been briefed by a U.S. Army press officer, because they were on their way, under military supervision, to Korea.

No use going into the club—it'd be empty. As I strolled to the Ginza it popped into my head. The innocent newsman's exclamation. The tide! Something's brewing near Inchon. Its tide is similar to that of North America's Bay of Fundy, where the sea level changes seventy feet in one cycle.

Soon afterward, General MacArthur executed his bold flanking move. His troops, transported by the U.S. Navy, invaded Inchon, recaptured Seoul, and cut the enemy supply line to the south. And I understood why military officers, in the presence of news hawks, feel uncomfortable.

It wasn't long before the troops pushed north and captured Pyongyang, the North Korean capital. I landed there at midnight, guided to touchdown by a U.S. Air Force team of precision radar controllers. The electric lights that illuminated the runway seemed luxurious; the coffee-can flares we had used in China were fresh in my memory.

An Air Force refueler drove up. Waiting for my tanks to fill, the driver looked over his truck. Pointing out a couple of bullet holes, he said casually, "Must've picked 'em up coming from the dump." Not until then did I know our side had captured the place a matter of hours before. In that short space of time a radar landing system had been set up and flight-tested and lights, fire and crash trucks, and maintenance stands had been installed.

A medevac sergeant said, "It'll be a few hours before we can get you loaded. Take a rest."

Tents sheltered cots, hot showers, towels, miniature bars of soap. A latrine's zigzag ditches looked like some sanitary engineering principle had been observed.

I recalled CAT's operations in China. How easily details were overlooked. And since that midnight landing in the North Korean capital I've had respect for American military logisticians.

I landed near Hamhung in the far north, near the east coast, soon after the capture of the airstrip. The operations officer said, "We just caught a sniper in the tall grass." I had been flying above clouds in moonlight. It was dark on the ground. Standing outside, in a grass field, waiting for the wounded to arrive, I heard a sergeant say something quietly, and eight skinny worn-out guys, carrying rifles, formed a single file. The sergeant raised his arm and lowered it again. Without a word, they followed him into the dark. They were going on patrol, one of the oldest tasks in military history. You keep going until someone shoots at you. It's how you tell where the enemy is. No background music or John Wayne shouts to stir their spirit; they just looked worried and very lonely. I would have looked terrified.

After I flew a load of supplies to some airport close to a battle I returned empty except for a lone Marine with fatigues and a stubble beard.

The night was clear and so cold that the engines drummed a crisp staccato. The airplane didn't run far down the strip before it grabbed the air and flew. I told the Marine to take the jump seat in the cockpit, where it was warmer.

"The Red Cross got word to me, my father died. . . . I got a good CO—he let me go."

"I didn't know the Red Cross came this far."

"They're pretty good at family emergencies."

"Sorry you lost your father. It's bad enough with a bunch of Koreans trying to kill you."

"Where're you landing?"

"Tachikawa Air Force Base, near Tokyo."

"Go near Iwakuni?"

"Right over it."

"Can you drop me off at the Marine Corps base? I'll pick up a uniform. These fatigues are all I got. MPs will pick me up."

"I'm sorry, I can't. The Air Force controls our movements—315th Combat Cargo Squadron." He accepted this philosophically.

"No sweat. I tell you what." He shifted his bayonet around so he could get to his hip pocket. From a thick wallet he withdrew a business card. "I'm one of the reserves who got called," he explained. "Got my own business. If you wire flowers to your wife or girlfriend, do it through my shop." The card was decorated with a bouquet of flowers. His first name was Renee.

Later, Willauer boarded one of my flights from Taipei, but he didn't take his customary place at the copilot's controls. He remained in the cabin with a group of Air Force officers. Halfway to Tokyo he brought a model of CAT's LST into the cockpit. "Look how she's changed since you sailed her out of Shanghai," he said.

The model reached three feet in length. Built by Chinese craftsmen, it came apart in sections to reveal a propeller shop, hydraulic shops, instrument laboratory, medical clinic, and a loft for hanging parachutes out to dry. "It's the best aircraft maintenance shop in the world. It goes where we go," he said. Willauer was wound up, and I had heard it before, but I enjoyed his enthusiasm. "If you have to take a shop to pieces before you move, it can take months to get it operating in the new place. Compressed-air hoses, electric and hydraulic lines have to be reconnected and adjusted. FEAMCOM is interested. The Air Force needs a couple off the Korean coast, the way the war is sashaying back and forth."

I didn't see Willauer for a long time after that, but I read what he wrote after his presentation: "I observed how badly off the Air Force was in maintenance equipment, which was coming over by slow boat and was gradually being assembled. When the Air Force officers saw this model they got tremendously excited about this potential for making the Air Force more mobile. However, one of the generals remarked, and I shall never forget this, that while this was a wonderful idea, since it was seaborne it would mean that the Navy would probably take it over and therefore they had better not think any more about it."

About four months into the Korean War we heard that Buol and his staff had been transferred from Mengtsz to a Red prison in Kunming. Bertram Hemingway, the British vice consul, took food, but was told, "Our prisoners don't need it. We feed them four meals a day." Eventually, they accepted canned goods. The prisoners couldn't write, but Hemingway sent news of them, and Sue was happy to learn that Buol exercised in a compound where military families hung their wash to dry.

Early in September, Jawbert and Lincoln Sun wangled a trip, under armed escort, to town. Pretending to fetch medicine for the foreign prisoner, they evaded their guards and hid in the British consulate. An employee of a trading company pointed out a disabled truck in a nearby shed. Jawbert worked on it for a few nights, while the trading company faked a couple of identity cards. Jawbert and Lincoln Sun drove the old truck through Kunming's gates and down the Burma Road. Fearing the Burmese would return them to China because they lacked passports, they stuck to byways and river boats, stopping only at small villages. By the time they reached the American consulate in Rangoon they were ill with malaria.

Sue cabled Ambassador Warren Austin to plead Buol's case before the United Nations. She beseeched Chou En-lai and even the National Press Club, trying to get safe passage to Kunming to join her husband in prison. Advisers warned her she'd probably wind up in some Canton prison, far from Buol, unable to help him whatsoever. She abandoned the idea.

Chennault kept her busy with projects to divert her from heartache. Assigned to Madame Chiang Kai-shek, who wanted to resurrect the run-down Grand Hotel, Sue turned it into a Mandarin showplace. Like a feminine Walter Mitty, Sue became an instant architect, landscape designer, interior decorator, assembler of all the fine artists who had migrated from the mainland. She transformed the dining room into a lavishly decorated restaurant that served succulent Chinese dishes. Tennis courts and a swimming pool appeared and then a club for local residents. Taipei's Grand Hotel became a subject of conversation among sophisticated travelers.

Snoddy and I dropped in to see Chennault. We looked into his open door and saw him writing with his customary yellow pencil. He looked up and seemed glad to see a couple of his pilots.

"I think Buol will be held until the war's over," he said. He pointed to a newspaper on his desk. "You can tell more from what's not said than what's said."

Chennault leaned back in his chair, happy for the break, it seemed.

"The Chinese should be denouncing us, but they've been mighty quiet lately. . . . Our friends on the mainland say artillery and ammunition are moving out of south China, heading north."

Snoddy said, "What about the rumors that China put soldiers in Korea, told them it was Manchuria and the Americans are invaders?

"It might be true. No one will know they're coming unless we drop flares at night. Chinese troops sleep all day, except for the scouts. The scouts move ahead in daylight to prepare the next camp. If they hear an airplane, they freeze. If anyone moves, an officer shoots him."

By Thanksgiving Day the U.S. Army was fourteen miles short of the Manchurian border. They saw the Yalu River. Marines east of them saw the Chosin Reservoir. General MacArthur announced, "You'll be home for Christmas."

Pessimistic, General Walker passed word to a colonel in the 21st Infantry, "If you smell Chinese food, fall back." A third of a million Red Chinese soldiers had marched over frozen roads from Manchuria. Eight hours a night. They made camp, camouflaged their equipment, ate, and bedded down before dawn. They covered 286 miles in three weeks. They waited in the mountains of North Korea.

Before the end of November, American soldiers heard bugles, whistles, gongs, and shrieks, similar to those heard by CAT pilots at the walls of Weihsien three years before.

In bitter cold, taking their dead and wounded with them, some of the American soldiers and Marines fought their way fifty miles southeast to a small landing strip where their wounded could be shuttled to Yonpo Airport on the coast. Larger planes took them to a military hospital in Japan.

Blustery winds shook the C-46 after I landed at Yonpo to pick up wounded. Sheets of rain obscured the coastline when I took off. A newly hired CAT pilot, inbound and eager to pick up wounded, made a GCA (ground-controlled approach) even though the team had just set it up and had not had time to calibrate the radar. His crash killed his only passenger, a medic of an evacuation squadron.

Rousselot ordered the plane torched, because Communist troops were advancing toward the airport. We weren't surprised when he fired the pilot for trusting a GCA that hadn't been calibrated. We couldn't imagine a circumstance when our chief would tolerate a breach of in-flight discipline.

On the following night I flew from Korea to Japan's Tachikawa Air Force Base near Tokyo and watched ice build up on our wings and windshield. We skirted the coast of Japan's Honshu Island, trying to get a navigation fix. Although snow static obliterated radio signals, a few intermittent signals hinted we had an unusual drift. Japan's winter winds were usually northwesterly, but this night brought strong winds with lots of ocean moisture from the south. Meteorologists had yet to discover a small yet deep low-pressure area over the sea. It seemed like we needed a twenty-degree drift correction to keep the wind from blowing us off our intended track, but I added another ten, because Mount Fuji waited twenty-five miles north of our course. I was descending into Tokyo when I heard Heising, another new CAT pilot, climbing out, bound to Korea, with an assigned altitude of eight thousand feet.

An Air Force radar surveillance team watched him drift off course, toward Fuji, and they called him on every available frequency without getting a response. Then his blip disappeared from the radarscope. In the morning, searchers found the remains of the crew and their C-46 at the eight-thousand-foot level of Mount Fuji.

Bone tired in Hong Kong a few days later, I was awakened by Cheong, who said I had visitors. The families of Heising's crew—the Changs and the Wens—wanted to talk to a CAT pilot. I showed them Mount Fuji on my chart and explained how the low-pressure cell had caused the south wind. The symbols on the chart and my meteorological explanation only confused the grieving families. They didn't want a science lecture; they wondered why a pilot struck a mountain that everybody knows is there. They didn't know a pilot can't see out of his windshield much of the time, or that unpredicted winds and snow static, in the days of low-frequency radio beacons, could form a booby trap.

From Hong Kong, I was scheduled to Indochina. Only a few days before, in Korea, I heard U.S. Marines sing a song of President Harry Truman and the war he euphemistically called a "police action." Sung to the tune of Australia's "Bless 'Em All," the Marine dithyramb ended,

> *We're Harry's police force on call,*
> *So put back your pack on,*
> *The next step is Saigon,*
> *Cheer up, all me lads, fuck 'em all.*

The spunky Marines didn't know how right they were, nor did I. The Korean War, only months old, would continue for three years, and when it was over the next stop would indeed be Saigon.

I found myself in that Paris of the Orient only six months after the Korean War began.

French Indochina

While the UN had its war in Korea, France had its own in Indochina, and CAT engaged in both simultaneously. So did American taxpayers. They paid 90 percent of Korea's tab and 75 percent of Indochina's. CAT pilots switched wars at the stroke of a crew scheduler's pencil and got breaks on peaceful passenger routes. Snoddy said, "Someday I'm going to meet myself going the other way."

A few days after the sad visit of the Chang and Wen families, Rousselot sent me to the Miramar Hotel to be briefed by Cox. CAT's room at the Miramar was used whenever we wanted more privacy than the frenetic head office afforded. Even though the hotel was owned by good Portuguese Catholics, I assumed our customer (the CIA) had swept it for bugging devices.

In that room I had seen Rousselot talk to a pilot or two while Cox took a different crew into the bathroom and sat on the lid of the toilet while the crew sat on the edge of the bathtub and listened to the briefing. Earthquake said, "CAT is the only airline with a hotel room for a head office and a toilet for a conference room."

A lot of missions were planned in that room. Rousselot made the first spy flight, dropping Chinese agents near Mongolia, where people were fiercely anti-Communist. A few who had been flying-boat skippers in the Navy before joining CAT landed PBYs off China's coastal islands by maintaining a slow rate of descent in the dark, without landing lights, until they hit water, hoping they wouldn't hit a log or some flotsam.

Bill Welk, who had flown B-17s in the big war, used one to penetrate deep into China and drop spies and propaganda leaflets. Other guys flew C-46s on flights that were shorter in miles but long enough to put them back at Taipei, low on fuel. Whenever I heard praise for CAT I thought it belonged to the guys who were assigned to those jobs. They deserved it more than anyone else. They got nothing more than ten extra dollars an hour in hazard pay.

Cox sat me in a corner of the Miramar room and said, "Keep your eyes peeled and avoid controversy. . . . This is our entry to Indochina. We've got a contract, but the French don't want us. They're looking for any excuse to kick us out. . . . You'll be flying for STEM"—the Special Technical and Economic Mission. "Medicines, mostly. Our stuff hasn't been getting to the Vietnamese. It goes via the French. Very little gets to the local people. We'll deliver it direct. Springweiler will fit right in. Lots of Germans there. He flew there before the war. He's known, and he speaks French."

On Christmas morning I bought a turkey at Tachenko's gourmet delicatessen in Hong Kong, knowing the C-47 would be *Saint Paul* and the copilot, Springweiler. The reunion deserved a feast.

After climbing out of Hong Kong I engaged the autopilot and unboxed the food. Springweiler said, "*Wunderbar*—I only brought two cans of beans."

"We'll eat the beans in Hanoi tonight."

Half a turkey and a few hours later we landed at Hanoi, where we met Frank Guberlet, our station manager, formerly a U.S. Navy pilot. "Merry Christmas," he said. "We're all invited to the American consulate for dinner."

"Christmas dinner with Foggy Bottoms," I told Springweiler. "I'd sooner eat beans." I was wrong.

The consul, whose name I forget (it sounded something like Blankenship), had been a concert violinist until arthritis cramped his hands. Courtly, as if bowing to applause, he accepted Springweiler's beans. He was a handsome, dark-haired man perhaps in his early fifties; his dignity was tempered with an easy manner and an inner peace that put us at ease.

I studied an oil painting on his living-room wall. A huge Sphinx-like stone head with a Buddha-like smile was entangled in jungle vines. In the foreground, minute images of Cambodians looked up at it. It was the essence of Angkor Wat. A watercolor of sparse green and black lines on finely crushed eggshells gave an impression of a graceful woman with long hair and a cone-shaped hat. She poled a slender barge along a canal lined with weeping willows, and I remembered the canals of Hue.

I didn't dwell on the paintings. Stunning Tonkin women, like nymphs from an ethereal forest, drifted quietly through the rooms with platters of steamed shrimp, spring rolls, sesame cakes that had been arranged in patterns, and rows of glasses of champagne. Never had I seen women move with such grace. Glossy black hair, waist-length, contrasted with pastel pink or green tunics that reached their knees. Satin pantaloons reached their ankles.

"Springweiler," I said, "our host has the soul of an artist. He has the capacity to love every kind of beauty on earth."

Willauer turned up the next day, and when his business was done he was anxious to get to Saigon, on the southern end of Indochina. Although it was a night flight, I let Willauer fly *Saint Paul*. The fluorescent glow of the instruments revealed his grin as he descended toward Tan Son Nhut Airport. He reached for the lever that would extend our wing flaps, but I put my hand over his and said, "Wait." I put my finger on the airspeed indicator to show he exceeded the maximum flap speed.

Willauer said, "Whoops," and Springweiler, annoyed, whispered, "Just because he's president you think you have to let him fly."

The Paris of the Orient

A fishing village two hundred years ago, Saigon grew with the French Empire. Like New Orleans, it sits on the delta of a famous river. Not precisely on the Mekong, it's on one of the watery fingers that splay out across the delta of silt. It's deep enough for oceangoing ships.

The Rue de la Paix, a grand boulevard with shade trees, ran from a twin-steepled cathedral—the Basilica—to the Majestic Hotel on the finger of the Mekong. Lei-Loi Boulevard sparkled with fountains leading to the National Assembly Hall. Nguyen Boulevard, framed by flower boxes, was called the Street of Flowers. Nightclubs with dazzling marquees bore names like Moulin Rouge, Arc-en-Ciel, Crois du Sud. Floor shows came from Paris, courtesy of Air France. Stone villas sat behind lavish gardens and fences of ornate ironwork.

Cholon, the Chinese suburb, provided a casino that rivaled Monte Carlo's, and a less splendid annex gave pedicab drivers and laborers a gambler's chance.

Everyone agreed that Saigon was the Paris of the Orient. Thirty thousand French citizens lived there, with other Europeans. Germans from Hitler's army had transferred their martial skills to the French Foreign Legion.

L'Amiral served French cuisine. The Kontiki, American salads and steaks. Pagoda's specialties were flaky croissants and coffee. I nursed Vichy water and absinthe at a sidewalk café while Springweiler admitted his first cool sip of French beer tasted almost as good as his country's brew.

Guberlet, our station manager, said, "I invited a Sûreté [French secret police] agent, but he wouldn't come. He was on my tail while I ran errands. I said, 'Come have a drink, you must be tired. You've been following me all day.'"

Our Belgian companion—a chemist on vacation from a rubber plantation—said, "You Americans take your wars too seriously. We've learned to live with it. Our laborers drift off for a spell with Red guerrillas and come back to work. Our supplies pass through Vietminh roadblocks—we just pay a toll."

I said, "Look at the women." French cyclists showed knees and elbows and effort while their Vietnamese sisters, with perfect posture, glided past. Those who perched behind motorcycle drivers didn't hang on even though they weaved through traffic. Silks fluttering, long hair streaming, they were relaxed and serene on their precarious mounts, and I wondered if the Vietnamese had a sense of balance that Westerners lack.

Three women strolled in white satin slacks and knee-length tunics of pongee silk. When they got a few meters past our sidewalk table, an urchin on the curb picked a slingshot off his lap. With an evil grin, he struggled to draw it to its maximum stretch and zinged a pebble at the trio, and quickly hid the launcher on his lap. Struck smartly on her derrière, the victim looked back angrily, only to see a ragged boy gazing forlornly into space.

Springweiler raised his glass to a Legionnaire officer at another table and said, *"Wie geht's?"*

Stiffly, the officer answered, *"Bon soir."*

Springweiler mumbled, "I thought he was German."

The Belgian said, "For dinner I suggest the Caravelle. The dining room's on the sixth floor, too high to lob a grenade."

We walked down the street and saw four officers of the French Foreign Legion on the other side. Springweiler called, *"Wie geht's?"* and bounded across, only to return, frowning. "I can't understand it. Eighty percent are supposed to be German."

We walked past the Caravelle and wound up at the Majestic Hotel, where an eight-year-old boy in a natty uniform ran a fast elevator to the top, and a French maître d' in a white dinner jacket seated us at a table covered with linen. Another Frenchman with a huge key presented a wine list; a white-gloved Vietnamese brought menus. Then a French headwaiter discussed choices as gravely as if we were a council of war.

For a moment I left the dining and dancing area with its glittering chandeliers and string ensemble and chattering Europeans in tuxedos and floor-length gowns, and I stepped to the outside balcony to lean on the railing to watch a freighter ply the river. Gunfire cracked sharply in the countryside across the river. I looked straight down where darkness had brought out teams of French soldiers and Vietnamese police who stopped pedestrians and cyclists at random to pat them down and look into handbags and packages while some of the owners complained angrily. Babies were also searched, because Vietminh hid grenades in their clothing.

By the time we finished cheese and cognac it was late, but the same boy, still alert, operated the elevator.

Taking me in tow the next morning, our station manager said, "It wasn't easy getting you a membership," and he ushered me into the office of the Cercle Sportif (the Sports Circle), whose French president, in a three-piece suit, rose and welcomed me with formal courtesy. I recognized bits of French and responded with the few words I knew.

Exiting his door, our station manager said, "I didn't know you were a tennis ace."

"Lucky if I get it over the net."

"He asked if you were competition class—you said, 'Oui.' He entered you in the tournament."

"I thought he was bragging about his tennis courts."

"And you guys bitch about locals saying yes when they don't understand."

Drawing a small package from my hip pocket, I said, "I bought this G-string the French call swim trunks."

Larger than Olympic size, the pool sparkled in an area of flower gardens and shade trees. I couldn't believe my good fortune. At Waikiki, women's swimsuits still had skirts. Chinese on Hong Kong's beaches were modest. But at the Cercle Sportif, voluptuous French and Vietnamese women were naked—almost—and they were not ashamed. They returned my glances with bold, liquid eyes.

"Careful," Guberlet warned. "Cozy up to a femme fatale, she'll be the mistress of some French general, and we'll both get evicted."

Sitting on the edge of the pool, idly kicking the water, I said, "It's snowing in Wisconsin."

"In Korea some guys are fighting their way back from the Chosin Reservoir."

In the morning, Springweiler and I waited at Saigon's airport for STEM's medical supplies. Tan Son Nhut was an aviation historian's delight. Old airplanes of Aigle Azur, the Blue Eagle Airline, cruised with canvas covers against the cockpit windows to shield the sun from its cavalier pilots, who flew instruments on clear days, never mind the traffic. French Air Force planes ranged from American torpedo dive-bombers to old JU-52s. Even though the planes were obsolete, the angular German trimotor transports with corrugated fuselages were popular with French paratroopers, Springweiler said, because their slow speed made jumping out easy. "Everything's ninety," Springweiler explained. "The old Junkers take off at ninety miles per hour, cruise at ninety, and land at ninety."

We flew an hour and a half northeast of Saigon's flat delta, crossed three-thousand-foot mountains, and touched down on Dalat's plateau. It was a summer resort for those who could afford a vacation from Saigon's heat. Our Vietnamese agent accepted the cargo. Perhaps this stuff will get to the people, I thought. He said, "Last night Vietminh kidnapped three headmen of villages nearby. Tied them to a stake and burned them alive."

Springweiler said, "It doesn't sound like a resort anymore."

We flew over to the coast, turned north, and saw bathers on Nha Trang's long white beach and in the gentle cobalt surf. "The Riviera of the Orient," Springweiler said.

We stopped frequently to drop off medical supplies. No matter how small the field, it had a bar, usually of plaited bamboo with a thatched roof.

French pilots said, "Have wine."

"Thanks, I'll have Vichy water."

Surprised: "No wine?"

"Can't drink. I got more flyin' to do."

Puzzled: "Wine is not drinking."

After reaching Haiphong—in the extreme north—we checked into the Metropole Hotel, whose narrow front garden included a private zoo with a caged, mangy, depressed bear.

In the morning I wandered the waterfront, where an American civilian recorded notes on his clipboard while he watched an American freighter discharge cargo. "She's from San Pedro," he said, and I remembered that America bore three-quarters of the cost of France's war in Indochina. "They're transferring the cargo to that one." He pointed at a French ship ahead of us. "It's going to Le Havre. This stuff is supposed to go to the Vietnamese."

When we got back to Saigon we saw French newsreels of their infantrymen battling guerrillas in jungles. Little did anyone know they'd eventually see, in color, almost identical scenes of Americans in the same jungles.

STEM's medicines weren't available for distribution for a couple of days, so a few officials of the American embassy utilized the *Saint Paul* for an overnight trip to Laos, and they asked us to fly via Cambodia so they could look upon Angkor, which was a vast area of crumbling stone temples and heads that were larger and more enigmatic than Egypt's Sphinx. They were the remains of an ancient civilization, partly obscured by jungle vines, that had lost one too many wars. Later, in the Middle Ages, the Khmers built a capital there and called it Angkor Thom.

We doglegged to the west to get there, not much out of our way. Cambodia's hills were brighter than the rest of Southeast Asia, and I could almost navigate by the varied shades of green. In about an hour we picked up the lake and the wats, descended low, smelled the jungle, and saw cracked stone heads with mysterious smiles sticking out of jungle growth. After flying over a long rectangular pond that led to the Khmer temple, we climbed up, and the cooler air made our sweaty clothes clammy.

We were soon over Thailand. The Mekong River, beyond our right wing, shimmered like a brown silk ribbon, separating Thailand from Laos. Long poles, stuck in the riverbed, supported fish nets. Small boats, some like dugout canoes, served the two countries. Many small villages lay on the banks of the river.

An hour and a half later we saw the characteristic bend in the Mekong that identified Vientiane, the commercial capital of Laos. We crossed the river and touched down on a red-clay strip that had been hacked out of the heavy foliage, and we taxied back through the red dust we had raised.

A black limousine with an American flag on the fender waited. A lone American driver stood at its open doors. We opened our cabin door immediately so our diplomats could escape the hot airplane, but they didn't disembark until they had tightened their neckties and donned seersucker jackets.

The last one in the long limousine closed the door halfway, hesitated, and said detachedly, "We'll take off at ten o'clock tomorrow morning."

"No transportation for the crew?"

"We thought you slept in the airplane." The door slammed. They drove off. It was dusk. Birds roosted. Bugs swarmed; it was malaria country.

A French Army officer lent us a jeep.

After a sentry raised a pole at the airport boundary our Lao driver jammed his foot to the jeep's floor and lurched us into a terrifying ride. Whitewashed *Beau Geste* forts at half-mile intervals were a blur, although I could identify a red ball at the peak of their flagpoles that meant the sector had been swept with mine detectors. Although Laos was an independent kingdom, it was protected by the French Army, which held the real estate in the daytime. Vietminh guerrillas owned it at night. Our wild driver skidded around bends in the clay road while we exhorted him to slow down. Springweiler, in front, hung on with white knuckles. Scared into losing my temper, I shook the driver's shoulder and hollered, "For Chrissake, why do you go so fast?"

He turned around, grinning, and shouted, "If hit mine, it go off behind us."

Vientiane was deserted. At a corner hotel a fat wordless Frenchman handed us two keys attached to wooden tags. Some of the steps leading to the rooms were missing. No shower, one toilet down the hall. The bed perched on four piles of bricks. When I flopped on the gray sheets a pile of bricks fell and the bed tilted. Too tired to get up, I reached up and dropped the mosquito net, and red dust fell over me. I slept all night on the tilt.

In the morning we sprayed away the mosquitoes that had assembled in the airplane and took our VIPs back to Saigon.

A powerful thirst drew me to La Croix du Sud, pronounced Crock of Suds by Earthquake, who had arrived with Snoddy. They wore new seersucker suits. "Mohan the tailor man gave us two choices," Earthquake said. "Black stripes or blue."

"Nobody will believe you're pilots—you're sartorially correct. Everybody in the State Department wears seersucker. It's a uniform."

"We'll get respect."

"Not from me. . . . They abandoned Springweiler and me to the mosquitoes of Laos." My tale kindled memories of imperious confrontations at various American consulates.

"My aunt in Ireland applied for a visa," Earthquake said. "A question on the application said, 'Did you ever commit adultery?' She answered, 'Not yet, because nobody asked me.'"

"I gave my passport to the American consulate in London for renewal," Snoddy said. "It had been issued in Guam. The clerk came back and said they confiscated it 'cause it was fake—there was no such place as Gooma."

"I'm takin' it off," Earthquake announced, "before somebody thinks I'm State Department." He stuffed the jacket under his bar stool.

"Leave your pants on."

"Mine's coming off too," Snoddy said.

I left early because I had to fly in the morning. When I returned from the next day's trip I checked their room. "You did the right thing leaving early," Snoddy said. "We piled our State Department suits on the floor, sprinkled lighter fluid, and set them afire."

"Didn't want to ruin our reputations," Earthquake said. I looked on the tile floor and saw remnants of ashes missed by a broom.

The next day I was scheduled back to Taipei.

Korea Again

At Taipei, Chennault had left word with operations for me to come to his house.

I knocked on his screen door and saw him eating something that looked like a Creole chicken dish. "Come in," he said, "Someone will think you're a stranger if they see you standing outside."

Chennault wanted a pilot's-eye view of Indochina, which I expected, and I sensed also that he got some contentment from keeping in touch with his pilots. By this time it was the summer of 1951 and the other war in Korea had seesawed up and down the peninsula for a year, with the Chinese Communists reveling in their sanctuary in Manchuria on the other side of the Yalu River. American statesmen had prohibited hot pursuit. They didn't want the fight to bleed into Manchuria, because the Soviets were expanding their arsenal in eastern Siberia. Our statesmen were wary of a third world war. General MacArthur had publicly disagreed with the policy, and President Truman had fired him for insubordination.

Chennault didn't say anything about the supreme commander's dismissal, but he agreed with his military strategy. "It's curious," Chennault remarked. "The Communists managed to hide their march to Korea but couldn't hide a buildup in Siberia. . . . I think Stalin planted the news to worry us. We're playing his game."

Chennault wasn't didactic; he just spoke in a matter-of-fact way, as if he accepted the fact that others disagreed.

Although I saw Chennault only briefly at times, I gained an impression of his beliefs. Knowing that Stalin was occupied with the Cold War in Europe, Chennault had reason to believe he wouldn't stir up trouble on two fronts. In the last war he wouldn't declare war on Japan until ninety days after the Germans surrendered, much as he wanted to attack Japan. And what Stalin had in Siberia wasn't sufficient for Korea. I had seen the railroads converge on Manchuria's capital—an obvious bottleneck, vulnerable to bombing. And the U.S. Navy could blockade the entire China coast. Chennault believed the Russians were bluffing. If our political wizards let us fly north of Yalu River, the war would end sooner, and that would save lives, he believed.

I knew nothing of military strategy, but I trusted Chennault. I believed America's State Department and militarists ignored him in spite of his experience in Asia.

I was glad to shove it from my mind and get into the air, above cloud layers where the moon and stars are brighter than I ever saw from earth. Navigating, watching continents appear on the horizon—this was the life.

It seemed as if I spent the next stage of the war, in 1951, flying overhauled B-29 engines from Clark Air Force Base to Okinawa and Japan. Wright engines failed often. World War II–vintage B-29s, designed for long range, bombed North Korea from Okinawa, which was a short flight for a Superfortress. Frequent takeoffs at full power and slow climbs with full bomb loads punished the reciprocating engines. I heard them call for air/sea rescue escorts to Okinawa because two engines had failed. I once heard a B-29 crew on one engine, which they were nursing while preparing to ditch at sea.

The B-29s were harassed by Communist prop-driven Yak fighters at the beginning of the war and later by MiG-15 jets. They were protected by American F-51s and then straight-wing F-80 jets. Eventually our sleek swept-wing F-86s turned up. I popped through the skies in a cargo plane, listening to excited calls—"On your tail!" "Break right, break right!" "Contrails, three o'clock!" I was amazed when I heard pilots far north over enemy territory head for home with an F-80 that had abruptly turned into a glider because the engine had died of battle wounds. Their buddies protected them until they reached friendly territory. When they got close to home they didn't even sound as if a flameout was a disaster. One of them told me, "We practice three-hundred-and-sixty-degree overhead approaches. If we wind up over the field with at least five thousand feet we've got it made."

Our fighter pilots were itchy because the enemy took off from bases in Manchuria and climbed safely to altitude before darting across the Yalu River. If disadvantaged, they scooted back across the river to the sanctuary of Manchuria. So our guys licked their chops, patrolled the river, and called it MiG Alley.

I had a copilot to navigate, a radio operator to communicate, and both to help with anything else. The fighter pilots did it alone, another reason why I respected them. My ultimate respect belonged to the fighters on the ground, where Korea's weather seemed harsh always, from its bleak subzero winter to its rain-drenched spring mud and humid summer heat. Just being there was punishment enough, let alone facing hordes trying to kill them.

Later that summer I rotated to our passenger routes and happened to be in Hong Kong on the queen's birthday. Great Britain's Privy Council announced its decision when Hong Kong was preoccupied with festivities. And CAT had agreed to remove the planes on that same day.

On the early morning of that significant day, the American aircraft carrier *Cape Esperance* anchored in deep water while the Kowloon dockyard's floating crane nestled against the airport breakwater. A third of the planes, the Communist flag still on their tail fins, were lifted to barges and shuttled to the carrier.

I wanted to taste the fruit of victory, the deliverance of planes from Communist control—planes that could transport Communist paratroopers to Taiwan. That afternoon I stood alone on the breakwater near my old office, where I had been station manager—where I had witnessed the defection, helped disable the remaining planes, confronted haughty cops, endured the decision of Hong Kong's court. With tremendous satisfaction I watched the USS *Cape Esperance* make way, bound for Los Angeles with the wings of DC-4s hanging over her flight deck.

Sensing someone behind me, I turned and saw Willauer. "Congratulations," I said. The aircraft carrier progressed through the gap at Waglan Island to the open sea. "Those damn British courts," I said. "Two and a half years on the ground. Hydraulic seals dried out, electrical contacts corroded—they won't bring much money."

Willauer kept watching the Waglan Island gap even though the carrier had disappeared well beyond. "Don't be too hard on the

Brits. Our goal was to keep them out of Commie hands. The shilly-shallying of the courts did just that. Remember, before the Korean War, our hands-off policy. Taiwan on its own. Those planes would have dropped paratroops." Willauer turned to me with his half-smile. His head tilted back, his eyelid lowered to half-mast. "If we don't get a dime for them we've won."

Days later, while flying, I was told another aircraft carrier, the *Wyndham Bay*, took more planes, and the American President Line's *Flying Cloud* took the rest.

An American senator called it the Free World's first victory in the Cold War.

Bob Lee, our supply chief, told us what happened to them. Two of the DC-4s were refurbished and became the Colombian government's hospital planes. Two Convairs were turned into executive planes for Standard Oil and the Imperial Oil Company, and the rest were absorbed by various American airlines. The sale of the deteriorated planes, minus colossal legal expenses, left Chennault with insufficient funds to cover his $4.75 million IOU.

Chiang Kai-shek's advisers suggested that Chennault made a bundle on the deal. Chiang summoned him and demanded an accounting.

I happened to be in Chennault's house when he returned. His mouth was a grim line. "Chiang tried to take my airline away from me," he said. His jaw clenched. "All my life I was taught to control my temper. I struggled to. This time I wanted to lose it, but I couldn't."

I nodded without saying a word and looked into his expressive eyes. I wasn't an executive, not even his confidant, but he trusted me because I was one of his pilots; and I knew why mavericks whose code precluded loyalty to anyone else were fiercely loyal to Chennault.

I left Hong Kong, headed for the Korean War, with Chennault on my mind. How strong and yet how vulnerable he seemed. His life was a series of reversals, yet he wasn't a loser, not by a long shot. He looked to the next challenge with conviction and confidence. He showed us the depth of the human spirit. I wondered what his next reversal would be. Surely he was destined for one, because that was his karma. Perhaps he was here to show us how to spit in misfortune's eye.

It wouldn't be long in coming. Surprisingly, it would be the CIA's mistrust—the hierarchy's, not the operations guys'. Rosbert said, "Perhaps they think he's too close to Chiang Kai-shek." I caught a hint of it on my next flight. I was scheduled to the island of Saipan in the Micronesia group.

The Third Force

I didn't blame the furious Air Force major who skidded his jeep to a stop to demand, "What the hell are you doing here?"

"Here" was a secure airport called Andersen Air Force Base on Guam, among the Mariana Islands in the central Pacific Ocean, about fourteen hundred miles due south of Tokyo. The obsolete C-46 I landed was disguised by aged camouflage. You couldn't see the ID numbers required by civil or military law. Not until you got close could you discern black undersized digits on the olive-drab tail fin that would let you know it belonged to Free China on the island of Taiwan.

All I knew, CAT had told me to fly it to Andersen. Before I could invent a respectable answer, a weapons carrier drove up with about fifteen civilians in aloha shirts or plain khakis; ten-gallon hats, sun helmets, or no hats; cowboy boots, rubber sandals, or tennis shoes.

One of the guys led the fuming major away from the airplane and produced a plastic card from a shirt pocket. The major drove off without another word.

My rescuer, a calm, soft-spoken, trim man, stuck out his hand and said, "Gilbert." By this time his buddies had loaded crates of stuff, and we filed a local VFR flight.

"To Saipan," they said. We flew north, over a hundred miles of Micronesia's coral reefs and islands and ocean, and when we sighted Saipan, Gilbert said, "Ignore the main runway. I'll point out the strip."

We reached their camp via a narrow road covered with migrating snails that popped when we ran over them.

We crewmen were given separate rooms in a corrugated-metal Quonset hut on a beach. "How lucky can we get?" we agreed. We had been flying night and day in Korea, and suddenly we were in a place where a breeze brought the scent of flowers and made the palm leaves clack. A surf thundering on a distant reef kicked up foam and spray.

The customers, some with their wives, lived in larger Quonset huts. A central building, decorated with shells, was a dining room and bar where we found casualness and camaraderie. Someone said, "Gilbert told the Air Force major to piss off, don't mess with our pilots."

"Sounds like him—a typical jarhead," someone else said.

"Oh, a former Marine," I said.

"No such thing as former. Once a Marine, always a Marine."

After dark I tagged along with two guys who drove to a village to pick up a couple of Micronesians who seemed to be old friends, and we all returned to a beach where other guys had assembled waterproof flashlights and snorkel gear. We groped around the coral and speared a few fish.

On the return flight we carried nine blindfolded passengers and three customers who were flight attendants. Over the Pacific at night, I was as relaxed as only a pilot can be when watching the sky and listening to the engines and the peaceful whistle of the slipstream that says everything is in equilibrium. A sudden sound of air rushing past the cabin, followed by a slam, told me the main door had been opened and shut. I said nothing, but noticed, after landing, that only eight passengers disembarked. I supposed our customers had discovered a double agent.

The passengers were Chinese Nationalists who had been trained as spies. Blindfolding was a way of keeping the location of the training base secret.

Guerrillas of a few other free nations in training had their own ethnic mess halls, which the customers enjoyed sampling.

They taught techniques of blowing up all kinds of structures, escape and evasion, the Morse code, the vagaries of small radio transmitters. Gold bars to be used for bartering or bribes were inscribed with the logo of whatever mint existed in the area. Cyanide was to be used at the agent's option, if torture was inevitable. I gained an impression they were advised to spill the beans if that's what it took to save one's self. The Communists would eventually extract any information with torture anyway. If anyone was captured, everyone else would assume this had happened and would adjust accordingly. The customers' protection lay in a policy of rationing information on a need-to-know basis. We were dissuaded from asking each other questions. And those in high places who had more than a fragmented picture were kept out of danger until their knowledge was stale.

The customers' interest in Manchuria lay in developing a Third Force, the First being CHINATS (Chinese Nationalists), the Second CHICOMS (Chinese Communists), the Third those who wanted no truck with the first two.

A rumor around Saipan said a CHINAT general claimed to be disillusioned with Chiang Kai-shek and had volunteered to organize a powerful Third Force, provided he had sufficient funds for his vast project. He disappeared with the funds and was found in comfortable retirement in Mexico. The customers didn't have to be threatened to realize he'd blow their secret if they harassed him.

Worrying over Chennault's loyalty to the CHINATS, customer headquarters invented reasons for him to be in Washington during a Third Force operation. In my opinion, had the customers known Chennault better, they would have relaxed in the knowledge that his loyalty to America superseded any other.

Rosbert wrote in his personal journal, "We'll never learn that we can't win the faith of a people by stupidly dividing the house. Why not get the Third Force elements into the First Force? Because we were divided before, the Second Force has all the mainland. I'm really burned on this type of thinking. . . . I'm disgusted with the so-called thinkers in Washington who work out these utterly stupid plans."

Rosbert seldom got excited, and his calm had been a stabilizing force all through CAT's trials on the mainland. He was slated to replace Chennault after the general retired. But handwriting on the wall, however faint, hinted that he'd be shoved farther into the background.

The Lights of Vladivostok

If love is felt between men, I sensed we knew it the afternoon I drove, with Bob Snoddy and Norman Schwartz, to a place called the menagerie. It was a secluded tarmac for all types of planes for special projects.

Aeronautical charts were in short supply, but these guys had privileged access to any they needed, and they picked up what I wanted, and I dropped them near a camouflaged C-47. I saw flame arresters over its engine exhaust stacks and knew that flame arresters, which usurp fuel, were used only on unarmed planes that penetrated enemy airspace.

I may be using hindsight to read a premonition that wasn't there, but I know that we three talkative guys were uncharacteristically quiet, and we felt comfortable with each other's silence.

Bob Snoddy and I had been close friends ever since our engine exploded and burned on a night takeoff in Shanghai years before. Our mutual hobby was celestial navigation, and I admired his U.S. Navy twenty-four-hour pocket chronometer. I shared his happiness when his wife announced her pregnancy by saying, "We finally got one in the hangar."

Schwartz was my quick-witted friend with rapier one-liners who saved me in Wellington, New Zealand, when I flooded the Royal Oak Hotel, henceforth dubbed the Royal Soak. I forgot the open tap on the bathtub. The main stream flowed down the hotel corridor while tributaries branched into adjoining rooms. The enraged manager splashed upstream to be defused by Schwartz, who drawled, "You folks have been bragging there's fish in every stream. Show us the fish!"

When we got to the menagerie I didn't ask where they were going, but after a long silence Snoddy said quietly in a matter-of-fact way, "I've seen the lights of Vladivostok."

I asked, "How about my going with you sometime?"

"Jeez, don't volunteer. Once you get on these you never get off. The customer figures the fewer that go, the tighter the security."

It wasn't their last flight, it was a test hop, but it was the last time I saw them.

A few days later, some of us were assigned to a search mission over the straits between Korea and Japan, while Mason flew to Korea to con Taegu's tower chief into faking his communications log to indicate that Snoddy and Schwartz had reported over Taegu, en route to Japan. Cover stories were vital to the security of wartime spy flights.

The true position of the remains of Snoddy and Schwartz was a meadow on the plains of Manchuria, not far from Vladivostok. They had gone to fetch the Manchurian they had dropped the week before, the recruiter for the Third Force.

Lewis told me, "I almost went along. I'd been training with them, reeling in the harnessed dummies they snatched off the ground with one of those rigs. They flew low with their hook dragging and grabbed the line. You had to be careful reeling it in, because the slipstream tended to bang the guy against the fuselage."

Cox had found out Lewis intended going and ordered him off the flight. "That's the customer's job, not yours," Cox said, and grumbled, "that damn Third Force operation."

Before the departure there was a concern that the Manchurian might have doubled or been captured. "His fist sounds different," a radioman warned. The cadence and rhythm of his dot-dash chirps raised a red flag. A good radioman recognized another's "fist" as easily as a layman recognized a human voice. However, the correct code name had been given, so the customer decided to dispatch the flight.

After it failed to return they assumed the CHICOMS had indeed set a trap. When the plane swooped low over the pickup rig the CHICOMS shot it down. It skidded along the ground in a fiery streak. Customers Downey and Fecteau, tending the reel in back, were thrown clear and lived to be imprisoned. The remains of Snoddy and Schwartz were buried in an unmarked grave in some Manchurian field, we presumed, because the USA denied knowledge of them.

The father of Snoddy's wife came to Tokyo to take her back to the USA. Many of us saw them off. Before boarding Pan Am, she cried, hugged me, and put something into my hand. It was Snoddy's navigation chronometer.

His daughter was christened Roberta. A few years later a stranger—probably a customer—knocked on the door, mumbled evasively in garbled syntax about an insurance policy, and presented a check that would take Roberta through college.

I don't know why I didn't weep. It was more of a dull, long-lasting ache; but I dreamed of Snoddy standing happily under an astrodome, sextant in hand. Years afterward I awoke to his voice downstairs, calling me to our favorite bistro. Not until I got out of bed and reached for my clothes did I realize I'd been dreaming again and there'd be no more cavorting with those guys.

And when I dream of Schwartz I see his wide grin and hear, "Show us the fish."

The French Air Force

The Korean armistice, signed on July 27, 1953, ended a three-year war. Korea was again cut in two at the 38th parallel, the same line that had divided it 400,000 UN casualties ago.

President Eisenhower proclaimed the armistice a victory for collective security.

A senator said it was hardly an example of collective security when 95 percent of the burden was borne by the USA and South Korea.

Senator Jenner called it "the last tribute to appeasement."

Senator Lyndon Johnson said, "An armistice merely releases the aggressors to attack elsewhere."

General Mark Clark said, "I cannot find it in me to exalt this hour."

Korea had its truce, however uneasy, and lapsed into the Cold War. But Indochina was still hot and France again called for help.

Our deeper involvement with France had begun on May Day 1953, before the Korean War ended. Every pilot in Tokyo who happened to have the day off got summoned to the Tachikawa Air Force Base with clothes for two weeks in a hot climate. "Take the train," the operations clerk warned. "May Day pinkos are blocking roads."

Five other pilots were exclusive passengers. I was preflighting the C-46 when the operations officer walked over with the weight and balance sheet, but no flight plan.

"Where are we going?"

"I can't tell ya."

"If I get this thing into the air I have to know which way to point it."

Cupping his hand over his mouth—the way he imagined spies talking—he said, "The Philippines. File for Taipei and revise your destination to Clark Air Base after you leave Tokyo's FIR [Flight information region]."

Six over-water hours later we penetrated Taiwan's control zone, and CAT operations advised us to land at Taipei, where we remained overnight.

In the morning, chief pilot Rousselot boarded, along with several other pilots he had rounded up. All of us had been in CAT long enough to refrain from asking questions. But Rousselot did say, "What you guys are going to be doing is very important."

We flew south for an hour, down the elm-leaf shape of Taiwan, continued south for another hour across the blue Straits of Luzon, and saw the Philippines. Its long green island of Luzon, its white sand beaches and coconut palms, glittered in the sun. Forty-five minutes more took us to Clark Air Force Base, fifty miles north of Manila.

We opened the door to a pungent aroma of tropical vegetation. A stern colonel, message in hand, looked up. Rousselot stepped down the ladder to introduce himself.

"These orders say we'll train your men on our C-119s."

Rousselot nodded.

The colonel asked, "How much time do we have?"

"Twenty-four hours."

"No one can check out in twenty-four hours!"

"The least experienced pilot is Porter, and he's logged seven thousand. The others have considerably more."

The colonel hesitated. Rousselot gave his notorious gimlet-eyed glare and said, "We've wasted five minutes already. Let's get going."

The colonel looked us over and said, "Follow me."

Bill Shaver chuckled and whispered, "Nobody intimidates our chief."

We wound up in a Quonset-hut classroom. Rousselot shook hands all around, said, "Don't relax discipline just 'cause you're a long way from home"; and flew the C-46 back.

Our ground school instructor, pointing a stick at various schematics, knew how to talk to pilots. "A C-119 is two corncob engines and a landing gear held together by tissue paper. Nobody ever ditched or belly-landed one successfully. Better to bail out. If you have to ride it down, don't land on the belly—it'll curl under and chew you up. Extend the landing gear."

After hours of following his pointer along lines of various colors, which distinguished oil, hydraulic, fuel, and oxygen systems, and memorizing pressures and speeds, we ate and bedded down, our heads full of numbers, in the   bachelor officers' quarters.

At the flight line, early in the morning, I saw why a C-119 was called a Flying Boxcar. It was close to the dimensions of a railroad freight car. Streamlined rear doors opened like a clamshell. The yawning opening was large enough to admit large trucks, small tanks, or cargo platforms that could be chained to parachutes. A boom ran along each side of the fuselage and extended far back to support twin rudders and elevators. Two engines—Pratt and Whitney R-4360s—were ringed with multiple rows of cylinders, like kernels on an ear of corn. The beefy landing gear had obviously been designed for landings on bumpy makeshift strips. As a C-119 taxied past, its thin fuselage vibrated, and I understood why mechanics had dubbed the beast "the dollar-nineteen."

One after the other, in a circuit, boxcars made touch-and-go landings. The trainees were second lieutenants whose planes bore U.S. Air Force insignia. But six planes waiting for the CAT pilots displayed the red-white-and-blue concentric rings of the French Air Force.

After CAT's C-46s, the C-119's flight deck seemed as spacious as a living room. From the way the U.S. Air Force captain relaxed in the right seat, I knew he was a good instructor. With no cargo on a bird that was designed for a colossal load, and with two thundering corncob engines, I pushed both throttles forward to takeoff power. It felt as if we were being shot out of a cannon.

At the practice area the captain said, "Let's see some three-sixties, forty-five-degree bank, hundred eighty knots." I knew he was checking my scan of the instruments. Your eyes have to keep roving. If you favor one indicator the others go wild. A steep bank while maintaining an altitude within plus or minus fifty feet, at a speed within five knots, requires rapid coordination between control pressures, engine power, and flight instruments. If you focus on airspeed the nose might pitch a hundred feet, and the bank can shallow out. By the time you've got everything restabilized you've shot beyond 360 degrees, a failure. Fortunately, the C-119 was easier than a C-46.

"Slow flight," he said, so I made S turns, ninety degrees left and right, alternately climbing and descending with the flaps at various settings. And then I reduced power, held the nose level, and watched the airspeed bleed off. The *whoosh* of the slipstream diminished and became silent. The plane shuddered with its own characteristic warning of a stall. I shoved its nose down and the power up and tucked the sound and feeling into my memory.

After a few touch-and-go landings with me jockeying the throttles to maintain a stable approach pattern, I got the hang of the power and sink rate, and the captain drawled, "Now you're flying the airplane instead of it flying you."

After parking we shook hands with me knowing he was one of the best instructors I'd ever had because he knew just when to keep quiet and when to point out some idiosyncrasy of the airplane. I learned sometime later that the Air Training Command handpicks its people.

He fitted me in with a group of second lieutenants who were listening to another captain tell how to drop stuff. "Aerial delivery," he called it.

He droned, "After takeoff, climb at humpteen knots to eight hundred feet, left turn ninety degrees . . ." I feared I'd forget half of the details until it dawned on me—all we had to do was drop dummy loads into a circle that was a helluva lot larger than Marshal Yen's drop zone at the siege of Taiyüan.

Bound for Hanoi, I was as enthusiastic as a kid with a new toy. Our fuselage was full of spare parts, ground power generators, wagons of drinking water, and a team of U.S. Air Force mechanics, which included a battle-scarred warhorse who sipped from a bottle of bourbon all the way. Never had I flown such a sophisticated bird.

So-called aerial delivery from our C-46s required many passes, but the C-119 dropped its entire load—seven tons—in one swoop, and the corncob engines zoomed the empty airplane away from ground fire.

Less than two weeks before, at a NATO conference in Paris, French delegates had appealed to the U.S. secretary of state for the planes. Two divisions of General Giap's Communist Army surrounded a French unit on the Plain of Jars, near the political capital of Laos. Men's lives and Lao freedom were at stake. The French Air Force suffered poverty with C-47s and obsolete JU-52s. The only planes capable of transporting tanks and artillery to the battle zone were Flying Boxcars. Moreover, Red guerrillas threatened French units in the Black River Valley, only 150 miles from Hanoi.

President Eisenhower granted the request provided that the airplanes, on loan, would display French insignia; the pilots would be American civilians flying under orders of the French Air Force. They would not drop bombs or napalm.

Although we didn't know these details, Rousselot had told us the mission was crucial.

After four hours over the South China Sea, we picked up Indochina's coast and the French Air Force base at Tourane, our fuel stop.

I feel sheepish, recalling my naiveté that afternoon. Told we wouldn't get fuel until noon the next day, I got a military driver to take me to the door of the commandant's house. A terrified houseboy answered my knock. "Don't make noise," he said. "Don't wake him." Having compassion for the quaking servant, I left quietly.

Somehow I discovered where the siesta-loving commandant and his entire officer corps were holding a celebration of spring. I wore sweaty khakis, but I doffed my red baseball cap and walked into a huge courtyard of long tables under strings of multicolored lights. French Air Force officers in immaculate white tunics with impressive epaulets and French women in chic sheer gowns watched me curiously.

I told the surprised commandant, at the head of a table, that we needed fuel for six Flying Boxcars, since we were bound for Hanoi and war.

We got fuel early in the morning, reached Hanoi before noon, and walked into a boxlike bamboo building with a control tower on top. Rows of chairs faced a chalkboard that had columns for times, aircraft numbers, crew names, sorties. I felt like an extra in a *Beau Geste* movie.

An operations officer, debonair as Adolphe Menjou, with a similar accent and a pencil mustache, stepped to a podium and smiled. "Americains, welcome to zee Anjou Escadrille."

After some general information he said he'd be "sharmed" by our questions.

Mindful of the coming monsoon season, a pilot asked, "What is your instrument approach procedure?"

Elegantly, Menjou raised his fingers to his nose and sniffed. "You smell zee runway."

Me: "What's the lost communications procedure?"

Amused, he pointed a forefinger at his head and cocked his thumb. "You zhoot yourself."

Someone said, "Iron-Ass Rousselot oughta hear this."

It was good the C-119's flight deck was roomy, because a crew included two American pilots and three Frenchmen: pilot, copilot, flight engineer, radio operator, navigator.

While introducing ourselves and shaking hands French-style— one vigorous pump—the radio operator said, "Sokolov."

"Sokolov?"

"I'm Russian." Eventually he spoke of his defection from the Soviet Air Force and his subsequent harassment by KGB agents who hung outside his apartment in Paris until the night he shouted, "Go away or I'll call the police. I'm a Frenchman now."

The navigator gave me a westerly heading to a French outpost, protected by several concentric rings of barbed wire, in hills an hour away. We reduced power and swooped to five hundred feet.

When we got over the white cloth T that marked the drop zone, I rang the bell and then heard the rattle of chains and rushing swoosh of air. The plane leaped up as if weightless. Obviously, our heavy cargo, chained to parachutes, had been released by the French Air Force "kickers" in back.

We added maximum power, pulled the nose up, circled back, and watched parachutes of various colors settle around the cloth T.

It was China all over again—tougher drops because of the hills, but the powerful engines compensated for that. We had just dropped near Na San, seventy miles south of China's border and only 130 miles south of the tin city of Mengtsz where Buol had lost his freedom three years earlier.

A French newsman rode with Kusak and wrote a dramatic description of swooping through antiaircraft fire. We didn't encounter much; the machine-gun fire was similar to China's—a bullet hole once in a while. During our morning sorties, French fighter pilots strafed the area, which suppressed the flak. Antiaircraft gunners were reluctant to reveal their position—they didn't want to get clobbered.

Our afternoon sorties seemed almost as safe, although the French pilots were away napping after lunch and wine. One of them told me, "This country is not worth dying for."

We called our early-morning sorties to Xeng Quong on the Plain of Jars the Dawn Patrol. Although five Boxcars had been scheduled to depart Hanoi at daybreak, French Air Force operations didn't have a weather report. The officer shrugged. "The radioman likes to sleep."

"The infantry is fighting and a radioman can't get his ass out of bed," a pilot said.

"Here's last night's report," someone said. "Wind calm, temperature seventy, dew point sixty-eight. An hour before that it was seventy and sixty-seven." We knew what it meant. The temperature and dew point were merging—a classic invitation to fog.

"It's probably still fogged in," someone said. "If all five of us go it could be five round trips of fuel wasted."

"I'll go and send you guys a report," I said.

The green mountains of North Vietnam and Laos looked peaceful in the early morning calm, and patches of ground fog decorated rice-paddy valleys. Three hours later, in bright morning sunshine I looked down at a thick blanket of fog and the strong radio beacon told me Xeng Quong was underneath. It was obvious it'd be hours before the sun burned it off. I carried my load of supplies back to Hanoi.

We flew the stuff to Xeng Quong early that afternoon. It was our last landing for a week. Instead, we dropped heavy stuff on battle areas. French ground crews had removed the clamshell doors. Although the entire back end was open, we couldn't see daylight. It was blocked by stacked palettes of ammunition and food or by a huge artillery piece. But when the kickers released the parachutes, the load disappeared in an instant and light flooded the empty fuselage. We climbed steeply while the back end framed green hills, and we saw the colored parachutes receding. The slipstream didn't sound its familiar whistle. It complained, *"Thuba thuba thuba,"* while the plane throbbed and fought the suction of the huge square opening and the fuel flow gauges revealed the exorbitant energy spent.

The battle must have favored the French, because we were scheduled to land at Xeng Quong. French ground crews were too lazy to replace the clamshell doors. I made a few quick mental calculations: six hours to the Xeng Quong and back, multiplied by the pounds per hour of fuel flow while sucking the air in back, *"thuba thuba."*

"I'll need more fuel," I said.

"You have plenty," a ground crewman said.

"Takes more with the doors off."

"That's all you get."

"I'll be in the café. Let me know when I got it." Sipping bitter coffee, nibbling a croissant, I felt like an orphan because the other guys were flying out.

Half an hour later the enlisted man came in to sneer, "All right, we got a Smith fuel load."

We took off and thub-thubbed all the way to Xeng Quong, landed, unloaded a field gun, and returned to Hanoi.

The tarmac was empty. "Where are the other guys? Did they get off on their second trip so fast?"

"They're sitting in Xeng Quong. Not enough fuel to get back. Three, anyway. The fourth is inbound."

We listened on the pilot's frequency. "Fuel warning light illuminated," he radioed.

"He's got fifteen minutes left," I said.

"We got our chutes on."

"A hundred miles out . . . Commie terrain," someone said.

He landed safely with almost nothing but fumes in his fuel tanks.

The next day's sorties halted while we flew fifty-five-gallon drums of gasoline to the stranded guys. Everyone, including me, acted as if the incident hadn't happened.

During the turnarounds I talked with Vietnamese meteorologists and civil aviation employees. Families didn't know if their soldiers were dead or alive until they bribed functionaries who held casualty lists. Emperor Bao Dai, oblivious to the suffering, belonged to the Vietnamese elite who were rewarded for loyalty to France.

I felt dumb because the Vietnamese meteorologists knew more about Thomas Jefferson than I.

"We believed you would champion our freedom," one said.

"That's our dilemma," the other Vietnamese added. "We kowtow to France or to Communists. But we don't want either in Vietnam."

"It's America's dilemma too," I said. "We believe in liberty but can't offend the French. The Cold War in Europe—we need their support."

The entire Indochina tragedy came from a little-known incident, I conjectured, at the end of the Second World War.

President Roosevelt had said, "[Indochina] should not go back to France. The case is pefectly clear. France has had the country—thirty million inhabitants—for nearly a hundred years and the people are worse off than they were at the beginning."

De Gaulle warned the American ambassador in Paris, "If you are against us in Indochina," it would cause terrific disappointment in France, which could drive her into the Soviet orbit.

"We do not want to become Communist. But I hope you do not push us into it."

After Roosevelt's death, America told France it didn't question French sovereignty over Indochina. And two American troopships carried almost two French divisions there from Marseilles and Madagascar. Secretary of State Acheson later said, "The French blackmailed us."

Even today, standing before the Vietnam Wall, I torture myself wondering. Had France not threatened America, had America not swallowed de Gaulle's bluff, would Vietnam, like Taiwan, be a prosperous showcase of democracy? And would the names of good Americans be absent from the marble of the Vietnam Wall?

In Indochina's demoralizing climate, the nobility of Vietnamese like those meteorologists—clinging to an ideal of liberty—reminded me of the courageous Chinese who gave up their mainland homes for a free but uncertain future on the island of Taiwan.

Emperor Bao Dai's loss of touch with his people; their mistrust because he was indeed a French puppet; his corrupt bureaucrats; Communist exploitation of the discontent; guerrilla control of the countryside; the brave infantrymen who died for want of good leaders—it all reminded me of our recent days on China's mainland.

We left Indochina as abruptly as we had arrived. I landed after a sortie and stepped out of the Flying Boxcar to hear our operations manager say, "Get aboard the C-46—everyone's waiting."

"I'll get my chute."

"Leave it; we're rushed. We'll put it in supply."

When I got back to Tachikawa in Japan, the Korean War still churned, and Rousselot asked, "Where's your parachute?"

"In Haiphong supply."

"You're supposed to carry it. You know the rules. You're gonna buy one: two hundred fifty dollars."

Iron-Ass Rousselot. I was home again and back in the Korean War. I didn't tell him, but I preferred Rousselot's discipline to French disorder. And USAF missions seemed the epitome of orderliness.

Korea got its truce late in 1953 and lapsed into the Cold War, but Indochina was still hot. The largest battle of its eight year war brewed. France again called for help.

The Last Flight of Earthquake Magoon

Every fragment of that day remains vivid, because it was the last I spent with Earthquake.

Up from Indonesia, where Cox had sent me to start a CAT subsidiary named Pioneer Airways, I walked along Hong Kong's Nathan Road, headed for Gingle's. I saw Lee, the orphan boy, on the sidewalk, outside the door. Straight black hair hung over his forehead. Mischievous brown eyes looked up at me in recognition. He followed me in.

Towering above the kid, Gingle bellowed, "Why aren't you in school, you little fart?" Lee edged closer to me. The bellowing continued, "You'll be running around with a goddam shoeshine box all your life."

In the restaurant section and working on a bowl of lima beans and butter, Earthquake Magoon bellowed, "Two Carlsberg and a lemon squash."

Lee gripped the glass with both hands and slurped. U.S. Marines in Tsingtao had adopted the war orphan, fitted him with a sergeant's uniform, and provided TLC until the unit left China.

Bill Welk had picked him up, paid a Hong Kong family to feed and shelter him, and enrolled him in school. But the excitement of Hong Kong's streets and the company of CAT pilots in Gingle's eroded his tolerance for school.

Earthquake told him, "You should have heard my old man holler when he found out I skipped school," and he bantered in his easy-going way. Never was Earthquake lighter hearted than in the company of children. I pretended I wasn't listening and sipped my Carlsberg. By the time the confab ended, none but the shrewdest observer would realize that Earthquake, in his offhand manner, had described the delights that school can eventually bring. Lee decided, on his own he thought, to return to spend the afternoon in school.

Earthquake then ordered a sack of hamburgers which would fortify him during the long movie we anticipated.

Halfway through the Clark Gable drama, Earthquake's stomach growled and he extracted a hamburger while Gingle's paper bag crackled and an aroma of onions and French mustard perfumed the area. A kid in a seat ahead turned around and gawked, and the giant gave him a hamburger. The kid grabbed it and said, "Ow-yaa."

The main feature was followed by a newsreel of a new guided missile intercepting a drone airplane. As pieces of airplane exploded across the movie screen, Earthquake grunted and leaned over to mutter, "Smees, it's time to get out of this racket." Little did I know he was prophetic.

We walked back to Gingle's, where we found the inner sanctum full of water policemen and CAT pilots at the long table and Gingle at the end, on his teakwood throne.

Earthquake sat next to him to jabber while I sat at the other end so I could hear Holden describe Earthquake's recent air rescue. Although the incident had occurred only a few days before, I hadn't heard of it.

Holden described a C-119 of the U.S. Air Force limping into Taipei on one engine and with seven passengers missing. The aircraft commander had been doubtful of reaching land and had ordered them to bail out. They floated in their life jackets in the open sea.

Holden said he was on the ground at Taipei when he got the Air Force's mayday. When he reached the area he saw Earthquake's C-46 circling the airmen. En route from Okinawa to Taipei, Earthquake had received the SOS, descended through the undercast, executed a square search, and found the guys. His copilot—Wang—had been the first to see the yellow dye marker from the life jackets.

Warming up to his story, Holden twitched a shoulder, gulped a portion of his scotch and soda, and continued, "The guys in the water, with the yellow dye marker all around them, were waving like crazy. Earthquake said Wang and Lai were in back of his cabin ready to toss out his twenty-man raft when he rang the bell. A more beautiful job of precision dropping I never saw. He skimmed the waves to get the hang of the wind and laid the raft right in the yellow water so close to the guys they didn't have to swim for it."

Talkative as he was, Earthquake hadn't told me about the rescue, even though I'd been with him most of the day. I recalled the time I happened to meet his World War II group commander, Colonel Ed Rector, at a reunion for China pilots. It was there I discovered that my friend had flown P-51 Mustangs with the 75th Fighter ("Flying Tiger Shark") Squadron in Chennault's 23rd Fighter Group, shot down two enemy planes and destroyed four on the ground. No one in CAT ever heard him mention it.

When we left Gingle's, slightly awash, Nathan Road was still bright with the lights of stores, and window-shoppers strolled in the warm spring evening. We were entranced by the sight of women in skintight, split-skirted, colorful dresses.

Earthquake raised his gull-wing eyebrows in mock delight, as if he were acting Falstaff on a New York stage. Hands forward like claws, he stalked down Nathan Road, pinching asses. His victims screamed and turned around, and when they saw him they laughed along with observers. I followed at a distance, wondering, How does he get away with it? The Chinese, who don't like touching, don't even like to shake hands, were laughing. If I or anyone else had tried it we would have wound up in "gaol" (as the Brits spelled it) with twenty strokes of the cane.

By the time I arose the next morning, Earthquake had left for Indochina. Cheong handed me the newspaper, which displayed a photograph of Earthquake and his crew, and a picture of the decoration they had earned—the Medal for Air Navigation. It was a huge bauble with bejeweled points of the compass around the white star of Nationalist China.

Copilot Wang and radio operator Lai attended the award ceremony without Earthquake, who was flying a C-119 out of the French Air Force base at Haiphong.

This time, all drop zones waited in a valley the size of Manhattan and were as flat. It was only 125 miles south of China's tin capital of Mengtsz where Buol had been captured four years earlier. The North Vietnam valley was near the Lao border, 230 miles west of Haiphong—an hour and a half in a Flying Boxcar.

A short Japanese airstrip, a leftover from the Second World War, lay in the middle, near a town called Dien Bien Phu. The name would soon be known around the world, and historian Stanley Karnow would write, "The Battle of Dien Bien Phu ranks with Agincourt, Waterloo, and Gettysburg as one of the great engagements in history."

General Navarre, commander in chief of the French Expeditionary Corps, planned to lure Red Vietnam's major force out of the mountain jungles. The valley was bait. Although it appeared vulnerable, its flat reach suited the static warfare at which the French excelled. They would wait with tanks and artillery and annihilate the jungle fighters as they attacked.

Experienced field commanders warned General Navarre against a showdown where the enemy held the high ground, but the proud general was intransigent. A graduate of the French military academy of Saint-Cyr, cavalry officer in the First World War, commander of a Free French armored regiment in the Second, General Navarre was an aristocrat of the French Army. Karnow wrote of the general, "A cold, solitary figure, convinced of his superior talents, he spurned intelligence accounts that did not fit his prejudices." He would monitor the battle from his headquarters in Hanoi, 185 miles away.

His man on the spot, commander of the troops in Dien Bien Phu, was the colorful General Christian Marie Ferdinand de la Croix de Castries. Also a graduate of Saint-Cyr, a cavalry officer, and a heroic figure in the Second World War and in previous battles in Indochina, General de Castries was described by American war correspondents as "an insanely brave, gum-chewing aristocrat."

The enemy commander, Vo Nguyen Giap, a former high school history teacher, had studied the campaigns of Napoleon, Kutuzov, and the Vietnamese generals who had defeated French forces on the Chinese border. He also ignored his advisers. The Chinese recommended a frontal attack, but General Giap told his soldiers, "Dig first, fight later." They shoveled tunnels and a spiderweb network of trenches toward the enemy. General de Castries' men heard the scraping and waited.

The people in France were disheartened. It was only six months after the armistice in Korea. If the United Nations couldn't get a clean win there, they reasoned, how could France alone hold Indochina? The French National Assembly demanded an end to "the enigmatic war." The French high command promised concerted action and a quick victory; and President Eisenhower increased U.S. funds to cover 78 percent of the cost.

The brave soldiers who waited in the Vietnam valley, anticipating a quick victory, resembled America's soldiers in Korea on Thanksgiving Day, three years earlier, when they saw the Yalu River and expected to be home by Christmas.

Again, China was a wild card. Under cover of darkness, for three and a half months, the Chinese ran convoys down the road from Mengtsz—Soviet Molotova two-and-a-half-ton trucks and American Dodge trucks that had been captured by the Chinese in Korea. They carried Stalin Organs (rocket launchers), bazookas, American mountain howitzers captured from Chinese Nationalist troops, and other artillery pieces. At Vietnam's border before dawn, they were dismantled and carried piece by piece over two hundred miles of jungle trails to the mountains that surrounded Dien Bien Phu. By early March, General Giap commanded a hidden ring of more than a hundred 105mm and 155mm artillery pieces and eighty 37mm antiaircraft guns. A Chinese antiaircraft regiment backed him up.

General Giap looked down at the cream of France's armed forces: bright young graduates of Saint-Cyr; nine parachute battalions; a third of all the Legionnaires in Indochina; the Red River Delta's mobile reserve; colonial troops from Morocco, Algeria, Senegal, Vietnam; Hmong hill tribesmen.

While General Navarre in Hanoi was confident of victory, General Giap spent sleepless nights wondering if he could win. So he would say, years after the battle.

By early March some of the Red trenches had reached within thirty feet of French outposts. General Giap attacked. A French redoubt fell on the first day, a second on the next.

Colonel Piroth, the French artillery chief, who had assured General Navarre he could silence any cannon the Communists might bear, lamented, "I am completely dishonored," and blew himself to pieces with a grenade.

Earthquake Magoon took off from Haiphong, flew west for an hour and a half, and descended into the valley while black puffs of exploding antiaircraft bracketed him. In a single pass he parachuted seven tons of supplies into the drop zone. On his climb out the Reds shot away his elevator control, and he roller-coastered home on his trim tab "like a jolly kangaroo." When a war correspondent asked if he was discouraged, he said, "When you're invited to a war you expect to get shot at."

General Giap focused on the airstrip, which would afford an excellent range of fire for his antiaircraft guns. The frequent shelling interrupted medical evacuation flights. Military observer Howard

Simpson, in his magnificent book *Dien Bien Phu: The Epic Battle That America Forgot*, wrote, "Close to five hundred wounded were now shoehorned into the available shelters. Blood, vomit, urine, pus, and solid excreta mixed underfoot with the mud to form a sticky, fly-covered paste. Maggots moved in undulating clusters over the damp mud walls and pulsated under dirty casts and soiled dressings. Normal cleanup tasks had to be abandoned as Girauwin's exhausted [medical] team fought to save lives, remove the dead, and prepare the seriously wounded for evacuation."

Tom Sailer descended into the valley, undeterred by black puffs of exploding antiaircraft shells. The gunners put a shell through a tail boom and shot away the rudder, but he continued his descent, parachuted seven tons of food and ammunition into the drop zone, and then returned to Haiphong.

Geneviève de Garlard-Terraube, a French Air Force nurse, was on the last plane to land at Dien Bien Phu. Shell fire destroyed it. Stranded on the battlefield, the blue-eyed nurse tended the wounded and became a legend, "the Angel of Dien Bien Phu."

France's chief of staff flew to Washington to ask for strikes from American aircraft carriers. If the valley fell, he warned, all of Indochina would go to the Communists, and British Malaya would topple next.

American aircraft carriers, the USS *Boxer* and USS *Essex*, steamed toward the Gulf of Tonkin, within striking range of Dien Bien Phu, and waited for orders.

Admiral Radford, America's chief of staff, wanted an intervention, and General Twining, the U.S. Air Force chief of staff, agreed. But General Ridgway, the Army chief of staff, believed that military action without political action would be futile. "There's simply no sense in fighting for people who won't fight for themselves," he maintained, "and the Indochinese won't fight for themselves as long as the only alternative to Communism is a continuation of French rule."

Congressmen balked and President Eisenhower soothed, "No American boys will be sent to fight in Indochina or anywhere else in Asia without the consent of Congress." The American carriers remained passive.

Antiaircraft shrapnel pierced Holden's hip and tore muscles from his arm. Copilot Wallace Buford, an Air Force veteran of the Korean War, stopped the bleeding with a tourniquet, completed the drop, and flew back to Haiphong, where French Army doctors wanted to amputate Holden's arm. He refused and asked a couple of pilots to remain at his bedside all night. He was afraid the doctors would anesthetize him after he fell asleep and amputate.

In the morning the French got a U.S. Air Force plane to fly him to Clark Air Force Base, where American doctors saved his arm.

Some of the French Air Force fighters, on flak-suppression sorties, flew higher than the Boxcars or not at all after lunch with wine. "Your Boxcars draw too much flak," they said. Helicopters based at Hanoi were supposed to pick up anyone who parachuted out. Bill Shaver said laconically, "Those choppers are as reliable as the fighters."

Frank Guberlet, CAT's station manager, visited a French aircraft carrier, the *Arromanches*, and told its pilots about the plight of the CAT pilots—the lack of support, namely flak suppression.

The next day, Fred Walker reported, "I saw two French Hellcats on my wingtips, and the antiaircraft guns didn't shoot—they were afraid of revealing their position."

Hugh Hicks didn't get an escort. A 37mm shell tore a hole in his wing and wiped out the aileron linkage. In a descending spiral, and bracketed by bursting antiaircraft shells, Hicks radioed for help. A plane from the *Arromanches* strafed the mountains and the gunfire stopped. Recovering from his spiral, Hicks asked the French pilot for his name. "I want to know who saved my life," he said.

Back at Haiphong, the wing was replaced. Fred Walker happened to be near the junk pile when a visiting U.S. Air Force inspector walked over and looked, with surprise, at the damaged wing. "Is that a shell hole?"

"Yep."

"No self-sealing tanks, no armor—you're not supposed to fly these in combat."

"We'll be glad to stop."

Another observer said the flak was thicker than in Germany's Ruhr industrial valley in World War II. A total of four French C-47s had been shot down.

Hanoi advised Paris that CAT crews flew *avec beaucoup de cran* (with great spirit), but there were days when everyone was grave, and even Earthquake lay on his bunk and stared at the ceiling with his own private feelings.

The French cabinet held an emergency meeting and asked for American intervention with B-29s, or American carrier planes. Secretary of State Dulles flew to London to request joint action, but the British refused because Dulles himself didn't know if Congress would approve.

John Plank returned from a sortie to report, "A shell fragment came through the cockpit and cut the handle off my briefcase as neat as if I had done it with a knife."

Secretary Dulles again flew to London, this time with the assurance that Congress would approve joint intervention provided the Commonwealth nations were included. But Lord Swinton, the colonial secretary, said none of the Commonwealth nations would agree to support French colonialism.

Hundreds of amputated wounded groaned in Dien Bien Phu's dank underground shelters. Bodies hung in barbed wire and rotted in the heat. There was no time to dig latrines. The stench of excrement mingled with the smell of death. New corpses piled on the hospital roof, one on top of the other.

At the peace conference in Geneva, the Russians stalled. They could drive a harder bargain after the valley fell.

Seven weeks into the fighting, France's portion of the embattled valley had shrunk to the size of Notre Dame's Ile de la Cité in the River Seine.

Hugh Marsh dropped a star of promotion and bottles of cognac to General de Castries. He suspected his Legionnaires had consumed the cognac and buried the stars until a Vietminh radio announced the besiegers had found French medals in a box that had drifted to their lines.

One of de Castries' officers fashioned stars from scrap metal. In a muddy shell-torn bunker, he got his stars, and then he pinned the Legion of Honor on the blood-spattered uniform of the Angel of Dien Bien Phu. It was her twenty-ninth birthday.

From Hanoi, General Navarre sent rescue troops toward Dien Bien Phu, but it was called "a quarter-hearted pretense," and cynics said Navarre was fearful of upsetting the Geneva Peace Conference.

Colonel Lelande, commanding two thousand Foreign Legionnaires at an outpost named Isabel—three miles south of General de Castries' command post—requested two artillery pieces. Art Wilson and Earthquake Magoon, along with their copilots, said they'd drop them.

Each huge gun was chained to three parachutes and placed in its own C-119. Flying low so he'd hit Colonel Lelande's small enclave, Wilson dropped his artillery piece and got out with a damaged tail boom.

Earthquake approached from the opposite direction to confuse the gunners. Three miles short of the drop zone, a shell hit his left engine. Oil streamed out. He shut it down and streamlined the propeller. The gunners had his range; he was bracketed. Another shell struck his tail. He lost directional control and spiraled down. He started his left engine, used partial power, and straightened his line of flight, although he drifted down toward a mountain ridge.

Steve Kusak, in another C-119, closed in to help in any way he could. Oil from Earthquake's shell-torn engine spattered over Kusak's windshield.

"Which way are hills the lowest?" Earthquake called.

"Turn right," Kusak answered.

"Have the choppers left Hanoi?"

"Not yet," Kusak said.

Earthquake drifted down, toward the Lao village of Muong Het, sixty miles ahead, where a short dirt strip lay alongside a river in a narrow valley.

Kusak called, "Bail out!"

"Shut up, I'm busy."

Kusak followed him down. A few miles short of the village, Earthquake spoke his last words. Calm, matter-of-fact, he said, "Looks like this is it, son."

It was.

Kusak watched a wing snag the peak of a hill. Earthquake's plane cartwheeled as if in slow motion and then turned into a ball of fire and smoke.

James McGovern, alias Earthquake Magoon, age thirty-two, was dead. Wallace Buford, his copilot, age twenty-seven, was dead.

They came within a hairbreadth of surviving. Dien Bien Phu fell the next day. CAT had flown 682 sorties.

On that day, May 7, 1954, General Giap's bullhorn blared in French, German, Arabic, Vietnamese, "Surrender or die."

General de Castries' men called, "Come and get us." They came screaming. Out of ammunition, de Castries' men fought with knives and sticks. At 4:45 P.M., he radioed Hanoi, "Ici Dien Bien Phu." Battle cries resounded in the background. De Castries continued calmly, "After twenty hours' fighting without respite, including hand-to-hand fighting, the enemy has infiltrated the whole center. We lack ammunition. Our resistance is going to be overwhelmed. The Viets are within a few meters of the radio transmitter where I am speaking. I have given orders to carry out maximum destruction. We will not surrender."

Hanoi headquarters radioed in reply, "You will fight to the end. There is no question of raising the white flag over Dien Bien Phu after your historic resistance."

General de Castries said, "*Etendu*, we will destroy the cannons and radio equipment. The transmitter will be destroyed at five-thirty. We will fight to the end. *Au revoir, mon Général. Vive la France.*"

General de Castries' radio operator announced, "In five minutes everything will be blown up here. The Viets are only a few meters away. Greetings to everyone." And then General de Castries ordered Colonel Lelande at Isabel to fire his big guns on the command post.

Nine hours later, Colonel Lelande himself radioed Hanoi, "I can no longer communicate with you." He yelled, "*A l'assaut!*" A French C-47, circling, maintaining a death watch, saw his Legionnaires, outnumbered ten to one, scramble out of their trenches and run toward the waves of Communists in a suicide charge.

A Communist radio crackled, "The victory is complete. There are many enemies lying on the ground."

A hush fell over France. A special mass was held at Notre Dame. If Saigon was the Paris of the Orient, and the beaches of Nha Trang its Riviera, then Dien Bien Phu was its Waterloo.

Le Monde's correspondent cabled from Hanoi, "'Let the enemy come,' said our troops at Dien Bien Phu, 'and we'll show them.

"'Show them what? We'll show them in Saigon where the people are busy sipping cool drinks on shaded café terraces or watching beautiful girls in the pool at the Cercle Sportif. We'll show the people of France, above all. They have to be shown what their neglect, their incredible indifference, their illusions, their dirty politics have led to.

"'And how best may we show them? By dying so that honor at least may be saved. . . .'"

Almost immediately, statesmen bickered over who had lost Indochina. A French general predicted that America's refusal to intercede condemned her to defend Southeast Asia alone; but it was inconceivable, even to him, that American children then in kindergarten would grow up to die in Vietnam.

The guys said Bill Welk cried a long time when he heard of Earthquake's death. I had just come from Korea when I heard. I wanted to cry but couldn't. Just a long-term ache that returns as I write. Once in a lifetime you know someone who deserves special dispensation from the Fates to live forever. Earthquake Magoon was my candidate, but he didn't live half the span of an ordinary mortal.

Welk and Doc Johnson sorted out Earthquake's belongings and found a letter from his father: "Always remember, son, you're Irish, and Irishmen can't drink."

I won't forget their thoughtfulness. They gave me Earthquake's uniform cap. I couldn't bring myself to hang it on the wall like some trophy. It waited in my clothes closet as if he'd walk in someday and growl, "Where the hell's my hat?"

Eventually it disappeared.

10

Buol's Freedom

Earthquake's death held alarming significance for Sue, because his fate and Buol's seemed to follow parallel courses.

The fall of Dien Bien Phu rekindled the on-again, off-again peace talks. Sue said, "I'm going to Geneva." It was a last resort. Chou En-lai, the Red potentate, had not answered her appeal for Buol's release. She went in the company of Rosbert and his wife, Lil, the gorgeous and vivacious Russian who carried the spirit of her father.

This is Sue's chapter, paraphrased from her book, *Oh, How They Lied*.

"I don't know what I'll do in Geneva," she said. "But all those delegates! Something's bound to happen."

The hotels were fully occupied by diplomats and news correspondents, so they settled in a hotel sixty miles away. Sue called on Secretary Dulles's delegation, and Walter Robertson unofficially blessed her mission. She was free to visit Chinese Communists and utilize the press. Fortunately, the diplomat didn't know Lil.

"I wanted to see what Communists looked like," Sue recalled. "So we waited outside the Soviet delegates' hotel, where black Cadillacs waited at the curb." The hammer-and-sickle flags inflamed Lil. She laughed at the drivers, who wore wide, square-shouldered overcoats, baggy pants, and wide-brimmed hats that bent their ears down. They looked at her with steely eyes. Molotov, in an immaculate suit, strode out briskly, and Lil gave him a Bronx cheer.

Sue and Rosbert calmed Lil, and they walked to the Chinese delegates' hotel, but Chou En-lai wasn't registered.

"Isn't the Chinese delegation staying here?"

"Oh yes, but we've given up on those names, and they refuse to let us see their passports. All we know, there're ninety-three of them."

While they were standing at the entrance, wondering what to do next, a Chinese entered and was beckoned by the concierge. After a brief conversation the Chinese cast a hostile glance at the American trio and disappeared into an elevator, and the concierge walked over and told Sue that Chou En-lai was ensconced in the largest villa on the lake and was refusing all visitors. Press correspondents, starved for news, were Sue's only hope.

Eddie Gilmore, of the United Press, who had covered Russia for years, told Sue she'd never see Chou En-lai. "But write a short note; ask for an audience to discuss the release of your husband. I'll do the rest."

Gilmore's photographer drove Sue along Lake Shore Drive until they came to an iron fence around gardens that were so vast they couldn't see Chou En-lai's villa. Swiss guards with traditional helmets and long pikes stood at attention outside the gate while a young Chinese sentry in a blue uniform stood inside. Sue knocked on the gate, and the guard ignored her. She pounded it and called in his own language. He came to the gate, and Sue held out the note. He backed away, shouting, "Who are you? Are you an English woman? Go away," while the Swiss guards looked amused and the photographer did his work.

The human-interest story got worldwide coverage. Taipei's newspaper proclaimed the resurrection of the legend of the loyal woman who traveled ten thousand miles, searching for her husband who had been kidnapped by soldiers. After enduring unspeakable hardships she came upon the Great Wall only to discover he had died of his labors and lay buried inside the wall. Overcome with grief, she threw herself off the wall to join her husband in death.

"I love the story," Sue laughed, "but the ending perturbs me."

"A modern Penelope," the *Florida Times Union* reported, comparing Sue to the faithful, beautiful wife of Odysseus, the Ithacan voyager; she waited, in the Greek myth, for twenty years.

No one knows the influence of the publicity, but months after Alexis Johnson and Wang Ping-nan discussed the release of American civilian prisoners, Sue's telephone rang at three in the morning. She answered with a sleepy voice and heard, "The Chinese Communists just announced they will free your husband." The voice belonged to Spencer Moosa.

Electric with excitement, she gasped, "I can't believe it. Is it really true? Oh my goodness, I don't know what to say. Are you sure it's truly true?"

"Word came direct from Geneva."

"No, I'm not crying, I'm too confused. I need time for it to sink in. I was praying the news would come and afraid it might not. I hardly dared hope anymore, it was such a long wait. . . . I don't know what to say, but thank you, oh thank you."

Sue ran to Rosbert's house. "Start packing, dummy," Lil said. "We're going to Hong Kong with you."

Hong Kong's American consulate told the trio a representative and a member of the Red Cross waited at the border every day to meet any arrivals, even though they were sure Red China would notify them in advance.

After several days without news, the consulate became as perturbed as Sue. "I think I'll return to Taipei and work," she said. " It'd be better than pacing the floor and driving my friends crazy."

Moments later a Royal Army jeep screeched to a stop and the excited driver said, "Your husband is free." He drove her to the border and told her to wait at the police station. She watched the British policeman and Red Cross man at the head of a long bridge. Two Red soldiers guarded the opposite end.

She saw Red soldiers carry a thin man and place him on the bridge. And then both sides watched while he clung to the rail and hobbled painfully on bony legs. When he got closer, a newsman said, "It's Father Ferrone, the Italian priest." British police lifted him into an ambulance and Sue heard that he suffered from beriberi.

And then she saw Buol. There was no break in his step after he hit the first plank of the bridge to freedom. Smiling from ear to ear, he fairly bounced off the bridge and grasped the hands of the American consul and Red Cross man. Wincing with the pain of Buol's grip, they steered him toward the police station where Sue waited.

Tears cascaded down her cheeks while a kind police inspector led them to a small room where they could be alone.

"After a few minutes of just looking at each other, we walked out arm in arm and faced the press," Sue told us. "I don't believe there has been another scene like that on the Hong Kong border. He held me tight while hardened newsmen looked at him with awe. They seemed deeply moved by the scene of our reunion."

Buol answered their questions vigorously and spoke scornfully of the most oppressive form of Communism on earth. "None of us values our freedom enough," he added. "We must fight to keep it."

"As the sun shone upon him—gaunt and shabby, with a bowl-shaped haircut—I saw only his dancing brown eyes and the impish grin that had charmed me years ago," Sue said.

On the drive back to Hong Kong, Buol seemed to be dazed until they rounded the top of Castle Peak Road and saw Victoria Peak, the harbor, familiar buildings, and he whispered, "It's really true. I finally made it."

The pilots decided to leave the couple alone for a few days, but Sue called and said he was starving for company.

I met them in Gingle's, unsurprised by his emaciated body, his cavernous eyes with dark circles, but was relieved to see the familiar debonair grin, the same cocky tilt of his head. Five and a half years in prison and his jaunty spirit was intact. The same cavalier disdain for peril that had bugged many of his fellow pilots sustained him during those interminable years of Communist harassment. It made him a hero to the same guys. Who of us would have emerged similarly unscathed? And I felt ashamed for my past anger with his small foibles.

"I can't describe the respect I feel for him," Sue beamed. "Five and a half years of brainwashing and he's still master of his soul."

"I never asked the Commies for anything," he said. "I knew whatever they gave me would have strings attached. I never showed interest in anything or anyone—I knew the bastards would use it for a weapon. . . . They didn't beat me, but they scared me by making me watch them beat Chinese prisoners. Tied their hands in back and hung them by their arms, all day in the sun."

I recalled the words of the Japanese general who said the Chinese are more cruel to their own people than to foreigners.

"Sure I got depressed. Worse than that. Despair. I got a grip on myself by dreaming up ways to bug 'em. Knitted a sweater with 'USA' across the front." Buol described how he stole olive-drab yarn from soldiers' socks that hung on wash lines in the compound where he was taken for exercise. He spent more than a year rolling the scraps into enough yarn for a sweater. And then he fashioned knitting needles from sticks. And when guards got lax he stole colored yarn from their families' wash line. Enough to knit 'USA' in bright colors into the olive-drab sweater.

Buol flashed his devil-may-care grin. "Here's something they didn't get." He showed us a knitted American flag. The stripes, about twelve inches long, were bright red and clean white. Each star, with a neat point, was perfectly positioned on its blue field.

It was a joy to hear Sue's gentle laugh, to see a sparkle in her eyes again. The golden hair that hung in waves to her shoulders had regained its former sheen. She looked at her husband admiringly as he ate shrimp cocktail, celery sticks, deviled eggs, steak, French fries, and salad, along with Bordeaux wine, and then apple pie, ice cream, cognac. She stroked his arm and whispered, "You can't make it up in one week."

"You can't imagine how it feels to be free," Buol said. "But excuse me—I'm going to the French consulate."

Sue said, "He won't rest till his friends get out of prison. He talked about them the first ten minutes he was out. He never saw two of them—they sent notes to each other.

"French records say they're missing, presumed dead," Sue continued. "You don't just walk into a French consulate and say their documents have errors. They need evidence."

Buol had discovered the presence of the three French prisoners after he struck something hard in his vegetable soup. It annoyed him until he discovered it was a medicine vial that contained a note from an inmate named George who worked in the kitchen. From then on they communicated by notes hidden in the wicker baskets that were used to carry pots of food to the prisoners, and Buol learned that a total of three Frenchmen were his fellow prisoners.

The kitchen became a clandestine message center. They played chess via notes—one move a day. Buol conducted a correspondence course in American slang and learned the French language from George, who copied a course outline from a German grammar book. Each of the foursome wrote a complete family history. Should anyone obtain freedom, he would bear news of the others. Should all four become free, they vowed they would hold a grand reunion in Paris.

The Frenchmen had been border guards at the Vietnamese village of Ban Nam Coum, which lies opposite southern Yunnan. Chinese soldiers raided the town, shot some of Pinky Boucher's men, and made prisoners of the rest. One of the wounded Vietnamese couldn't walk, so the raiders bayoneted him viciously. They confiscated six pigs and told the villagers there'd be more trouble if they helped the French. Pinky and a few Vietnamese survivors were herded to Muong La, China, where they remained on public exhibition.

Some weeks later a Chinese Army officer, with a white flag of truce, parlayed with border guards Bernard Lelièvre and George Eychunie, who were Pinky's replacements. The capture of Pinky had been a mistake, the officer explained. He apologized and said the Chinese wanted no part of the French Indochina war. Would Bernard and George come and get their comrade and escort him back to Vietnam?

Bernard and George crossed the border while the officer held the flag of truce. A few Chinese soldiers circled behind them, and their fear came true. The officer dropped the flag of truce and brandished a weapon, along with his soldiers. Bernard and George were arrested for invading China. With Pinky, they were imprisoned in Kunming; and George talked his way into the kitchen job.

In both Hong Kong and Tokyo, various military attachés, psychiatrists, and CIA personnel interviewed Buol. Primarily interested in the reaction of prisoners, they were surprised that Buol suffered so little trauma. "I have a feeling someone's watching me all the time," Buol told us. "I keep resisting a temptation to look back over my shoulder." He insisted on flying to Saigon to expedite the release of his prison mates, but the French consul in Hong Kong assured him the wheels were turning.

In between flights we celebrated. By the time Buol and Sue headed for the USA, he had a belly. "I can't keep up with him," Sue told us. "He wants to party all the time. I'm exhausted."

Waiting for their flight, Sue became reflective. "It makes me wonder. . . . Things happen in threes. My husband and Earthquake were on parallel courses. They were flying together when the Russian P-38 tried to force them down at Port Arthur—remember those early days when you guys flew troops from Tsingtao to Manchuria? That was the first coincidence. After the mainland fell, they were imprisoned about the same time, and they both got out. That was the second. And now Earthquake is dead. I hope the coincidences are over."

The city of Stockton, Bob's hometown, turned out for a parade, and the mayor said, "Bob Buol is a real American who lived up to the traditions of his country."

After conferring with functionaries in Paris, Buol and Sue looked for Pinky's mother in Tours, but couldn't find her, and learned she had remarried since her son's capture.

They continued by train to Bordeaux and found a hotel room before taking a taxi to George's home in a neighboring village. His parents wouldn't hear of them staying in a hotel and promptly moved them into their home. They were overcome with emotion when they saw, face to face, the American who had written the letters that brought them so much hope. They fed Buol and Sue food and wine until they couldn't breathe; and the visitors promised to return after George was home once again.

They went to Boulogne to visit the brother of Bernard. And then visited Britain's Isle of Man to thank Bertram Hemingway, who had been vice consul in Kunming.

After a prolonged second honeymoon, doctors pronounced Buol fit for work, and he tried to figure out what to do. The years of solitude in prison had ruined his ability to make decisions, even though he fought to overcome the problem.

He wrote an essay for others—how to survive brainwashing in case of capture and how relatives on the outside can help. Buol told Sue he could adjust to his freedom if he worked with his friends in Asia. They'd be more understanding than those in America who wondered why Communism was such a personal issue.

But first he had an appointment to keep. That reunion in Paris. The Frenchmen were free. Sue visited her parents in Albuquerque during the grand reunion, and then she'd join him in Paris.

George wrote in his journal:

Buol landed at Orly Field, a vigorous man with a smiling face, typically American. He carried a wicker basket, a symbol of the means by which we had communicated in our prison days.

This memorable moment was the culmination of a plan which had been in our hearts since the beginning of our clandestine correspondence. To meet in a free country, to relive our common memories, and to enjoy the maximum of freedom. The reunion was memorable. Though we had never seen each other, we felt kinship that could not be described.

Bernard was with me. We were immediately conquered by his conversation, his intelligence, his great love of life. Leaving Paris, we traveled together over the roads of France, going north to Boulogne, the country of Bernard, and then south to Tours, where Pinky had recently married. And finally into the province of L'Ariege, to the mountain village of Rabat-les-Trois-Seigneurs, my home.

We made the most of the days in the mountains, hiking in the Pyrenees, soaking in the hot springs of a village, and talking quietly for hours on end.

We talked, not only of the past, but of the future, and our friendship brightened as the days flew by. We found that there was a similarity in our outlook on life. We were encountering the same difficulties in the outside world and reacting in the same manner. We now found ourselves continually having to make adjustments in this wonderful world of the West. Life seems to be very complicated when you are free.

It was the day before our departure for Paris to meet Sue that the tragedy occurred. At 11:30 A.M. we discovered our comrade on the floor of the bathroom. Thinking he had only had a fainting spell, my father and I carried him into his bedroom and tried to revive him while Bernard fetched a doctor from the next village. For more than two hours we tried everything we could to revive our friend, but the doctor said he was dead. It was May 27, 1956, little more than eight months after his release from prison.

We later learned that a severe pulmonary congestion had brought his death. We held a ceremony, presided over by the American consul from Bordeaux. Most of our villagers attended. Buol had become a familiar sight. They had been captivated by the tall American with the jaunty grin who strolled their streets. They took him into their hearts. Sue arrived and the entire village turned out to grieve with her.

After Sue got back to America with Buol's earthly remains, George wrote, "He obtained our freedom and suddenly he is gone, this man—he had the strength to live a hundred years."

Sue replied, "Bob was an only child. In you he found the relationship one can have only with a brother. I am certain that if he had been able to choose the place of his death, he would have wished that it be in the small French village with you."

Months later, Sue again heard from George: "Time has passed since Buol's death, but the longer it becomes, the more we realize how much we owe to our dear friend. We think always of those who vegetate without hope behind the Iron or Bamboo Curtain, whose number is not decreasing, but growing. So long as we have a breath of life in us, Bob will be present at our sides. The poets have written, living in the hearts of men is not dying."

Sue wrote, "He was a true hero. He had faith in his heritage and grim determination to outwit his captors."

All of Buol's fellow pilots agreed. And we knew that Sue, also, was a hero.

Dr. Tom Dooley, USN

We were privileged to meet many others along the tortuous way. In contrast to the heroic, bedraggled, displaced peasants, an unlikely hero appeared. He looked like an American youth on a holiday.

The Geneva Peace Conference ended with Vietnam cut in two. Like Germany and Korea, it joined the Cold War. We went back.

A grace period gave people time to move to the regime of their choice: Communism north of the 17th parallel, or Nationalism in the south. Few moved north. There was an exodus in the other direction. We flew them and called it Operation Cognac.

After we parked at Haiphong our operations man walked over. "Where'd you come from?"

"Taipei."

"I didn't know you were coming. What're you here for?"

"Cognac. Didn't you get our position reports?"

"French Telecom said no messages. Hotels are full."

We got a jeep ride to the Metropole Hotel, where the mangy bear in the cage still looked depressed. Half a dozen CAT pilots were crowded into a room that contained its original double bed plus a pair of twin beds and a couple of iron cots and a mattress on the floor. Someone said, "Welcome to the zoo."

My copilot and radio operator muscled into a room that was equally crowded with other copilots. I walked down the street until I found a merchant who sold me two meters of cotton cloth. A hawker with no shop, just a place on the sidewalk, sold me a canvas cot with rickety wooden legs.

For the next couple of months we flew about twenty thousand people from Haiphong to Saigon to be placed in refugee camps: tribes from the hills, Red River Delta farmers, city dwellers.

On a day off a few of us bummed a ride on a French Navy landing ship that shuttled refugees to an American troopship offshore. With more time to talk to them—sometimes in English or halting French, most of the time with an interpreter—I was surprised to hear that a few looked forward to a new start in the south. However, most of them were anxious and bewildered. Some followed Catholic priests who had encouraged them to move.

Cruelties to come would prove my theory wrong, but in that phase I thought simple peasants would be better off at home, albeit in Communist territory, where the family had tilled the land for generation after generation, the land where the ghosts of their ancestors lived. Peasants felt like foreigners only forty miles from home. We took them hundreds of miles to where strangers spoke dialects they didn't comprehend.

I remember a slender teenage girl in cutoff black slacks and a brown cotton blouse, barefoot. Her only baggage was a bamboo carrying pole on her shoulder. It carried nothing. She walked off the airplane with a wistful smile. I watched her, alone, climb onto a crowded French Army truck.

The camps were supported by U.S. funds. After much money sifted through fingers before reaching the refugees, America decided to give funds direct to the camps. But the French government expressed righteous indignation, and so America continued to funnel the funds through it.

On a trip back from Saigon to Haiphong, several of us flew formation at ten thousand feet, above flat-topped clouds in a clear sky. I saw a bird large enough to be a goose, headed in the same direction. I throttled back to match its speed, but the bird's velocity was slower than my stalling speed. As I gained on it, the bird looked back momentarily and flapped its wings furiously. Someone radioed, "Hey! Do you guys see that bird?"

"Where do you suppose he's going?"

"He's looking for the Metropole Hotel," I said.

After the flight we slouched at tables outside the Metropole, sipped beer, and tossed *pommes frites* to the dejected bear.

An American voice shouted, "There it goes," while several guys in blue jeans ran past us with nets on long poles, on their way to snag a bat out of a tree. They were followed by a guy in his twenties dressed in khakis. He did a double take when he saw us and stopped at our outdoor tables. "You guys Americans? My name's Dooley."

"If you're Irish you can't be all bad," I said. "Sit down and try a French beer." His companions came back with the bat in a jar, and they joined us. They were NAMRU (Naval Medical Research Unit) personnel, looking for strange diseases and ways to cure them.

Their young leader was a physician, Lieutenant Tom Dooley, USN. "You guys come to our lab," he said cheerfully. "Get a stool test. Lots of amebic dysentery in this area. You'll never know you have it until years later. And you can catch liver flukes from snails. Don't swim in streams around here."

Dr. Dooley's research lab was the only interesting place to hang out in on our days off. He and his sailors found excitement in a tapeworm some peasant passed or in some unclassified vermin on a bird.

After days of getting acquainted, Dooley asked, "What's with your pilot Johnson?

"Johnson is our interpreter," someone else said, and everyone laughed.

"He's notorious for mangling our language," Welk said.

"I think he's got friction of the diction," I said.

Dooley hadn't yet learned Johnson's vocabulary. Mention dogs, and Johnson spoke of dober-pinchermans. Flowers? He liked Hawaii's anteriors (antheriums). He claimed he bought his girlfriend a one-calorie diamond, and a doctor injected him with five thousand BTUs of penicillin. His ambition was to own a condominio on Wacky Wacky beach on some island in Ha-Y-Ya.

"That's it," Dooley said. "Friction of the diction, a rare malady. . . . I found him outside my office waiting."

"I came to get castrated," Johnson said.

"Castrated?"

"Yeah, castrated. You told me to come over anytime.

Dooley said, "Might you happen to mean circumcised?"

"Ah, that's it."

We continued to see Dr. Dooley and flew him around Laos from time to time after he got out of the Navy. A devout Catholic, enthusiastic about the possibilities for improving public health, he joined a Catholic mission in Laos and opened a nursing school. Instead of the traditional capping ceremony at graduation, Dooley "bagged" them. He presented each new nurse with a shoulder bag of the tools and medicines she'd need for her new career.

Dooley spent the rest of his career in Laos. He wrote several books about his work and lectured in America to raise money for his medical missions in Laos. A few years after we met him outside the Metropole Hotel in Haiphong, he discovered a malignant tumor in his own chest. Although he could have spent his remaining days in the comfort of his home country, he supported his wasting ribs and spine with braces and continued his work in Laos.

He died young, indeed, but accomplished much. Instead of wearing a saintly mien, he appeared to believe his work in Laos was a lark.

11

The Kingdom of Laos

I didn't believe Laos was a lark, although its ethereal charm unfolded during my tours of duty. It was a fascinating part of our Indochina experience.

A landlocked never-never kingdom, Laos was surrounded by Burma, Thailand, China, and Vietnam. For six centuries it expanded or contracted, fragmented and mended, according to the belligerence of its neighbors, who exploited the jealousies of Lao princes.

By the time I got there it was three-quarters the size of Italy and the same shape without the boot. Its many mountains and few roads ran north and south. East-west communication didn't exist, almost. The royal family squabbled like children while three million languid subjects performed daily chores and delighted in their festivals. They didn't know what was going on in the next steep valley, let alone the outside world. They focused on their extended families and the spirits who inhabited their land and every object, animate or inanimate. A rainbow was the sky bending over for a drink; the Mekong River harbored a monstrous serpent; the moon eclipsed whenever a spirit started to devour it, and only the villagers' incantations and their gunshots, aimed at the moon, saved it from disappearing forever. Before an eclipse, our flight operations chief warned us to be wary of flying lead. Anthropologists labeled these interesting people "animists." They're the so-called primitive inhabitants, whereas many of the sophisticated Laos were Buddhists. Only one out of a hundred had an elementary school education.

The radio beacon at Vientiane, the commercial capital of Laos, in a characteristic bend of the Mekong River, wasn't working when I took off, nor is the beacon at my destination. So I'm flying like an old-time barnstormer, over or around jagged rock spires and vertical slabs of multilayered rock. They stand as white and tall as New York skyscrapers. Flat tops that aren't hiding in clouds show fractures that sprout gnarled trees and dark green leaves as broad as those in Madison Avenue offices. Wide grass valleys bear limestone cones larger than Egyptian pyramids. Steeper valleys are jungle-green with lighter patches that denote bamboo forests. I know the monsoon season is close, because clouds shroud the higher peaks and mist hangs in valleys. The kingdom has a mysterious aura.

Torrents of rain begin to pelt the jungle while lightning flashes a gloss on the canopy. I descend to a thousand feet over the Mekong, which looks like a river of molten lead. I hug every bend and leave it only when it's obscured by a cloudburst, knowing I'll pick it up again and it will lead me to my destination. Lowering clouds force me down to five hundred feet. I follow the river through light rain in a mountain pass and burst into a valley where sunshine sparkles silver on the water and temple roofs glint gold. It looks like Shangri-la to me, but it's Luang Prabang, the royal capital.

I land on its dirt strip, brake hard, and stop at the foot of a hill. A Buddhist temple rests on top. I've been told its roof is pure gold.

This is where Laos was born.

Only six hundred years before, a Thai prince, exiled from Thailand, migrated the same upstream route in a canoe, carrying his only treasure—an ancient golden sculpture of Buddha. When he came upon the fragrant valley and its scarlet blossoms of frangipani, he said, "This will be my court." He invited friends—Buddhist monks, scholars, craftsmen—and they called the valley Luang Prabang, the "Place of the Golden Buddha."

After it expanded, he called his realm Lan Xang, "the Kingdom of a Million Elephants," but now it was Laos, although the royal capital retained the name of the golden Buddha.

Aggressive neighbors grabbed at the kingdom and were still grabbing when I got there six centuries later. The steep mountains and few roads, with none connecting east and west, made invasions difficult; and the juxtaposition of Buddha and Mars made Lao wars different.

Westerners who returned home and tried to explain the mystical kingdom groped around their memories and discovered it would be easier to retrieve spilled mercury with their fingers.

I had progressed beyond the point of trying to fathom puzzles; I just accepted what I saw.

In 1893, Laos was designated a French protectorate, although France actually ruled it. The Empire of Japan occupied it during the Second World War but granted its independence before the war ended.

After the war, Thailand claimed a piece of it, but backed off after France threatened to veto Thailand's entry into the United Nations.

Laos went along with the reclaimed French domination because France's soldiers were needed to kick out Chinese troops who were looting the country. (The Allies had dispatched the Chinese to Laos to accept the surrender of the Japanese, who had already left.)

In October 1953, France signed a treaty that gave Laos full independence, although it remained part of the French Union. France kept troops there and dominated what little commerce existed.

Luang Prabang's small tarmac where I parked the C-47 was tended by women who scattered pebbles from flat baskets of woven bamboo. They wore sarongs. Long hair, spiraled in a bun of one style or another, told whether they were married or single. They walked sensuously, holding their straight backs and proud heads steady. The movement was in their hips. Their faces expressed inner peace, and sometimes they smiled to themselves as if they harbored a delicious secret.

I sat on the ground in the shade of a wing and waited for slow-moving men to unload the crates of hand grenades I'd brought—explosive stuff to ward off outsiders who wanted to take over the kingdom. Dismal-looking dogs roved and sniffed.

Passengers bound for Vientiane shared the shade of the wing with me. They held small stuff in shawls or tin pots or clutched live chickens by the neck. A few men, wiry and alert, wore floppy black pants and red sashes of hand-woven cotton that indicated they were Hmongs from the highest mountains in Laos. Some anthropologists believed they were cousins of Tibetans. And I recognized Kahs from the southern foothills by their dark complexions, which came from meat in the gourds from which the gods had poured them—according to legend. Others, lowland villagers, were fair-skinned, having descended from northern Chinese.

All of Laos seemed to be represented except "the Ghosts of the Yellow Bamboo," the Stone-Age wanderers who ate roots and slept in temporary shelters of bamboo leaves that wilted and turned yellow after they left. When villagers came upon a deserted lean-to they knew some shy nomads were transiting their neighborhood, so they placed a broken machete or piece of clothing on the trail and walked away and waited. The next morning the villagers found fruit in its place. Scholars called it silent barter.

After the grenades were unloaded from my plane, the people in the shade boarded and I flew them south to Vientiane in a beeline, in the comfort of a decent instrument altitude, because the radio beacon was now operating.

A few days later the king's DC-3 flew the same route, and I watched it arrive. Portly King Vatthana, in a white tunic with huge gold medals and a long-billed cap, emerged. A dozen or so stunning women in pastel silk sarongs with gold embroidery drifted out of the plane, smiled shyly, and waited beside their king. Others in the entourage slouched at half-attention while an oompah band played out of tune and off rhythm. Comic opera, I thought, but my grin faded when he spoke. I didn't know what the king said, but I saw him weep; and when I read the translation on the following day, I thought, Who among us would not weep?

"Lao people," their king had said, "our country is the most peaceful country in the world. . . . We have always strictly applied the teachings of Buddha concerning forgiveness, gentleness, and charity. At no time has there ever arisen in the minds of the Lao people the idea of coveting another's wealth, of quarreling with their neighbors, much less of fighting them. And yet, during the past twenty years our country has known neither peace nor security. . . . The misfortunes that have befallen us have been the result of disunity among the Lao on one hand, and of foreign interference on the other. Foreign interests do not care about our interests or peace; they are concerned only with their own interests."

The kingdom's twentieth-century misfortune was a road—the route for Soviet war supplies. It stretched from Red China to its North Vietnam partner, took a shortcut through Laos, and reached embattled South Vietnam. Strategic enough to acquire a name, it was called the Ho Chi Minh Trail.

Vietminh controlled rural Laos by terror. If a village school swerved from approved doctrine, a North Vietnamese soldier with pliers stretched the teacher's tongue while another cut it off with a bayonet. And they jammed chopsticks into the children's ears, splitting the ear canals and rupturing the drums so they'd never again hear evil.

When I was in Vientiane, Vietminh agents murdered Deforei, the French civil engineer who was famous for building most of the roads in Laos. They tied a schoolteacher and the pilot for an international peace commission airplane to a stake and cut their throats. They seized children of Lao peasants and indoctrinated them in some distant school in North Vietnam.

Vietminh did the dirty work because Lao Communists—Pathet Lao—were benign. Originally a collection of reformists, the Pathet Lao depended on the strength of the Vietminh. A CIA friend said, "Lao soldiers are good Buddhists, and they don't like to hurt anything. . . . When Royal Laos fight Pathet Laos, they fire over each other's heads, or withdraw out of sight and fire at random in each other's general direction." Fighting in the north was more fierce, he explained, because Vietminh officers followed Pathet Lao soldiers and threatened to shoot them if they didn't fight.

The Vietminh needed a Lao puppet, which they found in the form of the king's second son by his number nine wife. He married a

North Vietnamese woman and embraced Communism. Ill-tempered and warlike, he became a Pathet Lao leader and believed he impressed Lao peasants by entering their villages on foot while carrying his own pack. However, one villager told another, and the word was passed along, "He rode his horse until he got close." And when they dutifully gathered for indoctrination lessons they whispered, "The prince dances while the Vietminh pull the strings." During elections, the peasants voted by hand while spies watched for anyone who failed to raise an arm for the correct candidate.

The king's number one son—by his number one wife—remained neutral, as did the king. His minister of defense, however, was a gung-ho general who wanted to kill Communists. Because the names of the two princes and the minister were so alike—Souphanouvong, Souvanna Phouma, Phoumi Nosovan—I shamelessly oversimplified the matter by calling them the Evil Prince, the Good Prince, and the Mad Minister.

The Mad Minister persuaded his king to build an army, and France agreed to train it. But a revolt in their colony of Algeria gave the French a reason to pass the Thai burden to America.

The U.S. Joint Chiefs of Staff wanted no part of Laos. It was a general's nightmare—less than a thousand miles of roads in a country three-quarters the size of Italy, a quarreling royal family, and corruption galore. But the State Department pushed them into it.

The Mad Minister's officer corps laughed at American naiveté, acquired villas in France, and padded their personnel rosters. America suspected it was paying for soldiers who didn't exist, but many mountains and few roads precluded a fair census. America could, however, give a valid reason for refusing a pay raise for every soldier in the Lao Army. They were getting twice the pay of Greek and Pakistani soldiers, the minister was told. So he promoted everyone to a higher rank. The Royal Lao Army, defending a kingdom of three million subjects, cost American taxpayers almost $500 million.

Soon after I was assigned to the U.S. Army's White Star Mobile Training Team, chief pilot Rousselot came down for a hawk-eyed look-see. As usual, he showed up at the seat of the action and surveyed planes and pilots, ensuring there was no lapse in discipline. It was here he was most cheerful, away from the head office, in some jungle, bantering with everyone, seeing concrete evidence of the fight against the Evil Empire.

"I knew I could depend on you guys," he said, "no matter how far away you are from the head office."

"You have to hand it to the U.S. Army," I said. "Even though it didn't want any part of Laos, it sent its best troops. These guys are the best I ever flew with."

The White Star Team was a close group of about a dozen Green Berets. Although they wore civilian khakis and Hawaiian sport shirts, their muscles and jump boots gave them away. Too full of energy to walk down the C-46's tall ladder, they backflipped out the door and landed on their feet. Everyone spoke French, Lao, and Chinese and knew a lot about civil administration. By some incongruous alchemy, these big, enthusiastic guys fit unobtrusively into the village of Savannakhet, which was a small port on the Mekong, 160 miles south of Vientiane. We relaxed in wicker chairs at rickety tables outside a café on a dirt road where the Green Berets enjoyed bantering with villagers. No one drank too much or got boisterous.

They called one of their teammates "Border Crosser," because he had been a soldier in the Hungarian Army, part of the Soviet bloc, until the night he volunteered for duty as a border guard and then fled to the other side and joined the U.S. Army, where his linguistic skill got him into the Special Forces.

I billeted with my crew in a small hotel, while the Green Berets stayed in a clearing in the jungle in a rambling Victorian house with a machine gun on the veranda.

At one of their lectures to Royal Lao troops a bored Lao corporal pulled a slingshot out of his pocket, aimed a pebble at a bush, and zapped something that looked like a grasshopper, which he impaled on a stick and toasted with his Zippo cigarette lighter before popping it into his mouth. Later, when I told the lecturer, he laughed, "And I'm supposed to teach these guys jungle survival."

The young Lao paratroopers we took on practice jumps wore rubber sneakers. "I know they're tough," I said, "but isn't it hard on these kids' feet?"

"We sent jump boots, but didn't see a one. Bureaucrats in Vientiane sold 'em somewhere or other."

The bureaucrats of whom he spoke eventually found a better deal: positions in the foreign commerce and department of customs, where they skimmed funds from America's Agency for International Development.

The next day I flew a military adviser, a Green Beret, to the Plain of Jars to pick up a contingent of Lao soldiers. I circled the runway to check for water buffalo and noticed the first half of the grass strip had been reinforced with PSP (pierced steel planks). But newly painted boundary markers extended for the entire length of the runway. I assumed the entire strip was serviceable, which is where I made my mistake.

Instead of using a short-field technique (nose high, power on, over-the-fence speed of seventy-five knots), I made a normal approach at ninety. I could have braked hard and stopped before the end of the

PSP, but I let it roll normally. As soon as we ran onto the grass we sank through into mud. The plane wouldn't budge, not even with takeoff power.

The Lao soldiers had shovels. Instead of digging us out they lounged and jabbered, even though they didn't want to get stuck overnight. Because it was one of the only two broad meadowlands in their kingdom and was hemmed in by jungles, they believed all kinds of spirits roamed there after dark.

Anyone with imagination could believe the plain was spooky, because the huge ceramic jars were still there, where they had been abandoned two thousand years ago. Large enough for a person to sit inside, they might have been burial urns, archaeologists said, or containers for grain. If you looked inside you could see marks that had been made by iron chisels, which meant the jars had been made by the Chinese, because they were the only people who had iron tools two thousand years ago.

The Green Beret and I didn't fear ghosts. We worried about getting stuck with a bunch of soldiers who couldn't even shovel, and a lieutenant who couldn't lead them, in a place where Pathet Lao guerrillas came out of the jungle after dark.

That night, at Savannakhet's café, the White Star Team and I drank French beer while their medic bandaged the palm of my hand, which was raw from shoveling.

The incident induced a pilot to call me "Mud Cat." I replied, "That's what I get for flying our fancy DC-6. Away from the boonies for a couple of weeks, you lose touch." Although we old-timers had the privilege of flying CAT's plush Mandarin DC-6 on passenger routes, chief pilot Rousselot wanted us to share the bush flying. We switched caps at Bangkok and proceeded to Vientiane for a week or two in Air America. Each time I regretted leaving the comfortable life, but when I got to Laos I got hooked by the shenanigans and felt glad I had no control over my schedule—or I would have stayed north and missed a lot.

My paychecks came in pairs: $550 a month from CAT plus $550 from Air America. After sixty hours in the air we got $10 an hour overtime. Lots of time in an airplane—one hundred hours a month—brought a grand total of $1,500, not bad for the 1950s and 1960s, although it wasn't the fabulous amount rumored. If we picked up bullet holes from ground fire, the place was called a hazard zone and we got a bonus of $10 for each hour over that specific area. In a year's flying we averaged about half the income of pilots in major airlines in the USA.

The American consuls in Laos were an unexpected and pleasant surprise. Like Consul General Strong in Tsingtao during our China days, they were down-to-earth. They wisely balanced the vagaries of the local people with State directives and Air America's sensitive operations. The diverse dynamics pivoted precariously in the hands of America's sole representative in the boondocks of Laos. Among others who won our respect I recall the names, W. L. Sullivan and G. M. Godley.

On my next tour with Air America I found the guys so busy dropping supplies to Lao troops—4:00 A.M. to 10:00 P.M.—that Hudson said, "If I'm not scheduled out until eight I feel like I have the day off, and if I have a day off I feel like I got fired."

They told me they had seen one of CAT's old-timers, Woody Forte, get trapped in a valley. He circled northeast for his drop. A strong southwest wind caught him in his turn and drifted him toward a mountain. "He could see it coming," a CIA guy said. "He went into a sixty-degree bank, trying to get around, but the mountain peeled his right aileron off, his left wing mowed the grass, and he crashed down the hillside." Several CIA trainees were killed with the crew. It was all the more of a shock because Woody was a skillful pilot, tempered in the crucible of China.

"If it happened to Woody, it could happen to any of us," Walker said.

Rousselot, always the Marine, grumbled, "He let his attention lapse."

On my next Air America tour I delivered rice for U.S. AID. A white-haired New Yorker dispatched me with four soldiers of the Royal Lao Army, who would kick it out when we arrived over a besieged village. Close to the North Vietnam border, it was surrounded by Pathet Lao. Whitey scribbled the Roman numeral VII on his notebook, tore out the page, and gave it to me, saying, "They'll display seven." Roman numerals were standard because villagers could easily construct them with cloth strips, which they anchored to the ground with rocks. Whitey said, "Good luck."

"It makes you nervous when they say 'Good luck,'" I said. The copilot laughed. Our climb was slow because the day was hot. I had flown the same C-46 in China, and the border was only fifty miles beyond our target. "Here we go again," I mumbled. "I'm not progressing in this so-called career."

We got in the general area of our target and looked down through holes in billowy cumulus clouds. Eventually we saw the long white strips of cloth forming a VII. It was our drop zone. We circled until a big enough hole drifted over, and I pulled the power off, extended the flaps, and spiraled into the narrow valley. I rang the bell at a thousand feet, but didn't feel the familiar pitch that accompanied a change in our center of gravity. Guys on the ground waved, and I knew they, like me, wondered why rice didn't fall. Unstable hot air tossed us uncomfortably while the copilot went in back. He didn't return, so I sent the radio operator. Both returned to the cockpit with the chief of the Lao kickers. He waved his hand in front of his face and produced a stub of a pencil to write an arabic 7 on a scrap of paper. I wrote VII=7, while the copilot said, "Same, same."

After radio operator Chu managed a halting powwow in Lao, he turned to me with a grin so wide his eyes almost squeezed shut behind his horn-rimmed glasses and said, "His boss told him site seven. He doesn't know Roman numerals."

"Really funny," I said. "We'll have a helluva time climbing out of this valley if we don't get the load out." I told him to take the copilot back and toss out a few bags and maybe the soldiers would catch on. But after five minutes they returned to say the mutineer blocked the door.

"Fly the airplane," I told the copilot. "Don't be afraid to stick the wing close to the hill—when you start your turn you'll want enough room to get all the way around."

I put on my uniform cap with its winged badge, strode aft like Captain Bligh, pointed at the rice, and commanded, "Out." Although I alarmed the three junior kickers, their chief didn't know that an airplane commander, while airborne, is God. With great aplomb, he shouted above the roar of the engines and rush of air. I caught the gist. I was a Royal Lao Army chauffeur who had brought them to the wrong address. Neither exhortations nor demonstrations swayed the chief.

Our climb out of the narrow valley with the full load was arduous, because half our lift went into the tight climbing turns. The heat of the day made the air thin, which robbed lift from the wings and power from the engines.

When we got back to Vientiane the white-haired CIA guy kept biting his lip, and it was obvious that he had been trained to be courteous to natives. He ushered the chief to a Lao colonel's shed. We heard the bawling out, and Whitey said with satisfaction, "You won't have any more trouble with this clown."

We started out again, climbing north, through cumulus clouds and around thunderheads, and eventually found the white strips in the shape of a VII. Again we spiraled down and rang the bell. It was a repeat performance.

Red in the face, Whitey strode into the Lao colonel's shed and stayed inside for a while. He emerged to say, "We got a new chief kicker."

As I climbed the boarding ladder, Whitey asked how I stayed calm. I said, "In this place I expect nothing more than diarrhea and prickly heat."

During our slow climb out for the third time it occurred to me that the American's question was legitimate. Not long ago I had been like him. I recalled the assessment of a U.S. senator, after a quick visit to Southeast Asia: "The people walk around as if their minds are in another world." And I remembered sailors who returned from duty with the U.S. Navy's China Fleet. Atlantic sailors called them Asiatic. "Nothing you can put your finger on. They're just different."

When it came my turn to pick up CAT's passenger flight at Bangkok, I telephoned Art Wilson, who happened to be in that big city. Still hurting from Woody's death, I knew that gabbing with old-timer Wilson—the guy who dropped the field gun on Dien Bien Phu just before Earthquake Magoon was shot down—was better for my morale than a double scotch.

An American Original

"Sure I'll hoist a few," replied Wilson. "But I'll have none of your fancy bistros or drawing rooms."

By the time I got to the Red Door on Patpong Road, he was waiting outside. Wilson was tall and skinny, with a complexion that invited sunburn and a face that expressed resignation. His slouch and the way he hooked his thumbs in his pockets made him look like a beached seaman who knew the waterfront only too well.

Inside, we clinked frosted mugs of Singha beer and nibbled hot French bread with Roquefort cheese. "We're going to miss old Woody," I said.

"The best use for these airplanes is to cut 'em up for pots and pans and give 'em to the peasants."

I switched to the tale of my three trips to northern Laos to make one drop, thanks to the illiterate kicker, and then I suggested, "Why put up with this a hundred percent of the time? You've got enough seniority to fly the passenger routes up north. Live in clover at least half the time, keep up with the latest equipment. CAT's getting a Convair 880. Eight-tenths the speed of sound. A golden fuselage. A royal dragon, eating a flaming pearl, on the nose. Interior like a potentate's palace. A moon gate. Silk cushions to caress our passengers' buttocks. They're calling it the Mandarin jet."

"I'll have none of your fancy doodads and head-shed monkeyshines," he leered. "I like it better with Cobras hissing at me in the jungle."

Wilson's appearance and laconic speech masked uncommon talent. He lived in the pilots' hostel in Vientiane. For R&R he rented a walk-up cold-water flat in Hong Kong. The lucky few who were invited there saw sketches of people and places, an ivory chess set, and shelves of Shakespeare and other classic literature, including poetry. He had the soul of a poet. An outdated application for employment stated, under LIST ILLNESSES & INJURIES, "Fractured left femur, but now I walk good like a biped should."

Outside his home he chatted happily with peasants in their own lingo, which he quickly learned, and shunned loftier social gatherings. I lamented his throwaway talent and wondered how many of his cohorts saw beyond his footwear, which earned him the moniker "Shower Shoes Wilson." To me, his attire epitomized the simplicity of the Asia he loved.

MEMORANDUM
FROM: *President*
TO: *Chief Pilot, Vientiane, via Vice President Ops.*
SUBJECT: *Captain Wilson*
On my recent visit to S/E Asia I took note that Captain Wilson, in violation of company regulations, failed to wear jungle boots provided for the protection of our pilots; worse, he wore shower shoes in the cockpit.

"A disaster for us all," lamented Wilson. "The long arm of the head shed finally reached our jungle."
"I'll get us off scot-free," Walker soothed.

MEMORANDUM
FROM: *Chief Pilot, Vientiane*
TO: *President, via Vice President Operations*
Captain Wilson suffers with a fungus he contracted in line of duty. The Danish doctor in Bangkok prescribed medicated powder and advised Wilson to expose his feet to air until a cure is effected, which is anticipated soon.

At a party in Taipei, Rousselot told me, "Those guys think they're fooling me, but they're not. I know damn well Wilson isn't wearing his boots." Rousselot sipped his bourbon and added, "They're doing a damn fine job down there. I'll let the president worry about the boots."

After a luxurious tour of duty on CAT's passenger planes I was again scheduled to Vientiane and waited, with a few young new hires, for the flight to Laos. One of the innocents must have thought I was a recruit also. He said, "You know what I heard? A pilot down there is living with a native woman—right in the pilots' hostel—and she meets the crew bus with a cold martini. At the dinner table he just sits there and she feeds him with chopsticks." Merely telling the fable shocked him. It was pure Wilson. I stayed silent.

The newcomer nudged me. "What do you think of that?"

"You want to know what I think? I think when I get to Laos I'm going to ask if she's got a sister."

When we got there I flew a C-47 about a hundred miles north and landed on a mud strip next to a Hmong village. It was hemmed in by terraced hills on one end and a thirty-foot drop-off on the other.

Hmong boys helped their fathers unload sheets of corrugated metal for the construction of a school while women held their infants sidesaddle and watched. The men wore black pantaloons with vests and red sashes. The women dressed in black skirts and blouses embroidered with red or purple yarn. Both sexes wore necklaces and bracelets of heavy silver that had been hammered and carved into various designs.

Their weapons were crossbows and flintlock muskets. They were reserved but friendly; their intelligence showed when they unlatched cargo doors of an airplane they'd never seen before and helped me close an engine cowling that had come loose. They resembled American Indians I had seen in Wisconsin. Their family ties, their sensitivity to the mysticism of nature, and their unaffected dignity were captivating. They were high-mountain people. Chinese and Vietnamese called them Meo, "barbarian." They called themselves Hmong, "mankind," and resented the lowlanders who tried to regiment them. They needed no handouts. They farmed corn, eggplant, long cabbage, and opium and cured their ills with medicines they made from wild buffalo hide, the soft horns of deer, gall from bears, marrow from the bones of tigers.

Bob Weaver, the specialist who taught us escape and survival, said the Hmongs were the most adventurous people in Southeast Asia. A lone Hmong would travel for days on foot, and when he stopped to rest in some Hmong village he described the birds he had seen and adventures he'd encountered, and the villagers were spellbound by the tales of spirits he had encountered along the way, and they rehashed the stories long after his departure.

Air America provided the Hmong military leader with the latest state of the art—a single-engine STOL (short takeoff and landing) plane with large wing flaps and leading-edge slots that directed a smooth flow of air over the wings at slow speeds. A STOL wouldn't stall until its speed dropped below forty-five knots. And the fuselage, designed by a physics professor, absorbed the energy of a crash by breaking up in sequence, piece after piece, while leaving the cage of the beefed-up cabin intact. They were Helio Couriers, and Rousselot handpicked the pilot to provide transportation for General Vang Pao. He was Fred Walker, the six-foot-two redheaded Yankee whom the CIA loved as much as Wilson. Both pilots had served continuously and long enough in Laos to know every hill in the kingdom.

Like Wilson, Walker had the seniority to fly the big stuff on passenger routes, but he chose to remain in Southeast Asia. His excuse—he liked to sleep nights, and Laos was the only place left without runway lights.

If General Vang Pao wanted to visit a Hmong village, Walker buzzed it and the general dropped a note. The villagers grabbed their farm tools and hacked out their idea of a landing strip. It might end at a steep hill, which prohibited a go-around, or begin at the edge of a cliff, giving Walker the illusion of landing on a baby aircraft carrier. Gusty mountain swirls compounded the challenge. A fleet of Helio Couriers joined Vang Pao's. Walker trained his pilots until they could land on ridges that would dismay a mountain goat.

Whenever my rotation put me in Laos, I was glad to run into Walker, who'd fill me in on what I had missed. Like the day I stood in the shade of my C-47 wing waiting for the Hmongs to unload the corrugated-metal sheets I had flown in. I watched something that looked like a silver grasshopper—a Helio Courier—land. Six-foot-two, redheaded Walker stepped out.

Yesterday, he told me, he had landed at Xieng Dat to retrieve the propeller of a plane that had crashed months before. The accident investigation had been reopened. When Walker arrived over Xieng Dat, it didn't smell kosher. Too quiet, no kids, no animals. But it had been a strong Royal Lao Army base the night before, so he landed, although he swung around at the end of the runway, set the wing flaps for a short-field takeoff, and kept the engine idling—just in case.

A Royal Lao Army major he'd known for years ran toward him with two soldiers who held their rifles at the high-port position. The major stopped in front of the airplane and saluted smartly. French Army training, Walker thought.

Looking constrained, the major asked, in French, "What do you want?" After Walker explained, in broken French, that he'd come to pick up the broken propeller at the end of the landing strip, the major ordered his men to put it on the backseat of Walker's Helio Courier.

When Walker delivered the part to the CIA headquarters, he said, "Something funny's going on at Xieng Dat."

An agent replied, "Damn right—the Commies took it early this morning."

Although the turncoat Lao major was obligated to arrest Walker— a coveted prize—he let him take the propeller and go. Such was the esteem Walker enjoyed in Laos.

That night, Walker and I again met in our hostel in Vientiane. We heard a single-engine light plane. Walker recognized the sound. "There goes Air Opium," he said. Its owner and pilot, a Corsican, had lived in Laos for years and flew the stuff to Bangkok and Saigon. His silent partner was an adviser to Prime Minister Diem of South Vietnam.

The Lao Air Force—the other opium carrier—flew it to Vientiane, where Lao Army officers operated a so-called pharmaceutical company.

It is possible that we unknowingly carried opium, because many of our passengers were Lao officials who didn't have to submit to a search within the borders of their own country. Given this climate, it seemed inevitable that Soviet propagandists would plant rumors of Air America transporting the stuff. So the CIA, cooperating with American narcotics agents, searched crew baggage. We welcomed the protection. Nevertheless, the rumors were repeated until they seemed like facts, and more than once an otherwise responsible pilot, from some American airline, unwittingly served the Soviets by exclaiming, "Air America? That's the opium airline." Allegations that the CIA funded itself by smuggling narcotics didn't make sense, because it got adequate funds from the U.S. Treasury.

Kong Le's Coup

I again went to Laos in early August 1960, days after one of the great surprises in Lao history—the revolt of the 2d Battalion, led by its deputy commander, Captain Kong Le.

Kong Le, a Kah tribesman from the foothills of central Laos, joined the army at age sixteen and became an officer at nineteen. Five feet one inch tall, he smiled like an Eagle Scout.

Late in the summer of 1960, he turned his back on the Mad Minister of Defense; took control of Vientiane's police and radio headquarters and the airport; and declared his allegiance to the neutral king and the Good Prince. Lao would no longer fight Lao, he said; he and his men would stop the civil war. They would do away with grasping public servants and the officers whose villas cost more than their salaries. "Much as we like Americans," he announced, "they are foreigners. Laotians must not die fighting their battles."

Reminded that Americans shielded Laos from Communism, he replied, "No Lao could be a Communist. It is against our national character and the Buddhist religion."

Kong Le spoke in colloquialisms the peasants understood, and he wore the bracelets of string that symbolized their friendship. His rally at Vientiane's football stadium attracted more followers, and he asked the Good Prince (Phouma) to be Prime Minister.

Impulsive though Kong Le's revolt was, it unwittingly occurred when the entire cabinet was in Luang Prabang, conferring with the king. On August 11, the cabinet's envoy, General Ouan Ratikoun, flew from Luang Prabang to Vientiane to negotiate with Kong Le, who agreed to withdraw to specified points in the commercial capital. But the cabinet was reluctant to return. After the Good Prince became prime minister, the avid anti-Communist (Phoumi) conferred with U.S. and Thai officials who shared his sentiments. It was easy to imagine their dismay and the astonishment of the young Captain Kong Le, when he acquired, among many peasants throughout Laos, the aura of a giant-killer.

Eventually, Kong Le and his renegades would retreat to the Plain of Jars, sustained en route by food and ammunition parachuted from Soviet planes. The Soviets would turn the historic plain into a Red bastion where Kong Le would form an unholy alliance with the Patet Lao. But that lay far in the future. In the early days of the revolt we didn't know what to expect from Vientiane.

A few nights after Kong Le's coup I was spooked. Now it was a three-way war, and there was no moon and no runway lights at Vientiane. We'd pass it en route from Savannakhet to the northern border of Laos, near China. We had a full load of rice for the hill tribes near Sam Neua, a Communist-held village, only forty-five miles south of the place where Earthquake Magoon had crashed during the battle of Dien Bien Phu.

We climbed north in clouds, and when we crossed Vientiane's latitude our radio compass pointed to its strong beacon off our left wing. We were surprised that Kong Le kept it on. We cruised at eleven thousand feet to keep above the northern mountains.

At its beginning the sound didn't alarm us. It was a slight rhythm one hears when the propellers aren't synchronized. I glanced at the tachometers. The speed of the right propeller increased as if controlled by Lao spirits. I retarded the prop lever, but the rpms increased. So I toggled the manual electric control. The propeller didn't answer. It sped to 2,800 revolutions per minute. It was running away. I closed the throttle and pushed the red feathering button, but the blades didn't streamline. It was worse than a dead engine, because it windmilled in flat pitch. Its aerodynamic effect was that of a flat board, broadside to the slipstream. It felt like a powerful brake on our left side.

The Green Beret in the cabin heard the whine of the prop and came up to the cockpit. "Take the radio operator with you and kick out the rice," I said. "The higher we can stay, the less that prop's gonna drag."

Headed back to Savannakhet, I radioed for jeeps to illuminate the strip. The sound of air rushing past the open cabin door and the feel of the trim changing told me the rice was going out. The Green Beret returned to the cockpit, panting from the exertion at high altitude. "It's half out," he gasped.

"Half's enough, I think. Take a breather, and let's see how this bird performs." I didn't want to land at Vientiane even though our radio compass told us we'd passed abeam the place during our slow drift toward the jungle. Eventually I said, "We're okay; we'll reach Savannakhet in good shape."

Fortunately the clouds broke up when we got close to Savannakhet, and we saw the headlights of the jeeps. After we landed I asked one of the guys to drive his jeep under the propeller so I could climb up. I unlatched the brush block next to the hub of the propeller. The shape of a shoe brush, the block held four rows of carbon rods that were spring-loaded. They pressed against copper rings on the hub of the propeller and transmitted electrical commands to its dome, where a motor moved the angle of the blades. Some of the graphite rods had failed to perform their task because they were worn below their index marks. Others stuck down because the springs on which they were seated had lost resiliency. Apparently the brush blocks had missed an inspection or two.

Reflecting on the incident, I realized it was reassuring having that trooper on board. I could depend on him, no matter what happened. And I got a sense of what made the Green Berets tick.

The Royal Lao Army, in great numbers, drove Captain Kong Le out of Vientiane. With his army, he fled to Xeng Quong, on the Plain of Jars, where he was supplied by Russian Ilyushin cargo planes that brought artillery, ammunition, and trucks.

Months later I was scheduled to a strip near Udorn, which was a village in Thailand, close to the Mekong River. Although the commercial capital of Laos lay on the other side of the river, the Thai airport seemed far from everywhere, because it was a lone strip of concrete in a green jungle.

When I touched down I suffered a few alarming seconds, believing I had landed at the wrong place. Technical luxuries of a modern airport were tucked between trees and vines: a distinctive trailer and antennas of a radar landing system; forklifts, trucks, crates upon crates of supplies. Overnight, the U.S. Marines had landed. More were on alert in Okinawa.

Ex-President Eisenhower warned, "Laos is the principal domino whose fall will trigger the fall of the rest of Southeast Asia. . . . We are at the threshold of World War Three."

Across the river—in Laos—laborers lengthened Vientiane's runway.

More peace talks began, which held a major war at bay. Officially, Indochina remained at peace. I was scheduled to a different site of the Cold War, which was Taipei.

12

Chennault's Farewell

Each time I returned to Taiwan it bustled with more prosperity. A marble quarry got foreign investors. Textile factories introduced carpets. Potters and furniture makers expanded. Electronic manufacturers sprouted. Bookstores blossomed with the latest works—inexpensive and pirated. Novels and biographies cost a dollar. Medical textbooks could run as high as five. Enterprising Chinese somehow got copies of publishers' galley proofs from England and America and printed them in Taipei. Sometimes they appeared on bookstore shelves before they were available in New York or London. The government claimed exemption from copyrights because Free China was a developing nation whose students needed the subsidy.

The Nationalist Chinese Air Force was a tale indeed. Morale had been low. CAF pilots patrolled the Formosa Strait with propeller-driven P-47 Thunderbolts and P-51 Mustangs. Almost at whim, Red China's MiG-15 jets darted out and shot them down, until an image from the past appeared—a Flying Tiger ace, a flesh-and-blood original. Unlike the Hollywood version, he was slender, possessed refined manners, and spoke beautiful, precise English, which he salted in just the right places with fighter-pilot lingo. He was Colonel Edward Rector, chief of Air Section, MAAG (Military Assistance and Advisory Group).

As Chennault had taught his Tigers to beat Japan's maneuverable Zeros, so Colonel Rector told how CAF propeller planes could shoot down MiG-15 jets. He visited all five fighter groups, flew their planes, and lectured, "Your P-47s and P-51s can turn tighter than any damn fighter now flying. The next time you battle, turn into him and start shooting. If he wants to turn, he's dead meat. Just stick in there and shoot out ahead of him like you've been taught. That's your best way to survive. Work him down low—the lower he gets, the more fuel his jet engine uses."

The CAF pilots trusted Rector. They were kids when their parents told them the legend. Flying Tigers, losing only six pilots in aerial combat, destroyed 294 Japanese planes. Rector himself, during his entire career, had shot down ten and a half enemy planes.

Colonel Rector's disciples, in P-47s, shot down two MiG-15s. After that, Communist China's planes stuck close to the mainland.

Morale improved even more after Chiang Kai-shek changed the command. General Chow, chairman of the Joint Chiefs of Staff, had concurrently commanded the CAF. Although he was a capable army general, he understood little of aerial warfare and agreed with Rector's recommendations without implementing them. When the change could be made gracefully, General Chow retained the chair of the Joint Chiefs, and Tiger Wang (General Wang Hsu-ming) became commander of the CAF.

"We got along hand in glove," Rector recalled. "Tiger Wang had been in charge of Chennault's air warning system back in our Flying Tiger days. Working together on Taiwan, we turned the CAF around in eighteen months. It was the most rewarding period of my entire Air Force career."

Asia's temporary peace gave us time to reflect. Our stubborn stands in mainland cities had been more than hubris. Our makeshift headquarters in C-46s on Red-threatened airports bought time. The local authorities could maintain a semblance of order while evacuating people. Giving no thought whatsoever to caving in, we had been a source of hope. A stabilizing factor. And now these people were on Taiwan. Technicians, teachers, businessmen, bankers, and civil administrators. An important core. We had airlifted from Chengtu one of the best foreign ministers in China's history—George Yeh. We had been the air arm of Free China.

Heaven-sent, Yen Hsi-shan had been premier of China at precisely the right time. During the interval of Chiang's temporary retirement, frail Yen Hsi-shan, outwardly self-effacing and benign, smiling often, called upon his inner resources—the same down-to-earth awareness, the same steel will he had used to build his industrial complex at Taiyüan. Ruthlessly, he held the government intact while it fled from Canton to Chungking to Chengtu and finally to Taiwan. The old warlord, unlike the impenetrable Chiang Kai-shek, was not protected in a cocoon of unreality. Burrridge said, "Yen Hsi-shan brought discipline to government." By the time Chiang Kai-shek reclaimed the presidency, the government was lean.

Standing before the Executive Yuan, Chiang Kai-shek declared many things. Among them, "We must thoroughly reform our party. . . .

Do away with conflicts between cliques. . . . No longer tolerate the selfish behavior and ideas that have caused the collapse on the mainland and may cause the collapse of Taiwan if unchecked."

Political balderdash, I thought, while I recalled my mainland experience—kids crawling down holes in Mengtsz's tin mines, farmers taxed years in advance, soldiers unpaid while generals lent out the money. But I was wrong.

I was astounded at Executive Yuan's immediate land reform. Taiwanese sharecroppers had been paying at least 50 percent of their income to absentee landlords, and some rent was due even though crops failed. A new law required owners to sell their land to the government, which in turn sold it back to the tenants for ten-year mortgages to be repaid with 25 percent of the yield of the crops. Initially the money came from U.S. AID funds.

Having received a fair price for their land, many former landowners invested the proceeds in growing Taiwan's industries and became wealthy—a different deal than the People's Republic on the mainland, where landlords were shot.

Foreign observers discussed Taiwan's economic miracle and its gradual evolution to something close to Western democracy. Until then, I hadn't known a leopard could change its spots.

Few understood completely how the Nationalist Government changed so drastically so rapidly. Foreign devils aren't good at fathoming Chinese puzzles. Burridge laid it to Yen Hsi-shan's short but severe reform. Rosbert believed the tight security of an island made it easy to catch spies and racketeers. (We saw them in army trucks, tied to boards emblazoned with the Chinese word for bandit on their way to the racecourse to be shot.) Others said it was American aid (but previous aid on the mainland had been squandered). I believed it was enlightened Chinese pragmatism. Chiang and his son Chiang Ching-kuo noticed the Free Taiwan movement. They were savvy enough to know that good government would take the wind out of the militants' sails. And the mainland had shown them the bitterness of failure; they didn't want to fail again.

When Chiang first got to Taiwan, he sought seclusion in the mountains. He meditated. Perhaps he saw the light. Fishing a beautiful lake, he caught a large fish. "The longest ever caught in Sun Moon Lake," a fisherman said. It was a good omen.

Chiang Kai-shek gainsaid his critics. However, those who blamed him for the loss of the mainland didn't credit him with Taiwan's success. Nor did the cynics acknowledge that the new Free China repaid the U.S. funds it had borrowed to gain economic independence or that the people on Taiwan cooperated in a severe austerity program that banned the importation of unessential items until the currency stabilized.

During dark mainland days I questioned the corruption, and Chennault told me Chiang Kai-shek was a man of integrity, but who had difficulty finding honest administrators. I was glad Chennault lived long enough to see his dogged faith vindicated.

For the last couple of years, Chennault had spent most of his time in Washington, D.C. We heard he suffered a malignant tumor in a lung. Soon after his surgery we got word that he was on his way to Taiwan. All he wanted, he said, was a dinner party with his pilots. Rosbert and Lil arranged it at their house on Ya Ming Mountain.

It was obvious that he was happy to be home again with his airline. Craggy as his smile was, I'd never seen it broader, but he spoke in a hoarse whisper. He held a briar pipe as if it annoyed him and sucked it as if it were a sour lemon. I wondered why his doctor had denied him cigarettes at this late stage.

There was a bittersweet aura of a special farewell. No speeches. We just sat around, comfortable together, bantering like pilots.

Lil announced dinner, and twenty or so guys merged on the veranda. I hung back and was astonished and delighted when Lil grabbed my arm and pushed me into a chair beside Chennault. In between courses, the general leaned close and said, "I take a handful of pills every night, but can't sleep for pain." It wasn't a complaint; it was just his way—quietly matter-of-fact. I nodded. And then he said, "I remember the days you ran our New Zealand operation and the success you made of it." I nodded again.

I wanted to tell the splendid man how much he had taught us, the inspiration, the fun it had been. I owed him those words; I wanted to say them. But I sat tongue-tied. Now I'm dismayed at my dumbness, both literally and figuratively, during those last moments I spent with Chennault.

He returned to a bed in Bethesda Naval hospital, where the Air Force pinned on another star and promoted him to lieutenant general. "Too late," he gasped. He died on July 27, 1958, at age sixty-seven.

Six horses drew the caisson that carried his body to Arlington. Whitey Willauer and generals walked beside the casket, followed by honorary pallbearers including former Tigers Dick Rossi, Ed Rector, and Tex Hill. Members of Congress and more than a thousand mourners followed. The Air Force Band played "The General's March," and drummers beat three muffled flourishes.

Chennault was a general who lost many battles but never was defeated. I envisioned a rural Louisiana schoolteacher who wanted to fly, who loved his country. A pursuit pilot, discharged for damaged hearing, who went on to develop the Chinese Air Force. Invent the Flying Tigers. Make the Fourteenth Air Force a legend. Return to China with an airline to give freedom a meaning. He taught us, "You can't go back and relive the past. Look to tomorrow for the next challenge."

The persona of Old Leatherface masked a precious facet of Chennault's character. His personal code. In a letter to Anna not long before he died, he wrote, "I shall depend on you to cherish, guide, and teach [our daughters] to be proud of their ancestry and to lead upright, honorable lives. Teach them the true principals of life—to be moral, honest, loyal, frugal, and kind to all who need kindness. Live within your means, envy no one, enjoy both the comforts and privations on this earth. Be humble and work hard at anything you choose for a profession."

Chennault wasn't all we lost. Willauer's young son died in an accident near their summer home in Nantucket. Devastated, Willauer heeded urges of family and friends to become ambassador to Honduras, which was closer to home.

The customer selected our new head, we guessed, for his pedigree. Air Corps officer, Pan American captain, overseas administrative posts, an M.B.A. from Harvard—his name was Doole. Friend and foe alike agreed his was a fiscal genius. Our accountants and lawyers loved him because he brought order and convention to business matters as well as charm, which he turned on and off with alacrity. The customer's operations guys saw the off side. "Someone said Doole is a controversial character," one of them said. "But he isn't controversial at all; everyone agrees he's a son of a bitch."

Doole saw Chennault's portrait on the cover of CAT's magazine celebrating our founder's birthday. Summoning the director of public relations, he said, as accurately as can be recalled, "Why Chennault's picture? He's a has-been."

Our PR director, Marvin Plake—a former naval intelligence officer who had worked with Chennault in the big war—replied, "Mr. Doole, if that's the way you feel, I'll resign." Doole accepted, declaring Plake would never work in aviation again.

The new PR chief arrived. His name was Du Buque, but we called him Du Puke after he ordered the veteran PR secretary to burn the photographs of our China days. In tears, she piled the historical stuff in a spare room—Chennault with his Flying Tigers, P-40s galore, Fourteenth Air Force operations, CAT's inaugural flight, crews long dead, wives and kids on the mainland, our airdrops on Taiyüan—and spread the alarm: "Anyone who wants photographs, come quickly."

I got there in time to glean a few remainders and got angry when I found, in a wastebasket, a first edition of Chennault's book, *The Way of a Fighter*, with an inscription to Anna. Our Chinese PR assistant promised to send it to her.

Storming, "I told you to burn them," Du Puke fired the secretary. Rosbert assigned her to the engineering department and ferreted more boxes of photos, which he hid in his house, out of a storeroom. Eventually he sent them to our archives at the University of Texas.

Chennault had groomed Rosbert for the presidency, but now he found himself in an office with nothing to do. When I joked about his easy life, he didn't laugh. "You don't know how it feels to have talent you can't use," he said. He resigned, as did Burridge.

Doole wrote a summary claiming he'd fired them and even demeaned Willauer. In Doole's opinion, the entire bunch had mismanaged CAT with half-baked procedures, using vest pockets for files.

Like a crowing rooster claiming credit for the dawn, Doole didn't know the power of Chennault's long-term friendship with Chiang Kai-shek and his officials. Nor of Anna's, Willauer's, or Wang Wen-san's for that matter. Gently, behind the scenes, the way things work in China, they had bailed CAT out of many a sensitive situation.

Directing in detail all phases of CAT from his Washington office, Doole telephoned Taipei daily.

He even got to Fred Walker, eventually. The redheaded Yankee giant had served for eight years as chief pilot of Laos, assistant area manager, and personal pilot to Hmong general Vang Pao. He and his wife had raised four daughters in Asia.

Walker flew his Helio Courier to General Vang Pao's mountain redoubt. The general shook his hand vigorously and called him Captain Fred. "I just came up to tell you I'm being transferred to Bangkok," Walker said. "I don't want to go—I'd like to stay around here—but I don't have any choice in the matter."

Vang Pao looked crestfallen. He held out his handsome necklace of carved silver, which weighed about three pounds.

The redheaded Yankee said, "You gave me another one two years ago."

"I want you to have this."

Walker thanked him and said, "I must go now." Necklace in hand, he walked to the Helio Courier. Pausing for a moment, looking around, he thought, I'll never see this place again. Bittersweet memories had already begun. "I thought of my lunches with Vang Pao," Walker recalled, "in his huge field tent, where his number four wife cooked. A striking woman, slender and tall as Vang Pao, with glowing olive skin and high cheekbones. She cooked my favorite—meatballs the size of my thumbnail with a tasty sauce, and sticky rice." Sometimes Vang Pao put the whole serving bowl in front of Walker and said, "Eat!"

Vang Pao told his aide, "We'll never see a man like that up here again."

Relegated to a no-brainer job in Bangkok—a supervisor over just four pilots—Walker was honest enough to tell the company it wasted money on his administrator's salary. He'd return to flying the line.

Although Rousselot gave a year's notice before he resigned, Doole told a historian he had fired our chief. Vice president of operations when he departed, Rousselot had led the pilots from bush flying in China to sophisticated jet routes throughout Asia. A disciplinarian, he was just as tough on himself. He turned every flight of his into a learning experience. Through his gruff posture I saw an inner respect for pilots and a sense of decency. No one messed with his pilots. Although a few thought life would be easier with old Iron-Ass gone, it quickly became apparent that he had been our greatest champion. A pilot said, "Now that Rousselot's gone, any junior office clerk can harass a pilot more than he knows how to handle."

Lillian Chu, an elegant head office secretary, wrote to the Willauers, "Morale is at bottom low. As far as I am concerned they might as well not use the name of CAT, as it is not the organization that 'CAT' stood for and has certainly no esprit de corps as in the past. . . . I wish they would just have another name instead of CAT. . . ."

Our pity party ended when a Commie pilot jolted us out of ourselves. He called our attention to the civil war by flying his MiG-15 across the Straits of Formosa at eight hundred feet to stay below Taiwan's long-range radar. By the time the short-range scopes detected him, his landing gear was down. He claimed a million dollars, Chiang Kai-shek's standing offer. A million in gold for any defecting pilot.

The bloom died when a Nationalist training plane defected in the opposite direction. It was a small primary trainer, but it exposed a breach in the security system.

We soon got a memo from the Nationalist government warning us that any aircraft of Free China headed toward the mainland would be shot down without warning.

Welk exclaimed, "Do you realize what they're telling us? If our dragon wagon is hijacked, it'll be shot down, passengers and all."

"Sixty percent of our passengers are Americans and Europeans," I said. "Wouldn't they be pissed if they saw this friggin' memo? We're IATA [International Air Transport Association]. Our tickets cost the same as Pan Am's."

"Imagine the uproar in the States if Delta or American Airlines got a memo like this—if you get hijacked and head for Cuba, the USAF will shoot you down without warning!"

Two days later we got stern instructions to return the memos.

Doc Johnson said, "Someone must have told Shanghai Jack [Chiang Kai-shek] how the rest of the world would holler if the memo leaked out."

"They just recalled the memo; they didn't say they rescinded the policy," I said.

To us, the threat of a shoot down by any trigger-happy pilot in jittery Asia was real. Still fresh in our minds, even though it had happened years before, in 1954, was the downing of Cathay Pacific. My China National friend, Len Parish, with his wife, Fran, and their two sons, were on board, on their way from Saigon to Hong Kong. Of that family, only Fran reached the Crown Colony.

The Downing of Cathay Pacific

Red China had assumed a posture of contempt after the Korean truce and the fall of Dien Bien Phu. Mao Tse-tung crowed, "America is a paper tiger." Great Britain also suffered the vituperation.

Brazen as Red China appeared, no one expected it to shoot down an airliner on a civil airway on a flight plan in broad daylight in clear weather over international waters. Whatever bugged the Red Chinese, they didn't have to massacre innocent passengers. Pilots everywhere are familiar with international signals by which military planes communicate with civilian airliners. Wiggling wings by day or flashing navigation lights at night means "Follow me" or "Land at the closest airfield." A reluctant pilot can easily be herded by a fighter plane.

Red China's LA-7s had been cavorting off the south coast and occasionally buzzed a passing airliner, but we assumed they practiced ground-directed radar intercepts, which we called dry runs. Both Chinas denied it, but they used transiting airliners for practice attacks.

The ill-fated airliner belonged to Hong Kong's Cathay Pacific Airways, a respected British company that decorated its four-engine DC-4s with huge lettering and a British flag. On that July day of 1954, it was twenty miles off Hainan Island at nine thousand feet when Cathay's Australian captain was startled by cannon fire and the disintegration of his outboard engines. With burning fuel streaming from his right wing, he radioed a Mayday to air traffic control while he dived in an effort to blow out the flames.

"The guns were loud. We looked out and saw flames from the wing, and two fighters," Fran recalled. "Len put the boys in the aisle and covered them with his body. . . . Bullets streamed down the aisle. It killed them."

The fighters followed the airliner down, firing all the way, shooting away its rudder. Although swells ran ten feet, the captain ditched skillfully enough to save some of his passengers. They clung to wreckage, found an inflatable raft, helped each other aboard, and waited in fear of another attack.

They were in Hong Kong's flight information region, which meant their future lay in the hands of the British colony's search-and-rescue system. They waited for three hours, and when a Sunderland flying boat arrived from Hong Kong it couldn't land because the sea was too rough. Two SA-16 Albatrosses of the USAF 31st Search and Rescue Squadron at Clark Air Force Base, eight hundred miles away, headed for the survivors. The Reds warned them away from the crash site.

The rescue planes maintained their course and speed while Felix Stump, admiral of the U.S. Seventh Fleet, launched Skyraiders and Corsairs from his carrier.

They shot down two LA-7s while one Albatross landed in calmer waters near Hainan Island and taxied out through rough seas to the survivors.

By the time the Albatross reached Hong Kong, more of the wounded were dead. Only nine survived, including Fran Parish. The commander of the Albatross, Captain Jack Woodyard, received the Distinguished Flying Cross.

To this day no one knows why Red China, in broad daylight, shot down a silver passenger plane that displayed Britain's Union Jack. Some speculated that the Chinese fighter pilots mistook it for one of our planes because the first three letters of Cathay spell CAT. The Reds could have intercepted radio messages between our Bangkok and Hong Kong offices that confirmed, on CAT's flight that day, a seat for William Donovan, ambassador to Thailand (and former head of the Office of Strategic Services, America's World War II intelligence network). Communist news broadcasts had been lambasting Donovan ever since he helped frustrate their takeover of the China National planes at Hong Kong.

At a United Nations conference, the USA objected to the shoot down, but Red China contemptuously rejected the complaint and protested the destruction of its two fighters.

In that climate, Admiral Stump's quick response shone like a star. The admiral intrigued me.

Five years later I was CAT's temporary manager of Japan and Korea while Admiral Stump was temporary chairman of Air America. After his inspection visit I accompanied him to Tokyo's international airport. Unfortunately for Admiral Stump, but fortunately for me, Pan American's departure was delayed long enough for the rest of the party to drift off. The admiral's aide fell asleep. "Admiral Stump," I ventured, "I'm curious about the Cathay Pacific incident."

The admiral's eyes lit up, and I visualized him on his flagship. "I lined my pilots up on deck and told them, in all the four-letter words I know, English common law."

"Which one?"

"You don't have to wait until someone strikes you before you defend yourself. All you need is a threatening move in your direction."

No paper tiger.

The Stewardess

Chiang Kai-shek's memorandum regarding our own ally shooting us down—if we got hijacked—induced us to take the cockpit keys away from our cabin crew. "Anyone can overpower a ninety-pound stewardess and grab the keys," we said. The engineering department installed bolts and peepholes on the doors.

We got hijacked. Not our sleek jet or our plush DC-6; it was a C-46 on our around-the-island flight.

It was a cunning choice for the Communists. The captain, Benji Lin, was son-in-law to Tiger Wang, commanding general of the Chinese Air Force. The colorful general was proud of Benji for graduating from the Chinese Air Academy and serving as a CAT pilot for fourteen years. One of the passengers, Loke Wan-tho, the multimillionaire owner of Singapore's largest movie studio, was a socialite and friend of Lord Mountbatten. Loke had donated hefty sums of money to the Nationalist government.

Our newest stewardess—the first ever hired who wasn't Chinese—happened to be on the flight, although she wasn't on the original schedule. I first met her when I flew to Korea, before she became a stewardess. Her name was Cho He-yong.

After the last passenger disembarked at Seoul I slid open the side window and saw her standing on the ramp, staring up at the dragon on the nose of our Mandarin jet. Her hair, cut in a bob and shining black, curled inward at the ends to frame a porcelain-translucent face with high cheekbones scrubbed pink.

She walked up the steps and bowed slightly. "Good afternoon, Captain. May I look inside?" Her CAT badge read, "Cho He-yong, Passenger Service." She walked down the golden carpet, squeezed the silk upholstery of the seats, hesitated at the moon gate that separated first class and tourist, and swept delicate fingers over the carving. While she admired the teakwood phoenix and dragon, I admired her narrow waist, rounded hips, lovely calves.

She looked back suddenly and caught me staring. I quickly said, "It's an imperial dragon with five toes. Ordinary dragons only have four."

The corners of her mouth flexed, and her eyes glowed with intelligence. "Yes," she said. "And they eat flaming pearls."

Our station manager said, "She's been begging me to release her so she can be a stewardess. She's my right arm—speaks fluent

English, Japanese, Chinese—graduated from Columbia University. I don't want to let her go, but I won't stand in her way."

I happened to be flying on the autumn day when Miss Cho went to Taipei to attend CAT's stewardess school. Her family lined up side by side in Seoul's departure lounge. Her father, grave, in a Western suit, said, "I know our daughter will be safe in your hands." Mrs. Cho, in a high-waisted, ankle-length billowy skirt and an embroidered blouse, smiled, but her eyes looked sad. Miss Cho's two younger sisters giggled and looked excited.

Miss Cho arrived at Taipei, a stranger in a classroom of Chinese students. Even though CAT tried to preserve its Mandarin ambience with Chinese stewardesses, we had accommodated passengers on our growing Korean route by hiring Miss Cho. After two months of classes and apprentice flights around the island, CAT's president pinned a golden-dragon brooch on Miss Cho's new uniform.

In the roulette of crew scheduling, Miss Cho and I seldom shared flights, but during the few times we did, I was intrigued by her luminescent dark eyes and quiet, down-to-earth strength tempered by grace.

On a Wednesday in mid-June, Miss Cho checked in for her trip from Seoul to Tokyo. Her schedule had been changed. Instead of returning to Seoul, she would continue on to Taipei. So she telephoned her father to say she wouldn't return for a few days. Mr. Cho said the family would delay their vacation until she returned.

When Miss Cho got to Taipei, she was surprised to find herself in the middle of the 1964 Asian film festival. In addition to Loke Wantho, movie idol William Holden was present, with several Asian stars and producer Run-Run Shaw of Hong Kong.

Loke told newsmen he'd fulfill his dream to see the art treasures in China's National Central Museum in Taichung, which was only eighty miles south of Taipei. William Holden and Run-Run Shaw said they'd accompany him, and other celebrities decided to follow. The museum tour would leave Taipei on CAT's first flight of the day and return that afternoon, in time for the farewell banquet at Taipei's Grand Hotel. The announcement excited the two Chinese stewardesses who happened to be on the flight.

I had a beer or two with Joe Tang, a pilot friend who enjoyed relating the gossip. A stewardess, he said, had been consulting a *fung shui*. The professor of geomantics—aware of the delicately balanced forces in nature, sensitive to their vibrations—recommended the best site for her new house and the direction it should face. And he advised her to be wary of danger the next day.

Crossing a busy street, on her way home, she dropped her vanity case—the one she carried on her flights—and it was crushed by a passing taxi. Accepting it as a warning sign, she reported sick. Miss Cho replaced her.

The next morning, Taipei's passenger terminal was packed with fans, who jostled for a glimpse of the movie stars. Some were disappointed because William Holden wasn't there. He had decided to visit the museum a day early and travel on to Hong Kong. A messenger hurried into the terminal with an urgent cablegram for Run-Run Shaw, who read it and boarded the first plane for Hong Kong.

Miss Cho helped the other stewardess and the purser stow flight lunches. Kung, the squirrel-cheeked copilot with the peg tooth, climbed through the C-46's emergency exits to the wings, where he dipped a measuring stick into the plane's six fuel tanks and recorded the quantity in a logbook.

Captain Benji Lin, in the meteorology office, heard good news. The weather would be clear all day.

Amid waves and shouts, the movie celebrities boarded and were flown south for thirty minutes. When they disembarked at Taichung, Miss Cho smiled and told Loke Wan-tho and his museum group she'd see them on the return trip that afternoon.

Captain Lin continued down the elm-leaf-shaped island, over pineapple fields and rice paddies, with Taiwan's green mountains on his left. To his right, the sea sparkled blue, and the air was clear enough to reveal the faint line of the China coast, ninety miles west.

After his scheduled stops halfway around Taiwan, he reversed direction for his homeward journey. He put into Makung—the seaport town on one of the Pescadores Islands. A few American military advisers boarded, followed by a Chinese Navy lieutenant who was a radar expert at Makung's shipyard. He was accompanied by a friend, a former naval officer who had become a businessman. Although the Chinese Navy lieutenant was due back at the shipyard within seventy-two hours, he didn't take advantage of CAT's round-trip discount. Like his friend, he bought a one-way ticket. Assigned to a plush DC-4 going nonstop, the pair insisted on waiting for Captain Lin's C-46, which would make an intermediate stop at Taichung, saying, "We have a business appointment there." Told the plane would be on the ground only five minutes, hardly time for a business meeting, the pair said they required only a short confab.

An officer of the Peace Preservation Corps (the secret police) inspected the lieutenant's military papers and found them properly endorsed for a seventy-two-hour leave. The policeman had no way of knowing the lieutenant had spent the morning giving away his personal belongings. He and his companion had no checked baggage. The only hand-carried items were two U.S. Navy radar manuals.

Captain Lin took off and flew north over the rice paddies and pineapple fields and landed at Taichung, where the movie celebrities, tired from their museum tour, waited. Nobody was present to confer with the Chinese Navy lieutenant and his friend.

The plane left Taichung with fifty passengers. After a normal take-off, it climbed north for a few minutes and then turned toward China's mainland. It leveled off at eight hundred feet, the maximum altitude for evading long-range surveillance radar. It flew level for a few minutes and then descended in a gentle spiral as if no one controlled it. Close to the ground, it nosed sharply down and crashed into a rice paddy.

A piece of flying wreckage struck a farm boy. A passing helicopter radioed for help and landed beside the wreckage. The boy was the only sign of life. Badly frightened, with a grazed shoulder, he walked home in the company of a helicopter crewman.

Thirty minutes later, CAT's doctor, with his nurses, left Taipei with medical supplies. He later reported, "There was no indication of survival such as a voice calling for help, or any movement of the bodies. . . . The extreme painfulness in my heart could not be expressed in words. . . ."

Bodies were scattered over the paddy, beyond recognition. The local police cordoned it off and prohibited investigators from moving the remains until the coroner and district attorney arrived. Newsmen and relatives wailed and shouted disapproval until the officials arrived fourteen hours later.

Near the left engine, they found Captain Lin's body, with a small hole at the right side of his face. From that hole, a large part of his face and skull had been blown away, as if he had been shot.

Because some of the victims had been American military advisers, the American air attaché was allowed to investigate the site. He found a U.S. Navy radar manual with the inside pages cut out in the shape of a .45 automatic pistol. A few hours later he found a second manual, similarly hollowed out and empty. And then he found a .45-caliber pistol with its hammer cocked. After the left engine was lifted he discovered another pistol on top of the following items: Captain Lin's engine analyzer manual, copilot Kung's personal logbook and his crew baggage tag, a flashlight from the airplane's flight kit, a seat back from a pilot's seat, and a torn khaki shirt.

A laborer pointed to a sparkling object on the collar of the shirt. It was a double bronze bar on a black background, which is the insignia of a Chinese Navy lieutenant.

Serial numbers on the radar manuals confirmed the lieutenant had borrowed them from Makung's shipyard library. Numbers on the pistols indicated they'd been stolen from the shipyard armory a week before the crash.

By 7:00 P.M. the police said they'd withdraw from the scene, but CAT haggled with them until they agreed to guard the wreckage until it could be moved to CAT's maintenance base.

Although the bodies of the Americans were released, the remains of other victims were flown to Taipei to be held in a mortuary for further investigation. Hulse, our former station manager of Seoul and a friend of the Cho family, guarded Miss Cho's body while our manager of in-flight services watched over the remains of the other crew members. Relatives of other victims wailed in the mortuary all night. "A nightmare," Hulse said.

Korean newsmen picked up the gossip about the Chinese stewardess who refused to fly after the *fung shui*'s warning. Seoul newspapers blared, "Crash foreseen"; "Chinese stewardess replaced with Korean"; "Crash surrounded with suspicion and mystery"; "Korean stewardess' body held by Chinese government; cannot be prepared for proper burial." The ill will was magnified because Miss Cho was the first Korean stewardess, in Korean aviation history, to be killed on duty in a foreign airline.

By the time the government released her body, three days with temperatures above ninety degrees had elapsed. To spare her family unnecessary shock, her body was placed in a U.S. Navy coffin and Hulse jammed the lock.

I happened to be flying when the coffin was placed in the baggage compartment of the Mandarin jet. The stewardesses didn't talk much during the flight to Seoul, nor did I. Less than a year into her dream of flying, I thought, and now she was dead; and in her death the customs of her country had been denied her. Her face had not been washed in perfume or her body wrapped in silk garments or tied with seven silken ropes representing the Big Dipper, the lucky constellation. Her remains lay in a U.S. Navy coffin a few feet below the teakwood moon gate with the phoenix and five-toed dragon she had touched on the day I first admired her.

Before our intermediate stop at Okinawa, our purser came to the flight deck to whisper disconsolately, "We think we can smell something." I was sure it was only the apprehension of the flight attendants, but I nodded gravely, and when we landed at Okinawa I took him with me and we opened the door of the belly compartment. In silence we stared at the gray Navy coffin, sensed the closeness of Miss Cho's broken body, and felt the mystery of death. "It's okay," I said. The flight attendants settled down afterward.

When we landed at Seoul the station manager, looking glum, led us, in our best uniforms, to the VIP lounge. We walked slowly.

Mr. Cho, in a swallowtail coat, stood alongside his wife and daughters, whose dresses were covered with white kimonos. Candles burned nearby. We crew members removed our hats and bowed.

"We're very sorry," we said. The Cho family bowed and said thank you.

We returned to the airplane and flew out our schedule.

The station manager told me what happened.

The hearse with Miss Cho's photograph on its hood circled the Cho house several times and stopped. Mrs. Cho removed the photograph and took it into the house, loudly crying, *"Aoi, Aoi,"* which was an invitation for Miss Cho's spirit to leave her house. It was also a custom for a man in the household to announce the death in the neighborhood by climbing onto the roof to wave a garment of the deceased and cry out the name, but this was not done, because the Chos were Christian. It was a mix of two cultures.

After consulting the Cho family, CAT bought land for a grave near the top of a mountain near Seoul. Korean dead are not always buried in a formal cemetery. The preferred place is within sight of a rising ridgeline to enable the deceased to look upon a line of ancestors. CAT's Korean employees found a long, rising ridgeline near pine trees, which was good because snakes don't dwell in pines, and the grave was planned so that Miss Cho's head would face south without looking onto some other grave. All of these conditions made "a good advancing dragon."

The hearse and a busload of the Cho family and their friends started up the mountain road but got stuck in the mud of the summer rains. Ropes were tied around the coffin, and it was slung between bamboo poles that had been covered with red-and-blue bunting, the colors of the Korean flag. Laborers grunted and sweated and got it to the top of the mountain. Mourners followed on foot. Women in high heels slid and fell in the mud and cried. It took an hour to reach the top.

They overlooked the Han River. Nothing moved, not a tree branch or a leaf. Lazy stratus clouds hung in green valleys beyond. A Methodist minister droned on and on while the sun rose higher and beat down and the temperature climbed into the nineties. Soft-drink bottles exploded intermittently.

When the Navy coffin was moved over the hexagon-shaped grave it became obvious that it wouldn't fit because it was too big. Mr. Cho talked earnestly to the funeral director, who responded in staccato bursts of anger. The minister's face flushed as he joined the argument over where a new grave should be dug and the direction it should face.

After the argument subsided, the mourners heard the scraping of shovels and explosions of soda bottles.

When the new grave was ready, it faced south. Prayers were intoned while the coffin was lowered and covered with a mound of earth.

The mourners talked cheerfully while soft drinks and food were consumed in a feast of celebration with Miss Cho's spirit. After an hour of this communion the mourners walked down the mountain, slipping and tumbling again.

Hulse was the last to get on the bus. Someone had to call him. He was looking at the lonely mountain.

A Warrior's Child

In its eagerness to cover the breach in Taiwan's security system, the Chinese government blamed CAT's maintenance. There were rumors of a faulty engine, but an examination, assisted by the U.S. FAA, showed the engines operated normally until they hit the rice paddy.

The government denied the hole in Captain Lin's head was caused by a bullet. Ralph Turner, professor of forensic science at Michigan State, temporarily teaching at Taiwan's police academy, offered to examine the .45 to determine if it had been fired. "We know how to check weapons," officials indignantly replied, and they sent it to Japan for inspection. Their criminologists reported the results were inconclusive because too much time had elapsed.

CAT steadfastly refused to accept the verdict of maintenance error. Without warning, government agents stormed CAT's accounting offices and carried off boxes of records. "CAT officials and all the employees," the Chinese announced, had evaded taxes. Back income taxes were due immediately. Overnight, each of us owed overdue taxes, interest, and penalties. More money than any of us had. Chinese income taxes, like Sweden's, could exceed 100 percent. We had been paying 20 percent of our salaries because our work benefited China, but now the government denied the existence of the pact.

Neither employees nor their families could leave Taiwan—except crew members on duty. "They're not using the dirty word," someone said, "but they're holding American wives and kids hostage."

Another hothead guessed, "It isn't the crash—it's Doole's treatment of the Chinese."

Anna Chennault, always level-headed, told us the display of strength was merely a Chinese way of protesting the CIA's nosy intrusion into its domestic affairs. It would be resolved soon.

The U.S. State Department advised us to withdraw from the investigation of the crash because there were more important considerations. Highlighting a breach in the island's security system would be grist for Red China's mill. After all, the civil war was ongoing, however subdued, and we were Chiang Kai-shek's allies.

Both governments readily agreed that the American advisers who died on the flight were casualties of war.

In another incident, the daughter of a U.S. Navy officer reminded us that our warriors and their families endure hazards beyond battles. They live in the presence of our allies' strange customs and idiosyncrasies.

At Taipei International we were told the Mandarin jet's departure would be delayed for a U.S. Navy officer's daughter whose flannel nightgown had brushed against an electric heater and caught fire. If she got to the military burn center in Texas within twenty-four hours she had a fifty-fifty chance of living. She was five years old.

The clock had ticked away two hours of the crucial twenty-four at Taipei's naval hospital, where they prepared her for the long trip. It'd take twenty minutes more to get her to the airport. Our nonstop flight to Tokyo at eight-tenths the speed of sound would take little more than two hours, and her transfer to Yokota Air Force Base near Tokyo would take forty-five minutes. A U.S. Air Force jet waited. The runway, two miles long, would allow a takeoff with sufficient fuel to make Texas nonstop. The girl could get to the burn center in time for a fighting chance.

A stewardess told the passengers.

We removed three rows of first-class seats, made a bed on the floor, and curtained it off. Her mother and a doctor would sit across the aisle.

The Mandarin jet carried two captains, and it was the other guy's turn to fly. A tall Texan from a small town, he had been a football hero in college. Quiet, methodical, steady, his name was Bigony. We called him Big. After we executed the pre-start checklist, he looked out the left window and said, "The ambulance just pulled up." We started the two engines on our right wing. I radioed the tower and got an immediate response.

"CAT zero-eight cleared down the high-speed taxiway, cleared for immediate takeoff." The tower was helping. The high-speed taxiway—a shortcut to the runway—was normally used for arriving planes.

After taxiing a couple hundred feet, we were alongside a guardhouse. Instead of showing a green flag, the sentry waved a red one while his buddy, with a finger on the trigger of a rifle, drew a bead on Bigony's head. We stopped.

"Taipei Tower, we have a red flag." A Chinese Civil Aviation sedan drove up, followed by a Chinese Army garrison command jeep and a CAT operations station wagon. People emerged from all three vehicles and argued while the soldier held a bead on Bigony's head.

"Mah's on duty," I said. "He can fix anything." An intelligent, calm man with the courtly bearing of a north Chinese, Mah represented CAT at the airport. I called him the Noble Fixer.

Fifteen minutes passed with nothing happening. I opened the main cabin door and signaled for a ramp. When I got to the ground they were arguing over who controlled the taxiways—the army or the Aviation Administration. During a lull in the confab I asked Mah, the Noble Fixer, if they knew a burned child was suffering. He said yes.

"Tell the garrison commander I'll take the blame. When we get back from Tokyo he can throw me in jail or impound the airplane—anything he wants—but for God's sake let the plane take off."

Mah nodded. I stood alone, away from the harangue, and listened to Wong translate my message, and the argument between the three factions got more virulent and continued for ten more minutes.

North China Mah came over to me, shook his head disgustedly, and said, "This is the reason these people lost the mainland." Some trust! If I repeated what Mah said and the Peace Preservation Corps got word, they'd toss him in jail.

"See if you can get 'em to put down the rifle," I said. "Bigony might get a headache."

I reboarded the airplane. The doctor—a young Navy lieutenant—was clearly worried.

An hour and a half later, we were told we could depart, provided we maneuvered the plane into a 180-degree turn on the taxiway and returned to the tarmac and parked for a minute. Only then would we be cleared down the conventional taxiway.

Our flight plan with air traffic control had expired, and we had to wait for a new slot to Tokyo.

Eventually we departed and climbed east-northeast toward our first landfall in western Japan. When we got close to our cruising altitude—more than six miles high—our Doppler radar bounced its signals off the ocean's surface while its computer noted how long it took the signals to return. It calculated our speed over the surface of Mother Earth and displayed it to us. Obviously we had caught the jet stream, because our airspeed was 500 knots, whereas our ground speed was 650. "A hundred-and-fifty-knot tailwind," I said. Bigony nodded, and we watched it increase. For half an hour it read a hair over 700 knots (795 statute miles per hour).

I went back to ask how the child was faring. "We're in trouble," the doctor said. "See if you can have this waiting when we arrive." He scribbled a list: a French catheter with a number after it, and other equipment and drugs. Much as I tried on our long-range radio, the communicator on the other end couldn't understand the unfamiliar medical words. I tried spelling them, but static obscured them or they faded out.

"Damn," I said. "If those sons of bitches hadn't delayed us we'd be in Tokyo by now."

Our ground speed dropped off. We lost the jet stream over western Japan.

Before it was time to contact their control, Tokyo called us. "Yokota Approach Control wants you to contact them." Yokota was the U.S. Air Force base near Mount Fuji.

"Yokota Approach," I called, "CAT zero-eight. One-two-zero miles west of Tokyo, flight level three-seven-zero."

An American voice: "CAT zero-eight, can you land Yokota? We have an aircraft standing by for immediate takeoff to Houston."

I told Yokota to stand by. I sensed the wheels turning in Bigony's head. We weren't dispatched to Yokota; we had a passenger load for Tokyo International. The offbeat landing wasn't cricket. Bigony had always stuck to the rules.

"We can ask CAT ops for permission to divert, but hell, we won't get a reply in time. Let's just land there."

"Ask permission," Bigony said, "and we'll go in before they answer. That way we have a fifty-fifty chance of doing right."

I sent our request to CAT operations via Tokyo radio and returned to Yokota's frequency. "CAT zero-eight request land Yokota. Request keep number four engine running. Military air carts won't fit our plane." (It takes compressed air to start a jet engine.)

"Roger, keep an engine running."

"He's waiving the rules too," Bigony said.

It was a black night. We saw only our instruments, heard only Yokota's voice. "Steer heading zero-one-five, radar vector direct to runway three-six. Descend at your discretion. Maintain this frequency. Yokota Tower has cleared you to land. We have you five-seven miles out."

At the end of our landing roll a "Follow Me" jeep guided us to an Air Force C-141. It didn't take long to transfer our young passenger and her mother and doctor. We were cleared immediately to Tokyo International. I thanked our passengers.

An hour later the reply from CAT ops made its way through the communications systems to Tokyo. Our Yokota landing was approved, and it occurred to me that Bigony was smarter than I.

She died after reaching the burn center in Houston.

I couldn't fathom why the suffering of a burned child had failed to move the garrison commander. And then I remembered something the Dalai Lama wrote after Chinese Communists tortured his priests. "In spite of the atrocious crimes which Chinese have committed in our country," the Buddhist leader penned, "I have absolutely no hatred in my heart of the Chinese people. . . . I have known many admirable Chinese. I suspect there is nobody in the world more charming and civilized than the best of Chinese, and nobody more cruel and wicked than the worst."

That was it. The Dalai Lama gave me perspective. China was a look into a fun house mirror where everything was exaggerated. Highs were higher and lows lower than anywhere else.

Forced to read Shakespeare in school, I resented it until a marvelous teacher deciphered the strange language and fascinating characters became larger than life. Whose heart could be as pure as Desdemona's, wicked as Richard the Third's, logical as Portia's, or mixed up as Othello's?

Shakespeare with all his genius couldn't invent the rascality and nobility of Marshal Yen all in the same man. Or the forbearance and cheerfulness of Chinese who moved gracefully under burdens twice their weight, or sang while towing huge junks against the Yangtze's current, or the stout heart of Weihsien's militia leader. Or the colorful Christian general who baptized soldiers with a fire hose. Or the mean-mindedness of the garrison commander who delayed the burned child. Or the wisdom and generosity of my Chinese friends.

Was that why missionaries were drawn to retire in China? Why the rest of the world seemed flat?

The Mechanic

After the Chinese shenanigans, the Caucasian antics that followed didn't bother me. It was a metaphor for CAT's new regime. It may strike a familiar note with pilots everywhere in the world. Had Rousselot been boss, the last part would have been different.

It happened on the Mandarin jet, from Hong Kong to Taipei.

CAT was the first Asian airline to operate jets. Ours was the latest swept-wing Convair 880. It cruised eight-tenths the speed of sound and landed nose-high, like a fighter. Gold in color, the nose was decorated with an imperial dragon about to eat a flaming pearl. The company assigned two captains until we got experience. I had been pilot in command to Hong Kong; Holden was in charge on the way back.

When we saw Taipei's runway lights five miles ahead, we put the landing-gear handle in the down position and felt the familiar thump. Two green lights on the instrument panel said our main wheels were in place, but a red light in between said the nose wheel wasn't.

I raised the landing gear, dropped it, and the red light said no again. Holden retarded one of the power levers to fool the warning system into believing we were reducing power for a landing. The horn blasted. That confirmed it. (The nose wheel wasn't locked down.) I told the control tower we'd circle.

I opened the trapdoor in the cockpit floor and descended a ladder. A switch on the bulkhead illuminated the forward wheel well, which nestles the nose gear when it's retracted. I saw the wheel hanging in the darkness, but the ends of two white lines on the upper mechanism didn't meet. They were a couple of inches apart. It was the final physical check: The nose wheel wasn't locked down.

I pulled a pole from its brackets, poked it through a porthole, and pushed my weight against the gear. It wouldn't budge. Here I am in a six-million-dollar airplane, I thought, and I'm trying to push the gear down with a pole the way my mother used to prop up her wash line every Monday.

I climbed back up to the cockpit. "The index lines don't meet," I said. "I can't budge it with the pole. How about you trying." I circled the airport until Holden returned and said, "Damn, it won't budge."

A Convair 880's nose gear folds into its well the way a human's hip and knee joints bend when sitting on the floor, Japanese-style. When it extends, it straightens out and locks into place the way race-walkers lock their knees.

"The index lines are only a couple of inches apart," I said. "If the strut is past dead center, it'll lock when we put weight on it. We could land on the main gear and ease the nose onto the runway. If the horn stops and we get a green light, we can stop. If not, we can take off again."

Holden agreed. "Taipei Tower," I radioed, "please ask a CAT mechanic to come to the tower."

Fifteen minutes later we heard, "CAT zero-eight, this is Ritchie." I knew him slightly. He was a young guy, fairly new. Quiet, polite, neat.

"Check the schematics in your maintenance manual. Our index lines are only two inches apart. Does it look like the strut might be past dead center?

Five minutes later he radioed, "A fifty-fifty chance it's past dead center. It's worth a try."

I told the passengers what we would do, but when I requested permission to land, the control tower said, "We have a message from CAT operations. They want you to wait for their instructions. Hold on the Lima Kilo beacon. Standard holding pattern."

We made a racetrack pattern for two hours. All hands and the cook came to the airport: CAT's president, the new director of operations, the system chief pilot, the jet chief pilot, the Convair factory's technical representative. They wrung their hands, but no one wanted to make a decision. "The only thing that made sense," our PR man said later, "was your voice coming over our loudspeaker."

I told Holden, "We gave 'em two hours to come up with a decision. What do ya say we do it our way?" Holden twitched a shoulder and nodded.

"CAT Operations," I radioed, "we waited two hours. That's enough. We're going to follow our original plan. If anyone down there doesn't like it, now is the time to speak."

Nobody answered.

Holden made a steady approach. The landing-gear warning horn blatted. He touched down on the main wheels and eased the nose down until it brushed the runway like a feather. The horn stopped blatting, the red light went out, the green light illuminated. "Green light!" I shouted. Holden snapped the power levers shut and pulled the reverse levers, and we stopped. We had accomplished what we had wanted to do two hours ago.

After the passengers disembarked, I asked a stewardess if they had been worried. She said, "No, because you told them what was going on."

The lights of the tarmac showed the bigwigs all in a row. A reception committee.

I walked down the ramp and overheard the president tell the jet chief pilot, "They should have gone to Tainan, where the runway is longer."

The chief turned around, put his face close to mine, and said, "You should have gone to Tainan, where the runway is longer."

"You had two hours to tell us that," I said. "Why didn't you speak up?" He looked uncomfortable.

The chief mechanic came up, flashlight in hand, and told the president, "The gear linkage seems to be normal."

"One of those things that happens once in a million times and no one will ever know why," the president said.

Convair's technical representative followed me into operations. "Are you sure you had your glasses on when you looked at those lines?"

I was struggling against an urge to sock him when the director of operations walked in. Sizing up the situation in an instant, he told the smart-ass, "Get out of here."

The next morning's newspaper headline called it an emergency landing. The president wanted to know why we had circled the city, where we could be heard. And he questioned Ritchie's advice. Had the plane crashed, the president mentioned, the maintenance department could have been blamed.

A few days later a mechanic friend said, "You know what happened? A mech saw a lot of play in the drag strut—which is normal—but he tightened it with an extra nut. It was just enough to keep the nose wheel from locking in place."

"Did anyone tell the president or chief of maintenance?"

"Hell no."

Nor did I, not even Holden, because I knew the news would spread. I found perverse satisfaction in letting the know-it-alls guess for the rest of their careers.

Whenever I think of Ritchie's severe bosses, I recall him alone with his manual in the Chinese control tower, and I mentally salute his integrity and his courage to speak up. And the world seems rosier.

The Pink Airplane

I also realized my perspective was warping. The president didn't deserve my intense reaction. A perfectionist and man of integrity, he asked questions—why this and why that—and nodded if the answers made sense. Formerly our superb chief of maintenance, he was a major reason why CAT had become a fine airline. Presidential duties—thrust upon him against his wishes—burdened him. He seemed to miss the honest world of engineering where laws of physics prevailed.

After he became president, someone said he snooped because he walked around parked airplanes at night. I said, "He's not a snooper. He's rejuvenating his spirit—he finds solace in airplanes. Their performance is predictable, and when they go awry he can quickly find out why, and he knows the fix. Who can say that about the yahoos he works with now?"

We verterans lugged the dust of a shooting star. Enthusiastic newcomers saw good-enough company. Instead of burdening them with our old baggage we stuck to the fun stuff, like the tale of the pink airplane. They retold it in bars all over the Orient.

Years back, after Japan's national airline rose from the ashes of World War II—and got past the additional delay of the war in Korea—JAL president Matsuo wanted to begin overseas service with class. He leased America's newest pressurized airliner, a Martin 404, from Trans-Ocean Airlines.

Okinawa was the destination, but that first flight didn't get much more than fifty miles beyond Tokyo. The U.S. Air Force air traffic controller cleared the departing Martin to cross Oshima island at two thousand feet even though its volcano poked five hundred feet higher. Although the pilot was a stranger from America, he didn't refer to his navigation chart, apparently. He put his entire trust in the air traffic controller. Clouds hid the island and its volcano. The crash—at exactly two thousand feet—killed everyone aboard.

The air traffic controller—the star witness—didn't appear at the investigation. The Air Force had transferred him halfway around the world. A somber and disillusioned President Matsuo canceled Trans-Ocean's contract and leased CAT's DC-4. Our old four-engine

Douglas wasn't pressurized, but Matsuo was swayed by his knowledge that CAT had survived the booby traps of Asia's airways for years without losing a commercial passenger.

Welk said, "We don't have fancy uniforms."

Johnson said, "Matsuo knows most of our mistakes are behind us, way back in China."

Chief pilot Rousselot warned, "I want to see blouses pressed and neckties snug."

Lewis, Tachikawa's maintenance chief, said, "We'll have the bird ready in the morning." His mechanics towed it into our hangar and painted the fuselage enamel-white. Pressure nozzles sprayed red paint over stencils furnished by JAL. In traditional Japanese characters, "Japan Airlines" shined red on the right side of the white fuselage; Roman lettering appeared on the left.

Rousselot scheduled a crew to ferry the DC-4 to Tokyo International the next morning for an appropriate ceremony before it departed for Okinawa.

When the hangar doors opened, Lewis stared in disbelief. Red mist from the spray guns had dissipated into the air and then settled during the night. Instead of glossy white, the airplane was loathsome pink.

"Delay the ceremony," Lewis said. "Find some excuse—we have to repaint it."

Burridge, the only airline executive in the world who never worried, said, I'll handle it," and left the scene.

"Burridge always pulls a rabbit out of a hat," I said.

"You airdales are crazy," Lewis snapped. "I've heard a hundred times how Burridge inflated a life raft to raise a plane out of a grave, and how he drummed up so much business accountants begged him to stop the flights until they caught up with the paperwork, but there's no damn way he can bail us out of this."

Welk said, "President Matsuo will toss you one of those swords— you'll have to commit hara-kiri."

"It ain't funny."

"We don't know how he'll do it," I said. "We just know Burridge will find a way."

Welk, Johnson, and I drove over to Tokyo International with Lewis and got jostled by the crowd as we worked our way to the ceremonial platform close to the pink DC-4.

Burridge was seated up there, beside President Matsuo and his staff and other dignitaries. Expressionless, the Japanese stared at the plane and muttered to each other.

"They'd make good poker players," I said.

"Look at Burridge," Johnson said. "He's actually enjoying it."

"Look at the damn airplane," Lewis said.

After dignitaries intoned clichés, Burridge—the epitome of relaxed confidence—walked to the mike.

"Civil Air Transport is honored to participate in this first overseas flight of Japan Airlines," he began.

Lewis reseated his false teeth with his tongue.

"On this special day," Burridge continued, "our thoughts turn to Japan's gift to my country many years ago—the famous cherry trees of Washington, D.C., the trees that grace our national monuments. . . ."

Lewis gaped.

"The cherry trees are most beautiful when they blossom after a harsh winter. . . . After harsh years, Japan Airlines is reborn.

"This proud airline will bear its traditional colors, red and white. . . . However, to celebrate the first overseas flight we have decorated the airplane *cherry-blossom pink*."

JAL officials broke into smiles and shook hands all around.

Lewis said, "Whew."

Johnson laughed.

Welk said, "Burridge did it again."

That pink airplane seemed a hundred years in the past, because JAL had blossomed into an around-the-world airline with its own planes and pilots. And guys who looked very young were joining the CAT–Air America complex. And the Cold War was heating up again, almost silently. First, some more military advisers and then a few Marines to guard the perimeters of Vietnam's airports.

Voices

The night run between Hong Kong and Bangkok put us between two extremes. We were close to the tropopause, above all haze; the moon, stars, planets were our neighbors. Brilliant, familiar, transiting the sky with greater precision than our Convair 880, they said our universe is dependable, enduring. Even tranquil.

Seven miles below, magnesium parachute flares hung over the jungle while flashes of artillery said people died untimely deaths.

Danang, Vietnam, was a routine reporting point from which the U.S. Air Force relayed airliners' position reports to Bangkok's air traffic control.

Although personal messages were illegal, I added to our position report, "How're you doing down there?"

An American voice from Danang's control tower on the fringe of a jungle answered, "Almost stepped on a cobra on the way to work."

A faint whiff of perfume said a stewardess had entered the flight deck. She put a pillow on my lap and a tray with a filet mignon and trimmings.

On those trips some of our passengers were Air America pilots on their way to or from R&R in Hong Kong. Whoever rode the jump seat behind me was only a voice. It was dark except for the fluorescent glow of our weather radar sweeping the horizon. After landing, the guys were gone before I completed the logbook.

A new pilot named Riley had flown the jump seat. On the next trip I asked, "How's Riley?"

"Word's not out yet," a voice said. "He got shot down on an approach to the Plain of Jars. Had a clearance from Kong Le to land with supplies, but one of his soldiers got him with a mortar shell, just as he touched down. . . . Kong Le wanted to execute the soldier—he was a former Pathet Lao. But the Communist faction in his army is too strong."

On another trip I met a tall, freckle-faced redhead named Benjamin Franklin. "Yeah, I'm a descendant of the original," he said.

A few trips later I heard he was dead. Walker said, "I should have sent him home. I could tell right away he didn't have enough experience for this kind of flying. I figured he'd learn fast enough. . . ."

And I heard helicopter pilots. They joined Air America after their Vietnam tours in the Army, Navy, or Marine Corps. Allowed to fly in neutral Laos because they were now civilians, they soon learned every mountain that paralleled North Vietnam.

Before military commanders launched a strike they advised their pilots that if they had to abandon a battle-damaged plane they should maneuver across the border to Laos if they could. Air America was standing by to snatch them from the jungle.

Sometimes they were on the ground only minutes before Air America picked them up. Pathet Lao or Vietminh ground fire didn't deter the helicopters. They flew in pairs. If the first rescue chopper was shot down, its twin descended to pick up everyone. They were a new breed, these guys, and they perpetuated the spirit that originated with the Flying Tigers and endured in CAT. Their motto expressed it: Anything, Anywhere, Anytime, Professionally. "We get everyone we go after," they said, "dead or alive." The young fixed-wing pilots in Laos also captured the spirit.

We China Hands were downstream in the river of history. Arabs with crossbows; the Kaiser's one-man "Dragon Master" German air arm in Tsingtao during the First World War; Springweiler's Urasia; the incomparable China National; and now CAT. Each with its own legends. And now the new young pilots would make their own.

One voice stays with me. With the Mandarin jet on Bangkok's tarmac, ready to return to Hong Kong, I sat in the pilot seat and watched. Young neat American wives waited in a group near our boarding ramp. The one with the carry-on bag held a baby while a three-year-old girl clung to her free hand. A six-year-old boy stood silently nearby. Although I saw no tears, I knew from the quiet, accepting way they grouped together that Air America had another widow.

Her husband was George Verdon. He was a veteran of the Korean War, an armorer aboard the USS *Boxer*. He armed the planes and watched them catapult from the deck, leaving him behind. But it wasn't his nature to watch. He had to be a pilot.

After Korea, the GI Bill of Rights got George Verdon to flying school. Then he bought a war-surplus T-6 trainer for a pittance and earned a living by teaching and performing aerobatics in air shows. His wife and kids lived modestly and were happy. Their break came when a stranger named Pierre met Verdon at an air show and asked, "How'd you like to do some flying in Southeast Asia and wind up with an ATP [airline transport pilot certificate]?"

The voice of Stephen, his bright six-year-old son, stays with me. A grown man now, he recalls Laos as vividly as if it all happened yesterday.

"When the flight attendant opened the door to Vientiane, it was heat and bright light," he said. "We moved into a genuine Lao house on stilts, except it had screens on the windows and a gasoline generator for electricity." Other Air America families helped his mother find a Lao woman to do the marketing and keep house.

"On that first day," Steve recalled, "my dad saw a Lao kid with a deep gash in his leg. I had never seen such a deep wound. My dad put him in an Air America jeep and took him to the dispensary. Whenever he flew to Hong Kong he brought back medicine and toys and sports equipment for the neighborhood kids. They were always coming to the door. My dad taught me to doctor them with ear drops and antiseptics."

Devout Christians, the Verdons became members of Vientiane's Catholic church. Father Menger, a French Canadian priest, tutored Steve in the monastery three hours daily. When the priest made his rounds in a jeep, Steve sat beside him to be quizzed with mathematical problems.

On other days Stephen awoke with excitement. Cocks crowed, wheels of bullock carts creaked, smells of exotic food wafted through the screens and promised adventures he had never known in Philadelphia. And more freedom. George and Rose Verdon had discovered that Laos was safe for children.

Rose gave Stephen quarters, which were accepted in the marketplace because they were silver. "I was fascinated by Burmese men in sarongs, and Hmongs from the mountains," Steve said. "Muslims wore skullcaps, Buddhists with shaved heads wore yellow robes. Chefs balanced all kinds of goodies on bamboo poles. The food was piping hot and wrapped in moist leaves. Chestnuts, red beans, sesame cakes, rice."

Attracted by monotone chants of Buddhist monks, Steve followed Lao kids who sneaked through a back door and watched. Although they couldn't enter the monks' classrooms, they walked openly into the temple to stare up at a huge golden Buddha who looked at Steve with an enigmatic smile. "The mystical feeling, just the way Buddha looked, made me wonder how people worship—I learned that the Catholic way was not the only way.

"I played Ben Hur. Standing on the seat of a pedicab, I swung an imaginary whip and shouted for my chariot to pass everybody. . . . My parents told me it wasn't kind to pretend a pedicab man was a team of horses."

Near the marketplace, Steve knelt on the ground to peek through some seats and saw police beat someone they had captured. "I wasn't scared, because I knew he was a bad guy. The villagers were angry at him for whatever terrible thing he had done. They left their seats and swarmed over the compound and kicked him. Then I knew there was a different kind of justice in Laos."

Steve also knew that danger went with flying. One night they heard a plane circling low, so everyone ran outside and turned jeep lights in the direction of the airport.

But Steve wasn't prepared for that day when another pilot stopped Steve from playing on a rubber-tire swing. "Run home to your mother," the pilot said bluntly. "Your father is dead." Sternly, he added, "Don't cry—be a man about this."

Alone, Steve ran toward home, a mile away. He didn't notice the dogs sniffing at his heels. Ordinarily, he shooed them away with stones. They surrounded him and snarled. Steve's head had been in a whirl, but now he was terrified. "I thought they would tear me to pieces," he said. Two villagers came by on a motor scooter and took him home.

It was Verdon's day off, but he had donned his favorite souvenir from the UN war in Korea—an Aussie campaign hat with part of the brim turned up—and gone to the airport to see if he could do some extra flying. Although he was a captain, he offered to replace a sick copilot. The pilot in command—Prudhomme—flew into a rainsquall in a mountain pass and struck a tree. The plane exploded.

That was the first time I saw Rose and Steve, his younger sister Marianne, and two-year-old Patrick in his mother's arms. On the tarmac at Bangkok.

Rose's nobility won our hearts. She got a job. With faith in God, she steered her family through more heartbreaks. Rose's mother— her best friend—died, and Marianne succumbed to leukemia. With dignity, Rose raised her sons to be unafraid. A magnificent symbol of wives who lost their husbands to war, Rose is a hero, along with Sue Buol and countless others.

CAT'S Death

The death of CAT itself followed the loss of a passenger plane between Hong Kong and Taipei. CAT's president said, "Other airlines crash and lose the airplane. We crash and lose the airline."

February 1968. It almost didn't happen. Had the Boeing 727 been fifty feet to the left or thirty feet higher in the darkness and mist it would have cleared the house, and the farmer who found wide tire tracks in his rice paddy the next morning wouldn't have known what they were or how they got there. Nor would the pilots have known they were low enough to brush the plane's wheels through the rice paddy mud before they climbed toward the instrument glide path. But CAT's luck had run out. The right wing clipped the rooftop, and they crashed into an adjoining farm. Of sixty-three people on board, twenty-one lay dead. Others walked out of the wreckage to hail passing taxis and continue on to the airport, where they met relatives who'd been waiting and officials who bawled them out for failing to clear customs.

Like many airplane accidents, it was caused by a series of events. One link missing could have broken the chain that led to disaster. There was blame enough to go around: Taipei's ILS (instrument landing system); its communications antics; a vice president's indecision; the paltry training of flight engineers in Doole's cost-cutting policy. But blame was piled on a crewman who accepted it without a murmur.

A code of responsibility merged with Hugh Hicks's personal honor. They sprang from the 1930s when he first soloed an airplane and went on to teach. Although professional pilots faced starvation, there was the mystique of leaving the earth, an affinity with the wind, a sense of brotherhood with aviation's pioneers. Hugh Hicks would scoff at such lofty words. Asked why he flew, he'd probably respond like the French impressionist who replied, when asked where he found his muse for painting, "It's like having to pee."

Hicks augmented his instructor's pay by taking Pennsylvania's small-town gawkers for joyrides. Since he didn't own the airplane, his cut was ten cents per passenger. When the Air Corps Training Command picked him up his pay jumped to one hundred dollars a month.

After Pearl Harbor he was frozen to the job, but he wangled his way to wartime China and joined China National about the same time as I. We occasionally flew the Hump together. His straight spine made him look taller than his six feet. If I complained about the hardships of flying in Asia, he focused his level eyes on me and I shut up.

After the war, I joined CAT and Hicks wound up south in what had been the Dutch East Indies but was now the independent Republic of Indonesia. From scratch, he wrote training manuals for its fledgling air force, established a school, flew many of the training missions himself. One of his students, Wiweko Soepono, became famous as the father of the Indonesian Air Force. The time Hicks saw a Dutchman berate a young Indonesian Air Force officer he said, "You don't have to take that anymore."

Our paths crossed again when he joined CAT. By then he had married Gloria, a vivacious English woman who had served in the British Women's Army Service in Burma. A newsman called him an adventurer, and Hicks retorted, "Adventurer? I'm a family man—I'm responsible for a wife and three kids!"

I felt blessed sitting at this close family's long table while Hicks carved an English roast, prepared by Gloria. Her name suited her. She was cheerful and beautiful, and her eyes glowed with warmth. Speaking Taiwanese and Chinese, their young children delighted me when they had fun interpreting for vendors who appeared at their door.

In the accepting way of English women, Gloria didn't fret when Hicks left home for hazardous duty. When Communist antiaircraft guns at Dien Bien Phu bracketed him and tore a hole in his wing, a French fighter pilot dived down to silence the guns. From his crippled plane, Hicks asked his name, even though he knew they'd never meet. The Frenchman was based on a carrier at sea. "I'm obligated to know the name of the man who saved my life," Hicks said.

Some time after the battle, Hicks happened to attend a gathering of outsiders where a CAT executive crowed, "We're tough."

Hicks kept his counsel until we were alone, and then he said indignantly, "Tough? That executive flies a desk."

"It rubs the wrong way when ground pounders wear pilots' merit badges," I said. When it came to merit, I felt naked alongside Hicks, because he was nobler than I. I kept my mouth shut and flew where I was told, whereas he volunteered for dangerous missions because he felt a responsibility to share.

Hicks's sense of equity extended to management. Sensing an ever-widening gulf between the head office and pilots, he told me, "I think I can do some good," and he agreed to be an assistant chief pilot. Executives had eased his transition to a desk by promising he would fly CAT's latest acquisition, the Boeing 727, the high-tailed jet with three engines aft. However, he wasn't in his new job very long when a new vice president of operations—a veteran of American Airlines—moved the chief pilot's office downtown and declared, "You're on management's team. Stop flying."

Advised of CAT's promise to Hicks, his new boss evaded a decision. He didn't forbid Hicks to fly, but neither did he allow him time to keep proficient. It wouldn't have happened had Rousselot still been in charge. The new vice president of operations ignored the crucial phenomenon called "scan." Scan is the uncanny way a pilot sees the entire instrument panel as one unit instead of an over-whelming hodgepodge of instruments. Physiologists call it a psy-chomotor function. The closest thing to a pilot on an instrument approach is an organist whose hands and feet respond to symbols on sheets of music. Scan rusts when pilots are grounded, whereas other skills—maneuvering and judgment—have a long shelf life. Those who have become rusty are brought up to speed with a simulator or by a check airman monitoring their performance in an airplane and prompting them, if necessary, with terse comments: "Speed. Altitude. Two dots low." The check airman's silence is an indication that the airplane is within safe limits.

Flight engineers who operate the airplane's innards—its electrical, fuel, hydraulic, and pneumatic systems—are conventionally trained on simulators that duplicate problems a normal airplane can't. But CAT skipped the simulator. It was one of Doole's ways of cutting costs. The B-727 flight engineer trainees continued flying the older planes and caught ground school, piecemeal, in between flights. After approximately eight hours of training on the airplane itself they took the engineer's seat on passenger flights while an instructor monitored them.

When the budgeted training time expired, the instructors warned, "They're not ready—they don't know the emergency procedures," but Doole's policy kept them to budget, and the veteran flight engi-neers returned to Tachikawa.

Reminded that an inadequately trained crew member is a burden to the pilot in command, CAT agreed to a compromise. Veteran engi-neers monitored the new ones a while longer.

The flight engineer assigned to the flight, a CAT old-timer, was described by the instructors as "the best of the bunch." Nevertheless, the pilot in command thought it prudent to watch his performance, because it was his first trip without the company of a veteran engineer.

Another link in the chain to disaster was the design of the flight director—the most sophisticated instrument on the airplane. In addition to displaying an image of the plane above or below the glide slope, it had a command bar showing the best pitch (angle of the nose) to return the plane to the glide slope and keep it there. But the instrument had a booby trap. If a voltage fluctuation of the ILS ground installation released the command bar from the glide slope, it remained in its last position. Divorced from the influence of the glide slope, its last position could guide the pilot below the slope. The instrument's designers incorporated a "guide slope engaged" light and raw data information—lots of stuff that could be over-looked if the pilot's scan was rusty.

Although the ground installation of the ILS itself was satisfactory to those of us who were weaned on China's primitive airports, pilots of other airlines complained about its reliability. As for voice communication procedures, I called them "Taipei's rain dance." Conventional airports completed the dialogue as early as possible so crews could concentrate on the approach, but half of Taipei's controllers refused to release a plane to the tower until it reported, "Runway in sight." In low visibility there wasn't time to change communicators, so we acquired techniques of fudging. We called "Runway in sight" or "Over Outer Marker" ahead of time.

Taipei's Outer Marker had special significance. Seven and a half miles from the runway, it happened to sit near the dividing line between a high plateau and sea-level terrain. Only after a plane passed the Outer Marker was it safe to descend to sea level.

On that February night, the PIC (pilot in command) was a supervisory pilot and check airman. An excellent pilot with a cool head, he had flown through all our mainland adventures. On this night he carried a heavy load. It was the flight engineer's first flight without an instructor. The PIC assumed an additional burden. The flight from Hong Kong to Taipei carried Hicks and Gloria, who had been visiting relatives. It was Hicks's chance to brush up his skill. His duties in the chief pilot's office had allowed him but 145 hours in the B-727 seat in the previous eighteen months. The PIC offered him the captain's seat while he rode the jump seat.

The seating changed their status. Although the PIC retained command of the airplane, he also became a check airman, and Hicks was the checkee.

They flew due east on Airways Green Eight paralleling the south China coast until they were over the Strait of Formosa and then headed for northern Taiwan. A hundred miles out of Taipei they were cleared to descend, and the cockpit voice recorder preserved the countdown.

Minutes and Seconds to Impact
8:46
PIC   *That damn radio beacon off Makung always takes you quite a bit south.*

8:46
Hicks   *Yep.*
7:49
PIC   *To make it a little easier I'd suggest you go ahead and cut in the ILS here.*

7:47	
Hicks	*Yep.*
4:56	
PIC	*Reduce speed.*
4:55	
Hicks	*Yep.*
4:32	
Taipei Approach	*CAT 18 cleared to Outer Marker, 2,000 feet.*
1:30	
Copilot	*Taipei Approach, CAT 18 approaching Outer Marker.*
1:15	
Taipei Approach	*Contact Taipei Tower.*
1:13	
Copilot	*Taipei Tower, CAT 18 approaching Outer Marker.*
1:05	
Taipei Tower	*CAT 18, cleared ILS approach to runway one-zero.*

(The copilot's fudging worked. The plane is short of the Outer Marker. The crew is free to concentrate on the approach.) Having confidence in Hicks, who had made hundreds of DC-6 instrument approaches into Taipei, the PIC focused his attention on the new engineer.

No one will ever know what happened. A voltage fluctuation in the ILS ground installation might have disengaged the command bar from the electronic glide slope. Perhaps it emitted an erratic signal. Hicks's scan told him the instruments didn't agree. Had he been alone, he would have aborted the approach, but the PIC's silence, which had been interspersed with brief comments, gave Hicks confidence.

0:12	
PIC	*Hicks!*
0:12	
Hicks	*Yeah.*
0:11	
PIC	*We're low, aren't we?*
0:10	
PIC	*Hold your altitude!*

Hicks applied power. The plane's wheels stroked rice paddy mud for 517 feet and then climbed through a grove of thin trees.

0:02
Hicks   *What's going on here?*
0.00
PIC   *Oh God. (Sounds of the crash.)*

The PIC lay on the ground with a shattered arm while Hicks crawled out of the cockpit window and looked for Gloria. Unable to find her, he helped other passengers out of the wreckage until it exploded and he wound up in a hospital with an injured elbow and a gash across his face. He vaguely remembered being questioned by CAA inspectors who told him Gloria had been found strapped to her seat, dead.

Ten seconds before the crash, the PIC's final advice, "Hold your altitude," is good technique at a safe altitude. The plane will fly into the glide slope. Obviously the PIC, who would have been watching the engineer's panel, thought they were past the outer marker, over low terrain, or he would have shouted an alarmed "Climb" or reached over to execute a steep ascent himself.

A prosecutor charged both pilots with criminal negligence and manslaughter.

Students in the schoolyard stoned Hicks's son. He sent the boy and his sisters to Ohio with friends to attend their mother's funeral. Hicks was detained in Taipei, under house arrest. A policeman lived in his house.

When the two pilots were led into the courtroom, observers jammed the aisles, trying to strike the pilots. They spat on Hicks while he defended the PIC, whose arm was in a sling.

Playing to spectators, the prosecutor waved enlarged photographs of the victims.

The defense exhibited a life-size plywood mock-up of a Boeing 727 cockpit showing the instruments, and a CAT pilot showed the three judges how Taipei's malfunctioning instrument landing system could induce false displays on the plane's instrument panel.

Although a U.S. FAA technician had arrived with special instruments to check the ILS (an internationally agreed procedure, since an American plane was involved), the Chinese government denied him access to the ILS. "If our own technicians are considered questionable," the prosecutor asserted, "then we don't trust our government. And this implies the Republic of China has no experts."

Pilots of various international airlines waited to testify that the ILS system had been malfunctioning, but they weren't called.

The Chinese CAA investigating team testified that the ILS had functioned properly, because planes had landed safely before and after the crash.

Technicians changed some components of the ILS and claimed it was routine maintenance.

It was the first time in the history of aviation that airline pilots who had crashed were charged with a crime.

The International Federation of Airline Pilots sent its president to Taipei with commitments from pilots all over the world to boycott the island. I was surprised when even Japan Airline's pilots joined in.

At first the authorities laughed at the redheaded Finlander who claimed to represent the world's pilots. He couldn't even speak English, let alone Chinese. But when they realized he indeed held the power to isolate their island, the climate changed.

Eight months later the criminal court acquitted the pilots.

Hicks had no truck with highfalutin analyses. He was at the controls and that was that. He didn't even read the accident report. "I failed," he said, "maybe it was the ILS. Why couldn't I ride it down the glide slope?" His posture solved the dilemma of frantic executives. They heaped blame upon him, and he stood tall, while the PIC disclaimed responsibility by testifying he had been watching the engineer's panel. Inexplicably, no one asked why, at a crucial stage of the approach, in weather, at night, the PIC focused on the engineer's panel instead of watching his rusty crewman at the controls. The principle of command responsibility was ignored.

A historian's investigator wrote, "The help (the PIC) gave was the worst possible kind, analogous to helping a handicapped across a busy street; or helping someone lift a great weight and unexpectedly dropping his end."

The CAT hierarchy recalled the PIC to duty outside of Taipei's jurisdiction, but acted as if Hicks had vanished from the face of the earth.

He started an air ambulance service near his hometown and dedicated his life to his children.

Whenever I think of Hicks I see a staunch, grand man of aviation plumed in honor. A rare bird out of pioneer days when there was that code.

The Boeing 727 crash didn't kill CAT, but it accelerated its end. Plans had been in the wind to close it down and concentrate on the Air America operation in Southeast Asia.

The Chinese airline was my family. I had attended CAT's birth, grew with it, and watched it die.

The giants were gone. Like all gifted leaders, they didn't have to posture. I heard no stirring speeches or inspiring exhortations to the accompaniment of trumpets.

Chennault at the head office in his plaid duck-hunting shirt. I never heard him raise his voice.

Willauer, the Renaissance man, at the airport in his leather jacket, not afraid to show his shortcomings by copiloting a C-46 on which he had no experience or by murdering the Chinese language while conversing with laborers.

Cox, with his shy smile and mysterious charisma.

Rousselot, the disciplined Marine who ruled with a strong arm yet protected his pilots like a mother hen.

Rosbert, intelligent, unflappable Flying Tiger.

Burridge, with his inner peace. The masculine will-o'-the-wisp who turned problems into fun.

Different as they were, they were the same. They had a talent for leadership that sprang from fidelity to some deep conviction, plus an inner honesty that was unmistakable. Shining through it all was a respect for those they led.

And how would we ever forget Buol, our cocky Marine hero, who, unbowed, stole yarn and knitted an American flag under the noses of his captors? Or Snoddy, Schwartz, Earthquake, Buford, Miss Cho, and all the rest?

It didn't seem right. One day the airline flew, the next day it didn't. CAT had been such a cornucopia of colorful characters and events, I wanted a raucous Chinese funeral to celebrate its life. Like the ceremony I threw for Cheong during the Korean War. It was a funeral I'll never forget, nor will pedestrians who happened along Causeway Bay Road that afternoon.

Cheong's Funeral

I was in Korea when word came from Hong Kong: Cheong was ailing. His son was clearly worried, and Hsu, our amah, was in a skirmish to save his soul.

Hsu was a missionary's pet. Some frocked terrorizer had convinced her that heathens are doomed to hell, and she became notorious for dragging dying friends to the font to preclude eternal burning. And now, after years of indifference to his faith, she was railroading Cheong—ever since Dr. Carey-Huges said he had cancer in a hip.

Cheong said, "I die soon." I denied it. "I know I die—Hsu all time tell me I must be Catholic."

Apparently he wanted to show me where I could find stuff on my own, because he pulled open my top dresser drawer. Never had it been in such impeccable order. I saw Bob Snoddy's twenty-four-hour navigation watch his widow had given me; Hong Kong dollars, yen, kip, piastres, baht, old letters—things I'd left carelessly around our Hong Kong flat. A neat pile of Bill Welk's things lay alongside, and Doc Johnson's and Earthquake Magoon's. The second drawer held shirts and underwear that had been left by guests. It was washed, ironed, and neatly stacked. Cheong had written the owners' names on scraps of paper on top—Sims, Lampard, Gaddie.

Cheong knows he's going to die, I thought. I looked at his cropped gray hair, his immaculate white jacket with cloth frog buttons—he had the bearing of a general. I always felt he was more sensible than any of us carousing pilots. I didn't think of him as my servant. He was more like my father. We stood in silence at my open dresser drawer, looking into each other's eyes. Cheong finally blurted in his Mandarin twang, with uncharacteristic intensity, "You straight man."

Ordered back to flying, I was told I'd be notified if Cheong's health deteriorated. Days later I received word that he was dead. He had spent his last two days in the Queen Elizabeth Hospital with his sixteen-year-old son at his side and asking frequently, "Is Captain Smith coming?" Visitors said yes, but each thought someone else had sent word.

It felt like a kick in the stomach even though I knew this loss of touch was a pilot's lot. Unexpectedly scheduled four thousand miles one day, in a different direction the next, we lived a life made of fragments scattered among continents, loosely tied together with airplanes.

I sent word to arrange the best funeral possible.

In Hong Kong, Hsu told me through a cascade of tears, "I very happy. Cheong be Catholic before die."

My arrival at the funeral parlor was announced with a gong. I held my hands before my face, palms together, and bowed three times to the coffin in the center of the room; three times more to guests who were seated around the perimeter of the large room, where tables held sesame cakes and thermos jugs of tea. A brass band sat to one side. The musicians looked bored.

Cheong's body was dressed in a long Mandarin gown of blue silk. A black satin cap with a red tassel covered his head. The wedge-shaped coffin, carved from thick wood and lacquered black, was illuminated by a pagoda lamp.

At random moments, various guests walked over to the coffin, wailed for a few minutes, and returned to their seats to talk cheerfully again. I was the only foreigner. From time to time Cheong's friends came to me and said, "This is a very nice funeral. . . . This coffin looks very expensive. . . . How much did you pay for it?" The questions, I had learned, were not indiscreet. They were compliments.

Two hours later, attendants placed the lid on the coffin and turned cranks to drive in screws that were an inch thick and three feet long. Surplus lengths sticking out of the lid were sawed level. Screeching hacksaws resonated through the coffin and transformed it into a macabre cello. At the same time the band blatted "Dixie," "My Old Kentucky Home," "Swanee River." The music had been selected by the funeral director. Nobody conducted.

Cheong's son wept uncontrollably. I was astonished to hear myself blurt, "You'll see him again." I didn't know I believed that. Perhaps it was a shallow way of consoling him. Everybody cried. It was a crescendo of sobbing. The cacophony cheered me up. Cheong was going out with a bang.

The band switched to an earsplitting blast of "Marching Through Georgia." Eight bearers in green gowns with red embroidery lifted the coffin onto a truck and hung a three-foot photograph of Cheong on its cab.

It crept down Causeway Bay Road with Cheong's son and me marching ahead. Behind it, professional mourners in burlap capes flung their arms in agony and howled. Firecrackers exploded. The raucous band followed, and then Cheong's friends. Banners with verses of condolence brought up the rear. It was the best funeral I've ever seen.

Pedestrians stopped and commented. Had I been in America or Japan I'd have felt conspicuous, but in Hong Kong I felt comfortable.

Walking slowly with Cheong's son, leading the hearse, I thought of the time Cheong, without being asked, visited Doug and Ada Smith to show how to care for their first baby. I thought of how he remembered the favorite dishes of my friends. I never told him what to cook—just who was coming. When Charlotte Snoddy, with some illness or other, rested in the Miramar Hotel, Cheong baked a chocolate cake, put it in a fancy box, and sat on his heels outside her room until he heard her stir.

When he was too sick to work he resigned. I told him I needed him to supervise Hsu. "You just say because I sick," he said.

In Happy Valley the uniformed bearers lifted the heavy coffin to their shoulders, waved their arms for balance, and swiftly climbed the flight of stone steps to the lofty entrance of the church. Their natural grace and rhythm turned the long climb into a ballet, like a scene from grand opera.

The bearers stopped outside arched doors and waited with the coffin on their shoulders. An annoyed English priest appeared in the doorway and read, in a pained monotone, a brief prayer. The book snapped shut, the door closed. Left outside with the coffin still on their shoulders, the bearers carried it back down and through the iron gates of the Catholic graveyard.

Paper images, released by Cheong's friends, fluttered into the grave—gifts for his spirit—useful things he'd missed in this world: houses, money, cars, servants.

Hsu pressed a shovel into the hands of Cheong's bewildered son and helped him drop the first earth onto his father's coffin. The missionary had told her it was proper. Diggers filled it in.

We talked briefly, his friends and I, about sending Cheong's bones back to his hometown in Shantung Province when the Communists loosened their barriers.

A Summer's Day

Autumn 1968. Cheong was gone, and the China I knew, and so was the junior birdman who bumped onto an island in the Yangtze aeons ago.

Friends said, "You? Leaving?"

"I'm not leaving. CAT left us."

Little did I know when I first got to China what I would learn. And now I didn't know how much I had absorbed.

Not until I left would I realize I had adapted to the sociability that's uniquely Chinese. It's an enmeshing born of a sense of involvement with everything in sight. When I first got to China the people seemed nosy. "How old are you? How many children do you have? Are your mother and father alive?" Now I know the questions are an extension of a certain kind of caring, and I miss them. Although it's difficult to describe to one who hasn't lived among the Chinese, its impact was described by Dr. Lewis Richards, flight surgeon to the Flying Tigers and China National. "If I'm reborn," he said, "I hope I'll be Chinese." I once was a fellow passenger with a German Catholic missionary who had been kicked out of Red China. Sadly he said, "Someday I'll get back home." Home, to that German, was north China.

Packing to go, tiptoeing through memories, I discovered how memory mocks the calendar. How cunningly it rearranges events until the least mouthed becomes the most vivid. My secret reached out from the silence of years—from the summer we ferried Boxcars from a U.S. Air Force base in the Philippines to a French Air Force squadron in Hanoi.

Yes, it's a summer's day, and I'm ferrying a Flying Boxcar across the South China Sea to Indochina, which is dominated by France even though the people want their country back. Communists capitalize on the discontent. The C-119's twin tail booms glisten with newly painted tricolors of France. Close up, you can see the pentimento of the old American insignia. French Air Force pilots will soon discover that the airplane's rear end gapes wide enough for a Mack truck or artillery piece to pop out and parachute down.

Their comrades in barbed-wire enclaves throughout the French colony are waiting.

Seat tilted back, relaxed, I know I'm forty-five minutes from the coast because I see weathered shipwrecks that identify North Reef. Other evidence of age-old violence—sunken galleons, pirateers, steel warships, downed airplanes—is covered by the sea's calm blue. The sky ahead is lavender, with no hint of the calamity that will come. It will come before the sun sets.

An orange shimmer appears on the horizon. The glazed roofs of Hanoi.

I cross the coastline and descend over the familiar checkered patterns of rice paddies and villages and Catholic churches with tall spires.

A French colonel salutes, accepts the airplane, and lends me a jeep, and I head for town.

Hanoi is one of my favorite cities. Flower stalls decorate almost every corner. Strollers' wooden clogs clip-clop along the streets and echo around white houses that nestle under shade trees. Roof tiles glitter through the leaves. Weeping willows touch a lake. By the time I slurp noodles at an open stall it's time to return.

It's too late for my favorite pastime—wandering around neighboring villages with my camera. Catholic as they may be, Tonkin villages have a Buddha-like timelessness in which I steep, to return to airplanes, refreshed. Their open marketplaces are bright with vegetables that are arranged like flowers. Garlic is stacked in spiral columns. Elders gossip, kids ride sidesaddle on their hips. Strolling with feline grace, some of the women wear white slacks of see-through satin with pastel-colored high-necked blouses that reach their knees and are open at the sides. The flimsy silk drifts with the wind.

Some of the villagers say, "We're not Communists, but we hate the French, we want them to leave." I can't tell which ones, but I know that some of the men are Red organizers called "Vietminh" who are capitalizing on the discontent by making false promises of freedom under Communism. Some of the villages have fallen for the pitch. Tomorrow, perhaps, I'll have time to wander.

The airport is guarded by Foreign Legionnaires wearing white peaked caps with sun-shield bibs in back.

Senegalese giants, off duty, wear fezzes with red tassels. Others, shirtless, with ebony skin, load airplanes and sweat.

French Air Force pilots in khaki shorts walk around the strange airplanes, talk excitedly, point at the long tail booms that straddle the boxlike hulls.

A few Vietminh prisoners, hands tied behind them, sit in the shade of a hangar and glare.

It could be a scene from a movie. I sit in the shade of a hangar and watch. A U.S. Air Force major with a fresh-scrubbed face stands out. It's curious how you can spot an American fresh from home. Maybe it's simply a neater haircut or sharp creases in crisp khakis, or the lack of a Southeast Asia suntan; and there's an innocent demeanor, like that of a Boy Scout on parade. Something about the young officer reveals the long time I've been away. I suddenly feel like a hoary bush pilot.

He's one of the U.S. military advisers who have been sent here, although they're forbidden to fly under penalty of court-martial. America doesn't want to get entangled in another Asian war. Our soldiers are a year into the United Nations police action in Korea, and the conflict is escalating.

The major maneuvers his hands the way pilots do when talking airplanes. Any pilot can tell what he's saying just by watching his hands. He's teaching the Frenchman a technique of aerial delivery. "Nose up, add power, and the bird flies away from its load." On impulse, the major adds, "Come on, I'll show you."

They bound into an airplane, and when they taxi past I see their load. Layer upon layer of rectangular aluminum cans. The rear stack sparkles in the sunlight. Napalm.

Minutes after they roar down the runway, I'm still sitting in the shade. A few miles south, a column of smoke rises up and churns. A black pall hangs in the pale sky.

The news comes before the plane gets back. The major randomly selected a village for his demonstration. He buzzed it and dropped the jellied gasoline that clings burning to flesh and suffocates.

The village disappeared. It was the end of kids, graceful women, vegetables, and probably some Vietminh. All in one terrible *whuff*. As if an evil sorcerer had waved his wand.

I'm still in my shady spot when they land and park. The plane's empty fuselage yawns like a macabre cave. The major has changed also. He's a Kabuki devil with a gaudy orange face and green horns. I hate him. I want to rave and exorcise his demon, but I say nothing. My mouth tastes like brass. I tell myself this is the way wars are, the way the world is.

Ghosts

Back in the practical West, years away from *Alice in Wonderland*'s topsy-turvy domain, I hold memories fleetingly by their tails, wondering if those strange things really happened. The looking glass reveals only an aging face.

Sometimes, in the middle of the night, the past is confirmed by echoes. They seem like music. I awaken suddenly with the sounds still ringing in my ears. Chants that ease bitter labor. Choral harmonies of Yangtze River trackers. Exotic melodies of noodle sellers' flutes. Rustling sails of high-decked junks. Toots of laughter from Earthquake Magoon. The arresting silence when an engine, thundering like a kettledrum, fails on takeoff. The bass-drum boom of Hong Kong's noonday gun.

And sometimes, while we're watching a sunset at that special time of day, my wife looks at me curiously and asks what's wrong.

"Nothing," I say, although ghosts are paying a visit. They come from the village that disappeared in a fury of napalm.

They drift gracefully and whisper, "Why were you silent?"

Epilogue

October, 1979. C. Y. Chu wrote from the MV *Timar Star*, "Jailed at sea." It was his only feeling. He was the ship's radio officer. "I never really cared about money or clothes because I feel I am someone beyond my memory. I am Genghis Khan borrowing C. Y. Chu's body for a brief time. There are mysteries which childish persons do not believe.

"Remember the three copilots and one radioman who went to Red China just before CAT moved to Taiwan? They disappeared. I recently discovered that William Cheng hanged himself within the year, and sometime later H. Chu committed suicide by hanging. These were such cruel days. Many people in Shanghai committed suicide by jumping into the river from the Bund.

"I miss Suchow, my birthplace, so much—it was so beautiful. Surely, even in a dream, it always shows my old house and streets. I want to salute my father's grave. He missed me terribly until his last breath, my mother wrote. My life is so unworthy, my time so short."

More than two decades after the fall of French Indochina, historian William Leary unearthed documents from government archives that revealed what had happened to the remains of James (Earthquake Magoon) McGovern and Wallace Buford. They had been enshrined in a Buddhist tomb by the villagers of Ban Sot, in Laos, near the border of North Vietnam. A French graves-registration officer found the bones five years after the battle of Dien Bien Phu. Villagers had witnessed the crash. Kickers in the back of the C-119—a Thai sergeant and a French officer—had been thrown clear and lived. The officer endured several years in a Communist prison. Both survivors verified the villagers' reports.

The French Army notified CAT, but Doole saw no obligation to notify the next of kin. CAT stamped the report CONFIDENTIAL and attached a memorandum: "A review of the personnel files fails to indicate any outstanding liability on the part of the company." An accountant's figures proved it—the final pay had been sent to the parents. "Salary from May 1–6, 1954: 6/31 x $1,050 per month = $203. Plus $20,000 Death Benefit."

It became a well-guarded secret until Professor Leary cast sunshine upon it. Our buddies' parents went to their graves wondering if their sons' mortal remains lay scattered among the weeds of Asia. Had the pilots been members of the armed forces, their parents would have been notified and given the opportunity of receiving the remains on American soil.

The French Army deserves a nod. Even though it had lost Indochina five years earlier, its graves-registration officer, in completing its records, took meticulous care in locating the remains of these American civilians and in notifying CAT.

I still search for McGovern's and Buford's relatives so they will know. Perhaps they will receive a measure of comfort in knowing the remains were enshrined with reverence, albeit Buddhist.

The guilty conscience I suffered for sitting on the news of the napalmed village was somewhat assuaged when former station manager Frank Guberlet recently told me he had discovered the news the day it happened and had reported the major, who was subsequently court-martialled.

A few months before Air America closed its operations at the Tachikawa Air Force Base in Japan, Doole offered Lewis continued employment if he transferred to Saigon. Lewis asked, "What'll happen to these guys at Tachikawa?" Doole said they'd be terminated. "I'd appreciate it if you delay my transfer until this place closes," Lewis said. "Think how my guys will feel if I run out on them." Doole told him if he waited he'd be terminated with the rest. "That's okay with me," Lewis replied. "I'm not going to abandon my men just to save my job." He returned to his family in Pueblo, Colorado.

Sue Buol remarried and travels yearly to Hong Kong with her husband, John Hacker, to buy antiques for her shop near San Francisco.

Rousselot, realizing his dream, works his Oklahoma cattle ranch with his wife, their two sons, and their grandchildren.

Rosbert and Kusak turned a castle on Spain's island of Majorca into a resort hotel. Rosbert wrote two books about his life and lives with his wife—Shanghai Lil—in rural North Carolina.

Burridge became president of the Asian division of Sterling Drug.

Anna Chennault, with enthusiasm, chairs CIC, Inc., a nonpolitical, nonprofit organization working outside of governments to promote international goodwill.

Felicity Titus, the gorgeous red-haired German we met in Lanchow, is a professor of art in the United States.

Soon after Willauer became U.S. ambassador to Honduras, two local boys disappeared while swimming in a flooded stone quarry. Willauer grabbed his scuba gear and changed from his formal clothes while an automobile sped him to the scene. Although it was dark when they got to the quarry, Willauer dove to the bottom and groped around until he found the boys' bodies. He later became ambassador to Guatemala and died of a cerebral hemorrhage in his late fifties.

Rose Verdon, a successful realtor, is proud of her sons.

Stephen Verdon, who was six years old when he left Laos, combined his love of art and science by becoming a fine lithographer and printer. He is also a classical guitarist.

Patrick Verdon, two years old when he left Laos, grew up to realize his dream of flying. With courage, Rose respected his choice and helped finance his way through Embry Riddle Flying Academy. Today he is a proud Marine Corps captain in an F/A-18 strike fighter squadron.

I flew overseas routes for Japan Airlines. When regulations decreed I was too old to fly airliners, I became director of operations for South Pacific Island Airways, a Hawaii-based scheduled airline with four Boing 707s that flew to Tahiti, Samoa, Tonga, Hawaii, Guam, New Guinea, and Alaska. My wife and I now live in rural Wisconsin.

In 1993 the secretary of the Air Force determined that China National Aviation Corporation had been a division of the Army Air Corps' Air Transport Command during World War II. We Hump pilots received honorable discharges from the U.S. Air Force.

Upon reflection, my greatest satisfaction came in watching the development of Free China on the island of Taiwan. Its initial martial law, secret police, and austerity program seemed repressive until I reminded myself that it was in a hot section of the Cold War, with hostile Red China ten minutes away by jet. Eventually, the personal freedom and prosperity of Free China became a testament to democracy. The Republic of China on Taiwan is the only nation I know of that has repaid the aid funds loaned by the United States.

Although the CIA eventually owned the corporate complex, we maintained our private identity. I believe that no more than five CIA professionals worked in our ranks at any one time. When CAT–Air America disbanded, approximately $23 million were given to America's GSA (General Services Administration). The complex turned out to be the only CIA-owned organization that earned more money than it cost taxpayers. Nor is it saddled with paying us a pension. When I left, I received a "retirement benefit" of $40,000, half of which I contributed through payroll deductions.

The spirit of CAT and Air America still lives through our biannual reunions, which include the children who were born in Asia and grandchildren who listen to the tales.

However, Memorial Day in Dallas, 1987, was more than a reunion. It was a ceremony for our dead.

We lost 242 comrades in Asia. The bones of some lie in unmarked graves. Their loved ones wanted tangible evidence of the last years of their lives and deaths—something that could be seen and touched. None of the names could appear on the Vietnam Wall in our nation's capital because that memorial is for members of the armed forces. So we chipped in and honored our own.

We commissioned Dominico Facci, the principal artist for the President Johnson Museum, to sculpt a bronze memorial from images of our history. A C-46 over China, a C-119 dropping parachutes on Dien Bien Phu, an eagle over Korea, a mountain strip in Laos, refugees climbing toward an Air America helicopter atop the U.S. embassy in Saigon. Below the panorama these words appeared: DEDICATED TO THE AIR CREWS AND GROUND SUPPORT PERSONNEL OF CIVIL AIR TRANSPORT, AIR AMERICA, AIR ASIA AND SOUTHERN AIR TRANSPORT WHO DIED WHILE SERVING THE CAUSE OF FREEDOM IN ASIA—1947 TO 1975.

And then the names: BENJAMIN FRANKLIN, CHO HE-YOUNG, THANOM KHANTHAPHENGXCAY...242.

The University of Texas accepted it for a permanent display in their McDermott Library, a Mecca for aviation historians.

Among the six hundred who attended the ceremony were two granddaughters and two great-granddaughters of General Chennault. More than fifty were relatives of our lost ones.

Robert Snoddy's sister, Ruth, and his daughter, Roberta, recognized some of us from the photos he had sent home. Born after her father died, Roberta is married and has three children. She manages a private elementary school.

Norman Schwartz's brothers and his nephew said it was gratifying to meet Norm's old friends.

Seven Verdons came to honor George. Among them, his mom and dad, and brothers Kenneth and Stephen.

We assembled in the university auditorium. Souvenir programs bore accolades from the president and from the governor of Texas.

The sculpture, covered by a veil, waited center stage while flags of Asian nations, so familiar to us, hung in the background. The president of the university welcomed us and said our archives were important to scholars.

Aviation historian William Leary, giving a summary of our history, was eloquent. "Secret soldiers of the Cold War" was one of his phrases.

William Colby, former director of the CIA, spoke. "We shared a common profession...courage in civilian clothes...the customer could rely upon you...professionalism...discipline of behavior."

Helicopter pilot John Merkel's widow tugged a string and the veil fell from our sculture. Our history, in bronze, shone. There was applause, and then a moment of silence.

Douglas Dexter piped "Amazing Grace" on the same bagpipes he had played while waiting with his helicopter to rescue downed pilots. The drones echoed from the auditorium walls like they had echoed among Lao mountains.

A bugler sounded taps. Muted sobs were heard.

When it was over, relatives mounted the stage to examine the memorial more closely. They stroked the names.

After almost everyone left, someone returned, leaned over, and kissed a name.

In the McDermott library, where we were invited for refreshments, we saw keepsakes loaned for the occasion: a Hmong crossbow; ancient Thai pottery; a bronze Lao drum; a portrait of George Verdon in his jaunty Aussie campaign hat; a photograph of a helicopter crashed in a jungle; Terry Wofford's painting of the Mandarin Jet on a night approach to Hong Kong.

At the end of the day we heard comments from relatives. "I now truly feel he is at rest and I can finally let go."

A daughter said, "This is the first time I felt like I know my father."

One of our families said their son, who had never known his father, had been taunted with jibes from schoolmates repeating what they had read in the tabloids: "Swashbucklers...mercenaries...soldiers of fortune." But now he walked proudly. He had paid rapt attention when the value of his father's work was assessed by the historian; the director of a government agency; the president of the United States.

Stephen Verdon said, "I lost something in Laos—I lost my father." Stephen lost something else, also—as did many of the CAT children. They lost certitude—the narrow yet comforting conviction that their way is the only way. Raised overseas, outside the insulation of military bases, they played and attended school with children of diverse cultures. They developed the capacity to love the world. They can assess our planet with evenhandedness, a healthy detachment, a sophisticated perspective. Like me, they feel at home almost anywhere, yet outsiders everywhere.

Many follow interesting careers. Among them are two physicians, an anthropologist, a producer of documentary films, a professor of Asian studies, a champion and teacher of horsemanship in Madrid, two Marine Corps pilots, naval officers, and Air Force pilots. Aerospace engineers. International bankers. A daughter who's an Air Force major and teaches at the Air Force Academy. A daughter who administrates a refugee camp on the Cambodia-Thai border. Her sister teaches the refugees how to make artificial limbs from local material to replace the flesh and bones blown away by mines that still lurk in the fields.

They show a remarkable zest for life. Although some may not feel rooted in any one piece of geography, they pay in that price a service to their country, for they lead us out of provincialism and bigotry. They remind us that different trails lead to the same mountain, and splendid people are where you find them.

Addendum

Even after death, James (Earthquake Magoon) McGovern is a magnet for spectacular events.

In 1998, while searching for a missing USAF plane, a JTF-FA (Joint Task Force—Full Accounting) came across the French C-119. By now—thirty-nine years after the French discovery—the bones of the pilots lay beneath one of the few super-highways in Laos—Route 6 leading to Vietnam and the valley of Dien Bien Phu.

The JTF-FA will build a detour around the site, tear up part of Route 6, recover the remains, and rebuild it. For lack of funds, there's a backlog of cases, perhaps two years. Relatives await their turn. Buford's brothers will bury his bones in the family plot in Kansas. McGovern's brother, also a veteran of World War II, will see the remains laid to rest, with military honors, in Arlington.

Richard Fecteau and John Downey, the Third Force case officers who survived Schwartz and Snoddy's spy flight, were released from their imprisonment in China, Fecteau in 1971, Downey in 1973. Fecteau became a university athletic director, and Downey, a judge in Connecticut.

In 1999, Downey attended a ceremony that was otherwise limited to Schwartz and Snoddy's next of kin. They received a medal of valor and the Distinguished Intelligence Cross.

Two unmarked stars, representing them, have been carved into the marble façade on the north wall of the CIA's headquarters, beside plain stars of other unsung heroes.

Snoddy's widow died and his daughter, Roberta, has four robust children. I placed into her hands Snoddy's navigation chronometer.